Environmental Discourse

Environmental
Discourse

A critical analysis of 'environmentalism'
in architecture, planning, design, ecology,
social sciences and the media

Necdet Teymur

?uestion Press   London

First published in Great Britain in 1982 by
?uestion Press
P.O. Box 162 , London N2 9LZ

Printed in Great Britain by
Blackwell Press, London and Worcester

© N. Teymur, 1982

*British Library
Cataloguing in Publication data*

Teymur, Necdet
    Environmental discourse
    1. Architectural criticism
    I. Title
    720'. 1   NA2599.5
    ISBN 0-946169-00-7
    ISBN 0-946160-01-5 pbk

Contents

Foreword

It is an unfortunate fact of academic publishing that there can often be a gap of several years between the completion of a book and its publication. This book is no exception. It is also a known fact that some books may 'age' before they are published and read, some may, however, remain as fresh as when they were written. *Environmental Discourse*, as it happened, did not become one of those in the former category — and nobody can yet tell whether it is firmly in the latter. It is true to say that, whatever its worth, it has so far not been superseded by alternative works, or made redundant by historical developments in the four years since its completion. This delay was partly due to my own mistake — giving priority to new productions and leaving the accomplished ones to their own fate; and partly the pitiful state of academic publishing in this country — questions of sale potential, listings, print-runs and, of course, the author's name . . .!

As amply discussed in the *General Introduction* and the *Conclusion*, the text is a product of its conjuncture — personal, historical, theoretical, political . . . It could therefore be suggested that as the conjuncture might have changed over the past 4-5 years, so should the problems that the study tried to deal with. This is a plausible argument, but to my satisfaction as author of its critique (but disappointment as a committed progressive) the ideology of environment has neither been transcended or abandoned, nor has it been rigorously analysed or criticized. In fact, whilst environmentalist movements in ecology, planning and architecture have, to a certain degree, lost their fervour all the negative effects of the concept of 'environment' have been internalized by a whole generation of professionals, political activists, bureaucrats and academics as well as many institutions all over the world. 'Nature' was effectively replaced by 'Environment' — and it would not be convincing to suggest that we became any wiser as a result. Nor do I see any sign that the 'public', the 'experts' or the media manage to talk about issues such as housing, energy, pollution or urban life in any more intelligible and accurate terms when they talk simply about 'environmental crises'. The ahistorical discourse on environment became a historically identifiable ideology in architectural, planning, design, art and communications, as well as political, practices. The concrete indication of the last case is the emergence of political parties with the primary (and often the sole) object of 'environment' which managed to get a considerable number of votes — as if that were a significant measure of anything. In short, the *object* of the book has neither disappeared nor has it become marginal or redundant.

On the theoretical front to which the book addresses itself the unfortunate fashion-following habits took their toll, discarded some of the most significant contributions to our understanding of society, and not fully replaced them by other alternative problematics. I am glad to say that at least the vocabulary and the approach(es) employed in this study became more commonly recognizable in the English speaking world over the last few years. The belated recognition, for example, of Foucault's work, however much it was often misunderstood or taken simplistically or literally, provided some support to my often repeated criticism that there was more to language than a convenient analogy for architecture, and that there was more to the relationship between architectural practice and society than a simple determinism, artistic individualism or ill-conceived reflectionism. Most of the uses made of Foucault's work in architectural circles have been literal and selective, 'quoting' what superficially are architectural aspects of his research and ignoring the profound philosophical, discursive and institutional observations that he makes. The non-architectural use, on the other hand, has hardly gone beyond commentaries and there appears (at least in Britain) no significant attempt to employ and extend the discursive approach in areas not defined by Foucault himself.

One important factor has been the specific meaning of the word 'discourse' in English and how that meaning was carried into the ways in which 'discourse analysis' has been carried out — resulting in a social psychological approach to conversations and to extremely small scale utterances. Both in the course of analysing the environmental discourse and of various projects on which I have embarked since then it has become clear that neither the English concept of 'discourse' nor the modes of its analysis referred to above could do justice to the specificity of a social/ideological/practical problem exemplified by what I chose to call 'environmental discourse'. Being the first of its kind it carries with it *both* the weaknesses, eclectic inclinations and signs of experimentation, *and* the excitements, potentials and possibilities. It is with this awareness that I believe the study may present possibilities not only for architectural, urban and artistic discourses, but also for several other practices, disciplines and fields of communication.

Finally, the reader might like to know that I know how difficult the present text is. Its language is rather contrived, formal and overstructured, and in places exhibits problems of style as well as grammatical curiosities characteristic of non-native speakers. Moreover, it is full of seemingly repetitive but absolutely essential methodological discussions and somehow overburdened procedural explanations. Part of the reasons for these have been given in the *Introduction* and the *Conclusion* pointing, in particular, to the inevitable problems of developing and using a new mode of analysis on a newly constituted object. But, whatever the apparent difficulties are in reading a text of this sort, it is necessary to recognize the importance of reading and evaluating it in its entirety — with its rather unusual emphases, patient pace and cross-disciplinary observations.

If the book opens up one or two alternative possibilities of seeing and talking about the world *as well as* about other people's ways of seeing and talking; if it can change the level of discussions in the field of its concern or introduce to them new objects; and if it can draw attention to the inherent materiality of discourse, ideas and words it will have justified its publication.

Acknowledgements

A study of this sort could not but be a product of many inputs, influences and contributions − theoretical as well as non-theoretical. Whilst the theoretical, discursive and professional inspirations, loans and conjunctural factors are discussed in the *General Introduction*, and whilst all bibliographical references are credited in the text, the 'non-theoretical' and non-textual contributions are not and could not be expressed equally explicitly. The historical, institutional and personal factors that shaped my position were constituted by 'positive' and/or 'negative' forces and agents the effects of which can be traced back to my pre-PhD period of professional and educational life and even to my childhood.

The 'negative' factors and agents are responsible for my development (and its outcomes) in a way that they have certainly *not* intended − by repressing, ignoring or misdirecting my abilities and options. Yet, they will not be named here as they do not deserve credit for what may have been achieved *as a reaction to*, or *in spite of*, them.

'Positive' forces and agents, on the other hand, include those institutions and persons (many of whom I have befriended in the process) who, in various ways, supported, inspired, criticized or contributed to, my quest for knowledge: Some allowed me to join their institutions, courses or seminars, or to use their resources, while some let me read their (often unpublished) writings, or discussed with me, or criticized my ideas and writings. They all contributed to the long process of clarification and formulation of my own approach especially after 1971 when I started my research with many difficult questions.

Without any claim to completeness I must express my gratitude to some of these institutions and persons:
The University of Liverpool (Schools of Architecture, Civic Design, Social Sciences and Politics), University of Surrey (Department of Environmental Psychology), Architectural Association, International Institute of Design, London School of Economics, University College London (School of Environmental Studies /Bartlett); Portsmouth Polytechnic (School of Architecture);
and
Francis M. Jones, John B. O'Malley, Frank Horton, Robert Simpson, Barry Hindess, Mehmet Adam, Bill Hillier, Adrian Leaman, Alan Beattie, Alvin Boyarsky, Geoffrey Broadbent, Tomas Llorenz, Zeynep & Haluk Pamir, Cecilio Sanchez-Roblez, Doreen Massey, Anthony Wilden, Paul Mugnaioni, M.Ali Dikerdem, Frederik Herweijer.

The study was supervised by Mr Francis M. Jones. To me, Mr Jones represented, and actively participated in, the transition from classical architectural education with its emphasis on professionalism to the developing awareness of the need for critical, research-oriented and multi-disciplinary approaches to the architectural profession and education. And, with an appreciation of this development, he criticized and supported, warned and encouraged, my difficult, complex and often confusing endeavour. His patient and encouraging attitude made it possible for me to survive the intense strain in which I   developed my approach, and overcome immense psychological, as well as theoretical, difficulties. If, therefore, the study proves to be a 'useful' one, Mr Jones's contributions to it should be seen as fundamental to its existence in the first place.

The late Dr John B. O'Malley whose 'social theory' seminars I attended during my first two years at The University of Liverpool continued to show a close and friendly interest in my work until his early death in 1976. Despite his obvious distance from my professional background, and despite many fundamental differences between our theoretical positions; he enjoyed helping me and seriously responded to my (often naive) 'philosophical' ventures. He saved me from 'textbook' theories, directed me to the sources of a wide range of theoretical systems, gave me the conception of what a 'discourse' could be (much before I came in contact with Althusser and Foucault), enabled me to understand the specificity of 'theoretical' work, made in-depth criticisms of my writings, and helped me   develop my capacity for abstract thought and theoretical analysis. I hope this work will be a tribute to his memory in the best of his teaching method: by its fundamental disagreements with, and questions on, many established theoretical positions − including that of O'Malley!

My friends Berna & Savaş Basatemur and Ali Tınay spent several days helping to prepare the original manuscript. Without their co-operation we could not have borne the weight of the work involved.

Finally, I can hardly specify or categorize the contribution and co-operation of my wife, Emel. She shared, with remarkable patience, my test of endurance during my years of struggle − often full of stresses and despair. She always renewed my confidence and hope, and not only supported me financially, and not only shared the immense amount of labour involved in the last phase of producing a 200-page text out of about 5,000 pages of notes, she also critically appreciated,and intellectually contributed to, my work. My only regret is that despite her constant interest and wish to co-operate with my work at a wider scale she had to spend most of her energy and time earning our living. It is perhaps the irony of the present study − or, perhaps the confirmation of some of its propositions − that this study could materially be possible only by Emel's toil in a field which this very study uncompromisingly criticizes and wants to transform.

* * *

During the period between the completion of the study and its publication several individuals contributed to the development of my work and to the publication of this text. In particular, I would like to mention Dr Michael Naslas whose critical assessment and appreciation of the study encouraged me to publish it; Hans Heinlein who, as my Head of Department at the Polytechnic of the South Bank between 1978-1982 provided the support and the platform that enabled me to concentrate on my research and teaching interests, and who therefore was instrumental in the continuity of my work, and Gerrard Ryan who patiently read the whole manuscript and made useful corrections which at least reduced the number of grammatical or stylistic curiosities that, as a non-native speaker writing on the most abstract of subjects, I could not fully avoid. John J. Scott too was very helpful in making some last minute corrections. I thank them all and many others who convinced me that I should not leave the book unpublished.

* * *

The nature of the analysis in this book required an unusual number of illustrative examples, quotations, graphics and references from a wide range of sources. This very fact made it materially and practically impossible to obtain permission from all or even some of the authors or publishers concerned. However, all sources are duly credited in the footnotes as well as in the *Bibliography*, and I would like to gratefully acknowledge here the contributions that the discursive illustrations as well as the theoretical borrowings made to the overall composition of the study.

1 General Introduction

*"One cannot speak of anything
at any time; it is not easy
to say something new; . . ."* [1]

1.1 About this *Introduction*

This *Introduction* is a rather long one. This is because it is more than an introduction
to a study. It is a major *part* of the study. It tries to fulfil the combined functions of
(what are conventionally known as) a *'Preface'* and an *'Introduction'*. Thus, it is the
only part of the study which has some personal references, though for theoretical
reasons.

It is part of a study which claims a place and an audience in a difficult and equally
barren terrain – though not by answering the questions of that terrain, nor, in fact,
repeating the given answers in a different way, but by *questioning* the whole terrain.

Secondly, this *Introduction* is meant to be the locus of explaining a (personal *and*
theoretical) transition – an attempt at a transition from a dispersed, unsystematic
and highly speculative mode of analysis to a tidy, systematic and rigorous, in short,
theoretical, one.

It tries to *locate* the study in its proper context. It opens its cards, explains its
approach and its method. It tells where *problems* lie and what contribution this study
can make to the understanding and tackling of those problems. In a self-critical (and
not apologetic) way it admits the possibilities and impossibilities, advantages and disadvantages, difficulties and hopes of the project that it took upon itself to realize. It
tries to discuss the vital questions of why a seemingly 'hair-splitting', yet, a *potential*
mode of analysis has been employed, or, rather, *developed,* and why a ready-made
mode of analysis, method or approach could not have been as useful and productive.

Furthermore, this *Introduction*, if it succeeds in its intended task, is meant to
reflect its author's position vis-a-vis his work and present conjunctures in their often
contradictory unity. In return, it calls for the need *to consider the study as a whole
– a whole that is irreducible to isolated arguments or statements in it.*

1.2 The conjuncture(s): Personal, theoretical, social

At a first reading the present text may appear belaboured, complex and difficult.
Complexities and difficulties are present not only in its objects and its method of
analysis, but also in the way it is presented, i.e. its *writing*. This needs to be said at the

1 Foucault, M. (1972): 44.

1

beginning, as writing an *Introduction* to such a work is no less complex and difficult than writing the text itself. The *Introduction* is expected to introduce the text in a way that enables the reader to locate it properly.

With 'location' I mean the spectrum of past and present fields of inquiry, the range of theoretical as well as other forms of arguments and institutional, social and professional contexts of these inquiries and arguments. We can call the instant that is defined by these locations, spectrum, range and contexts the *'conjuncture'*. Due, mainly, to the nature of this study its conjuncture should be seen as a complex structured whole constituted by *theoretical* as well as *professional, social, political, historical* and *personal* conjunctures. Thus, *the* conjuncture of this study cannot be reduced to any one of these conjunctures, nor, in fact, any one of the latter is reducible to one or more of each other.

Therefore, the complexities and difficulties referred to above must be seen in terms not only of the *internal* problems of the study or those of its object, but also of the conjuncture within which the study is done. However, this is not to say that conjuncture is 'external' to the study. Nor does it mean that it is the conjuncture which carries the responsibility for all the shortcomings, mistakes and difficulties.

This study is about a *Discourse*. For the moment, a discourse can be defined as a formation constituted by all that is said, written or thought in a (more-or-less) determinate field. This definition will be elaborated later on in this *Introduction* as well as in various sections of the study. Now, by locating the object of study (i.e. *Environmental Discourse* 1) and the study itself in a conjuncture it is expected that the present study is *not* treated as a closed, finished and self-standing piece of work with definite boundaries.

First, a brief note on the *personal* conjuncture — however much this note may seem to be paradoxical vis-a-vis the method of discourse analysis developed in the study, namely, the principle that no statement or text can be evaluated in relation to the personality of its author. With the awareness of this possible paradox it must be noted that in the case of the present study the 'personal' level of the conjuncture is inseparable from other levels that will also be discussed in this section.

The central question is a simple one: *How is it that this study has been possible?* In other words, how did it form or define its *object?* Was that object readily 'given', and already talked about? If not, in what theoretical mode was the object (i.e. the 'Environmental Discourse') identified and approached? What 'approach', 'technique', 'method' or 'theory' were there in hand to start with the analysis? . . . .

It must be stated here that the study began with a refusal to accept a ready-made 'approach' to or 'framework' for an already constituted object. This refusal had two main sources:

1) I have always been sceptical of orthodoxy, fixed schemas and *'the'* correct perspectives — especially when I became aware of their socio-economic bases on the one hand, and theoretical blind-alleys they often lead to, on the other. Therefore, for me, beginning a research had to be marked by a *search* rather than an *adoption* or application.

2) In the specific terrain that I was to *begin* my research, namely 'environmental practices and disciplines', there was no framework or approach that could change my mind and attitude towards fixed schemas and 'best' approaches. As far as the questions I was asking were concerned, that terrain was *barren, diffused* and *confused* with a set of *multiplicities*. My knowledge of the'environmental practices', 'disciplines', 'education', 'studies' and 'theories' made me pessimistic on the one hand, and eager to overcome

1 Hereafter referred to as ED except for the purposes of emphasis or clarity.

that barrenness on the other.

'Environmental' studies and researches in the sixties and early seventies were either following the traditional conception of architecture and planning, or were looking for *external* approaches often with disastrous and mystificatory consequences. Whilst the one assumed and advocated the purity of what is known as the 'Art of Architecture', the other had to dirty its hands in the unresolved controversies of various sciences which it could very seldom comprehend. However, it was my conviction just as much as my experience that *it wasn't easy to solve problems*. My negative attitude to the 'approaches' of the day was not, therefore, based on any underestimation of the difficulties that my colleagues had to face in their work — whether they were studying the slum areas in Liverpool or squatters in Ankara, noise problems of M1 or industrial location in Midlands or were designing a university complex in Kuwait, a housing estate in London or entering a competition for Centre Beaubourg. Having worked in architectural practice, done research on architectural products and on design and production of industrialized housing I had no intention of convincing others to stop what they were trying to do in those fields. Simply stated, *I was asking some radically different questions on seemingly obvious problems that neither academic nor professional tradition seemed to me to be capable of offering answers to.*

What I was asking then can hardly be summarized now especially after a long period of theoretical work which *changed not only my approach to those questions, but also the questions themselves.* To put it in the terms I used then, I was concerned with the social definition of architecture and planning, intending to dispel the myths created around the products and activities in those practices, and trying to make sure that the so-called 'scientific approaches', 'design methods', 'systems theories' or 'quantitative models', . . . were actually justified, and I was interested in understanding the political pertinence of professional radicalism, environmentalism, participationism, etc.

These were difficult questions despite their obviousness. After all, everybody was talking and writing about them! Did I have to rediscover America? It was precisely at that point that the *thesis* has started taking its structure. I realized that 'America' had indeed been discovered long ago, yet (a) there seemed to be thousands of different 'America's depending on thousands of different points of views and approaches; and (b) as far as I could see, the whole continent was badly obscured under fog. *There was an apparent paradox in the presumed obviousness of the object* and *the multiplicity of its conceptions.* Similarly, there was an anomaly in the fog-infested precision with which my inevitably confused arguments on seemingly obvious questions were confronted: I was accused of being *too* 'abstract', 'vague', 'idealistic', 'revolutionary', 'pessimistic', 'academic', . . . I was advised to be less of these things. My questions about the *social specificity* of (so-called) 'environmental issues' were met with similar reactions. While the 'rightist' opposition reminded me of the fact that they do things differently in this country, the 'leftist' opposition found my critical approach a wasted effort. Yet, they were unified in one, very significant, way: They were both trapped by an ideology of *'immediate relevance'*. The former translated this ideology as *'technicism'* (e.g. "we must do our best for the community, design better buildings and towns") while the second group's conception of relevance ended up in *'moralism'* (e.g. "we must provide better housing for the working-class", "what is the use of theoretical work on 'environment' — everything will be OK after the revolution").

In the traditional circles, on the other hand, it was *assumed* and *argued* that architecture was an art of building, that space was defined by distance, that squatter settlements were illegal, yet 'imaginary',creations of 'native' genius, that urban sociology studied modern cities while anthropology studied primitive villages, that space reflected culture, that vandalism was caused by high-rise buildings, that 'environment' had to be 'humanized', that local government structure had to be reformed, that decentralization was essential, that prefabrication was the only solution, etc, etc. The differences of opinion on these arguments were the *variations* on the same themes. Given issues were discussed in seemingly *opposing approaches* but in *similar terms.*

Designers and planners were justifying their products in various ways — from divine proportion to modular co-ordination, from artistic inspiration to mathematical models, from user requirements to universal principles, or from professionalism to humanism. Once I observed this rather confusing state of affairs I could not ask just *one more* question which would probably imply its own answers.

Another problem was that the fundamental questions that I dared asking could not be posed, let alone answered, in the theoretical conjuncture of the 1970-71 (at least in the English-speaking world): For example, a materialist understanding of architecture and planning, buildings and urban phenomena were yet an un-realized possibility. In fact, I have later seen that the initial questions that I posed regarding the *'society-space', 'society-environment', 'society-architecture' relations* were only possible as wrongly-posed questions based on what I identified as 'Man-Environment' problematic. The present study was therefore initiated as a prolegomenon to the study of those questions; yet, later on, it has   enabled me to see their inadequacies. When, for example, I wanted to study the possibility of an 'architecture' which would be 'social' I soon realized that I was formulating an equation with two unknowns. What was 'architecture', and what was 'social'? Once again, what *seemed obvious* to everyone else I discovered, in effect, to be two unknowns (or lacunae) owing their existence and their presumed connexions to a *denegation.*

With these observations I started formulating *my* tasks: First of them was to understand the natures of 'architecture' and 'society' not as two separate phenomena to be correlated, but the first as an element of the second. This 'discovery' (which is *now* a fairly common knowledge) led me to the study of social phenomena, that is, to the social sciences, and more specifically, to a historical materialist conception of society. Second of my tasks had to be to understand how it was that all those talks and texts, all those easy answers to difficult questions were possible in the first place. Surely, conceptual mistakes were not 'falling from the sky'. There must have been a set of mechanisms enabling people to make certain statements and to adopt certain frameworks with confidence. These two tasks found their expression in some topical issues such as 'participation in housing process', 'design methods', 'environmental perception', 'professional ideologies', 'urbanization', 'education', etc.

Yet, it was here that the two tasks *had to* be discriminated. I could not choose just one or both of them *at any order.* Although they seemed to be closely related (which I still think they are) as far as theoretical strategy was concerned, they represented different choices. To tackle the first without doing the second would presume an *understanding* that is the object of the second task. To tackle the second, on the other hand, seemed to be possible without committing myself to one of many existing positions on the first question.

These strategic decisions involved much more than the specific study that I was to embark on. It was a question of whether numerous positions on the relationship between spatial organization and social structure were legitimate/tenable/viable/ sustainable/ . . . *And,* it was a question of how one could decide *which* position or *what* approach was to be adopted as the basis for a specific study.

Having seen the subtle and fundamental differences between the two tasks it was no longer possible for me to behave *as if* that difference did not exist. Thus, despite my desire to do so, I could not simply attempt to study some architectural/urban problems from a chosen (say, Marxist) theoretical point of view, yet, in *given* terms.

For, unlike most of the 'environmental studies' I couldn't help asking:
a) What is the *basis* on which one chooses a theoretical system, an approach or a method?
b) What is the *nature* of the object to be studied?
The first question required an understanding of what a 'theory', an 'approach', a 'method' or a 'technique' was; and the second, an understanding of *what*, exactly, 'city' 'housing', 'settlement', 'environment', 'space' or 'society' were.

Now, if the existing arguments were *not* asking these seemingly obvious, yet subtle and fundamental, questions, were they aware of the inevitable *relativism* that they were working within, and often, reproducing? After all, *any* chosen theory or method could be 'applied' to *any* conception of these socio-physical phenomena. Moreover, the fact that (like weather) *everybody* was talking about the 'environment' could either mean that everybody knew what it was, or that (unlike weather) *nobody* actually knew what it was. It was one thing to one person and another thing to another. So, what was *really* 'environment'? And whether theory A's definition of it was compatible with profession B, or practice C? How were problems related to the definition(s) of 'environment' on the one hand and to specific differences of professions, practices and domains on the other? Were all problems, practices, theories, approaches, definitions, environments, spaces, cities . . . at the *same level*? If not, how were different levels defined and determined?

These and other questions marked the end of the beginning: I could see that all these questions were indispensable, and that they could not be ignored if one did not want to produce a self-justifying (and ultimately redundant) study. At the same moment I also realized that neither architectural nor planning practices were able to discuss such questions that were vital to their development. These practices were basically *technical* though with strong social determinations. They did not possess the tools and terms for *theoretical* analysis of their own activities while being capable of producing highly complicated and precise technical schemes for given problems. Besides, whether the practitioners of these practices liked it or not, earlier-mentioned problems were being defined, theorized, studied and institutionalized often *without asking the very questions that I found indispensable.*

Secondly, the disciplines and sciences (such as social sciences, systems theory, ecology, engineering) to which references were made would themselves need to be questioned. There was no guarantee that these 'external' aids possessed *the* way out of the architectural and urban problems. And, there was *no* indication that those who borrowed wanted to know whether those disciplines and sciences solved all their own internal problems. These borrowings assumed the source disciplines as 'advanced' and thus useful to more 'inferior' practices of architecture and planning. As in all direct and uncritical borrowings the whole enterprise remained (with some notable exceptions) to be a 'transfer of (conceptual) technology', and in many cases nothing more than a vocabulary. Of course, this had origins in the ongoing debates in the philosophy of science where a *physicist bias* was (and still is) dominant. The conception of 'science' was based, in those debates, on a scrutiny of how theories in physical sciences were produced. When, however, borrowings were from social sciences they too remained as uncritical transfers by appreciative outsiders. The so-called 'interdisciplinary approach', on the other hand, often remained an uncritical incorporation of two or more approaches. Yet, while this strategy enabled 'environmental scientists' to base their studies on seemingly firm and indisputable grounds, they also remained (at least formally) within the traditional mode of analysis in architecture and planning (namely, adopting styles, fashions or models, and 'explaining' their choices in terms of 'beauty', 'scale', 'function', 'cost yard-stick', etc.)

All these and many other arguments (often with myself) produced a gloomy picture of the field in which I happened to have been trained. In my previous education and research as well as in a period of office practice I had already observed stark theoretical naivety coexisting with elaborate technical detailing, second-hand social theorizing providing ammunition for many anti-social arguments, and pseudo-social concern covering up established modes of exploitative relations. I had also observed that these contradictions, in turn, were being isolated, institutionalized, neutralized and hypostatized through so-called 'environmental studies'.

To return to the distinctions made at the beginning, it was now necessary to tackle the *second* task to avoid a premature preoccupation with the *first* one. In other words, in the then *theoretical conjuncture* the first task could not be tackled without some inevitable pitfalls or anomalies. Yet, this is not to say that it was also easier to tackle the second task first. On the contrary, and as far as the academic requirements were concerned it would have been much 'easier' to choose an 'environmental problem' and a reasonable theory/method to study it — without necessarily asking the type of questions mentioned earlier on. It was here that the *personal conjuncture* overlapped with the *theoretical* one. My refusal to take up the easier (yet, theoretically inpermissable) route proved to be the best possible strategy as far as my research programme is concerned. I was not to make statements about so-called 'environmental problems', but to question how those statements were being made. As we will see in detail this did not involve a linguistic study, nor one detached from the socio-political and institutional contexts.

It is now possible, with the hindsight, to say that it *was* a correct decision. Yet, at the time of making that decision the theoretical conjuncture was much less favourable for a study that had to be concluded at a limited time. In order to be able to *situate* my study I had to review:
— *existing* approaches, trends, frameworks and theories in history and theory of architecture, environmental psychology, urban sociology, industrial design, etc.
— *existing* modes of analysing (a) practical issues, and (b) theoretical and discursive formations. In both cases it involved a *method of reading* — whether made explicit or not. In the first instance, my method of reading was dominated by an (over-)critical look at the architectural and planning practices as a whole. This included what designers and planners *say* about their activities and products, how 'scientists' or researchers *explain* problems associated with these practices, and how several sub-disciplines like histories of art, architecture, and urbanism, environmental psychology or urban sociology *operate* as sub-disciplines.

Furthermore, as this 'survey' progressed, certain common threads of argument and analysis in non-academic and non-professional discourses were discovered. Yet, at no stage did I have the illusion that my survey was conducted with an explicit theoretical framework. I took all material in their own terms. Though I certainly had some views about all these problems I never classified them as 'correct' or 'wrong', as 'legitimate' or 'inpermissable', as 'scientific' or 'rubbish' — i.e. in an *a priori* system of classification. It now seems that it was a correct strategy in the absence of a definite method of reading. If it delayed the formulation of the object of study it nevertheless had the advantage of not committing me to a (possibly ill-) chosen method.

Parallel to this survey was the development of my insight into areas such as social theory, psychology, scientific methods, epistemology, philosophy, theories of art, literature and semiotics. Thus, by the time I was able, *in my own terms,* to have achieved a sufficient level of theoretical formation I simultaneously achieved a comprehensive (if not fully specialized) understanding of the practices and discourses I surveyed. This saturation point was reached in 1974 after which I began *structuring* the study.

In the first instance it involved developing a mode of reading and analysis. This, on the other hand, had to be a non-environmental, non-social scientific and non-technical mode of reading in order to avoid the inherent and inevitable reductionism in such 'approaches'. In other words, *the object of study* had to be not specific positions, styles, theories, books, persons or schools of thought, but, the *discourse* that is dominant in all these practices and approaches. This point will be appreciated when we see what a 'discourse' is and how it can be analysed.

But now, we must look at the *conjuncture* further. When I refused to adopt an 'external' framework on the one hand, and professional ideologies on the other, I was aware of the fact that either I had to find another, but 'better', framework, or I had to develop a framework for my own study. In view of the confusions, dogmatism, barrenness and uncertainties that I had observed earlier on neither of these possibilities was any easier. What I was refusing to accept was so pervasive that I had to risk the possibility of producing nothing — nothing,that is, with respect to the widespread notions and protocols as to what constitutes research. Moreover, I also realized towards the middle of my research that the limits as well as the extent of these recognized frameworks were not *universal* — as they let one believe in the first instance. While it was inconceivable in one country to define urban problems in terms of Marxist theory, it was, however, a common knowledge in another. Of course, linguistic, political and ideological differences, rather than geographic ones, were the main factors in these differences.

This discovery too confirmed my earlier insistence on the non-existence of a *single* framework. This was also in line with my criticism of the discrepancy between the *globality* of environmental arguments and the extreme *narrowness* of 'environmental studies'. I was convinced that this was due mainly to the nature of the discourse within which these arguments were produced. Here too there was a theoretical barrenness and poverty, if not void, in the discourse that I was looking at. It was not only disinterested in, but also largely incapable of, discussing its own theoretical problems, its own epistemological status and its own shortcomings. In other words, there were approaches of all sorts: moral, formal, technicist, humanist, speculative, . . . yet, hardly ever epistemological. Moreover, any statement which seemed to touch the questions of epistemology did so with considerable confusion of the practical and epistemological, real and theoretical, levels.

Some isolated, yet notable, efforts started to appear in Europe and England after 1973-74 which tried to transcend these confusions by establishing for themselves genuinely theoretical bases. In other words, instead of ignoring, reducing or confusing the levels just mentioned they took upon themselves the difficult task of tackling the two strategies that I have differentiated at the beginning. Due mainly to their over-ambitious projects (— similar in a way to what I wanted to embark on at the beginning of my study) they had to attempt, from rather different positions
a) to produce critiques of existing spatial/urban discourses,
b) to propose 'alternative' theoretical frameworks (i.e. *problematics*),
c) to analyse mainly urban problems within the 'alternative' framework(s) proposed.
In this process, however, they *had to* stop short in the task (a), and resort to a quick *application* (or, a 'theoretical pragmatism') in the tasks (b) and (c). The conditions of these developments are too complex to be examined here. Moreover, as I am aware of the objectives and limitations of the present discussion I do not intend to turn it into a superficial critique of some substantial and ongoing efforts. I only want to relate these developments to the question of conjuncture.

The appearance of these works had profound effects on my attitude towards my own work. I became assured
— that my early questions on the *social specificity* of spatial organization were relevant, valid and possible,
— that my decision to start with the discursive/theoretical analysis (i.e. the second task) was a healthy one,
— that practical questions could only be formulated and tackled on the basis of explicit theoretical frameworks.
— that theoretical conjuncture was a *material* force that had to be understood alongside social, political . . . conjunctures.
It was after these observations that I noticed a flourishing trend, specifically in the field of planning, which broke its ties with previous ones and tackled the theoretical and/or empirical problems on a *materialist* basis. Though all carried with them the limitations of a developing framework they nevertheless are the welcome forerunners of significant new approaches.

My study can only be located within this development in the light of the developments in non-urban and non-architectural domains. This is so not because it is just one more 'interdisciplinary' study, or the 'application' of an external theory or a discipline.It is because the object of the study (i.e. the Environmental Discourse) is definable only *theoretically* and analysable only as a *discourse,* such a mode of inquiry cannot be confined within the limits of a single theory, a single discipline, or, for that matter, to a combination of these.

As we will discuss in Sec. 1.5 below in detail, what is involved in a *discourse analysis* is the conceptualization of the discourse as a *practice* and as a *formation* with its own object(s), structure, rules and mechanisms. Furthermore, there is no homology, parallel or correspondence between a discourse and a particular theory or discipline. Yet, a discourse analysis is not a 'general theory' to analyse all and every conceivable discourse either. Each discourse or theory may not need a completely different mode of analysis, but each discourse analysis may be different. It is in this sense that my approach to the dominant discourse in architecture, planning and ecology movement is *related* with the theoretical developments in social sciences, philosophy of science and theory of art. Thus, the theoretical conjuncture of this study is constituted by these fields of inquiry alongside the ones that we provisionally call 'environmental'. In the case of this study, the conjuncture is chiefly determined by the 'non-environmental' fields as the 'environmental' ones were (and still are) *incapable* of comprehending the discourse which they are operating within. It is at least in this sense that this study analyses the ED from *without.*

It must be emphasized that there is no intention here to survey the theoretical developments in social sciences and philosophy of science in the early 70's. This is neither necessary nor   possible in this context. What I could say here is that a series of theoretical works particularly in France and later in England had profound effects on *the conception of social phenomena* ranging from physical objects to class-struggle or from works of 'art' to state apparatus. Thus, the formation of this study owes to this development a particular, yet hardly describable, debt. It neither 'adopted' or 'applied' a particular theory or method for the reasons explained above, nor was it, in fact, an 'extension' of one or more of such theories or methods. Although it may sound as a rather abstract explanation, I would say that this study's debt to these developments is in the latter's creation of a *theoretical field* (much more than a framework or a problematic) which enabled me *to repose, to formulate* and *to analyse* the questions which I was asking at the beginning of my

research. In other words, most of the questions that are posed in the final text are
neither given in the ED itself, nor are they presented by those 'non-environmental'
theoretical developments. Nor, in fact, are most of them ever considered in the
recent developments in urban discourse mentioned earlier on. My use of the 'terms'
from the developing theoretical sources is largely independent of their origin not due
to any 'inspired originality' on my part, but due to my attempt to *establish a discourse
analysis* that would meet the requirements of analysing a complex, pervasive and
confused discourse – hence, an adequate and effective, if not tailor-made, mode of
analysis. It was only through such a mode of analysis that the question of 'applicability', i.e. *theoretical pragmatism,* and *shift of domain* (e.g. Marxism applied to
'environment') is avoided – if not ignored. What is thus achieved poses the question
differently and in different terms.

Finally, there is another component of the conjuncture which hasn't been discussed
yet. That component is constituted by the basically *non-discursive* domains and forces
with unignorable effects on both the ED *and* on the formation of its present critique.
In other words, they have determinant relations with what is said, written or thought,
in particular contexts. It is in this sense that the theoretical conjuncture of this study
is to be seen in its connexion with the *non-discursive conjuncture*[1] too. As a *social*
practice the ED emerges, is recognized or supported by, and criticized,in particular sets
of social conditions. These conditions will be examined in Ch. 5. Suffice it to say here,
by way of example, that if there is a shift of emphasis from 'progress' to 'environment'
or a shift of attention from 'capitalist crises' to 'environmental crises' we cannot
ignore the social (i.e. economic, political, ideological) conjuncture within which such
shifts occur. Similarly, if in certain societies well-established theoretical systems are
banned, repressed and *persecuted* we cannot speak about a 'free' milieu in which the
nature of certain problems can be redefined. Thus, if identifying some problems as
'environmental' (and nothing else) becomes the official truth, arguing *against* this
'truth' may well have to face certain non-theoretical and non-discursive consequences.
Or, (and this is a warning against misplacing this very study) a critique that distinguishes (without separating) the *epistemological* from the *political, ideological* or *professional* levels neither reduces the latter to the former, nor (even as an epistemological
critique) is it unrelated with other levels.

However, the nature of this relationship is itself a question worth studying separately.
What I can only suggest here is that so long as a discourse analysis shows
the fallacies in established truths in arguments so long as it deciphers, demystifies and
lays bare self-justifying propositions or obvious-looking assumptions, it *is* political.
Similarly, so long as it questions, *by analysing,* the tautological and pragmatic modes
of explanation in socio-technical practices such as architecture or planning, it *is*
relevant and useful. What determines the 'usefulness' of a discourse analysis is *not* its
apparent distance from political struggles or professional practices. For, that 'distance'
itself is defined and determined by those struggles or practices *or* by the theoretical
analysis of their dominant discourses. It should at least be recognized that there can
be no struggle or practice that hasn't got theoretical, educational, discursive, artistic,
scientific, as well as speculative, instances. Yet, these instances are not secondary
accessories that can be ignored at will: *They are, often, what struggles or practices are*

---

1 The concept of 'non-discursive' does not imply a conjuncture which has nothing to do with
discourses. On the contrary, all domains and practices *contain* or *use* discursive means. Here, it
simply denotes those conditions whose objects, structures, and mechanisms do not constitute a
discursive unity – such as the 'religious discourse', 'political discourse' or 'artistic discourse'.
While the religions, politics and art include discursive forms and tools they are not, however,
discourses, but are *practices, institutions* or *activities.* (See Sec. 5.3.4 for a more detailed discussion
on this point).

all about. In short, a discourse analysis *can* be vital in understanding, criticizing, participating, developing, demolishing or transforming . . . struggles and practices.

Leaving the examination of these questions to other sections we may now return to the theoretical conjuncture and see in what ways the present analysis is related with the ED itself. Following the strategic decisions and choices made earlier this study was constituted *outside* the ED which, in return, is nothing more than the *object of the study.* Therefore, the study deals mainly with the nature of arguments of the discourse rather than that which these arguments are about. Similarly, the objects (e.g. 'Man', 'Environment') of the discourse are *not* recognized as theoretically specified empirical objects, but as the *discursive objects* of the ED. This study neither recognizes nor uses these terms as its own terms. (Hence, the consistent bracketing of these terms in the text.) For, to speak in 'environmental' terms would in no way contribute to an understanding of the discourse on that object. After all, *everybody seems to know what the 'environment' was!* Thus, instead of attempting to contribute to this common *(and* confused) knowledge just one more treatise on how 'Man' and 'Environment' interact, or how 'Environment' and 'Behaviour' are related (questions preoccuping most of the ED), this study began with a well founded suspicion of the *ease* at which such a 'knowledge' is assumed to exist. That is why it was necessary to go *outside* the ED itself — though not exactly *its* outside[1] as this would be a *recognition* of the objects and arguments of the discourse. The reasons for this strategy has already been examined. One more reason is that it was only by such a strategy that the ED as an object of study could be *identified.* Consequently, *the study is not about 'environment' or 'Man-Environment relationship', but about a pervasive discourse constituted around these terms.* And, it is neither an 'environmental' nor 'sociological' study, but a 'discursive' and 'theoretical' one. Furthermore, it is *not* based on a criticism of a single book, a theory or a person. A discourse exists in all forms of statements. It can therefore be analysed in terms of its objects, structure and mechanisms, not in terms of where, or by whom, it is reproduced.

This study does not criticize the *conceptions of 'environment'* in the ED and does not propose *alternative* definitions or theories of 'environment'. Instead, it criticizes the *nature* of these conceptions and definitions. *It does not, therefore, address itself to the so-called environmental problems that this study identified in that discourse.* This does not mean that the present study (or its author) is not concerned with the practical issues and problems that are *presently designated as* 'environmental' problems. It is (and I am) certainly interested in and concerned with socio-physical problems of all sorts. But I am also concerned with the serious theoretical, professional and ideological effects of *denegated* formulations of questions and tautological explanations of these problems. For the reasons which are partly described at the beginning I found it both *impossible* to tackle empirical problems without a theoretical understanding, and *irresponsible* to answer certain existing questions *as if* they were legitimate. These were the main reasons for my shift into a theoretical/discourse analysis. In short, whatever the apparent concern of the study seems to be, a careful reading should not miss the *relevance* of the analysis vis a vis the central problem it identifies.

---

1 cf. "It is impossible to leave a closed space simply by taking up a position *outside it,* either in its exterior or its profundity: so long as this outside or profundity remains *its* outside or profundity, they still belong to *that* circle, to *that* closed space, as its 'repetition' in *its* other-than-itself. Not the repetition but the non-repetition of this space is, the way out of this circle: . . . the radical foundation of a new space, a new problematic which allows the real *problem* to be posed . . ." (Althusser, L. (1970): 53).

Making no attempt to establish an 'alternative' to the ED this study analysed *what exists* and *how*. In view of the immense task that it has taken on itself this study neither attempted to be the documentation of an ideology (or a worldview, or a profession, . . .), nor did it attempt to present an exhaustive analysis of a discourse. Being the first of its kind in a particular field it had to be *general* if not *complete*. This was not a choice, but an inevitability. Having hardly any base or an earlier work in the fields of architecture and planning on which to build up an analysis of the ED *it had to establish a base for, and by, itself.* Therefore, it carries with it the disadvantages (as much as the potentials) of this specificity.

With an awareness of this specificity it tried to be *open-ended* and *self-critical*. As such, it *can* be developed, rectified and extended. It can also be the basis for other studies — discursive or otherwise. It proposes to be such a basis in its arguments
1) that even most commonly recognized statements and terms may be highly questionable,
2) that reluctance to question even the most obvious-looking positions is an indication not of strength, but of weakness,
3) that inability to see the weaknesses and fallacies of a field is only remediable through a theoretical analysis of its nature, status, discourse and methods,
4) that to achieve a self-critical, open-minded and progressive field (or a profession, or a discipline) that field must be able to look at its own 'problems' not in terms of fixed schemas and terms, but as complex objects that cannot be approached without prior theoretical (or technical) analyses.

Thus, this study analyses not only the structure and mechanisms of the ED — as a prolegomenon to further analyses, it also presents *how* such an analysis can be done. In other words, *it is not simply a study applying a given method or approach, but one which develops a specific mode of analysis.* Similarly, it is not a *survey* of given ideas, theories, approaches, statements . . . (as formed into a discourse). Neither is it a *history of ideas.* Furthermore, it must be emphasized that the ED, as identified and analysed in this study, *was not given as an empirical object only to be studied, nor was it readily deducible from a mass of statements or quotations.* Recognition of this point is absolutely necessary to be able to appreciate the *specificity* of the study. In fact, this point should be a logical consequence of
a) *an understanding of the ED as a discourse,*
b) *an understanding of what is involved in the analysis of a discourse.*

The text of the study is not simply an end-product of a research project. Nor is it the end of a process. It represents the *process itself.* It *is* the process whereby the unity of the ED is identified and analysed, its objects and assumptions are questioned, its structure and mechanisms are dissected. It is also the process whereby a *discourse analysis* is developed and tested. The resulting text, then, can be considered not as a set of finished products but as the *production process* itself. Thus, it can be likened neither to the goods in shops (ready for uncritical consumption), nor to a shop window (where finished products are exhibited). Instead, it best resembles to a set of products, and more specifically, to manufacturing tools under the process of production, and, in another sense, to a shop floor (where all processes take place).

With such a *self-awareness* (implying openness rather than pretentiousness) and self-analysis (implying uncompromising criticism rather than unfair arrogance) this study makes no attempt to criticize how designers design or planners plan. Neither does it want to tell them *how* to design or to plan. This does not mean, of course, that the present analysis lacks a conception of these activities. On the contrary, it would not be possible in the first place if it lacked such a conception.

But, seeing all *productive activities* as complex and overdetermined wholes, and identifying the important place that discursive modes of expression occupy in their structures, this study shows designers and planners the *nature* of their use of these modes without prescribing universal design or planning 'methods'. It also calls them *to be careful in how they think and talk about their activities.* Thus, it attempts neither to discredit those practices and disciplines nor to underestimate the difficulties involved in their operations. This is quite consistent with its conception of the reality: *Nothing is simple to do, nor anything is simple to express.* If it discusses, deconstructs, scrutinizes, criticizes and/or transforms nearly all modes of expression (from speeches to drawings, from theoretical texts to newspaper advertisements) in the field of the so-called 'Environment' it is mainly because it sees the serious implications of simplistic reductionism and schematism, circular arguments, second-hand theories . . . that are dominant in that field. If it uses a *theoretical* mode of analysis (as opposed to speculative, moralistic, pseudo-philosophic or technicist ones) it is not because the study thinks this mode is 'superior' to the others, but because the effects of them can only be *exposed* through such an analysis. Besides, theoretical analysis is done at a theoretical level, and not in a concrete mixer. Nor can theoretical and epistemological problems be handled by shovels or even by T-squares. But, it is also important to recognize the fact that one cannot construct houses by concepts and statements alone. As to the difficulties and relations between these practices, it is precisely an object of *theoretical* analysis. That is why epistemological and discursive levels are the ones to which the primary attention is directed. Otherwise, it would be difficult *not to reproduce the terms and arguments of what is being criticized.* It would also be difficult *to question what seems to be so obvious.*

One question that may be asked is whether the ED is worth this long and difficult effort, and whether it would better be ignored. The answer to this question would be simple: The whole argument at the beginning of this introduction was that if these problems which are presently called 'environmental', 'spatial', 'architectural', 'ecological' . . . are to be *tackled,* then they must first be *formulated* and *understood.* In the pervasive existence of a specific discourse, dominated by a misleading 'ideology' and a 'problematic', such formulations had to be *within* the ED. Yet, I had several strong reasons for refusing this framework: First of all, it is the *terms* and *structures* with which formulations are made in these fields that are suspect. It was therefore impossible to propose radical formulations on the basis of given terms, schemas and ideologies. Once this theoretical observation was established, it was a theoretical duty to pursue the search for healthier modes of formulation. Secondly, as the study progressed and new observations were made it was clear that a study on the ED had far more implications than the ones for architectural and planning practices. It was one more domain where the social formations could be understood in terms of their determinate structures and elements. For, the ED was much more than a technical discourse. It was the locus of a widespread ideology – *the ideology of environment,* which was a prominent supporter and component of the political ideology. Similarly, the discourse was not simply about brick-and-mortar. It was carrying with it overt or covert *assumptions* on society, on politics, on 'human behaviour', on professional functions, etc. Moreover, presenting its arguments as 'scientific', it was giving a false confidence to its adherents and a protective veil to its mystificatory statements. Due mainly to its highly complex and confused structure it was not readily possible to reform or rectify it. It was too large to handle. And those who were in the day-to-day activity of producing plans, projects or programmes for implementation could not be expected to see the scope, the nature and the implications of their arguments.

It was therefore necessary to analyse the position of these arguments in the practices and disciplines, and consequently ask *how it was that these practices manage to work on an object which they can hardly define, or upon which there is no agreement.*

Pausing here for a moment, we may introduce the *field* at which the ED is situated and which it constitutes. This diversion is necessary to clarify and to explain certain notions that have already been referred to above (such as 'epistemology', 'discourse', 'problematic', 'ideology', 'unity'), and to facilitate the transition from the arguments on conjuncture to the actual study which is a product of that conjuncture. This will be followed by a *Detour* on the notions referred to.

1.3   The field of the 'environmental' question

To open up the discussion we must start with a set of *provisional* observations on a *tentatively recognised* field — the field of architecture and planning: There are, and there have always been, many 'approaches', 'styles' and 'trends' in the field of architecture and planning. In fact, each generation of practitioners and professionals keep witnessing several 'new' approaches or 'new' ideologies. Even a superficial observation would indicate the variety of the sources of these approaches: they come from arts, from industrial design, from social sciences, physical sciences, computer technology, systems theory, political arguments of the time or the everyday discourse prevalent at particular conjunctures.

Whatever their origins, these trends and approaches possess some distinct notions or concepts, use specific terms, or refer to problems. In short, they work on some *objects.* While some trends have no explicit objects, or have 'new' objects, some   keep working on objects which are transferred or borrowed from other disciplines, trends, approaches or professional practices. Some rely on 'common sense' to pursue their arguments or to evaluate their physical products, some, however, tend to be more subtle, less explicit or more technical. Some speak the language of the sciences, some, of moral ideology or of 'sister professions'. As to the *effects* they have, they vary, some remain in the books, some in drawings while some enter into the codes of practice and shape the products. Yet, some others get condemnations, or, are   demolished with the physical objects they once helped to shape. Moreover, they exert different types and degrees of influence on the practices of these professions. They penetrate into, or sometimes originate from, educational establishments of these practices. The degree to which they find their place in the physical and/or visual aspects of the products of these practices vary too: while some approaches and 'styles' disappear before they gain any wide recognition some, however, persist, get into several new forms, are transformed, recognized and remain influential. Some even find their way into official policies.

Now, it is assumed, for the purposes of this section, that these rather abstract and general observations *assume,* if not *define,* a 'domain', a 'field' or a 'level' at which all these transactions, developments and movements take place. Or, they seem to provide answers to questions which are not yet openly posed. They refer to an activity without specifying its rules, its object, its 'subject', its aim or its 'beneficiary'. They even regard the name of this field as rather tentative.

In order to improve what was said, at the beginning, to be 'provisional observations' we may proceed by posing some equally provisional and general questions — this time without attempting to give any answers:
— *Where* do all these transactions and transformations take place (i.e. at what domain or level)?
— If they constitute a domain or a field, what kind of domain or field is it?

– How are they possible (i.e. what are their conditions of existence)?
– What status do they have (i.e. are they scientific, technical, ideological, . . .)?
– What governs their emergence, disappearance, persistence, effectivity or trans-
formation (i.e. what structural properties, mechanisms or relationships)?
– To put several problems into a more 'down-to-earth' question: what distinguishes
or unites those approaches that are called after the names of persons such as Vitruvius,
Alberti, Le Corbusier or E. Howard, or after the names of groups such as Team X,
Utopie or Archigram, or that are known as neoclassicism, functionalism, constructivism, utopianism, or that are studied within the frameworks or design methodology,
history of art, architecture and planning, urban sociology, environmental psychology,
or that involve professional practices of engineering, architecture, political economy,
ecology, geography, art, or that are the objects of codes of practice, books, 'imperial
decrees', artistic impressions, religious imagery, popular movements, or last, but
not least, that are identified with pyramid building, council housing, shanty towns
or Bororo village?
– Or, another set of problems: *What exactly specifies and relates* these terms,
problems, concepts or words which, for ages, have been the objects of arguments, or
objectives of approaches and practices: function, style, symbol, need, satisfaction,
ownership, environmental quality, environmental imagery, privacy, attitude, participation, new towns, segregation, migration, destruction, speculation, measurement,
occupation, living, expropriation, prevention, emancipation, revolution, harmony,
balance, community, nature, unity, choice, freedom, roofing, garden fence, prefabrication, space standards, utility, spatiality, territoriality, vandalism, class-struggle,
intuition, precision, creativity, innovation, systematicity, interaction, interface, discrimination, racialism, spirit, flow, movement, development, growth, decay, obsoles-
cence, conflict, reflection, anarchy, ecology, culture, economy, art, climatization,
filter, expansion, transformation, renovation, bathroom, living room, city square,
flexibility, green areas, overcrowding, population density, environmental perception . . ?
   These rather randomly selected terms, problems and concepts are not meant to
bring into the disciplines and professions any more confusion than there already exists
in them. In fact, it is a relatively small list if one considers the number of such 'items'
that exist in the vocabulary of these professions and their practices. *Why,* and *how?*
   Now, as it has been stressed in the introductory discussions above this study does
not intend to provide *practical* solutions to all these problems, nor does it aim to
bring   all these terms and concepts into an all-embracing general framework (i.e.
a 'general theory of everything' with which such solutions can be achieved), nor, in
fact, is it convinced that such a project is possible. To repeat what has already been
said earlier on the first thing that this study aims to achieve is to provide an analysis
which lays bare
a) the *nature* of these questions – whether actually posed, or existing by implication;
b) the *conditions of existence* of these terms, notions and concepts; and
c) the fundamental *mechanisms* which produce, transform and relate them.
And, most significantly, to identify the only level at which this analysis is possible
without any reductionism; in other words, without choosing the point of view of
some in expense of others, and without establishing an arbitrary hierarchy of these
terms by declaring some as privileged over others, or explaining them in terms of others.
This level is the level of *epistemology,* and the domain at which this can be analysed
is the *discourse* which they constitute. This level and the domain are far from being
the individual choice of a person or a 'school of thought', but a result of a fundamental understanding of the complexity that occupies the field that is presently referred to as *'the environmental'*.

1.4 *A detour:* **On epistemology, ideology and problematic**

The present study carries within it the tension between its complex and ever-changing conjuncture and the task of producing a precise, if not definitive, account of an immensely vague and pervasive discourse. On the one hand, the theoretical developments that helped the formulation of the initial questions did not stop at a point, nor are they ever to do so. On the other hand, the impossibility of covering the whole ED (if such a 'whole' is ever conceivable in a nutshell) in one study is more obvious at the end of the long effort than at its beginning.

While this study would contribute to an understanding of the nature of arguments in the ED it is expected that it should not be taken as a *finished* statement on that discourse. Neither is it correct to deduce from it the idea that there is only one possible position from which to analyse it. It is possible to produce several analyses of the same discourse with differences in
a) the epistemological position of each analysis,
b) the differential emphasis of the aspects of the discursive structure,
c) the particular non-discursive domain, practice or formation they address themselves to.
It is not, however, permissible to suggest (as in empiricism) that there can be as many analyses as there are those who attempt to produce them, or that there are as many discourses (as 'objects') as there are analyses (done by 'subjects'). What is briefly remarked above is not to suggest such a relativism, but to stress the *conjunctural materiality* of discourses as well as their analyses.

Thus, the following notes on epistemology, ideology and problematic are not meant to describe finished and constant positions, but the theoretical framework that articulated *the beginning* of the study. In fact, these can be seen as already rectified and clarified in various discussions in the text especially in Chapters 5 and 6 on the *Relations* and the *Status* of the ED. They should therefore be seen as nothing more than introductory information, or as an index of positions that articulate my mode of critique. Furthermore, while they are made of brief remarks on certain positions, they are not axiomatic.

Epistemology

Epistemology is the study of the process of knowledge production. As such, it is concerned with special problems of this process. Yet, while epistemology analyses the processes and methods of sciences it is not itself a methodology[1], and does not constitute a privileged level. This conception of epistemology should be distinguished from the one which is associated with 'the theory of knowledge'. The latter is concerned with the study of acquisition of knowledge in terms of a 'knowledge' and a 'reality' to be known. Thus, theories of knowledge involve an 'object' (or 'world') to be known and a 'subject' (or 'man') who knows it. Although there are many 'theories of knowledge' they all assume, or are based upon, such a conception.[2]

In the classical philosophical traditions, all the way from Aristotle, epistemology (i.e. 'theory of knowledge') is contrasted with *'ontology'*. Ontology is said to be the study or "doctrine of being in general, being as such, independent of its particular forms".[3] Kant, for example, criticised ontology as being tautological in that, an "ontological argument is based on the concept of necessary existence, i.e., an exist-

---

1 cf. Latouche, S. (1970): 216.
2 On this conception of 'theory of knowledge', see, for ex., Hamlyn, D.W. (1971).
3 Rosenthal, M. & Yudin, P. (eds) (1967): 324.

ence it would be impossible to deny".[1] For Kant neither a subject nor a predicate can have necessity. Hegel, on the other hand, constructed the 'unity'of ontology (dialectics), logic and theory of knowledge only to end up in the 'Idea'. This philosophical trap of 'epistemology-ontology' couple is present in the ED though, mainly, at a physical context[2]. In fact, it is precisely this trap which leads to the confusion of 'real object' with 'theoretical object' and to the empiricist domination in the whole field. Husserl, on the other hand, resolved ontology into a phenomenological analysis, and saw it as "the self-revelation of the meaning of experience",[3] or as a "phenomenologically directed understanding of what fulfils the intentionality".[4]

As to the Marxist philosophy, 'dialectical materialism' is claimed to answer the ontological questions of idealist philosophy[5] simply by substituting 'matter' for 'existence' or 'being'[6] This brand of 'Diamat' reproduces the idealist problematic on the one hand, and a dualist position on the other. In fact, such an ontology "can be discussed without any reference to Marx's works, and is no longer essentially concerned with the analysis of the capitalist mode of production"[7] Such an epistemology implies a relativist position too, especially in claiming the 'primacy of matter', that is, the primacy in terms of the mechanistic dichotomy of mind and matter. Furthermore, it leads to the empiricist fallacy of subject-object problematic, and to the reflectionist theory of knowledge[8] . Moreover, a general ontology transforms the specific scientificity of Marxist theory into a 'general theory of everything', and finds itself looking for dialectics in microbiology, biology[9] or in boiling water, or 'applying' it to 'tomato' production or transportation[10] However, identifying Marxist theory with a 'regional' or a 'material'[11] ontology does not resolve the risks involved in the ontology-epistemology framework. There is also an empiricist confusion that arises out of an attempt to answer ontological questions at an epistemological level and epistemological questions at an ontological level.[12] Finally, such approaches tend to displace the questions from science to philosophy and ignore the fact that "science is the only means of apprehending reality, the only means of gaining knowledge of the world. There cannot be two (qualitatively different) forms of knowledge."[13]

The epistemological position that constitutes the problematic of the present study is one which *refuses to confuse* sensory experiences, everyday recognitions of events or objects, and the cognitive processes *with* a process of knowledge which is based on the production and movement of concepts and theories. In other words, an understanding of the processes whereby sensory perception takes place is not an explanation of the way in which scientific knowledge of the real is produced.

1 Hartnack, J. (1968): 133.
2 cf. Tschumi, B. (1975). 1-2.
3 Paci, E. (1972): 465.
4 O'Malley, J.B. (1971): 1.
5 For example, B. Ollmann presents a conception of reality which is essentially a conception of 'expressive totality' of Leibnitz, or 'totality' of Hegel. In this conception each of the parts in 'totality' "in its fullness can represent the totality" (Quoted in Harvey, D. (1973): 288). See, also, Ollmann, B. (1971). For a critique of this conception of 'totality', and a formulation of another one see: Althusser, L. (1969): Part 6. For an attempt to approach urban problems from the position of Ollmann, see: Harvey, D. (1973): 288-302.
6 cf. Bonjour, G.P. –(1967); Schmidt, A. (1971): 11, 164 ff.
7 Schmidt, A. (1971): 165.
8 cf. Cornforth, M. (1963): 26ff. For a critique of the reflectionist position, see Lecourt, D. (1973).
9 See, for example: Sandow, A. (1972).
10 Workers and Peasants (1972).
11 O'Malley, J.B. (1971): 1.
12 Bhaskar, R. (1975): 46.
13 Colletti, L. (1975): 29. However, this does not rule out the existence of other forms of knowledge in different practices such as architecture. The difference that is difficult to conceive in the same word

This and other problems concerning the epistemological position of the environmental discourse will be examined in their relevant sections. The present discussion will be limited to a brief statement on the epistemological position of *this* study as it operates in the analysis of the ED.

In most theories of knowledge the process of knowledge is one which takes place between a knowing subject and a known object (e.g. an interaction between 'Man' and 'Environment'). In this sense knowledge is related with individual subjects, whether concrete or ideal[1], and knowledge of the real becomes a subjective matter. As it will be shown later, the epistemological structure of the environmental discourse is such a structure. An immediate question that should be asked is whether the dominant epistemology, or the problematic, of the environmental discourse can answer questions regarding the structure and the status of the discourse? Or, does this question disappear when the locus of knowledge is shifted from individual human beings to books, libraries, sign systems or to the "objective contents of thought"?[2] *Which* books, or *whose* 'thoughts' are to be the object of the present analysis? Is there any mechanism in the ED to specify the difference between the *knowledge* of an object and the *real object?* And, does it specify precisely what its object is?

In the face of such an ambiguous discourse *this study attempts,* as argued earlier on, *not to analyse the 'knowing subject', nor 'known object', nor their supposed interaction.* Neither, for that matter, does it study the point of view of one or both of these sides. *It attempts to study the discourse itself* to be able to answer all these questions that have been posed above. It also attempts to *re*pose some of the questions that are *absent* on the surface while effectively *present* in the constitution of the discourse.

Ideology

The question of *ideology* has always been settled in the abstract and in general. Despite the fact that it is one of the most fundamental questions as far as the theories of social formation and political practice are concerned, it has often been assumed to be a matter of common knowledge. The same term 'ideology' stood for science, (as in the misconception of Marxist theory) as well as the opposite of science, for false consciousness as well as for what is written, said, and thought, or for things which should be put right as well as for those that one must be prepared to die for!

There are many 'theories' in sociology and psychology which relate 'ideology' to the individual subject, to mental states, social relations, or to social structure. On the other hand, it is also conceived of as a *misrepresentation* of the real, or as an effect of the nature of the human mind.[3] This last view is quite close to the view that the knowing subject's relation to the known object is distorted by deliberate and *external* forces (e.g. by one class)[4]. This, basically, is what is called a 'conspirational' view of ideology[5], and one which disregards the specificity of the latter as a relatively autonomous instance of social formations. For, if ideology is seen as a 'false conception' of the

---

'knowledge' is conceivable as *'connaissance'* and *'savoir'* in French. The former denotes the knowledges produced in sciences, the latter the ones used or produced in technical, artistic, . . . practices. The former consists of theories and concepts, the latter the know-how, rules, information, . . . (see Ch. 6 on this point; and Teymur N. & E. (1978) for a detailed discussion on the status of 'knowledge' in architecture.) /[I would in fact formulate the question differently today. N.T., 1982]

1 cf. the 'double status of subject', Althusser, L. (1969): 227 ff. See, also Sec. 3.3.2.

2 cf. Popper's 'Third World', Popper, K.R. (1972): 106.

3 cf. Durkheim, E. (1966), and Hirst, P.Q. (1975): 53-89.

4 cf. Northrop, F.S.C. mentioned in Bose, A. (1975): 45-7.

5 On this view, see: Mepham, J. (1972) and Althusser, L. (1971): 123-173.

real imported and imposed from *'outside'* the class, group or social formation, then, ideology would be reduced to an entity produced independently of the determinant structure of a social formation, and imported into it. But, if, on the other hand, ideology is an agent with a mechanism of 'self deception'[1] , it would be necessary to avoid the type of explanation which traps this mechanism into the dead-end of methodological agnosticism.

With these positions in mind, it becomes essential that our analyses should avoid reference to 'society *in general'*,[2] 'class *in general'* or 'ideology *in general'*. They should, instead, study *particular* social formations and *particular* modes of production as well as *particular* instances of these formations. Thus, for example, the determinate position of ideological instance in feudal social formation(s) should clearly be distinguished from that of economy in capitalist social formation(s). In that case, for example, the bourgeoisie not only needs *its* ideology to 'mystify' the working class, it actually *lives in it.* Yet, this is more than a self-deception or a psychological dilemma at individual level. If the political economy of the bourgeoisie 'sees' economic activity and economic instance in terms of 'economic man', market forces, private property, human needs, etc. or considers capitalist mode of production as eternal, [3] it is precisely because that is how capitalist mode of production is desired to be maintained by the class which dominates it. Ideology, understood as "the representation of the imaginary relation-ship of individuals to their real conditions of existence", implies that men represent *not* their real conditions of existence, their real world, but "their relation to those conditions of existence which is represented to them there".[4] It is the imaginary relationship of those individuals to the *real relations* in which they live that governs their existence.

An analysis of ideology, then, would involve an analysis not only of the structures and mechanisms by which an ideology is constructed, but also its material conditions of existence. And, that is where the relationship between discursive and non-discursive practices, and between ideologies and the real relations and problems which they are called upon to represent, can best be understood. This would also require distinguishing the 'theoretical' from the 'practical'[5] ideologies. Finally, in the fact of the as yet un-developed state of (general or particular) theories of ideology, it is necessary to be over-cautious in conducting, assessing and 'using' discourse analyses, analyses of ideologies and modes of 'reading'.[6]

Problematic

A theory, a discourse or a text[7] does not exist in an epistemological or theoretical void, or by itself.   They are the products of their theoretical conditions of existence – their *'problematic'*.[8] The problematic defines a field, a system or a theme. Yet, it must be

1 O'Malley, J.B. (1972): 252.
2 For a non-sociological critique of this conception, see: Lenin, V.I. (1970a): 9-11.
3 "In so far as Political Economy remains within that horizon, in so far, *i.e.* as the capitalist regime is looked upon as the absolutely final form of social production, instead of as a passing historical phase of its evolution, Political Economy can remain a science only so long as the class-struggle is latent or manifests itself only in isolated and sporadic phenomena." (Marx, K. (1970) v.I:24).
4 Althusser, L. (1971): 153-54. / 5 See L. Althusser in Lecourt, D. (1975): 210-11.
6 On these questions, and for a comparison of history of ideas, Althusser's theory of 'reading', structuralist theory of reading and Foucault's 'archaeology', see: Williams, K. (1974). For the limitations of the latter from a historical materialist point of view: Lecourt, D. (1975). See also Hirst, P.Q. (1976) for a critique of Althusser's concept of ideology.
Though the whole analysis of the ED here identifies an *Ideology of Environment*, Ch. 6 on the *Relations* will specifically deal with the ED as an ideological formation.
7 'Text' refers to literary or theoretical texts which are being 'read'; and to "the focus of thematic awareness/inquiry" (O'Malley, J.B. (1970): 14-15).
8 The concept of 'problematic' should not be confused with the same word which is used in everyday

distinguished from the concepts of 'thematique',[1] 'paradigm',[2] 'anomaly' or 'scientific research programmes'.[3] A problematic is a theoretical/conceptual structure, not a scientific ideology *agreed upon* by a 'scientific community'. It is a "determinate articulated system of concepts, instruments and modes of theoretical labour" whose unity is "that of a complex structured whole which is reducible neither to its elements nor to some essence of which its parts are just so many different expressions."[4]

Scientific research "demands the setting up of a problematic. Its real starting-point is a problem, however ill-posed".[5] Yet, a problematic may be ideological, moralistic, technical, as well as scientific. But, this cannot be determined solely with reference to the internal consistency, or structure of concepts. An ideology may be coherent and consistent too (such as religions). According to an idealist interpretation, the development of ideology "brings out within the thought *the objective internal reference system of its particular* themes, the system of *questions* commanding the *answers* given by the ideology". Yet, when the problematic itself is *"an answer,* no longer to its own internal questions − problems − but to *the objective problems posed* for ideology *by its time,"* the internal consistency of an ideology cannot be the criteria for its status. And. that is why "the *problematic of an ideology* cannot be demonstrated without *relating* and *submitting* it to the real problems to which its deformed enunciation gives a false answer".[6] Every ideology is a real whole, and is unified by its own problematic internally, and by the meaning that depends on its relationship to the existing ideological fields as well as to the social problems and social structures that sustain the ideologies.

An ideology must be understood by its social effects too.[7] As it is the problematic, i.e. the system of formulating *problems,* that governs the nature of *solutions,* and since an ideological problematic may provide solutions to real problems which may not (or, does not) "correspond to any of these real problems",[8] it is necessary to understand the problematic of an ideological discourse in order to be able to see the nature of solutions that it makes possible. However, it must be made clear that this conception does not resurrect the so-called 'problem of knowledge', i.e. the problem of *correspondence* between the reality and knowledge; or of 'truth' and 'falsity' of statements (as linguistic and analytic philosophy is concerned with). Nor is it meant to propose a unitary point of reference with respect to which *all* discourses and ideological systems can be assessed. This is also different from relating an ideological (or 'scientific') system to the 'consensus' of a 'scientific community' (i.e. *'paradigm'*). A paradigm is not primarily a problem-based conceptual system, but, rather, a *sociological field.*[9] It is a kind of 'worldview' of scientists. Its ideology is implicit, and is difficult to detect. It is taken for granted. And, most significantly, the relationship of a paradigmatic ideology to real problems is itself decided *within* the 'community' which holds it (hence, the *closed nature of* all ideologies).

Finally, it can be asked whether the ED is based upon a 'problematic' or a 'paradigm'. It was suggested, for example, that "man-environment studies are still at a pre-paradigmatic stage of development,"[10] or, that "there are, among other paradigms, three basically

discourse to denote doubtfulness. It is not also reducible to a linguistic sense as in "problematique: forme interrogative; dilemmatique: forme dubitative". (Lefebvre, H. (1971): 390.)
1 cf. Castells, M. (1973): 307, Foucault, M. (1972): 35-7.
2 Kuhn, T.S. (1970), also see: Lakatos, I. & Musgrave, A. (eds) (1970), and Tribe, K. (1973).
3 Lakatos, I. (1968).
4 Hindess, B. (1973b): 322.
5 Bachelard, G. (1949): 51 (translation quoted in Lecourt, D. (1975): 80).
6 Althusser, L. (1969): 67n.
7 Castells, M. (1975): 238.
8 Althusser, L. (1969): 80n.
9 For a critique of this aspect of Kuhn's position, see: Tribe, K. (1973).
10 Rapoport, A. (1971): 4.

different paradigms in planning and environmental design as well as in various fields of science . . . "[1]. The fundamental structure of the environmental discourse, namely, 'M-E relationship' has also been identified as a "man-environment paradigm".[2] Of course, the levels at which these three suggestions involve the term 'paradigm' are not the same, and from a similar point of view it might be possible to distinguish the *sociological* aspects of environmental ideologies from the *epistemological* ones. There have been some attempts to do this for architectural ideologies, in sociological at the expense of epistemological, terms[3]. This may seem to be quite possible and acceptable especially with regard to the nature of the domain, i.e. a non-scientific practice and a non-scientific 'community' of designers, architects, planners and 'users'. But, studying the prevalent ideologies in the terms given by that very ideology, or, indeed, in terms of empirical psychology and sociology, is bound to reproduce those ideologies only in a different vocabulary. In short, an ideological discourse like the ED cannot be analysed in sociological terms, and as a 'paradigm'. What is absolutely essential is to identify the conceptual structure, i.e. the problematic, of it in order to be able to *transform* it. This is what the present study attempts to demonstrate, if not fully achieve.

Principles and propositions

As pointed out at the beginning of this chapter, this study proposes to tackle the problem at the levels where it is generated, i.e. at epistemological and discursive levels, and to be guided by a set of principles which would enable it
a) to avoid presumed solutions in posing questions,
b) to break the pre-scientific domination of philosophy and cosmology in the analysis of real problems,
c) to question the questions themselves,
d) to 'read' what is absent in a discourse as well as what is present and obvious,
e) to avoid a 'theoretical empiricism' or 'pragmatism' in favour of analysing problematics by a distinct and explicit mode of discourse analysis.
Although these principles are discussed on several occasions in the study, it would still be useful to expand them briefly. In the light of what has already been said elsewhere in this *Introduction* it is possible to see
a) that a scientific research or a discourse is based upon a problematic which enables us to pose questions rather than to reproduce and perpetuate given answers;
b) that philosophy provides most of what goes on in theoretical ideologies (within or without sciences) mostly by referring the real problems to some ideal relationships, pure principles, moral values or to subjective judgements;
c) that it is necessary to identify the discrepancy between the questions that can be asked of real problems in science, and mystifications and deformations in the answers given in ideological discourses;
d) that a close, 'symptomatic', reading[4] of a discourse is necessary in order to see not only what is present in words, concepts and 'obvious' looking answers, but, also, what is *absent*, as it is after this that it may be possible to identify the specific knowledge effects of a discourse;
e) that in criticizing an ideological problematic and in showing *what* is ideological in it this problematic should be attacked by another problematic, thus, instead of searching for

1 Maruyama, M. (1973): 18ff.
2 Hillier, B. & Leaman, A. (1973).
3 For example, Lipman, A. (1969); (1971); Broady, M. (1968).
4 cf. Althusser, L. (1970): 19f, 28, 32.

discrepancies between 'facts' and 'concepts' the nature of the problematic which defines those 'facts' should be analysed.[1] These 'principles' signal one, very significant, intention: that of *anti-relativism* vis-a-vis the real object. This intention involves two propositions both of which are relevant to a critique of the ED:

1) *it is necessary, if not always possible, to give a definitive account of a real problem,* or a set of real problems;

2) *it is necessary to attempt to produce an account of the systematic organization of an ideology,*[2] i.e. a problematic, and to distinguish this account from a 'history of ideas.'

1.5 Discourse and discourse analysis

A discourse is a formation that consists of all that are expressed, represented or meant, (that is, 'statements' which may or may not have been said or written) around some objects. It exists under the positive conditions of a complex group of relations.[3] Yet, these relations are neither simply internal (i.e. between concepts, words, etc.), nor simply external (i.e. limitations, impositions, etc.), but relations that establish discourse *as a practice*. This then begs the initial question of exactly what the analysis of a discourse actually refers to: to a referent, to an object outside it, or to things? Yet, to recognise this question, which inevitably invokes the subject-object structure, and which tends to reproduce it, would be a mistake. It is this very question that is being criticized here.

A discourse can and should be analysed without reference to a *referent*[4]. Yet, a discourse analysis should not necessarily imply dropping the referent (i.e. 'object' of the subject-object couple).[5] In other words a discourse analysis should be related with its referent theoretically: as a 'theoretical object' is related with the 'real object' - through concepts and theories, *not* as empirical elements confronting each other. This relationship with material conditions (e.g. historical determinations, institutional definitions, class domination[6]) cannot be reduced to a relationship between things and words, or between things and their 'origin',[7] 'foundation', genesis[8] or subjects[9] nor, for that matter, between an 'original unity' and its 'false consciousness'.

The relevance of this emphasis to the analysis of environmental discourse is obvious. Especially considering what this analysis *would* do about *real problems* it is of critical importance to free it from the empiricist temptations of the environmental field on the one hand, and to be able to get rid of the ideologically given object(s) (i.e. 'referents'), on the other. In doing this it must be borne in mind that:

a) discourses are practices that "systematically form the objects of which they speak".[10]

b) a discourse analysis should not be seen as a substitute for the 'concrete analysis of concrete situations'.

c) it must not be assumed that "the knowledge of an object might ultimately replace the object or dissipate its existence", for the knowledge of this ideology . . . is simultaneously the knowledge of the conditions of its necessity. [11]

1 Poulantzas, N. (1972): 241.
2 cf. Williams, K. (1972): 461.
3 Foucault, M. (1972): 45.
4 ibid: 47.
5 For example, F. Choay attempts to avoid the traditional modes of analysis of histories of art, architecture and urbanism, or of urban and architectural semiotics by dropping the referent in her textual analysis. (1974): 1.
6 Piccone, P. (1971): 123.
7 cf. Foucault, M. (1972).
8 cf. Choay, F. (1973): 298.
9 cf. Williams, K. (1974): 52, and Foucault, M. (1972).
10 Foucault, M. (1972): 49.
11 Althusser, L. (1969): 230.

It can now be asked: how can   all those real problems in which several 'practices'
are involved with   be identified? Or, what is it that makes them available to analysis
(as opposed to speculative or empiricist approaches)? Do they appear in books,
statements, theories, buildings, institutions, regulations, rules of conduct, construction
manuals, technical specifications, by-laws or descriptions of real objects . . . ? How
is it that all those topics, concepts and problems some of which will be mentioned below
form a *unity* which we can study? It is not necessary, at this stage, to extend these
questions further. Instead, an attempt will be made to see what answers can (or cannot)
be given to them. As this study does not try to develop any 'general theory of discourses'
these comments will be brief and limited to the requirements of this study.

Perhaps the most important condition for an analysis is that it should avoid taking
as its *starting point,* or as *given*, the object(s), books, disciplines, styles, knowing
subjects, psychological subjects, or the collection of things and words, of the discourse
that is being analysed. (This is what the 'history of ideas' tends to do). What it should
instead try to define is a *'field'* (or, a 'space', 'terrain', 'area','domain' – all, however,
carrying with them the obvious risks inherent in metaphors). This field is the "field of
the facts of discourse on the basis of which those facts are built up . . . " It is "the
laws that govern the differential history of sciences and the non-sciences", and "all
actual statements (whether spoken or written)"[1]that constitute 'discursive events'.
These events, however, are quite unlike the objects of the 'history of ideas' which is
characterized with its postulates of 'genesis', 'continuity' and 'totalization'. Whilst
the 'history of ideas' refers to a subject and   assumes a continuity of development
and a homogeneity of parts, a 'discursive event' enables one to determine "the connexions of one or more authors, or 'connexions between statements or groups of statements
and events of a quite different kind (technical, economic, social, political)."[2] A
connexion, on the other hand, is a set of relations of "coexistence, succession, mutual
functioning, reciprocal determination, independent or correlative transformation" which
"determine the bundle of relations that discourse must establish in order to be able to
deal with them, name them, analyse them, classify them, explain them . . . "[3], and
characterize the *discourse as a practice.*

In the realization of this practice, there may appear several diffractions, incompati-
bilities,   contradictory developments and inconsistencies. It is through these and other
points that the nature of a particular discourse can be identified. Whether it is a discourse
of scientific, or technical, philosophical or artistic, nature this approach implies a close
examination of the structure, mechanisms and the relations that make up that discourse.

This is the main reason behind the organization of the present study. But, the order
of its sections, starting from the unity and the object of the ED, and ending with its
status, is not a fixed order. In different discourse analyses different orders may be
possible. Moreover, there is no fixed number of elements that make up an analysis. In
one analysis mechanisms may be extremely important while, say, the structure may
not. Or, in one it may not be possible at all to separate structure from relations.
Secondly, the order in which the discourse is analysed may not necessarily be reflected
in the order of the text in which the analysis is presented. In the present study, for
example, the analysis of the ED has been presented in a way that would help the reader
to build up an understanding of the discourse while, in fact, the analysis has been done
in a much more complex, and often difficult, way.

As stressed earlier on, the ED was not *given* to the author as an object ready for

1 Foucault, M. (1972): 26.
2 ibid: 29.
3 ibid: 46.

analysis. It had to be theoretically (i.e. not simply textually) observed. Then, the *elements* of an analysis had to be established and justified. Yet, the laborious survey of literature had to begin much before these advances were made. The *mode* of analysis, its *order* and *elements* and the existing *discursive material* had to be composed into a coherent whole. It is in this sense that this study is neither a simple *application*, nor a *survey*, nor, for that matter, a *speculative* treatise. It is a complex text *representing a process of understanding through an internally developed mode of analysis.*

The specific nature of the study is partly reflected in the presentation, that is, its *writing.* For example, it is not a descriptive text as its conception of discourse analysis would rule that out. It does not *describe*, but *analyse* and *criticize* the ED. It is not a *linguistic* or *textual* analysis either. It analyses the *discursive* objects, structure, rules and mechanisms, rather than linguistic ones. As a discourse cannot be reduced to language, the former's analysis cannot also be reduced to that of a language. It is in this sense that a discourse analysis deals not only with what is said or written, but also what is *not.* It lays bare what is *not* said in what *is.*

Furthermore, a discourse analysis does not have to follow the dichotomy 'etymology/ meaning'[1] in dealing with the notions of 'environment', 'space', etc. If 'etymology' is concerned with the origins and the linguistic existence of a word, and the 'meaning' with its conceptual and semiological content, then, a discourse analysis deals with all these, though not in the same terms. For, a discourse analysis takes each object of a discourse as a unit, and tries to examine its structure, relations and status which may include its content, its use, variants, semiotic function etc. as necessary features of a discursive formation. Thus, for example, the 'etymology' of the word 'environment' which includes 'surrounding' or 'encircling' is not subordinated to some supposed 'meaning' of it. Instead, it is shown that the common notion of environment (as "that which surrounds 'organism' or 'man'") is the *dominant* component of the discursive object 'environment'; and the spatiality of the term is functional in readily accepting it as a term in architectural and planning practices.

The second sense of the language, i.e. the mode of textual expression, used in the text of such an analysis has to be *theoretical.* This is not a matter of choice but of necessity. The concepts used in it are to be theoretical concepts. Neither the objects of a discourse are conceivable in terms of brick-and-mortar, or molecules-and-atoms, nor does its 'structure' resemble that of an office building, a bridge or a firm. (Briefly, even the objects and structures in physics, engineering, biology or economics are quite different from the *everyday objects.* They are abstract and theoretical, rather than purely empirical.)

As this study is not a 'text-book', a 'guidebook', or a 'history of ideas', it does not need to simplify its arguments for intelligibility (probably) at the expense of *precision.* A theoretical text has to be precise even though this is only possible through an abstract (and often intricate) language. Thus, the precision of everyday speech and writing cannot be a model for that of theoretical writing. What is at stake is not a choice of style, but of effectivity. (As one cannot have a haircut by a pair of garden scissors, or repair a watch by power-drills, nor can a quasi-theoretical discourse be analysed in everyday language.) In fact, there are many examples in the text to suggest that most of the questionable arguments in the ED are due to its imprecise and a-theoretical use of language. But, an imprecise discourse cannot be analysed in an imprecise manner. However, this is not to suggest that theoretical language is the *sufficient* condition for effective analysis, though it is a *necessary* one. Especially when this analysis is considered as a 'shop-floor', as suggested earlier, rather than as a 'shop-window', the specificity of its language would be appreciated better.

1   cf. for ex., Mason, H.L. & Langenheim, J.H. (1957): 333 who suggest that the former must be regarded as wholly secondary to the latter.

It must be emphasized that in the course of the study there was no attempt to *create* problems (or non-problems as is the case in 'environmental studies') to be studied. There were sufficient problems in the discourse itself to justify more than one study. Nor was there any attempt to *complicate* what could be understood more simply. *However imprecise (and often trivial) the arguments of the ED are, it is still a complex discourse that cannot be understood without a sufficiently rigorous and complex analysis.* This understanding is reflected in the way the present analysis is organized; and identifies theoretical problems in the ED. First of all there is no necessary correspondance between the structure of the discourse and that of its analysis. Secondly, on the one hand, many individual problems of the ED are examined in more than one section or context due to their complex nature, on the other hand, each section is concentrated on specific aspects of the discourse which are not necessarily present in all the discursive examples cited or referred to. Yet, at the same time the ED is characterized by a series of pure principles, cosmological schemas and homogenous fields (mostly concentrated around the 'Man-Environment relationship'). It is these contrasting and often impossible-looking properties of the ED which create so many complex (theoretical) problems. In short, there is a *displaced* and *uneven* structure both within the ED and in its present analysis. Thus, while there is an apparent tidyness in the organization of the study, there is also a diffused unity which makes the organization rather redundant. In other words the object of study (i.e. the ED) is not actually compart-mentalized into five or six parts each of which to be studied by a separate chapter. On the contrary, there are no clear demarcations between, for example, the object, structure and certain mechanisms or, similarly, between all mechanisms. *The organization of the study is not meant to provide a 'grid' to divide and subdivide the discourse, but a textual means of presenting the confusing totality of the discourse that had already been understood prior to writing.*

Another relevant question is the status of the sources, examples and quotations in the analysis. There is a large number of examples in the form of references either to phrases, terms and concepts, or to full statements. They are not the only ones that could be found in specific contexts. There could be more, but also less. The validity of the arguments do not depend on the number of quotations especially as far as a discourse analysis is concern-ed. It cannot rely on the school or personality of the owners of the quotations. The terms, phrases, concepts or statements quoted in the study are *discursive examples* or *illustrations,* and not evidences or proofs of arguments. Consequently, most of the arguments in the study could stand without the support of examples. For a reader who is familiar with the ED the analysis would readily invoke necessary examples. Those references and quotations that provide theoretical support to the analysis from outside the ED are either *sources of inspiration* or can be considered as *theoretical loans.* Yet, they are not responsible for the arguments and the theses developed here. To avoid confusions on these points nearly all references are given in the footnotes. (This also avoids creation of a hierarchy among the sources and their interference with the continuity of arguments, and allows the reader to ignore them if such references are not necessary to their comprehension.) Moreover, this mode of writing provides for the admission of debts (to the extent of single phrases or concepts) while at the same time not committing the mistake of absolutizing isolated concepts or statements.

The statements, etc. that are quoted are not necessarily the *representatives* of the sources they are taken from. They are quoted simply as discursive examples, and are of interest to this analysis to the extent that they are *components* of, and located *within*, the ED. This approach also rules out the wholesale 'labelling' of authors or theories on the basis of some isolated statements, and is equally necessary in reading the *present* study which cannot be understood and criticized on the basis of isolated statements in it. A work is a whole, and should be read as such. Yet, this does not rule out the possibility of associating isolated passages of it with some external theoretical positions. This, of course, would *not* be a reading of the study *as a whole*, but construction of a unity in which those passages have places.

Besides, many examples or statements are not consciously *within* or without the ED. Some of them may not even be observable as unities. Only a discourse analysis with a wide field of operation could incorporate them into the arguments. This may give an impression of an 'eclectic' approach. But, if a discourse is eclectic, widespread, and all-embracing, and is present in every conceivable field its analysis cannot afford to eliminate certain examples simply because they are taken from supermarket carrier-bags, or newspaper advertisements, or from sources like *Reader's Digest*. It would then be an incomplete analysis. If a privileged level of discourse is not desired, then *all levels at which a discourse operates should be analysed*.

A discourse analysis is not an *a posteriori comment* on existing material, nor is it a *collage* of some selected material and their interpretation. In fact, it also deals with material that may only be thought of, and not expressed, in verbal or graphic statements, or that may be present in the absences of a text. As a social practice, a discourse may involve all sorts of levels and domains. A discourse analysis, or a critique, has to see its object as a whole and in its structural totality, if not in its empirical mass. The limits of its specialization is the discourse itself, rather than this or that position, point of view, disciplinary framework, cultural barriers, etc . . . What is to be observed is the *problematic* which makes a discourse possible as a unity. Furthermore, a discourse analysis does not dissect the complex whole of the discourse into simpler unities. It only analyses the elements and properties of a discourse in view of the conception of that whole. Thus, no chapter or section of this study is conceivable separately. In fact, it is not possible to study isolated aspects of a discourse without an understanding of *all* the aspects. This is particularly so in the ED as this is the first time that it is identified and analysed as a discourse. So, there couldn't be a question of a limited analysis.[1] This is particularly so when considering the case that the features of a discourse may not (as in 'expressive totality') be present in each and every element and each and every object. Thus, while generalizing from specific cases or elements is not a sound strategy, to expect discursive critiques of single elements (as present in specific architectural, urban or design problems) to represent a complete discourse analysis is equally vulnerable to misunderstandings, if not always to inconsistencies.

Now, we can return to the question of field that we introduced in Sec. 1.3. Every discourse or ideology is defined by two kinds of fields:
1) The field which contains the discursive facts and events; and on the basis of which these facts and events are built up: *'discursive field'* or *'ideological field'*,
2) The field which makes it possible for an ideology to exist, which provides the meaning of a particular ideology, and which establishes its relationship with the existing field(s): *'problematic'*.

Discursive fields consist of arguments, statements, discursive rules and regulations, themes, disciplinary definitions, empirically or theoretically established domains of study, problems discussed as unities, and whole range of variations on the invariant structures of such unities. As to the field itself as a *unity*, it must be analysed only in its relationship to the problematic which defines it. This would be in marked contrast to those modes of analysis which simply 'dissect' complex problems into their *obvious* elements and attributes,

---

1 This is, in fact, a major point of criticism that can be directed to some,otherwise valuable,theoretical studies.For ex., the criticism of the ecology movement by Galtung, J. (1973) and Enzensberger, H.M. (1974); the urban and regional ideologies by Harvey, D. (1973), Castells, M. (1975) and Massey, D. (1973); or industrial design ideology by Wolf, L. (1972) and Bonsiepe, G. (1975) (with no comparable work in architecture) are all done with a knowledge and awareness of the discursive nature of what is being criticized.Yet, these knowledges and awareness are not sufficiently formulated to form *discourse analyses* of their whole respective fields. This limitation is not only a question of scope and subject matter, but would in certain cases have serious effects on what is being presented.

and which reduce or correlate them as empirical givens. For example, it is possible for some to identify and to analyse 'problems' such as "The spatial ecology of stripped cars"[1], "Belief and behaviour as determinants of environmental attitude"[2], or "City size and unemployment"[3] as given 'facts'. This is done either analytically (e.g. space/room/psychological state/value systems/built form/function/social structure), or linguistically (e.g. correspondence or contradiction between terms, nature of terms (such as 'privacy' 'environmental attitude' etc.), variables, adjectives.) Yet, although a discursive field may contain several empirically derived elements (e.g. technical terms, empirical **data**, representations, drawings) the field itself is not an empirical entity. Thus, it is only appropriate to examine it and the studies which it consists in, as the *loci* of theoretical and epistemological structures, and the latter as discursive illustrations for such structures.

1.6 Unity of the Environmental Discourse

As was rather sketchily pointed out at the beginning of Sec. 1.3, and illustrated by examples elsewhere, the questions, notions, terms and 'problems' of the discourse *somehow* exist as a *unity*. How is it that such a diversity is conceivable as a unity? What is it that unites the immense variety that can be found in the ED?

The discursive field that has been specified above is not necessarily a *uniform* field; that is, it comprises of not only the uniformity of a discourse or an ideology but, also, of the possible range of variations in them. This range of variations is determined by the problematic which defines the field in the first place.

A problematic may be adopted or 'crossed' by several thoughts which may be affected by that problematic in different ways and, as a result, different effects may be produced. But, these different effects carry with them some identical features in common: the features of the problematic they have come upon (or from).[4] From such an identification the elements of the discourse can be seen as so many different realizations of the same problematic. The unity of a problematic, on the other hand, is a complex structured whole which is neither reducible to its elements nor to some essence of which its parts are different expressions.

It is on these bases that a conception of the environmental problematic should be developed. In such a conception the 'obvious' elements of the ED, namely, 'environment', 'man-environment' or 'society-environment', should be taken as ideologically given objects of the discourse. But even in a conception like this the ED should not be assumed to allow a 'dissection' of its elements in an analytic manner. Its unity is to be understood before it can be analysed. Furthermore, it is neither a long-established discourse, nor has it got a science-based unity, instead, it is one which is constituted at the intersection of several diverse discourses and domains. Thus, overlaps, confusions, interchanges and shifts of domains in arguments are inevitable. These and other mechanisms will be examined in greater detail in the study.[5] The question of discursive and non-discursive relations will also be examined.[6] These discussions will try to clarify the theoretical conditions of social-science-based intervention into environmental studies, confusion of the 'object' in several environmental disciplines, intrusion of ideologies into the ED, similarities in the positions of radically different theories vis-a-vis the environmental question, and the institutionalization of the ED in professional and educational frameworks.

How is it, then, that the environmental problematic can be identified as a *unity* in the

1 Ley, D. & Cybriwsky, R. (1974).
2 Bruvold, W.H. (1973).
3 Vipond, J. (1974).
4 On this question, see: Althusser, L. (1970): 135-6
5 cf. Ch. 4.
6 cf. Ch. 5.

light of above observations? Such a question involves another unity – the *unity* of the ED. As it is the problematic of a discourse which defines its unity, it is essential that these questions are examined together. Firstly, how can a discourse that is as diffused, as vaguely defined and as widespread as the ED be viewed and analysed as a unity? It involves so many domains and so many diverse objects that this question is almost inevitably answered with reference to those domains and objects which are about, or identified with, a single object: *'environment'*. But such an answer should be taking as *given* what it is supposed to be questioning. In other words, what we should be trying to look at is not what is called 'the environment', but *the discourse on it*. Thus, the unity of this discourse cannot be based upon a conception of those domains and objects which are themselves 'environmen*tal*'. Secondly, there is a strong possibility that the problematic of the ED may not be identifiable without in some way freeing our analysis from its 'circle' all together. It is a problematic which survives the *generality* of the discourse while crossing a large number of domains and objects, and survives its *particularity* which enables it to feel at home in all those objects and domains. In fact, in analysing it in terms of its objects, structure, mechanisms and relations what we   do is to bring out this generality or unity, and exemplify them with particular discursive cases, events and relations without being trapped by a recognition of its objects.

2 The Objects of the Environmental Discourse

"Alors l'Environnement?
Stendhal aurait pu en dire:
  La seule excuse de l'Environnement,
  – c'est qu il n'existe pas."[1]

2.1 'Discursive objects' *(Introduction)*

This study is an attempt (and the only one, to the knowledge of its author) to analyse the 'environmental discourse' in terms of its problematic, and thus, of its concepts, structures and mechanisms. Leaving the problematic, structure and mechanisms to other chapters, this chapter will deal with the *object* of this discourse.

As stressed above, and as it will be discussed later on, such an analysis is *not* done by reducing the discourse, or its problematic, to their object(s). This is particularly inappropriate in a discourse as complex as the ED.

This analysis stems from a set of initial questions, such as:
— *What* is it that constitutes the environmental discourse?
— Does it have an *object* (comparable to sciences or other discourses)?
— Do 'environmental' disciplines and practices have object(s)?
— What is the difference between the objects (if any) of the ED and of disciplines and practices?

As stressed earlier, none of the elements of a discourse, nor the discourse as a whole, can be viewed as empirically given entities. They are complex wholes with complex sets of concepts or terms, relations and rules which are organized by a specific problematic. Thus, a discourse is constituted by all these elements. But, what is the *specificity* of its object?

To start with, the object of a discourse is a *'discursive object'*. As such it should be distinguished both from the 'known object' of the theory of knowledge, and from the

---

1 *"Then, [what about] the Environment?*
  Stendhal would have said:
    The only excuse for [the existence of] the Environment,
    – is that it does not exist."
                    (*Architecture*, no. 397, June 1976, p. 107.)

28

'real object' and 'theoretical object' of scientific practices. (The environmental discourse is, in fact, a *'field of confusion'* of all such distinct objects).[1] *A 'discursive object' is that which a discourse as a practice forms and deals with.* Just as discourse cannot be reduced to a 'linguistic' sense [2], discursive object cannot be reduced to what someone or some books say about something. What is at stake is an identification of the field and its conditions that *enable* a discourse to form and to function.

Perhaps in accordance with these conditions *(including the non-discursive ones)* it is hard to find any trace of an awareness in so-called 'environmental practices' (e.g. architecture, planning), 'environmental studies' (e.g. 'environmental science', 'environmental psychology'), or 'environmental theories' (e.g. 'territoriality', 'spatial imagery', 'environmental determinism') of *what exactly it is* that they are dealing with, let alone of the discursive rules and formations within which they talk about 'environment'. Of course, this is not to say that they have no 'idea' on 'environment'. On the contrary, it is this very idea, this very presumption, which makes them unaware of the scientific conception of what exactly they are dealing with.

On the basis of these two observations a critical analysis of the discourse is bound to avoid referring to persons or books on the one hand, and to *unspecified* conceptions of 'environment' on the other. What is referred to in this analysis is, then, the *discursive object* of the ED.[3] Thus, any division, classification or grouping that is introduced as a part of the analysis *does not* necessarily belong to the discourse and its ideology, but is a requirement of *this* analysis. For example, a question like "Whether 'environmental phenomena' can be classified in terms of some nominal scale" is not to be accepted as an inherent question of the real (so-called 'environment'). Instead, it must be seen as a *discursive question* or, at best, a theoretical question that can only be settled at that level. Therefore, schemes like 'Ekistic Grid' or 'Anthropocosmos Model' which divide the 'environment' or the 'World' into the 'Elements' of Nature, Man, Society, Shells, Networks, or into the 'Ekistic Units' of Man, Room, Dwelling, ... Megalopolis, Urban Region, Urbanized Continent, Ecumenopolis[4] do this at a discursive level (though claiming that they are actually classifying the World). It is in the professional/technical/economic practices of planning, architecture and commerce and in their discursive processes that such schemes are accepted, rejected or transformed. And it is there that they produce their *effects*. This approach to such schemes is in line with the objectives of the present critique which is to identify their status, structure and variants, and to specify their objects to prepare conditions for the development of a discourse with *scientifically specifiable* objects.

With these objectives in mind it is now possible to approach the *'discursive field'* which provides the initial material for an analysis of the *'object'*. This field is one which comprises of parts of a large number of disciplines (e.g. architecture, town and regional planning, geography, industrial design, ecology, physical, biological and social sciences), techniques (e.g. quantitative techniques, topology, drawing, modelling, experimentation, speculation), discourses (e.g. technical, popular, political, literary, religious, artistic) and problems (e.g. housing, transportation, 'pollution', migration, 'urbanization'). It is in the ED that this complex field finds its expression. But, is this possible, as it may seem to a superficial observation, by insisting on a *single object*: *'environment'* (or 'space'), or on its *derivations*: 'Man - Environment', 'Society - Environment' relationships?

As discussed above, neither a discursive object can come about independent of several

---

1 cf. Sec. 4.6.1
2 cf. Williams, K. (1974): 65.
3 Hereafter referred to as 'object' unless otherwise specified.
4 *Ekistics* Journal; or Bell, G. & Tyrwitt, J. (eds) (1972): 23.

conditions and mechanisms, nor can a single object form a discourse. 'Environment' as a discursive object is not an exception to this. Yet, its specific characteristics make it the central object around which a complex discourse exists. This is made possible (a) by *representing different concepts* (as far as the *'regional'* discourses of each science or discipline are concerned); and (b) by *pertaining to a general discourse of environment which has no determinate object for the words 'Environment' and 'Man' to be the concepts of*[1]. These points are particularly relevant to an examination of the status of the environmental discourse in Ch. 6. For the moment, however, they should be sufficient to explain the scope and the imprecision of the discourse, and how it was possible for it to 'combine' several borrowed or imported philosophical notions, techniques, professional jargon, moralist notions, pseudo-political rhetoric, etc. — all under *one* framework: *'man-environment relationship'*.

Regarding all these 'combinations' of domains and elements a set of questions may arise:
— how is it that all these different domains, disciplines and elements can *co-exist* in a single discourse?
— how is it that different domains and disciplines are *distinguished* within the problematic which they share?
— can they constitute a *'scientific'* domain merely on the basis of such a problematic — (as there can be 'ideological' problematics too)?
— what is the 'specific coherence'[2] of the object which is assumed to be the object of an 'environmental science', or more modestly, a discourse, on a single object?
As with many questions that were posed in this study these questions are *not* the questions which environmental discourse ever poses, or indeed can pose.

Instead, a general conception of *'interdisciplinary'* research and an empiricist and positivist conception of science are believed to be sufficient. Interdisciplinary research, for example, appears to be nothing more than an arbitrary cooperation of two or more disciplines. Yet, as the status of each discipline is itself questionable and as the conditions of such a cooperation is hardly ever specified, domination of preconceptions or the problematic of one discipline over the other tend to replace any such question that, in return, may radically alter the nature of the endeavour.

First of all, the object(s) and problems are defined *prior to* the cooperation, often with a vague notion of the discipline(s) whose cooperation is sought. Therefore, this initial definition tends to dictate the mode of cooperation. In the ED, for example, the prior definitions of 'environment' and 'man' (however implicit they may be) dictate all stages of the 'environmental' research. For example, a research on "bedroom size and social interaction of the psychiatric ward",[3] or one on the "socioeconomic status and residential locational choice"[4] both attempt to study a 'relationship' between an 'environmental variable' and a 'psychological variable' (or 'socioeconomic', or 'geographic' ones). There are other attempts to study 'environmental phenomena' by conflating these two variables at the level of the object and method. While only one variable is apparent, the other is somehow included into a 'dimension' defined as a relational object of study (as, for example, in "Measuring environmental dispositions with the environmental response inventory"[5] which attempts to isolate a "significant environment - related personality dimension").

1 On these conditions, see: Althusser, L. (1970): Ch. 7.
2 cf. Levi-Strauss, C. (1967): 10-11; and Mepham, J. (1973): 110.
3 Ittelson, W.H. *et al* (1970).
4 Moriarty, B.M. (1974).
5 McKencnie, G.E. (1973).

It is obvious that the conditions imposed by an *a priori conception* of the object are often more powerful than the contribution that a cooperation of disciplines may eventually make. Interdisciplinary research can be seen as a result of two sorts of inquiry, one relating to "common structures and mechanisms", and the other to "common methods".[1] While most of 'environmental' research treat their objects in some sort of 'method', that method is seldom common, and almost always the method of either one or the other of the 'disciplines' coming together. Thus, for example, environmental psychology is basically a *psychological* study of so-called 'man-environment relationship' or simply 'environment'. Or, history of architecture and urbanism is a linear *history* of architectural and urban 'objects'. Architectural and urban semiotics is, as yet, nothing more than a *semiological* study of some objects, signs or patterns.[2] What seems to be common to all these 'branches' of environmental discourse is their *unquestioned* conception of 'architecture', 'city' and 'environment'. This unquestioning attitude is precisely what the *problematic* of 'environment' requires with its fixed schema of 'Man', 'Environment' and their relationship.

2.2 The unity of the object(s)

After all these discussions, observations and definitions the question of the *unity of the object* of environmental discourse can now be posed.

As argued earlier, the unity of a discourse cannot simply be based upon a *generalized object* – whether it is primarily 'real' or 'discursive'. But, can such a generalized object provide the initial basis for a discourse as, for example, a whole discipline of urbanism or urban sociology is constituted by a generalized object of 'city' or 'urban' ?

$$\odot \longrightarrow D$$

And, more significantly, if such a single object is not sought, can a *multiplicity of objects* lead to a *single* discourse?

Moreover, is it possible to suggest that one (real) object may provide the basis for more than one discourse simply because that object is a *complex* one with many instances and variants?

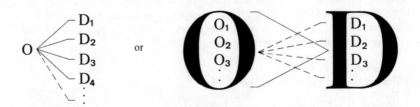

---

1 Piaget, J. (1973): 9.
2 For a detailed discussion on the relations between disciplines and discourses, see Sec. 5.2

(This last question, however, is bound to be redundant in the sense that it presupposes a single object to start with, proposes to establish discourses on the sub-objects obtained by splitting that single object, and in so doing reproduces the pervasive mistakes of analysing a discursive formation and its object as empirically given entities).

Finally, as in the geographic discourse, a single discourse attempts to deal with a large number of phenomena which are already analysed by different geographical or non-geographical discourses and practices:[1]

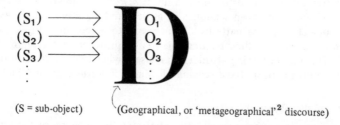

$(S_1) \longrightarrow$ O_1
$(S_2) \longrightarrow$ O_2
$(S_3) \longrightarrow$ O_3

(S = sub-object)   (Geographical, or 'metageographical'[2] discourse)

Actually, what happens in the case of a 'complex real object' is that that object is studied by various disciplines and practices which *share the same problematic* (e.g. 'Man-Environment' problematic). It is that problematic which then provides the basis for a discourse on the real object. Therefore, *it is not that there are many discourses on the same object, but, rather, one discourse constituted by a problematic which is shared by several disciplines, domains and 'regional' discourses.* (The discussion on the specificity of the 'environmental' will be concerned with the consequences of this process.[3] But, before that the question of a 'single object' needs further clarification).

As a study of psychopathological discourse and medical profession showed, there existed in these fields a complex set of mechanisms whereby 'madness' was ensured to be the singular object of psychopathology. For example, certain individual differences were socially labelled, conceptually coded, theoretically categorized, institutionally defined, and, by this process, were accorded the status of 'disease', 'alienation', 'anomaly', 'dementia', 'neurosis' or 'psychosis'.[4] Also in that process, the discourse *appeared to be* on *one* object, 'madness', despite the fact that it involved a large number of different problems, and different discursive and non-discursive, scientific and institutional, fields. In other words, a single discursive object that was constituted by a generalization from a large variety of real problems was recognized as *the* object of the medical/psycho-pathological discourse. While there was (and, there still is) a great share of yet unknown factors in the understanding of psychic phenomena, and while every domain claimed its superiority as well as jurisdiction over the discoveries on that phenomena, there was, however, a consensus on the existence of a 'malaise' called 'madness'. It was on this consensus that medical profession and religious, legal and literary authorities united their efforts to explain, to classify and to 'solve' this problem. Needless to say, this unity was accompanied by unified attempts to establish causal relations, resemblances and cures.[5]

1 cf. Lacoste, Y. (1976): 75
2 For this term see: Gokhman, V. (1976): 70
3 cf. Sec. 2.4.
4 Foucault, M. (1972): 40-2, see, also his (1965), (1973).
5 For the institutional relations of discourses, see Sec. 5.3.

This example illustrates the gross discrepancy between the *singularity of a discursive object* and *multiplicity of 'real' objects (or problems)* which that discourse is supposed to deal with. While this example is not meant to provide an analogy, or a support, to the particular discourse we are examining; it however, illustrates the claim of this study that a *discourse analysis* (in a non-linguistic sense) can provide the kind of insight which, say, sociological, historical or even technical, approaches fail to do.

The ED, when analysed in this manner, can be seen under the total domination of several fallacies among which the *singularity of object* and the *confusion of real with discursive objects*, are most pervasive. But, is there any contradiction in this explanation if it is suggested that,as it stands, the ED is based upon a single object (and its derivations or variants)? To be able to clarify this question two explanations are needed:

1) It was shown earlier[1] that discourses could be identified (a) through their dominant problematic(s), and (b) through their discursive objects, structures and mechanisms (that exist in accordance with (a)); and *not* through an analysis which takes discourse as an empirically given object. Therefore, there is no attempt here to identify (i.e. to accept) a discourse based on a dubious set of terms as a *legitimate* discourse. This study does not take 'environment' as a real-concrete object, nor does it recognize all the contents of the ED as real objects. The latter is taken as an object which is constituted within some theoretical and practical ideologies and discourses. In this sense, the differences of approach and opinion *within* the ED are not the main concern of this study. *It does not try to solve their problems* (unless those problems are shown to be scientifically specifiable without resorting to preconceived words like 'environment'). Moreover, it does not attempt to redefine,reform, rectify or improve the *given* objects of the ED.

2) The aim is to analyse the ED, locate its problematic, its mechanisms and its effects so that,
(a) *Confusion of real object(s) and theoretical object(s) of the field (that is presently designated by the ED) is eliminated,* and
(b) the *conditions for the establishment of a scientific discourse on the real problems of this field are prepared.*

It is in this sense that 'environment' and 'man-environment relationship' are identified as *ideological non-objects. Ideological,* because they are produced in, and used by, theoretical and practical ideologies,[2] and because, like other ideological objects, they are lived in, talked by,and taken for granted. They became 'natural' and 'invisible', thus 'obvious'.[3] Unlike scientific objects, these ideological ones are *not specifiable.* They are *presumed, known by everybody,* and *applicable to nearly everything* (as in the case of 'environment'). Moreover, and not too surprisingly, the ideology of environment has become an integral part of the dominant ideology in most social formations.[4] They are *non-objects*, because there is no real object for them to be the objects of, or at best, the real objects which they claim to be representing are too vague to be specifiable. (They are as vague and as general as the words 'nature', 'world', 'life', 'human' etc.).

To open up the analysis further, it can be asked:
— If there is *not* a real object 'environment' (which the environmental discourse assumes there is), then *what is it that the environmental discourse is about* (i.e. what is the nature, structure, mechanisms of *what* it is dealing with)?

1 Ch. 1.
2 For this differentiation and their relationships, see: Lecourt, D. (1975): 210-1.
3 As Hillier, B. & Leaman, A. remark concerning "M-E Paradigm", (1973): 507-8.
4 cf. Ch. 5.

This question requires an examination of:
1) The *formation* of the objects of the environmental discourse,
2) The *specificity* of the 'environmental',
3) The *status* of the object of the environmental discourse.

2.3 Formation of the objects

Object formation in a discourse involves several mechanisms, processes and stages. Yet, there may be variations in these processes in different objects of a discourse. Secondly, discursive objects should be seen as the locus of potential *change.* No object is ever finished or frozen. On the other extreme, however, an object may never get formed. The following analysis is concerned with indicating some of the complex mechanisms by which the objects of the discourse are formed and maintained. Some of the mechanisms will be examined in greater detail when the mechanisms of the discourse as a whole are analysed:[1]

a) The objects of the ED are formed by adopting ordinary words or terms
A *word* is not a *'concept'.*[2] A word is the means by which a concept, just as well as any notion, denotation, name, object etc., is given a distinct, *discursive,* existence. Sciences work on concepts. It is necessary for a scientific discourse to adopt and produce concepts which are derived by abstraction from the real,[3] and not by ordinary generalization or designation.

The ED, however, is constituted around some words such as 'man', 'environment',[4] 'space', 'M-E relationship' which are given to it by non-scientific practices and discourses; or are imported from other disciplines within which they usually have different status. Besides, some attributes of 'E' and 'M' are carried over from other discourses, and new objects are derived from them (e.g. 'crowding', 'noise', 'territoriality'.)

b) The objects of the ED are formed by reference to same empirically given   real objects
In the absence of a scientific problematic and a set of scientific concepts the ED relies on an observational 'recognition' (i.e. not a theoretical cognition) of some real objects. These objects are either given to sense organs, thus, are 'obvious', or are given by theoretical and practical ideologies which accord a double status to their subjects and objects.

In the first case, it is the 'obviousness' which is key to the inability of the ED to analyse the reality which is *not visible.* In the second case, the real object is seen as the embodiment of a 'concreteness' *and* an 'ideal essence'[5] which alternately, or simultaneously, inhabit 'M' and 'E' of the 'M-E' couple. This mechanism operates whether the real object is a building, a city or a region, a single person or a group of men/women. The confusion of the *real object* with the *discursive object* leads to a confusion in comprehension of what it is that the discourse is actually about.

Also in this context is the reliance upon 'facts' as absolute givens, i.e. as the reality itself. These 'facts' provide not only the substance of the discursive objects of the ED, they also support the inherent empiricism of the social and 'environmental' studies.

c) The objects of the ED are constituted by arbitrarily determined   points of view.
The main focus of the ED is a relationship which is presumed to exist between 'M' and 'E'. These elements are the representatives of 'ideal beings' on the one hand, and concrete men, women and physical objects, on the other. In this way, whether it is the first or the

---

1 In Ch. 4
2 Canguilhem, G.: in Lecourt, D. (1975): 173.
3 cf. Marx, K. (1971): 206-7; Althusser, L. (1969): Ch. 6.
4 Hereafter referred to as 'M' and 'E' except for the purposes of emphasis or clarity.
5 See Sec. 4.2 in this study, and Althusser, L. (1969): 183f.

second sense in which they are used, their relationship is considered first and foremost as a *separation* of a whole. Secondly, each of these elements is viewed from the *point of view* either of 'E' or of 'M'. (In fact, even the sciences concerned with 'man' are divided along these lines).[1]

This mechanism originates in the basic epistemological structure of these discourses, namely, the one which is constituted by 'subject-object', 'organism - environment' and 'M-E' couples. It must be stressed that these are not merely abstract conceptions. They represent the way in which real objects of ('environmental') practices are *looked at* and worked on.

There is hardly any exception in architectural and urban criticism which views, describes, photographs *and* evaluates buildings *from outside.*[2] Recent 'environmental studies' do, in fact, reproduce this attitude. Just as social sciences view individual man as 'nodes' from outside, environmental studies view 'environmental objects' from outside, or from the point of view of the subject.[3]

d) The objects of the ED are formed by generalizations
Generalization is an empiricist substitute for rational abstraction. Instead of producing and transforming concepts, empiricist social and environmental discourses rely on generalizations constructed out of some empirical findings[4] or, simply, set of observations.[5] Empirical generalizations claim to be describing "observable regularities of nature" and "permanent relationships between observable events".[6] In this sense, so-called 'concepts' of most empirical studies are either the "common response(s) to dissimilar stimuli" (as in behaviourism), or groupings of "seemingly different objects and events into catagories".[7]

In fact, the objects of many disciplines also rely on generalizations often on a criteria that is itself the result of a generalization. For example, a discipline like geography is "concerned with the *synthesis* of everything within the areal context",[8] or with studying "the grand open book of Nature",[9] or 'environment' is defined as a "specific set of measurable physical phenomena . . . "[10] The term 'environment' is a generalization of everything that is "external to man"[11], and 'M-E' relationship is a general term for nearly all human activities as no such activity can take place out of, or independent of, a physical context.

The ED makes judgements and statements on *generalized objects.* This process is coupled by the 'double status'[12] of the terms in such a way that the singularity of concrete 'M' and 'E' is provided not by any scientific specification, but by a *general, homogenous and ideal essence.*[13]

e) The objects of the ED are formed by reductions and simplifications
In the absence of a set of scientific procedures the ED relies on reductions of complex problems into simple oppositions, theoretical problems into empirical issues, and social

1   cf. Hillier, B. & Leaman, A. (1973): 508.
2   cf. Fitch, J.M. (1970) who criticizes this, yet,in saying "in architecture there are no spectators; there are only participants" (p.76) he reduces the question to that of 'building - user' dichatomy in which the latter 'participates' instead of 'views' the former.
3   On 'point of view' see Sec.s 3.3.5 and 4.6.3.
4   O'Malley, J.B. (1972): 63.
5   Willer, D. & Willer, J. (1973): 23.
6   Wolman, B.B. (ed) (1965).
7   Abel, C. (1974): 2.
8   Hartshorne, R.: *The Nature of Geography,* 1939, mentioned in Harvey, D. (1969): 127.
9   Lacoste, Y. (1976): 173-4
10   Boutourline, S. (1970): 498.
11   For example, see: Fuller, R.B. paraphrased in Jardine, B. (1971): 38
12   cf. Sec. 3.3.2.
13   cf. Sec. 4.2

problems into technical ones. For example, complex relations between the physical, economic, ideological, technical, political instances of a social formation which are operative in any 'socio-spatial' problem are reduced either to a 'society - environment interaction',or to technical solutions.

At another level, it reduces real phenomena to an 'ideal essence' (e.g. to 'environment' as an original and ideal being). This essence co-exists with the real and is invoked as a substitute for concrete analysis. Moreover, it forms its objects by reducing relations to things, distinctions to oppositions, differences to separations, or diversities to typologies.[1]

f) The objects of the ED are formed by reference to 'ideal' and 'original' objects, or to 'pure principles'

The 'man - environment' problematic which constitutes the ED is based on a system of original, ideal and pure states or principles. This involves two distinct levels:

1) the level at which real objects are defined on the basis of an 'essence' which is conceived as *whatever* the knowledge of those objects are believed to be. In other words, it is this essence which is assigned to be the origin of knowledge[2] and, consequently, it is the 'goal' of the ED to discover it. Thus, it becomes quite legitimate for many diverse phenomena such as architecture, agriculture, settlements, atmosphere . . . to be *conceived in terms of 'their essence'*, i.e. 'environment'.

2) the level at which the presumed essence is projected upon an 'ideal' state which embodies the ('lost') 'origin'. This is the level at which *utopias*[3] are formulated, and it is the framework within which environmental (as well as social, economic, political) practices are expected to *realize* them.

The first level finds its expression in the current M-E studies — though, sometimes, in a rigorous[4] technical manner. They believe in, and propose, a 'M-E relationship' which is *essentially* present in all 'environmental' situations. The second is indicative of the way in which so many utopian and anarchist theories are produced. Although a comprehension of the 'present' in such theories superficially identifies problems with a socio-political system, and often with the 'moral state of man', the 'future' state is expressed in physical forms and patterns and *in total isolation from any concrete social order.*Finished products or 'models' are justified with reference to the 'ills' and 'alienation' of the present, and are projected into an indefinite future as "imaginary treatment(s) of real problems",[5] or philosophical speculations are used to present architectural and urban experiments of *formal* nature.[6]

The common features of these include an idealist/moralist stance accompanied by a domination of 'representational fallacies'[7] in which geometric or visual patterns are granted the status of real objects, or are substituted for theoretical analysis.

g) The objects of the ED are formed by the variations of the basic epistemological structure

The ED is concerned with describing and constructing certain phenomena called 'environment's on the basis of a relationship that is assumed to exist between 'M' and 'E', or between a *'subject'* and an *'object'*. This is precisely the epistemological structure which dominates the discourse as will be shown in Chapter 3.

---

1 See Sec. 4.5.
2 This origin is often thought in ideal geometric terms, e.g. *'Golden Section'* etc. cf. Tyng, A.G. (1969).
3 cf. large number of utopias from Thomas More to the urbanistic theories of the 19. century; and to the religious and ecologist utopias of 1960s, and 70s. (On a discursive analysis of More's Utopian urbanism, see: Choay, F. (1974): 301, 308. See also Sec. 4.3.4 on Utopianism).
4 Rigour, however, is not a guarantee of correctness by itself, (cf. Parsons' system).
5 Althusser, L. (1969): 247.
6 cf. for ex. P. Soleri's 'city of man', *'Arcology'*, (1969) (1973).
7 cf. Sec. 4.6.7.

One of the basic features of this epistemology is that nearly all other variants within the discourse are the variants of this basic schema. Thus, a common mechanism is the *substitution* of variants into the subject - object structure. For example, *'subject'* is replaced by 'man', 'individual', 'me', 'organization', 'society', 'user', 'designer', 'client', while *'object'* is replaced by 'nature', 'environment', 'external world', 'life space', 'cosmos', 'building', etc.

While this process does not necessarily supply *new* objects to the discourse, it, however, produces *sub-objects* which give the false impression of 'universal applicability' of the 'M-E' schema. In fact, it is the invariant structure of *this* schema which provides the variants, and it is these variants which are adopted as discursive objects in various discourses and practices.

h) The objects of the ED are formed by analogies and metaphors
Although analogies and metaphors may enrich literary or everyday discourses by their suggestions of similarities[1] or substitutes[2], they, however, are two of the major *obstacles* to the development of a scientific discourse. They tend to subordinate *real* differences between domains and objects to *formal* similarities, mostly in appearances. They also help to oversimplify the reality. They provide 'methods' of *organizing radically different objects,* such as life, world, a city, a house, a theatre, a wall, or a column . . . [3] in similar fashions. Thus, for example, 'biological analogies' may be used to organize design[4] and planning[5].

Analogies and metaphors, on the other hand, can serve as the prescriptive tools and basis of styles in architecture , or may be used as the method of criticism.[6] In the latter case they function as the principle of explanation and artificially fill in the place left by the lack of theoretical analysis. Moreover, the specific coherence that *may* enable such shifts and reductions remains to be specified.[7]

While metaphors cannot stand in for notions or concepts [8] they, however, represent the basis of 'environmental' vocabulary. This point will be examined in greater detail later.[9] One significant problem, however, must be mentioned here concerning the double effect of *spatial metaphors* in the ED. It involves using spatial terms (e.g. in-out, territory, boundary, spacious, . . .), or spatial representations (e.g. circle)[10] to denote spatial phenomena (e.g. territory, 'space', in-out, size, . . .). Before all else, *the term 'environment' is a spatial term and a metaphor*[11] *for all spatial objects and phenomena.* Thus, *the ED is a metaphorical metalanguage*[12] *which is constituted around, and is about, a set of metaphorical confusions.* The latter include a conflation of metaphors with what is meant [13] or the real with the conceptual and representational.

i) The objects of the ED are formed by shifts of domain, amphibologies and borrowings
It was emphasized right from the beginning of this chapter that the ED exists at the

1   cf. O'Malley, J.B. (1972): 48; Simon, H.A. (1969): 85.
2   cf. Wilden, A. (1972): 46ff; Barthes, R. (1967): 60.
3   cf. Choay, F. (1974): 314-5.
4   cf. Yeang, K. (1974): 53f.
5   cf. Lynch, K. in Battisti, E. (1975): 243, fig. 95; see also: Harvey, D. (1969): 14-5, 169-172.
6   For example, 'linguistic analogies' (see: Collins, P. (1965) ; Daru, M. (1973): 1-3-4).
7   "Appeal to analogy cannot function as a principle of explanation in the absence of a theory justifying the analogy by reference to similarity of forms of internal coherence." (Mepham, J. (1973): 111).
8   Bachelard, G. in Lecourt, D. (1975): 64, see also, 173.
9   Sec. 4.6.6.
10 cf. Sec. 4.3.2.
11 Lefebvre, H. (in response to a question by the author, London, 19.3.1973), see also: Lefebvre, H. (1970): 245-6.
12 cf. Barthes, R. (1967): 61.
13 cf. Bateson, G. in Wilden, A. (1972): 59-60.

'intersection' of many fields, practices and disciplines. This can be said to be a major determinant of its nature. Secondly, the ED is based upon a problematic whose elements are generalistic, imaginary and metaphorical. Thirdly, its elements possess a multiple status which results in a confusion of the real with the imaginary[1], and real object with theoretical object.

These three factors are operative in the discourse by means of shifts of domains, amphibologies and borrowings. These factors as well as the mechanisms which follow are supports and representatives of other modes of object formation examined in this section.[2] These operations or mechanisms form objects (or non-objects) of the ED

− by *'bracketing'* concepts and terms of other discourses, disciplines and practices and using them in 'environmental' context (as one of the necessary conditions of shifts and borrowings),

− by *shifting* domains, disciplines, discourses, levels, instances, practices, points of view, fields or terms, (for example *to* and *from* moral, psychological, political, technical, subjective, economic . . .),

− by *confusing* objects, requirements, objectives, structures, tools, levels, issues, scales, or modes of representation and expression, (for example, real, theoretical, visual, functional, individual-social, discursive-non-discursive, drawings, structures . . .),

− by *conflating* aspects, questions, levels, (for example, sociological, epistemological, psychological, biological[3] . . .),

− by *substituting* or *displacing* elements, terms, objects and problems with others, (for example, variants, metaphors, examples, classes) − (e.g. 'classes' substituted by 'people'[4], 'tenant', 'user' or 'man'; 'appropriation' or 'ownership' substituted by 'use' etc.),

− by *borrowing* from other domains, discourses and disciplines mainly to satisfy the requirements of a general problematic of a particular discourse, (for example, from art, systems engineering, physical sciences, religious discourse etc.),

− by *transposing* the terms and problematic of one domain into another without yielding any new knowledge ; in other words producing 'amphibologies'[5], (for example, by transposing an anthropological   problematic into economic, (e.g. alienation of man); or, a religious one into environmental, (e.g. M-E split) to 'explain' questions as diverse as environmental crises, starvation of the 'Third World' people, destruction of forests, or ill effects of high-rise housing).

j) The objects of the ED are formed by means of some graphical representations
In addition to the conceptual effects of metaphors, substitutions and shifts that have been discussed briefly, the modes of representation in these mechanisms have significant effects on the objects of the discourse. For, a representation is not simply a tool. It carries the presumed meaning of the object represented while imposing upon it a certain degree of conceptual content.

In nearly all domains where the ED is operative, graphical representation[6] (as well as schematic diagrams) is a common means of expressing 'M-E', 'in-out', 'container-content' relations. In fact, these representations often become *the only 'evidences' of the validity* of the relationships which they are supposed to represent. It is mainly because *spatiality of the graphical shapes tends to coincide with the spatial objects that the latter represent.*

1 cf. Wilden, A. (1972).
2 For detailed examinations of these mechanisms, see Ch. 4.
3 See, for ex. how the epistemological relation between subject and object is assimilated to the biological relation between organism and environment by such a mechanism, (Hindess, B. (1973a):251).
4 On this, see Faye, J.P. (1976): 59; Castells, M. (1975): 238-9; Castells, M. (1974): 8.
5 In other words, doing nothing more than a "terminological round trip", (N.L.R. (1972): 65, also, Glucksmann, A. (1972): 87-8). See also Rancière, J. (1973): 19.
6 This subject will be treated in greater detail and with examples in Sec. 4.6.7.

Therefore, a conceptualization of 'E' as the 'surrounding', 'habitat' or 'context' of 'M' seems unquestionable when, say, a circular shape shows this relationship to be physically possible. Similarly, it makes little difference whether 'E' is substituted by 'world', 'nature', a stadium, a living room or a prison cell. This usually appears like this:

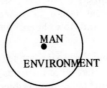

Beside the spatiality of this shape, its direct, realistic and *experiential* nature as well as its ease of reproduction is functional in its being the most common tool of the *circular* logic. It is this logic, on the other hand, which turns the 'obviousness' of the explanation into a relativistic fallacy.[1]

Other, less graphical, but equally common form of representation is schematic diagrams. For example, arrows are used to convey, as well as to impose, types of relations that are believed to exist between 'M' and 'E'.

e.g.

$M \longrightarrow E$
$E \longrightarrow M$
$M \longleftrightarrow E$
$M \rightleftharpoons E$ etc., or

NATURE

MEN $\longleftrightarrow$ MEN[2]

As these and other problems will be dealt with in greater detail, it would be sufficient for the moment to suggest that it is not only the graphical and spatial nature of the graphical representations which is instrumental in their effects, but, more important, it is the nature of the M-E problematic which is responsible for their utilization in the first place.[3]

k) The objects of the ED are formed by non-discursive interventions, ideological promotions; and under institutional and historical determinations.
The ED, like any other discourse, is a *practice*. It is neither a finished product, nor a mental process, nor simply a set of books or statements. As such, it exits amongst other (discursive and non-discursive) practices in society. That is, it is a *social* practice.

This last point, however, should not be left at its simple and often misunderstood implications. What is invoked here is neither a reduction of the discursive practice to a vague 'sociality', nor is it a determinism of some sort — as is common in empiricist sociology and social psychology. What is aimed at here is an identification of the *discursive existence of a discourse (and its objects) as a necessary and determinate practice of social formations*. Briefly stated, this position implies an understanding of:
a) particular social formations in terms of their dominant instances and modes of production, and how particular (economic, technical, ideological) practices involve a *discursive appropriation* of their real objects, (e.g. the relationship between the ED in the framework

1 cf. Sec. s. 4.3.2 and 4.6.7.
2 Biolat, G. (1973): 12.
3 Graphical representation is indeed a necessary means of expression in scientific discourses as well. Where would chemistry be without 'ties', and polygonal representation of compounds and molecular structures? Similarly, where would architectural and planning practices be without drawing? (See, for example, the theoretical significance of tetrahedral representation of carbon in Bachelard's discussion on "secondary objects" that are preceded by theories, in Lecourt, D. (1975): 53).

of urban and architectural production and the capitalist mode of production in English social formation, and how the latter institutionalizes and utilizes the former),

b) how the dominant institutional structure produces, promotes, influences, prohibits, censors or distorts certain discursive practices and their objects, (e.g. how 'environmental' institutions, government departments, schools, professional bodies, research establishments and media treat the objects, terms and judgements of the ED; how they prefer one object or set of objects to another, and how they establish 'official' discourses and institutionalize them),

c) and, how some objects appear and disappear, are formed and transformed under certain historical conditions, (e.g. under what historical circumstances 'nature', 'man', 'God', 'space', 'milieu', 'environment' become the objects of discourses/what is the relationship between the history of the ED and those of particular social formations, or of sciences),

d) and, how some objects are granted 'importance' while others are ignored or undermined, (e.g. how and why 'environment' is so important in Western capitalist countries, how, for example, starvation of millions of people in other places is less important, or is transformed into a natural and 'environmental' hazard),

e) and, in short, *how is it that some real or theoretical objects (and non-objects) become discursive objects,* (e.g. how cities, but not villages, how architectural objects, but not theoretical concepts, become the objects of the ED).[1]

2.4 Specificity of the objects

While discussing the unity of the ED and of its object it was argued that it is not that there are many discourses on the same object, but, rather, one discourse that is constituted by a *problematic* which is shared by several disciplines, domains and 'regional' discourses. It was also argued that the ED was under the domination of several fallacies among which the illusion of the singularity of object and confusion of real with discursive objects were most pervasive, and that the object(s) of the ED were ideological non-object(s), and could not be taken as real or theoretical objects[2]. As a result of these arguments two questions emerged one of which was "if there is *no* real object 'environment' (which the ED assumes that there is), then what is it that the ED is about?"[3]

On the basis of these arguments and questions, and following the analysis of object formation above, it can now be asked: *What is the object of the ED?* If the object of the ED is seen to be 'Environment' and its variants, such as 'Space' or 'Nature', and its relation with subject, 'Man' or 'Society'; it may then be asked: *"What is Environment?"* But, *is it a legitimate question to pose?* Before answering this question a brief detour is necessary:

In view of many confusing mechanisms which dominate the ED some strategic decisions expressed in the form of postulates must be made concerning the specificity of the discursive object:

1) It is not possible to define a discursive object at a level which is defined by that object *in the first place* (e.g. defining 'Environment' at an *'environmental'* level),

2) It is not possible to define an *exclusively 'environmental'* problem at a level which is *exclusively 'environmental'* (that is, there can be no problem which is 'environmental' and nothing else),

1 All these and other questions regarding the relations and determinations of discursive objects as well as those of the discourse itself will be examined in Ch.5.
2 Sec. 2.2.
3 ibid.

3) Specificity of a real problem cannot be obtained by *reducing* its complexity to one of its levels (e.g. to the physical or psychological),

4) or, by *ignoring* some of its main levels (e.g. the social specificity of physical problems, etc.),

5) Some identifiable properties of complex problems cannot be accorded the status of *problems in-themselves* (e.g. 'noise' presented as a specific problem, or as an 'enemy').[1]

The first decision is to be expounded as it carries with it one of the principles followed by the present critique.

A discursive object which is not a scientific *concept* but a descriptive and general *notion* (like 'Environment' and 'Man') cannot be asked to specify what it specifically refers to in the domain of real objects. Thus, questions like *"What is Environment?"* or *"What is the relation between M and E?"* are redundant if they require designation of some real objects or real relations. It is because what is at stake is not simply what the words 'Environment' and 'Man' designate or name, but, whether they are scientifically specifiable concepts in the first place. Thus, the questions may be reposed as *"What is 'environment'?"* and *"What is the 'M-E relations'?,* and on the basis of these questions, *"What exactly is the object that so-called 'environmental practices' deal with?"*[2] In this modified form the questions are concerned with

a) *the specificity of the discursive objects* of the ED,

b) *the status of these (discursive) objects,*

and, finally,

c) *the specificity and the status of the objects that 'environmental' practices deal with* in a variety of ways.

The first question involves a specification of the *level(s)* at which the phenomena are dealt with in the ED as well as the question of *defining* the objects of the ED. The second involves a specification of the *nature* and *type* of the discursive objects. The third, which this study does not primarily aim at answering, involves an analysis of all objects ('real' or otherwise) that 'environmental practices' deal with or the ED refers to. Yet, to avoid reproducing the problematic of 'environment' in such an analysis, first the *present* analysis of the ED needs to be completed.

The specificity of a discursive object is not determined solely by identifying some *words* or *concepts* – however commonly they may be used in a discourse. This is so even if some of these words or concepts happen to represent the discursive object at the same time. It is the problematic and the mechanisms of a discourse which define the domains, the field of relevance, thematic range, levels, names and status of objects. No definition can be made without a problematic within which that definition is formulated. Therefore, this critique analyses *that* problematic, instead of any *a priori* recognition of given definitions. Finally, institutional delimitations provide a certain degree of specificity to the rather fuzzy set of objects in the ED[3]. This is done in a tautological manner: some institutionally recognized practices define their own objects which are then institutionalized only to establish the scope and object of those practices. In other words, some practices reproduce the 'Environmental' objects by accepting and legitimizing their givenness. All 'environmental problems' *become* environmental because they *belong to* an 'environmental level'.

1 cf. Castells, M. (1975): 241-2.

2 In the course of the following analysis these questions will mostly involve the terms 'environment', 'M-E relation', and 'M' in the order of emphasis. This is so mainly because the ED is essentially a discourse on 'environment'. 'M' on the other hand, is the necessary *counterpart* of E in the M-E couple, and is implicit in all statements on E and M-E relation. Moreover, the conception of M will be examined in greater detail on several other occasions.

3 cf. Sec. 2.3 on formation of objects and Ch. 5 on discursive relations.

The strategic decisions above are based on a close observation of the practices and discourses which operate around the 'Environmental' objects. In formulating these decisions it was asked whether it really mattered what a practice, discipline or discourse was called, or the level at which it is conceived of, as long as it 'delivered the goods'. The conclusion was that there was a peculiar coincidence in the abundance of 'Environmental' practices dealing with 'Environmental' problems and the number of obvious failures in 'delivering the goods' promised. Moreover, the question remained with those 'goods' which seemed to have been delivered: do they actually deliver what they say they are delivering, or is it *something else* that they deliver? (i.e. are they knowledges of scientifically specifiable objects, or technical information on technique-dominated problems, or an understanding of complex socio-technical problems?). For example, what exactly the objects of architectural practice, design or planning are? Are they 'environment'[1], space[2], *the* 'Environment'[3], brick-and-mortar, people[4], 'unconscious codes and theories',[5] or behaviour.

This question is relevant in another respect too. Since the 1960s there has been an immense amount of attention paid to design methods often in a highly sophisticated manner, yet, with an astonishing lack of attention to the *object* that is assumed to be designed. Similarly, some fundamental questions have been ignored altogether: *What* exactly is that which is said to be polluted in 'environmental pollution'? *What* is the object of an 'environmental policy'? Or, *what* precisely is 'the Image of the City'[6] the image of; or the 'environmental perception' the perception of?

Before going further into the analysis of such questions it must be said that it seems quite futile to tackle real problems in such a circular manner. Real problems concerning the practices that we are examining here must be seen as complex wholes whose determinate levels should not be reduced either to one of them, or to a generality such as 'environmental'. It is on the basis of these principles and strategic decisions that we can now return to asking the ED the question 'what is *'environment'?*

The question 'what' implies a definition. It must be remembered, however, that definitions, formulations and descriptions do not carry universal truths. Nor are they to be self-justifying statements on what, in fact, are perfectly questionable positions. They are made possible by conceptual systems, i.e. by *problematics*. Thus, it is on the basis of an understanding of the latter that they can be evaluated. Especially if the definitions persistently contain the elements which are referred to in the strategic decisions above, there is every right to be suspicious of their status. Thus, no argument on 'environment' should be immune from questioning on the basis of a statement 'by definition' (of 'environment'). (This implies an ideal or goal-state which any conception of 'environment' should refer to if it wants to be 'correct'!). As it will be partly exemplified in the collection of definitions and statements in the *Appendix,* there are definitions that are made intuitively, sensorially[7], culturally[8]. with or without perceiving persons[9] or linguistically[10].

1 An 'environment-in-itself' as a 'thing-in-itself' is not *knowable*, (cf. Colletti, L. (1974):11 on the knowability of 'thing-in-itself'.)
2 'Space-in-itself' is no more possible to analyse than time-in-itself, (cf. Castells, M. (1975): 475).
3 cf. Medawar, P. (1960): "Although we cheerfully speak about *the* environment of an organism or a population; we know very well there is no such thing".
4 "Materialet for arkitektens skaperverk er menneskene, ikke bare betong og jern". ("The material for architects' creative work is men, not merely concrete and steel".) (Candilis, G. (1968): 419).
5 Hillier, B. & Leaman, A. (1976): 32.
6 cf. Lynch, K. (1964).
7 For ex., Thiel, P. (1973): 377.
8 For ex., Rapoport, A. (1969): 127.
9 For ex., Boutourline, S. (1970): 498.
10 For ex., De Long, A.J. (1973): 5.

Definitions carry with them the *problematic*, the *ideology*, or the *worldview* that is dominant in the respective discourses. Moreover, definitions are made possible by a large number of *mechanisms* which will be dealt with in Ch. 4. The ones which are most relevant to the question of specificity are the reductionism, generalization, individualization, substitutions, shifts, metaphors, pure principles and conceptual couples. Therefore, the following collection of definitions and statements should not be expected to dispel the questions that are being asked of these definitions in the first place. Without an understanding of their common problematic it would give the impression that there is a systematicity, consistency or coherence in the variety of definitions. Their variety would even be taken as the index of the inherent complexity of the 'environment' (rather than the latter's dubiousness). Moreover, such a collection of definitions should not lead us to ignore the fact that the *notion* of 'environment' may exist in a discourse in forms other than words, such as in graphical representations, drawings, or in statistics about certain phenomena.

This plain set of definitions should not, however, obscure some significant facts of the ED, namely the *lack* of definitions[1], *difficulties* of defining (recognized even by the environmentalists[2]), and the *multiplicity*[3] of definitions. The lack of definition is closely related with a serious *lack of theory* in the ED.[4] Without an established theory it is hardly possible to expect a discourse to produce reliable definitions of its objects. Thus, the specificity of the object largely depends upon the state of theory in that discourse. To compensate this *a-theoretical* state of the discourse various attempts are being made to bring in a systematicity or a structure of principles. For example, 'environment' and 'space' are often described as *'systems'*[5] as if describing it as such would guarantee its validity[6]. Or, similarly, certain concepts are refused validity. Yet, using them in different senses or combinations would hardly dispel the *inherent conception* that persists in the term[7]. Lack of definition is coupled with an uneven presence of the word in some languages[8]. While the recognized difficulty of defining 'environment' is partly due to a lack of theory, it is partly due to a number of other fundamental factors. It is these factors which need to be scrutinized in terms of the *status* of the objects (which will be done following the Appendix).

1 cf. Baladier, C. (1976): 43.
2 cf. Sonnenfeld, J. (1972): 244f.
3 cf. Sec. 3.3.
4 This will be examined in Chapter 6 on Status of the ED. On this question see: Koseki, S. (1972): 64; Gould, P.R. (1963): 290; on the lack of social theory, see Enzensberger, H.M. (1974): 17.
5 For ex., Ecologist (1972): 24; Broadbent, G.   (1973): Ch. 18; Tekeli, İ. (1969): Part 2; Chizhov, N. & Lipets, Y. (1976): 138.
6 cf. Hirst, P.Q. (1975): 75.
7 For ex., M. Castells's introduction of the term 'urban system' after his demolition of the term 'urban', cf. (1976).
8 For ex., the term 'environment', though used with great misconceptions in various discourses in France, does not even exist in some dictionaries (cf. Baladier, C. (1976) while the word "environer" was present in old French (The Concise Oxford Dictionary, (5th ed.): 406). It is reported that in most Australian 'aboriginal' languages a concept of 'space' or 'environment' does not exist. (cf. P. Memmott in a lecture at the UCL, 10.3.1975).

Appendix: A collection of definitions and statements

In addition to what has already been said above regarding the nature of this collection, a couple of additional points must be made here:
— This collection of definitions, statements and quotations is not meant to be an exhaustive survey of existing (or possible) statements on the subject. Nor such a project is believed to be possible or necessary.
— It is not meant to constitute any *unity* other than a *collection of statements* from a complex and diffused discourse, or, in fact, a field. Moreover, it has already been argued that a discourse or a discipline cannot be defined in terms of its *object* alone.
— There is no deliberate classification, order or evaluation of statements.
— It is not assumed also that they possess any systematicity, coherence or consistency.
— Such a simple collection of definitions is not in contradiction with the fundamental nature of the present study which is expounded in the General Introduction, in the general discussion on discourse and problematic, and in several other occasions. Simply stated, it is *not a history of ideas,* a semantic analysis, a history of architecture, art or planning, or a survey of what others think about 'architecture', 'environment', etc.
— Statements and definitions are mere *examples,* and *not proofs* of any thesis. In fact, no thesis can be proven on the basis of a set of statements.
The discourse of which this collection has been isolated from for the purpose of illustration can only be analysed in terms of its epistemological structure, mechanisms, status, relations and effects which this study attempts to tackle.

"The environment of the organism is the class composed of the sum of those phenomena that enter a reaction system of the organism or otherwise directly impinge upon it to affect its mode of life at any time throughout its life cycle as ordered by the demands of the ontogeny of the organism or as ordered by any other condition of the organism that alters its environmental demands. This definition expresses operationally a time-space-organism concept of environment where constituents form a class".[1]

"For Fuller, environment is everything that is not man. But other people, their actions and ideas form part of his environment. He is part of theirs. Is it not possible that parts of him should be part of his own environment?"[2]

"Even though people no longer build their own houses, the houses they buy reflect popular values and goals more closely than do those of the design subculture — and these houses constitute the bulk of the built environment".[3]

". . . they have bought quality of environment and space as well as a roof over their heads."[4]

"All people are builders, creators, molders of shapes of the environment; we are the environment".[5]

"To the geographer, the environment is; 'a range of conditions; without reference to any specific creatures'." . . . "To the biologist; 'cells or matter external to any micro or macro structure, from extra-nucleic matter of the cell to geographical or climatic conditions in which an entire species exist'." . . . "To a psychologist it is 'a combination of social/economic/religious/political influences'."[6]

1 Mason, H.L. & Langenheim, J.H. (1957): 332.
2 paraphrased in Jardin, B. (1971): 38.
3 Rapoport, A. (1969): 127.
4 J. Hillman, in *The Guardian,* 28.6.75, p.9, (on Eric Lyon's designs).
5 Sommer, R. (1969).
6 Wells, B.W.P. (1965 b).

"The unmodified term 'environment' broadly signifies any condition or influence outside the organism, group, system, or whatever entity is being studied. In the heredity-environment controversy, for example, the environmentalists countered genetic variables not only with physical environmental variables, but all variables outside the organism that influence its development. In the growing literature on educational environments, research is typically focused on institutional variables, such as administrative practices, teacher-pupil ratio, or aptitude level of the student body, rather than on physical environmental variables".[1]

"Consider the skin of the earth — air, water and soil — all presently endangered by the greed and pollution of a ravenous society. Relate the wonderful riches of the world and the marvellous brain of man to the disgrace of poverty, hunger and deprivation. This is the politics of environment.
And only socialism can make sense of it".[2]

"The Golf. . . buy it. A car that makes sense. Sound financial sense. Sound family sense. Sound traffic sense. And sound environmental sense . . ."[3]

"Architecture of a far more acceptable kind with an inbuilt sense of place, of identity, of environment for people with the human connotations."[4]

". . Ricardian economy made the environment in the form of 'the original and indestructible properties of soil', the basic capital that society has to work with, and the limiting factor in man's ability to improve his economic lot by accumulation of material capitals in the form of factories and machines".
"The environment, therefore, is a form of social capital . . ."
"Contrary to Ricardo, environment is not 'original and indestructible".[5]

"We may not be able to define it [the word 'environment'] precisely, but we can still perceive its limits more or less clearly: our environment is everything that is not us. We do not confine its use just to the physical universe, but include the social universe and the universe of ideas in our meaning".[6]

"This paper represents an attempt to briefly identify the environment as a system of communication which is hierarchically organized, with each level of hierarchical complexity characterized by an aspectual integration".[7]

"Traditionally, psychology has treated the physical environment as either the source of physical stimuli to which an organism responds or as an object to be perceived or cognized. Rarely has it been treated as an inextricable part of the life processes of the organisms studied".[8]

1 Craik, K.H. (1969): 13-14.
2 Labour Party (1973): (back cover).
3 VW — Golf 1975 pamphlet, p.1.
4 Broadbent, G. (1975): 416.
5 Johnson, H.G. (1973): 7.
6 Jardine, B. (1971): 38.
7 De Long, A.J. (1973): 5.
8 Ittelson, W.H. *et. al.* (1970): 419.

"The 5 definitions he [D. Watson] proposes are of the:
1) environment as bounded processes,
2) as a field of human activity,
3) as a field of message cues,
4) as a set of limited resources,
5) as a means of structuring communities . . ."[1]

"Environmental Cycle:
An electric bicycle which runs for up to 30 miles on four pence worth of power has
been developed by a British team led by a former Ford chairman, Sir Leonard
Crossland."[2]

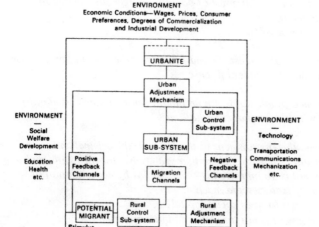

ENVIRONMENT
Governmental Policies—Agricultural Practices,
Marketing Organization, Population Movement, etc.

A system schema for a theory of rural-urban migration.[3]

"We define environment for a given population of human beings as the system of
spatial and temporal regularities of non-human structures, which influences the biologi-
cal and behavioural processes of this population."[4]

"Environmental quality comprises the twin aspects of character and amenity. Amenity
is concerned with the nature of appearance, and character with the distinguishing
features of areas, places or objects. High environmental quality exists where distinction
and delight combine . . ."[5]

"At Stockholm [UN Human Environment Conference in 1972], the developed nations
were somewhat vague on just what they meant by the environment. But they all agreed
it had something to do with pollution; everybody except Japan agreed it could be
stretched to include whales; and all but the French agreed it meant not letting off
atom bombs in the Pacific" . . ." . . . the Swedes . . . spoilt the whole thing by saying
that Vietnam was environment, and You-Know-Who ought to stop dropping bombs on it.

1 quoted in Barbéy, G. & Gelber, C. (eds) (1973): 323.
2 R. Rodwell in *The Guardian*, quoted in *Readers' Digest*, Jan. 1977, p.12.
3 Mabogunje, A.L. (1972): 195.
4 Reichardt, R. (1970): 661.
5 G.L.C., Dept. of Arch. & Civic Design: 'Thames-side Environmental Assessment' (1968).

The developed nations resigned themselves to the environment involving everything from multi-national corporations to ecocide in Indo-China, and comforted one another with the thought that if the subject was really as broad as all that nobody would ever be able to do anything about it." . . . ". . . the rich nations went back to explaining the poor ones that environment meant smokeless zones and salmon in the Thames . . ."[1]

". . . a new environmental game . . . which aims to help children measure the quality of their environment street by street. The Streetometer . . . gives children . . . the means to assess the nuisance caused by such aspects of the environment as litter, 'floorscape' . . . wirescape and landscape. . . ."[2]

"An open system is such that its relationship to a supersystem (which may be referred to methodologically as its 'environment' or as its 'context') is indispensable to its survival. There is an ongoing exchange of matter — energy and information between them".[3]

"Neither the human/nonhuman distinction, nor the natural/artificial distinction was seen to have any functional relevance when behaviour in environment was at issue. The only clear difference between environments . . . is the existence or non-existence of social interaction.[4]*"*

"Environment is a relational concept defined with respect to what is surrounded [çevrelenen]. *The concept of environment enables us to pursue analyses without much error by including factors which are outside the geographic spatial dimensions into a container and content type of spatial perception.*

Environment does not contain all that is outside the 'çevrelenen', *yet, contains the perceptions, units and variables which effect* 'çevrelenen'. *Environment is an operational concept defined according to the way in which the object of study is effected.*

In such a distinction of environment and 'çevrelenen', *some of the variables used to explain the pheomena are in the environment and some within* 'cevrelenen'[5]*."*

"The term 'environment' implies two things: that there is a set of phenomena, facts or things, and that they are experienced. In the built environment we have on the one hand a set of physical facts (a physical system); on the other, a system of human experience of them (an experience system)."[6]

"Help save our trees with this free Safeway bag. Safeway have sponsored this bag to assist in preserving the environment and to save natural resources . . . let us all help to protect our environment."[7]

"The physical world may be described as an aggregation of locally differentiated spaces, each determined by a perceived invariance in sensory pattern in a given sensory mood. Thus we have visual, olfactory, auditory, thermal, and tactile space. Scene may be defined

1 **Tinker**, J. (1975): 600.
2 *The Guardian*, 15.1.1975.
3 Wilden, A. (1972): 203.
4 Sonnenfeld, J. (1969): 137.
5 Tekeli, İ. (1973): 6-7.
6 Hillier, B. (1970): 27.
7 Safeway Supermarkets.

as the combination of all the multi-modal spaces coexisting at a given point; at a given moment. This physical environment is experiencable only in the course of our movement through it, from scene to scene. . . ."[1]

"Environment can be considered as a complex system of relations between processes, themselves more or less complex . . ."[2]

"Environment is where you live and where you work. It is intolerable housing conditions, where noise from the TV upstairs or the children next door can be worse than Concorde. It is unacceptable factories and pits and workshops all over the world. Environment is a big word and we must accept all that it means to all people. It is a word with many levels. It leads some of our friends to campaign for world wild life, to protest against factory farming, to be vegetarian and not wear furs. Others translate their concern in demonstrating against chemical defoliation in Vietnam. For some it is not having an airport or a motorway too near; demonstrating against planners who want to pull down old houses. To others environmental progress is having an indoor lavatory and being put on main drainage; or having somewhere to park their car, without necessarily wanting everybody else to have a car. The spectrum of concern ranges from the person who drops his picnic papers on the ground to the factory owner who hopes that the local river can drink up all his problems."[3]

"To Jack Mundey . . . 'environment' covers a large area".[4]

1 Thiel, P. (1973): 377.
2 Spizzichino, R. (1971): 9.
3 Labour Party (1973): 3.
4 *Building Design*, 16.1.1976: 10.

2.5 Status of the objects

While the specificity of discursive objects involves a *'what'*, the 'status'[1] of the same
objects would require the questions *'how'*, or *'what kind of'*. Furthermore, while
what is meant with 'specificity' is the specification of discursive objects, the question
of status involves a specification of the epistemological, scientific and discursive
nature of objects as well as a reference to the mechanisms which specify them.
This must not, however, be taken to mean that status is a question regarding the
'object' alone. It is a question involving all practices, discourses and objects at several
distinct levels. This, in return, does not mean that there is a necessary identity of the
status(es) of these different unities. These status(es) are closely related and are
observable at staggered levels of each unity. There is no one-to-one correspondence
between their structures and status(es)[2].

Having said that, the question of the status of the object can be posed as:
− What is the nature of the object(s) of the ED?
− At precisely what levels do these objects exist?
− How are they sustained in the form that they are in?

This section will examine these questions, and will deal with the *dominant* objects
of that discourse, namely 'environment', 'man', 'M-E relationship', and their variations
(e.g. buildings, city, user, nature). This will be done in the form of a series of propositions
which will be illustrated by some exemplary cases or statements[3]. Yet, as there is no
product without process, and no object without a process of its formation, it would
be useful to remember the postulates and observations that were discussed earlier[4].
The objects of the ED are formed
− by adopting ordinary words or terms,
− by reference to some empirically given (real) objects,
− on the basis of arbitrarily determined points of view,
− by generalizations,
− by reductions and simplifications,
− by reference to 'ideal' and 'original' objects, or to 'pure principles',
− by substitution of the variants of the basic objects,
− by analogies and metaphors,
− by shifts of domain, amphibologies and loans,
− by means of some graphical representations,
− by non-discursive determinations, ideological promotions, and under institutional
and historical conditions.

It is also useful to remember some of the 'strategic decisions' made in the context
of the specificity of the central discursive object, 'Environment'. It was suggested that
it is not possible to define an object at a level which is *defined* by that object in the
first place. Secondly, there can be no problem which is 'environmental' and nothing else.

Following these arguments it can be seen that 'Environment' is a term which has no
definite unity, specificity and autonomy (which are the minimum conditions to make
it an identifiable object). The questions of whether the terms 'environment' and 'man'
refer to some empirical objects, or whether they are theoretical concepts are never
posed in the ED. Thus, these two radically different types of objects are continuously
conflated and confused in order to sustain them as discursive objects. Especially,
'environment' is conceived both as a *relational and systemic   notion,* and as a *spatial*

1 For an explanation of the concept of 'status', see Ch. 6.
2 For a detailed examination of this point, see Teymur, N. & E. (1978).
3 In addition to these illustrations, the definitions and statements in the *Appendix* in this Chapter
can also be consulted.
4 cf. Sec.s 2.3, and 2.4.

and physical entity. The same term denotes both a *frame of reference* against which an object can (or, should) be conceptualized, and that which physically surrounds an organism. The first is a *notion,* the other a *name.*

The term 'environment' is an *imprecise,* and for this and other reasons, an *inadequate* object. This 'inadequacy', however, is not sought between the discursive object and a presumed 'real object' according to a criteria established prior to a discursive analysis. It is one that is internal to the term 'environment'. The set of physical objects cannot be adequately conceptualized by the conceptual or notional content of the term.

In the professional discourse as well as in the economic sphere 'environment' is conceived as the set of objects that are directly accessible to visual perception, measurement, transactions, and transformation, i.e. to direct appropriation. In the academic discourse, on the other hand, a deep *dualism* separates the professional and economic conception from the one that is too abstract and too general to signify anything specific, (i.e. 'environment' as *everything*[1]). This is due, partly, to the epistemological structure of the discourse which embodies simultaneously an idealism of the subject and an empiricism of the object[2], and, partly, to the type of institutional and ideological relations between the professional practice and the academic one.[3]

The ED is incapable of *producing new concepts for newly recognized problems.* Thus, these 'problems' are either expressed in 'old' terms; or new terms are borrowed or made up to meet the immediate requirements of the discourse[4]. This leads to some immense confusions and misunderstandings not only in the discursive field, but also, in the non-discursive modes of tackling the problems themselves.

The terms 'man', 'environment', 'society', 'nature' . . . are all *transhistorical* and *extra-historical.* They are conceived to be the substitutes for   'subject' and 'object' in a linear conception of history. Thus, they embody a peculiar paradox. On the one hand, their transhistoricity   seems to deny history a place in their conceptual universe: 'man' is 'man', 'environment' is 'environment', and 'society' is 'society' whatever the time dimension in the phenomena is. On the other hand, they stand as the *variants* of subject and object which, in linear conception of history[5], are the substance of historicity. Moreover, M-E schema does hardly imply a process, or a movement. They are two elements, or two 'things', one of which is a 'subject', the other an 'object', and they are counterposed to each other in a variety of ways[6], yet almost always without a history. They are infinitely variable, yet *structurally invariant,* elements.

The only apparent movement is the frequent shifts of points of view: one is always viewed from the *point of view* of the other[7] this movement too takes place at a horizontal level. Whereas "the verb is the indispensable condition for all discourse"[8] in the case of the ED it comes only through a *post factum attribution* of a particular type of relationship that the M-E couple is expected to possess[9].

1 cf. Sec.2.2.
2 cf. Sec. 3.3.2.
3 cf. Sec. 5.3.
4 For ex. the term 'crowding' has been employed in expressing many diverse problems or producing several spurious correlations. (For a criticism, see Mercer, C. (1976): 64-5; for a review of 'crowding researches', see Fischer, C.S. *et.al.* (1975)). Similarly the term 'territoriality' has been introduced and used to explain what, in fact, are ideologically determined social relations and behaviour.
5 i.e. one which is based on the continuous, evolutionary, non-contradictory and even, succession of human subjects and events, (cf. Althusser, L. (1970): Ch. 4).
6 cf. Sec. 3.3.
7 cf. Sec.s 2.3.c, and 3.3.5.
8 Foucault, M. (1970): 93.
9 see the list of *Relations* in Sec. 3.3.7.b.

The objects of the ED are imprecise, vague, fuzzy and highly variational terms. They are too general to be of use in the analysis of specific phenomena. Especially the word 'environment' refers to nearly *everything* (thus, to *nothing*).[1] This *'allness'* is quite similar to, and closely related with, the earlier ideology of Nature which is being replaced by the 'ideology of Environment'.[2] The *globality* in this conception is often perpetuated by taking it as a matter of fact, and accepting its varied connotations as a positive richness (rather than as a source of confusion). Moreover, several other terms that are introduced in order to account for this globality and allness tend to function as their confirmation (e.g. 'Total Environment',[3] and 'Life Space'[4]).

'Environment' is a *metaphor*[5] for 'space' and for 'physical', 'natural' and 'built' phenomena at one and the same time. As a metaphor it is not a concept, and it "cannot stand for a notion".[6] More significantly, as a metaphor, it cannot be *known*. The knowledge of a metaphor results in its dissolution.

'Environmental' objects are conceived of, in the ED, as *the* 'Environment' *in general* while studied in terms of *specific* facts and data in different disciplines[7].

'Environment' is a pseudo-concept[8] which is *assumed* to designate a whole range of other concepts (and/or 'real' objects) such as 'nature', 'milieu' and 'space'.

The multiplicity of the senses in which the term 'environment' is used defies a clear conception of *what*, exactly, to tackle with in real problem situations. When, in the context of so-called 'environmental studies', many overlapping but distinct senses of the word 'environment' are used, it becomes quite difficult to relate such a single term with, for example, the precise content of education[9]. As pointed out on several occasions, the immense variety of objects and the multiplicity at epistemological, terminological and semantic levels make the ED a discourse with *unmanageable* objects. Such objects cannot be accorded the status of 'richness'[10], but, rather, 'poverty' (as far as its adequacy is concerned).

Mainly owing to the confusion of the real and the conceptual, 'environment' cannot be *physically* measured or dimensioned. (Even when it is destroyed it gives way to yet another thing which is also an 'environment'!) On the other hand, the effects or factors that *are* measured refer to the unmeasurable conception of 'environment' in order to establish correlations between 'man' and 'environment'. Thus, the question of *what* exactly is   studied in an 'environmental study' remains to be settled especially considering the huge amount of studies produced during the last decade.

---

1 On the question of 'everything', see Sec. 2.2. and quotations in *Appendix* in this Chapter as well as in Sec. 3.3.7.a., in particular, those from Tinker, J. (1975): 600; Labour Party (1973): 3. See, also, Brown, H. (1973): 13; Castells, M. (1975): 238f; George, P. (1973): 5f.
2 cf. "The most inclusive sense of 'nature' is the 'physis' of the pre-Socratic Greeks: it designates the All or Everything. Modern philosophers retain this all-inclusive meaning of the word. To George Santayana, nature is the "public experience . . . the stars, the seasons, the swarm of animals, the spectacle of birth and death, of cities and wars . . . the facts before every man's eyes". Another philosopher resorts to the nonsense lines of Lewis Carroll. The talk of nature is "To talk of many things; Of shoes – and ships – and sealing wax – Of cabbages – and kings –"." (Tuan, Y-F. (1971):3).
3 See, for ex., Craik, K.H. (1969): 5: "the total contemporary physical environment". See also Klausner, S.Z. (1972): 335; Proshansky, H.M., & Ittelson, W.H. & Rivlin, L.G. (eds) (1970): 33.
4 or 'Lebensraum' in German, 'l'espace de la vie' in French. On these notions, see Koseki, S. (1972): 54; Lacoste, Y. (1976): 9.
5 cf. Sec.s 2.3.h., and 4.6.6.
6 Lecourt, D. (1975): 64 referring to Bachelard.
7 cf. for ex. Craik, K.H. (1969): 15: "environmental entities can be considered in terms of the underlying facts of physics and chemistry".
8 cf. Lefebvre, H. (1970): 245-46.
9 cf. for ex., "the whole experience of the child; the character of the school; features of the classroom and the school used in active learning, the physical and social characteristics of the child's home, neighbourhood and natural surroundings used in teaching" (Watts, D.G. (1969): 2).
10 cf. for ex., Craik, K.H. (1969): 5.

The terms, notions and concepts of the ED are often *relativistic* as they have different definitions for different professional practices, sciences, discourses as well as for different socio-cultural formations[1]. This relativism in disciplines and discourses is inherent in the very way in which those terms and notions are conceived: that is, as *subjective* phenomena. For example, 'environment' is said to be "an artifact created in man's own image . . . What is environment under one mode of analysis may not be environment under another".[2] This relativism is even carried into materialist analysis where the correct identification of this subjectivism is pointed out — though on a wrong terminological basis[3]. Relativism dominates disciplines too. Each discipline studies different objects under the heading of 'Environment'.[4] As it is briefly shown here, and will be expanded   in later sections, 'environment' is often said to be the focus of attention in, say, transport surveys as well as in window sizes, or in conservation of wildlife. Or, for example, 'economy' is said to be constitutive of the 'environment' of a firm.[5] Or, the word 'city' implies the concept, the imagery, the specificity, as well as the physical existence of an object at one and the same time. Yet, when the term is employed all these different senses are assumed to be contained by it.[6]

'Environment' is often specified only by the act of *surrounding*. It is "nothing without something to surround".[7] As it is a part of a 'conceptual couple' it is both *dependent* and *relative.* It is defined with reference to another object (an organism) which it 'environs'[8]. The obvious spatial connotation of the act of surrounding is readily recognized in some discourses[9] while being denied in others where the etymology of the term is seen as secondary to its meaning[10]. Yet, the discursive effects of the term undeniably perpetuate its relative spatiality.

The term 'environment' is constituted by a widespread ideology which is part of the dominant ideologies in particular social formations[11]. Its position in the latter is determined by an ideological problematic rather than by reference to a real object. Thus, for example, current *concern* with 'environment' is not necessarily with scientifically specifiable nature of *problems*, but with an imaginary set of relations (e.g. 'M-E relations'), or with distorted and isolated issues defined in terms of the M-E schema. Similarly, certain ideological contents are presented as 'theoretical concepts' in terms such as 'vernacular', 'noise', 'crowding', 'natural harmony' which, in return, are used as the basis of understanding and solving problems.

Due mainly to the mode of defining 'problems', as has just been discussed, 'environment' cannot designate phenomena which can be handled, and whose 'problems' can be solved. It is a metaphoric and imaginary discursive object which is largely *transparent*, i.e. in its

1 cf. Sec. 4.6.3. for an examination of relativism.
2 Ittelson, W.H. (1973): 18.
3 cf. for ex. Biolat, G. (1973) who suggests that 'environment' means 'needs' for a worker, but 'profits' for a capitalist. (p.47).
4 On the question of the disciplinary relativism of 'environment', see Sec. 3.3.4, and Baladier, C. (1976) :42.
5 cf. Harvey, D. (1969): 458.
6 cf. Mumford, L. (1966) begins with the question "What is the city? How did it come into existence? . . . The origins of the city are obscure . . ." (p.11). On questioning the status of the term 'city', see Harris, N. (1974): 346; Castells, M. (1975): 102 ff; Harvey D. (1973): Ch. 6, Lefebvre, H. (1970): 80.
7 Campbell, R.D. *et. al.* (1974): 89.
8 In English it is not very usual to express the relation between 'organism' and 'environment' by words derived from the same etymological root. In other words, there is no substitute for 'organism' as 'that which is being surrounded by environment', except perhaps *'the environed'* (as in Morrison, B.M. (1974) :171). In Turkish, for example, it is possible to replace 'organism-environment' by *'çevrelenen-çevre'* couple (as in Tekeli, İ. (1973): 6-7) based on the same root denoting the act of 'surrounding'.
9 for ex., in architectural one: "it is important to note that the structure of the environment . . ., is *spatial*" (Rapoport, A. (1973a): **30**).
10 cf. Mason, H.L. & Langenheim, J.H. (1957): 333.
11 cf. Ch. 5.

present conception it defies scientific observation, analysis and appropriation. As to those empirical problems which the ED refers to as 'environmental', they can and should be tackled without reference to a generality like 'environment' and 'M-E relationship'. Finally, the term 'environment' is not, and cannot be, an explanatory concept. It is, rather, a means of referring to something without actually conveying a new knowledge.

2.6 Concluding remarks

This conclusion will not attempt to summarize the chapter, but, in a very brief way, rephrase its possible effects within the framework of the study. The analyses of this chapter had to be rather brief mainly because more detailed treatment of various aspects of the objects is reserved for the following chapters. Despite this, one thing can surely be asserted: *it is possible and necessary to give a definitive account of a discourse and its objects.*

The examination of the objects of the ED here was done with reference neither to any pre-conception of the objects, nor to their apparent givenness in the discourse itself. Thus, no alternative conceptions or definitions of *given* objects were offered.[1] Instead, the frame of analysis was constituted by the formation, the specificity and the status of the *discursive objects*. Similarly, whether objects were actually real objects or theoretical ones, they were taken as discursive objects, and examined as such — the discursive object being that which a discourse as a practice forms and deals with. The theoretical reasons for this strategy is implicit in the *discursive,* as against historical, formal, empirical, semiological, comparative . . . approaches.

It was stressed that the ED embodies the structure, the objects, the mechanisms, in short, *the conditions, of a unified way of looking at things.* It carries with it, implies, or changes (if not transforms), a corpus of knowledge which presupposes and divides the 'perceptual field'[2] of 'environmental practices'. It supplies the *terms* (i.e. objects) and *principles* (i.e. problematic, structures, rules) and *hypotheses* (i.e. assumptions, problems) upôn which studies are done, institutional regulations and codes of practice upon which much of 'environmental' production takes place, and, to a certain extent, the curricula upon which the 'environmental' education is conducted. All these discussions and conclusions should, of course, be seen in the light of the methodological and strategic decisions that were made explicit in the General Introduction as well as in the introduction to this chapter. Specifically, however, this chapter offered not a recognition, but an *analysis* of the discursive objects. Some of the conclusions derived from this analysis are that

— There is *no* specifically *environmental* phenomena or *environmental* process.
— It is necessary to distinguish the questions of the specificity of the *real* object and of the *discursive* object.
— It is not that there are many discourses on the same object, but, rather, *one* discourse constituted by a problematic which is shared by several disciplines, domains and 'regional' discourses.
— Finally, there is no doubt that conception of an object (whether real or theoretical) develops in the course of the specific practice whose objective is the transformation of that object. In this sense it may be suggested that environmental practices develop the conception of their objects just as other practices do with their objects. Yet, there are two major problems here:

1 As is done, for ex., by Spizzichino (1971): 4.
2 Foucault, M. (1972): 33.

1) Does the ED make explicit *what* exactly it is that it is transforming?
2) Does it actually *transform* that object? If not, *what* does it do with (or, to) them?

The first problem was examined in this chapter, though to a limited extent. The second problem, however, is the subject matter of later chapters. Nevertheless, it can at least be suggested that in the absence of a scientific specification and 'definition' of the presumed objects (e.g. 'environment'), it is not clear *what* it is that the 'environmental practices' actually *transform*. In that sense the conception of 'transformation' that develops within the given limitations of these objects is bound to be as imaginary, as general and as vague as the presumed objects themselves. This is not to say that there is a correspondence between the real and its concept, or the object and its processes. What is peculiar here is that the presumed real object in the ED is *everything* that is presumed to be 'environmental' or 'environment-related'. Thus, to ask the same question from the opposite direction, if a large variety of problems — from aesthetic appreciation to hygiene, from engineering production to urban processes or from ecological issues to architectural detailing are all considered under a single 'word', how is it that the *product* of the transformation can be identified? And, what can the object of that transformation be called? Leaving the rest of the discussion to other sections of the study, we can conclude by suggesting that only sciences *transform* their objects, and produce knowledges. Ideologies, on the other hand, *repeat* some ideological objects that are often borrowed from other domains. Moreover, it must be clear by now that an understanding of the formation, specificity and the status of the objects of the ED is a necessary, if not the sufficient, condition of answering these fundamental questions, *and* understanding how so-called 'environmental practices' transform their objects.

3 The Structure of the Environmental Discourse

"And if ECOLOGISTS are merely going to strengthen the GROUP OF EXPERTS giving advice to OTHER EXPERTS so that THEY can structure OTHER PEOPLES' lives more effectively, i.e. interpose THEM-SELVES between the ORGANISM and its ENVIRONMENT, then how are WE ever going to get a SOCIETY which is responsive to the WORLD in which WE live? . . . . ."[1]

3.1 'Structure' of the Environmental Discourse and its analysis *(Introduction)*

As the present study is aimed, as a whole, at producing a critical analysis of the ED, it can be asked what *specific* analysis can be done under the heading of 'Structure of the Discourse'. This question can be answered with reference to the conception of 'discourse' that is implicit in the problematic of this study[2]. In that conception of discourse, the distinction between the *'internal'* relations of the objects of a discourse and its *'external'* relations with other discourses, or with non-discursive formations, does not imply a similar distinction in the real-concrete which that discourse refers to. Secondly, there isn't any 'boundary' between 'the internal' and 'the external' of a discourse. Thus, to avoid any misunderstanding, the structure of the epistemology and problematic of the ED is examined under the heading of 'Structure of the ED' whereas its relations with other discourses or with non-discursive formations are examined under the heading of 'Relations of the ED' in Chapter 5.

The ED, like all discursive formations, has a structure. In fact, our knowledge of it is only possible on the basis of an understanding of its structure. A *structure* is a system of relations and of transformations which also involves 'wholeness' and 'self-regulation'. To grasp it, we do not have to make references to extraneous elements[3]. It is *what* a formation owes its existence and its effects to. A discursive formation, then, is identified more with its structure and effects than with any of its other properties.

1 Ray, P. (1976), (capitals added).
2 cf. *General Introduction*.
3 See Piaget, J. (1971): 4-5; Rambourg, C. (1973): 138ff.

What is most relevant to our analysis here is the questions of:
1) Whether the structure of what is referred to as 'Environment'[1] is 'visible',
2) Whether that structure is conceivable in the terms of the ED,
3) Whether, in the case of the ED, the structure of the discourse is analysable separately from the structure of the objects in that discourse.

To start with, structures are *abstract* systems. They are not (necessarily) visible in the formation they constitute. An analysis of the discourse is principally a question of identifying non-visible system of relations between visible (or non-visible)elements[2]. The question of 'the visible' is relevant to the present analysis not because it is internal to the problematic of the study, but because it is the basis of several fallacious mechanisms of the ED itself. In more specific terms, 'the ED' structures its arguments so as to refer to 'visible' objects while in fact the problem is one of *theoretical* relationship (the opposite is also quite common when visible phenomena are approached in terms of an abstract, conceptual schema, such as 'M-E relationship')[3]

The notion of structure is often reduced to visible sets of elements (as in engineering and architectural discourses), or sought in the mental constructs which structure the speech, culture[4] or the way in which people perceive their surroundings. *Sciences, on the other hand, produce knowledge about objects which are not necessarily visible.* Then, how is it that structures are identified if not by visible properties? And, how is it that the structure in the 'real' is discriminated from the structure within discourses?

It is here that a distinction[5] can be introduced between "structural models" and "paradigmatic structures". "Structural models" are superimposed constructs which cannot be obtained from an analysis of the data. "Paradigmatic structures", on the other hand, are ordered arrangement of a body of empirical data and are extracted from the data[6]. Structural models enable a discourse, through a set of rules, to make statements, assumptions, explanations and descriptions, but have nothing to do with the configuration and nature of the data themselves. Paradigmatic structures, on the other hand, are based on and derived from data — they are empirical generalizations.

It is precisely here that the set of confusions with which the ED is constituted can be seen at work. It commits two types of confusions: The structure of E and M-E relations (which the discourse takes as its object) is (1) the locus of a *confusion of two types of conceptual tools,* namely structural models and paradigmatic structures; and (2) the locus of a *confusion of empirical relations and discursive structures,* or *real objects and theoretical objects.* In the first type of confusion the ED fails to discriminate between (a) a M-E relation which is supposed to be *inherent in the real world* (i.e. empiricist epistemology), and (b) a M-E relation which is *an ideological or cosmological model* that is superimposed on the elements of the real (i.e. idealism, schematism, etc). In the second type of confusion, the ED ignores the necessary *non-correspondence* between the real (i.e. empirical man/woman or physical objects), and the discursive (i.e. the formation whose objects are discursive elements).

1 cf. Sec.s 2.2 and 2.4 .
2 The visible-invisible dichotomy must be kept as a *provisional* schema, and not as a fully specified, scientific one. It is provisional in view of the multitude of mistakes committed in the names of visible-invisible, manifest-hidden, appearance-essence, etc.
3 cf. Ch. 4.
4 For Levi-Strauss "the universals of Human Culture exist only at the level of structure, never at the level of manifest fact", (cf. Leach, E. (1970): 27).
5 following Nutini, H.G. (1968): 11f.
6 In anthropology, for example, Levi-Strauss's use of the term 'structure' corresponds to the former, and Radcliffe-Brown's use of the term corresponds to the latter sense.

In the first case it becomes impossible to approach a problem, a set of data or an observed event in terms of M and E. The reasons for this limitation is the object of this study. In the second, it becomes impossible to discriminate *what is* from *what is said* or *thought*.

To put the problem in semiological terms, the structure of the discourse is at the level of the *signifier,* not of the *signified.* The discourse may be constituted by a problematic in which the referent (i.e. the given, the real, the facts) may not be 'reflected' at all. This is due, mainly, to the different natures of the real and the conceptual[1] or the real and the discursive[2]. This is perhaps the most fundamental point in attempting to analyse a discourse and, in fact, a precondition for such an analysis to be possible.

The third question that was raised at the beginning is the one concerning whether the present study analyses the *structure of the ED* or *the structure of the object of the ED.* Though, obviously, these two structures are closely related, they, however, could and should be analysed separately. However, a discourse (especially one as complex and as widespread as the ED is *not* constituted on the basis of its object(s) alone[3]. A discourse is constituted by several formations, mechanisms, relations, problematics as well as objects. Secondly, the structure of a discourse involves its epistemological and conceptual properties; in other words, its problematic(s) and its (internal) relations. The structure of discursive object, on the other hand, is limited to its *place* in the problematic of the discourse, to its relations with other objects and to its variations in the discourse. In short, the difference is one of level and scope. But, besides this precise relationship between the structure of a discourse and that of its object(s), there exists a peculiar confusion in the ED precisely at that relationship.

For a discourse to be analysed clearly it must be a discourse which leaves no ambiguity as to the nature of its object(s). Secondly, if it deals with objects whose status are not clear (i.e. as to whether they are real or conceptual), it must clearly distinguish them in *its conceptual,* as well as *textual,* structures. The ED takes as its object a set of elements which are *simultaneously* empirical objects as well as ideological notions, or borrowed concepts. Thus, *a critique of the ED is bound to take as its object a discourse whose objects are indistinguishable in terms of real/ concept or real/discourse.* (As shown elsewhere they are ideological non-objects)[4]. Moreover, it is bound to take these (ideologically given non-) objects, and to study their structure, status and relations *rather than what is supposed by the ED to be its real object, namely, 'the Environment'.*

It is an unresolved problem of the ED that it deals with birds and blocks of flats, images and buildings, forests and hospital corridors, ecology and interior design, ideal forms and sewage problems *in one and the same term.* Mainly due to (and, in spite of) this conflated content of environmental notions, there is a peculiar congruity (or, homology) between the *structure of discursive objects* and the *presumed structure of the empirical objects.* This congruity is achieved through a complex set of mechanisms that will be examined below, and in Ch. 4.

---

1 cf.'the concept of dog does not bark . . .' (Spinoza).

2 In addition to all these problems, it is important to remember that there is also the question of whether the term 'environment' refers to a real concrete or to a concept. As it was argued in Ch. 2 it is a spatial/empirical term and a metaphor at one and the same time.

3 cf. Foucault, M. (1972): 32f.

4 see Sec. 2.5.

The *present* analysis of this discourse, on the other hand, is distinguished by its materialist dialectic base which tries to "explain without deducing reality from the concept, and without reducing reality to the concept"[1], and which implies taking reality (whether physical, social or discursive) in all its concrete determinations, in its *specific order*. The present theoretical and professional conjuncture requires that without such an analysis it would be inevitable to reproduce some of the earlier mistakes encountered in attempts to tackle problems in the field of social and physical reality. The whole discussion on theory/practice, knowledge/action, science/ production, words/deeds, design/building, etc. is therefore transcended by *refusing* to adopt them as the preliminary problematics of the present study, which, in fact, is concerned with the very status of these schemas and problematics. It is hoped that these preliminary observations and statements of principles should establish a sufficiently cautious approach to the analysis of a complex discursive structure.

The analysis will be done in terms of
1) the problematic of the ED,
2) the epistemology of the ED,
3) the mechanisms of the ED.
Briefly stated, the problematic will be identified as one of the 'M-E', or 'Organism-E', relationship. The epistemology will be shown to be a Subject-Object epistemology on the basis of which the problematic was established, and from which the variations of the subject-object structure are derived. The mechanisms will include the division of reality, conceptual couples, and the multiplicity of object and subject.

Finally it should be apparent by now that *all these confusions take place within a discourse,* and, that *the present discursive critique proceeds independent of the discursive structure of the discourse that is being analysed*[2]. It is also significant to remember that structures are not visible entities, but sets of relations that are known by their *effects*. These effects, on the other hand, may not always be visible although some may theoretically, and others empirically, be observable. The conditions of this process is too specific to be dealt with here. Suffice it to say that without a recognition of these effects, none of the theoretical, professional and political problems in discursive as well as non-discursive domains (that will be discussed in the following chapters) can ever be formulated.

It was shown in the *Introduction* above that the analysis of the structure of the ED is bound to go together with the analysis of the *object(s)* of that discourse. This analysis will be done on the basis of the problematic, epistemology, textual structure and mechanisms of the discourse as far as they are involved in the *constitution* of the structure of the discourse. As a preliminary guide to the following analysis, these elements can be schematically presented as below:

The STRUCTURE of the ED:

1) the problematic   :M-E relationship, Organism-E relationship,
                            S-E relationship;
2) the object(s)   :M, E, M-E relationship, Organism-E relationship,
                            Nature, M-N relationship, Society, Space, Society-
                            Space relationship;

1 Godelier, M. (1972): 118n-119n.
2 See the *General Introduction* on this independence.

3) the epistemology   : empiricist epistemology;
4) the epistemological structure : subject-object relationship;
5) the textual structure   : conceptual-couples, variants of the invariant structure,
                                       variants of the invariant objects.

3.2.1 'Man-Environment' problematic

The central problematic of the ED is constituted around the relationship that is supposed to exist between two elements, M and E. This relationship as well as the elements
themselves are mainly *presupposed*, that is, they are hardly ever *theorized*. When they
are presupposed they constitute the implicit structure of the discourse. Just like
thousands of words used in daily speeches and writings, they possess a certain *obviousness* and *givenness*. They are left unquestioned, and seen as *natural* as the names people
have, or the blueness of the sky. However, when they are theorized, though this is
done very seldomly, they are first presupposed as 'given's, and then fitted into some sort
of problematic which provides them with a legitimacy. It is on such a basis that 'new'
theories, disciplines and discourses are constituted. Whatever subject matter these
theories or disciplines deal with, the 'M-E' schema is present in their assumptions,
if not always in their formulations. In other words, *'M-E relationship' is an invariant
structure of the M-E problematic which exists in all its variants.* Moreover, even in
different domains with completely different objects and themes the 'M-E' problematic
cuts   across their practices as well as their discourses. Yet, as shown in Ch. 1 and
Ch. 2, this is quite normal for the ED as, in fact, *its unity is constituted by several
contradictory elements.*

    The variations of the invariant structure, and some of the mechanisms which allow
them, will be examined in this chapter. Now, as a curtain-raiser to the analysis, a couple
of cases can be introduced here.

    The invariant M-E structure is held together both by its binary nature (that is, by
'M' and 'E' mutually presupposing each other),[1] and by a very large number of relationships between them.

    The most common type of relationship is the *determinist* one according to which
either

a) environment determines the formation, evolution and the behaviour of the organism
(e.g. man):

$$E \rightarrow M$$

This position is known in biology and sociology as 'evolutionism', in psychology and
economics as 'behaviourism', and in environmental psychology and geography as 'environmental determinism'[2] or,

b) man determines the environment:

$$M \rightarrow E$$

or,

c) there is a two-way relationship depending on the situation:

$$M \rightarrow E$$
$$M \leftarrow E$$

or,

d) when this two-way relationship is simultaneous, it is often referred to as 'interaction'
or 'interface':

1 The binary nature of M-E structure produces what can be called 'conceptual-couples', which will
be examined in detail below.
2   cf. Sec. 4.6.2.

$$M \rightleftharpoons E$$

or,

e) a more sophisticated version of this interactionism specifies the types of relationships, e.g. 'against', 'opposition', 'struggle':

$$M \times E$$

or,

f) the primacy of either M. or E is replaced by their unqualified 'togetherness' and 'unity':

$$M \And E \qquad\qquad\qquad M + E$$

This last schema is shared by a large range of positions, from scientific to the mystic. It constitutes the problematic of several 'cosmologies', and is based on an ideal conception of the world which is believed to possess an 'original unity'.[1]

In the face of this rather large variety of schemas, discussions on E tend to take up one of these positions once they have uncritically accepted the *terms* of the discourse. Taking the point of view of M or E[2], or changing their order in the text, does not change this fact[3]. Thus, whatever the position they remain *within* the 'M-E' problematic: any type of variation (including those that claim to be *outside* the debate while recognizing and repeating the notions of 'man' and 'environment') is bound to reproduce this problematic as "it is impossible to leave a closed space simply by taking up a position merely *outside it*, either in its exterior or its profundity: so long as this outside or profundity remain *its* outside or profundity, they still belong to *that* circle, to *that* closed space, as its 'repetition' in *its* other-than-itself".[4] Whatever their apparent differences as to the way in which they believe M and E are related, the *structure* of the discourse remains the same. More specifically, they all operate within the subject-object epistemology, they see M and E as elements which are distinct, yet related, but always constituting a 'conceptual couple'. Moreover, they all extend this couple to other domains where the variants of the terms carry the same problematic. For example, organism-environment, man-nature, user-building, society-space, us-them, private-public, response-stimulus, activity-space, culture-nature as well as many other conceptual couples in a large variety of fields operate on the epistemological basis of subject-object, and within the problematic of M-E. And, it is precisely on these bases that many social and physical problems are seen and formulated as *'environmental problems'*, and conceived in terms of *'M-E relationship'*.

The whole range of such 'problems', their functions, mechanisms, the 'ideology of environment' that they constitute and their place in the whole social structure will all be discussed, criticized, or simply pointed out, in this and other chapters. But, in order for these necessary analyses to be done the epistemological basis and the structure of the ED must be examined further.

1 As will be shown in Sec.s 4.2.4 and 5.2, the striking similarity of such 'environmental cosmologies' with religious ones is not coincidental. Remember, for example, the religious conception of unity, that is, of man and God, man and world, etc. Similarly, religious search for the 'divine order' and 'harmony' are present in the ED with all its closed logic, and paralleled by the identification of the 'environmental crisis' by the 'original sin'!

2 cf. Hillier, B. & Leaman, A. (1973): 508. See also Sec.s 2.3.c, 3.3.5 and 4.6.3.

3 "Notice that Whitehead says 'nature and man' whereas we shall be considering 'man and nature'. This re-ordering is not arbitrary. By putting nature first, man is viewed objectively: he is objectively, in quantitative terms, an insignificant part of the totality of nature, although worthy of separate and special treatment because he exhibits nature's plasticity in its most intense form. By putting man first, we stress the fact that nature, except for the pinpoints of consciousness in man, is essentially non-reflective; it is incapable of 'declaring' itself apart from man". (Tuan, Y. (1971): 3).

4 Althusser, L. (1970): 53.

It was said that the epistemological structure of the ED is one which is predomina-
ted by the interaction of a subject and an object, and that the M-E problematic is
based on such a structure. These relationships can be specified (1) as *epistemological*
conditions of the discourse, and (2) in terms of their *textual* structure. To put it in
more specific terms, what this analysis is to be concerned with is not only that the
ED is made possible by the M-E problematic, and not only that the latter is basically
an empiricist problematic based on the subject-object couple, but also that *the
subject-object couple is present in all the conceptual couples of the ED regardless
of whether the context is one concerning the conception of knowledge or not.* Of
course, this is not to say that the conceptual couples and binary oppositions of the
ED have nothing to do with the knowledge process of which they are a part. In fact,
they are the variants of the subject (i.e. knowing subject) and the object (i.e. known
object), or/and as the carriers of the dualist structure which counterposes a subject
(e.g. man, society) and an object (e.g. the world, the building, the city). Nor is this
to imply that the knowledge process *(as recognized by the ED)* is separate from the
way in which that discourse conceptualizes and organizes the real. On the contrary,
*it is the dominance of the empiricist conception of knowledge in the M-E problematic
that determines the structure, mechanisms and the status of the discourse.*
    Without this precise and complex understanding, it is difficult to see
a) the internal structure and processes of the discourse, and
b) the position and the effects of the discourse as a practice.
These assertions can be more meaningful in the context of the conception of knowledge
and discourse *of this study.* That conception is implicit in the organization and the
arguments of the study from beginning to end, and it is explained at the very beginning, in the *General Introduction,* as well as on several occasions. We can, therefore,
make only a brief note on the process of knowledge production vis a vis the structure of the object of this production. In our case, the process at work is *the critical
analysis of the ED.* It is expected that the study will contribute to an understanding
of that discourse. The *object* of this process, therefore, is the ED itself.
    If the object of this study (i.e. the ED) is constituted by a *complex* set of episte-
mological, textual, ideological and non-discursive elements, *its analysis must not
reduce that complexity to any one of its elements.* In other words, if the ED is concerned
a) with the production of the knowledge of the environmental phenomena,
b) with the reproduction and utilization of given conceptions (and, occasionally,
knowledges) of that phenomena, and
c) with the practical   problems of that phenomena (i.e. with 'environmental',
'architectural', 'urban' problems),
it cannot be reduced to, say, psychological processes of cognition, literary merits of
its texts, cultural patterns of its use or ideological currency of its statements. Consequently, the knowledge that is in the process of production in this study is the
knowledge of that complexity before all else. Secondly, it tries to expose this complexity to a critical scrutiny which considers *each aspect* of the discourse in all its
complexity, and the *whole* as irreducible to any one of its aspects.
    Finally, the 'subject' and the 'object' of the ED, are not reducible to the 'knowing
subject' and the 'known object'. The subject(s) of the ED are said by that discourse
to be appropriating the 'object'. (Even assuming for a moment that these problems
are possible in these terms) these appropriations take place not only cognitively, but
also physically, economically, administratively, etc. In other words, *they do not
only 'know' that which is called 'Environment'; but, build, use, see, buy, sell, plan,
destroy, and in the course of doing these, they talk and write about it.* This is pre-

cisely why the *subject-object structure of the discourse is analysed in this chapter first-ly as an epistemological structure,* secondly, *as the terms of a problematic, and finally, as the textual and terminological structure of the ED.*

Accordingly, the analysis can continue now. Yet, before tackling the complex epistemological problems of the structure, a detour is necessary. This detour will look at the *apparent textual nature* of the subject-object and M-E structures, (i.e. the final aspect mentioned) treating the latter as 'conceptual couples'. After this diversion we will examine empiricist epistemology, its subject-object structure and effects of this on the overall structure of the discourse.

3.2.2 The textual structure of the discourse: 'Conceptual Couples'

What the textual structure of the ED implies, basically, is a *division of reality* at the level of words, terms, and concepts — all as discursive elements. This division process includes classifications, organizations and demarcations which all take place at several levels from simple to complex, from naive and fallacious to sophisticated and scientific. This is not, however, the occasion to analyse these processes, or pass judgements on them[1]. What concerns us here is the constitution of the subject-object structure and its effects in the M-E problematic. *Subject-object structure is a form of division of the real.* This division is ensured by the empiricist conception of knowledge[2], and is realized in specific problematics, ideologies and discourses as in the case of M-E problematic, environmental ideology and environmental discourse.

The apparent, textual, structure of the ED consists basically of a *couple* of terms, 'M' and 'E' (and their variants, such as organism, milieu, society, space). As such, it constitutes what we can call a *'conceptual couple'*[3]. A conceptual couple is basically a couple of two words (or, terms, concepts). They exist in a determinate relationship with each other. In all discourses, from the everyday chats to the theoretical texts they serve differing purposes. Yet, they are distinguishable by some particular rules which make them possible. Before seeing these rules, we can mention a few conceptual couples selected from several discourses:

good - bad	knower - known	ruler - ruled
ideology - science	nature - culture	beginning - end
origin - telos	truth - error	practice - theory
recognition - cognition	wisdom - ignorance	past - future
right - wrong	raw - cooked	giver - receiver
symmetry - asymmetry	appearance - reality	latent - manifest
appearance - structure	poor - rich	subject - object
form - content	form - function	unity - split
split - integrated	public - private	sacred - profane
real - thought	Being - knowledge	reason - experience

1 Division of the real will be examined in Ch. 4 in greater detail. However, we can mention here one or two processes of division as examples: *Physical* and *spatial* divisions include horizontal - vertical, in - out, as well as boundaries, borders. *Epistemological* divisions, on the other hand, include unity - split, subject - object, real - imaginary as well as concept - real, scientific - non-scientific; *social* divisions include public - private, individual - social as well as property relations, social classes; *arbitrary and ideological criteria* include architecture - building, art - artifact, me - other.

2 cf. Sec. 3.2.3 below.

3 This term has been introduced in order to avoid possible connotations of similar terms in other domains, such as 'binary oppositions', 'binary taxonomies', 'dual structures', 'dichotomy', or polar oppositions (on these, see Leech, G. (1974): 106-8).

town - country	death - life	fact - value
cause - effect	Gemeinschaft-Gesellschaft	urban - rural
spiritual - physical	proletariat - bourgeois	us - them

As can easily be observed, most of these couples constitute some (more or less closed and self-justificatory) *wholes*. These wholes imply 'original unities'[1] or complementarities[2] that are then assumed to have been split[3] and divided into oppositions, dichotomies etc. It is especially these properties, among others, which enable so many discourses to use them so frequently. Similarly, that is why their mere utterance is often seen as a substitute for scientific analysis. They are *finished schemas* about   reality — often untheorized and untheorizable. A conceptual couple is a *simplification* of what may be a complex question. It reduces[4] a large number of variables[5] into two camps or two elements (e.g. in-out, M-E, me-other) the effects of which cannot be explained away by resorting to the 'principle of parsimony'[6].

The implicit opposition in conceptual couples often produce either/or situations that lead to some epistemological mistakes which are only too apparent in M-E discourse, (for example, the boundary between M and E, even assuming for a moment that there are two such elements, is an *imaginary* boundary and not a real one)[7].

Obviously an either/or situation excludes the possibility that the reality may possess 'both/and' differences or, in fact, 'complex structured wholes'[8].

An immediate criticism of binary distinctions (or discriminations) on the basis of the attempted divisions would be that there is no such *separation* in 'reality'. Similarly, it is suggested, often with power and rigour, that there exists no classification and no boundary in 'nature'. It is 'we', the human mind, which imposes upon the 'world' a system of classification which, in return, makes the world *appear to us* as separate, binary, and classified. As put forward in the context of the Taoist philosophy, classification is a 'human invention' and "the world is not given to us in a classified form. ."[9]

1 cf. Sec. 4.2.4.
2 cf. Tibbetts, P. & Esser, A.H. (1973): 458.
3 cf. "The subsequent process of conscious differentiation, with its dual schema of inside and out-side, psyche or world, splits the unitary symbolic image in two: on the one hand an inward, 'psychic' image, on the other an outward, 'physical' image. Actually neither can be derived from the other, for both are partial images of an original symbolic unity that has split in two". (Neumann, E.: *Art and Creative Unconscious*, quoted in Stewart, T.C. (1970): 55).
4 cf. "The relations within a structure can be reduced to binary opposition, not necessarily in the logical sense of mutual exclusion and exhaustivity, but in the sense of synergic inclusion and complementarity, best symbolized in the Chinese principle of Yin and Yang". (Tibbets, P. & Esser, A.H. (1973): 458.
5 and often reduces this large number of variables into two, 'dependent' and 'independent', variables usually leading to a discussion on whether M and E are dependent or independent variables. (For differing positions on this controversy see Wohlwill, J.F. (1973): 177f; Tekeli, İ. (1973) (1969)).
6 'Principle of Parsimony' is the effort of the theorist to introduce only as many constructs as necessary to explain his/her object of study (cf. 'Ockham's razor') (Rychlak, J.F. (1968): 65).
7 cf. Wilden, A. (1972): 219-20, see also Sec. 4.4.4.
8 cf. Sec. 4.5.2.
9 Watts, A.W. (1973): 35.

When it comes to analysing this process, there appears a large variety of views ranging from mystic to pragmatic, vitalist to psychologistic, phenomenological to structuralist, or idealist to materialist. In fact, the whole question is one of the fundamental points which distinguish different epistemologies. It is suggested, for example, that 'primitive' language(s?) combine(d) opposites in simple terms from the outset[1]. Or, Ancient Chinese epistemology is known to have emphasized totality, or, rather, unity of opposites (Yin-Yang etc.) as opposed to the analytic separations which are characteristic of Western philosophical traditions[2].

On the other hand, L. Straus's structuration of myths into 'binary' oppositions (e.g. culture-nature, raw-cooked, private-public) is *assumed* to be relevant to the analysis of contemporary social realities[3]. Most of the 20th Century social theories (outside Marxist tradition) is dominated by conceptual dichatomies. (For example, Tonnies's Gemeinschaft-Gesellschaft, Weber's types of rational action, Durkheim's organic-mechanical solidarity.Redfield's folk-urban continuum, Becker's sacred-secular[4], or, individual-collective, thinking-feeling, special-universal, body-cosmic[5]).

At another level, classification and separation are seen as purely cognitive processes. Or, the distinction between A and not-A, or between organism and environment are said to be made *within* consciousness[6].

Whatever their differences on the type and locus of the couples, most of these interpretations have one thing in common: the recognition of the *original unity* of the world, nature, environment, etc., and the reproduction of the couple or opposition in all levels and instances[7]. Dividing the reality into (often mutually exclusive) couples is an empiricism in a profound sense. It either assumes *that the world is 'given' to 'us' in two parts* which are in opposition (or in correspondence, or in co-operation),or, it claims to be dividing *a world which is given undivided, yet, dividable.* What we are concerned with here is not the question of *what* divides the world (a causal question at a substantive level) but, rather, the *effects* of such divisions, and whether that 'world' and its 'parts' are legitimate objects of inquiry in the first place. To look for the causes, or beginnings, of divisions would be likely to create not only some 'origins', it would also create misleading correspondences between the assumed causes and effects of conceptual couples. Thus, it would seem as if the causes of one event or object would also be *the causes of the effects* of that event or object[8]. For example, if the suggestion that "language is .. that which divides reality"[9] is taken as a statement of causality, it might follow that the language is responsible for the results of this division. Actually, it is also possible that in the very act of dividing reality, language keeps assuming that the imaginary division was only possible and conceivable simply because there remained an interpenetration of the divided elements, or a relative co-existence of them in a 'unity'.[10]

1 Rychlak, J.F. (1968): 354 who calls on Freud to support this 'theory'.
2 cf. Wilden, A. (1972): 166n.
3 cf. Leach, E. (1970); Glucksmann, M. (1974): 76.
4 cf. Goddard, D. (1972): 69-70.
5 cf. Giedion, S. (1969): 721.
6 cf. ". . . since encountered and encounterer are such only in their encountering, distinctions between 'me' and 'other than me' are made 'within consciousness'"(O'Malley, J.B. (1972): 122).
7 cf. for ex., C. Caudwell, for whom "the 'subject' of the historical process is the economy, which is constituted in the struggle between man and Nature. This polar contradiction reproduces itself at every social level, in a series of homologous, epiphenomenal oppositions: subject/object, affect/cognition, art/science, Beauty/Truth". (Mulhern, F. (1974): 53).
8 The conception of 'effect' in this study is not synonymous with the one in cause-effect relationship. cf. Sec. 4.6.2.
9 Barthes, R. (1967): 64.
10 cf. Cassirer, E. (1955), v.1; 178 who talks of the 'indifference' of the language towards this division. See also, Whorf, B.L. (1963) for the relationship between the language and the worldview that people develop.

On the other hand, it is not also correct to assume a social determinism of all real and conceptual groupings and classifications. For example, the statement that "it was because men were grouped and thought of themselves in the form of groups that in their ideas they grouped other things"[1], or that "the classification of men into groups is at the origin of the classification of things into different, logically distinct, classes"[2] seem both to be implying some sort of materialism which however, is full of untheorized correspondences between the divisions in social whole and in the domain of artifacts. Leaving aside the detailed criticism of these ideas for the time being[3], attention must be paid to the effects of these ideas on an understanding of conceptual couples, cosmologies and ideologies specifically in the ED[4].

The elements of a conceptual couple are not only related with each other by an assumed relationship. Certain characteristics are prescribed for them. While certain couples are defined primarily by their particular *relationship* (e.g. subject-object, past-future, giver-receiver) some others are predominantly defined by the nature of their *elements* (e.g. part-whole, A-non A, M-E). The relativistic fallacies in part-whole relationship; the linear fallacy of simple-complex, or the simple determinism in M-E are results both of the particular relationship on which they are based, and of the implicit nature of elements which they are made of.

At still another instance, even the relationships between the elements of the conceptual couples themselves are conceived as binary opposites. For example, 'against' is *counterposed* with 'for', 'competition' with 'co-operation', 'determinism' with 'indeterminism', etc. (i.e. $A \times \bar{A}$).

$$x \quad \bar{x}$$

But what mechanism is there to produce so many simple, clear-cut (and often, all-purpose), conceptual couples in the midst of a reality, especially social reality, which is full of complexities? To take just one, but significant, case, even the most fundamental of all social contradictions, i.e. the one between labour and capital is not a *binary* discrimination, but a *complex, structured, and overdetermined, contradiction* surrounded by and including in it several other contradictions[5].

This criticism of the division of reality into conceptual couples should *not* be taken

1 Douglas, M. (1973): 12. She also takes "goods as a way of people relating to one another", reported by P. Brennan in *New Society*, 24.4.75, p.189.
2 Harvey, M. (1972): 88, (on Durkheim).
3 More will be said about the 'division of reality' in Ch. 4.
4 We know that in class societies ideologies act as material forces to constitute and to consolidate the rule of the dominant classes. We also know that ideologies are *not external* to social reality. They are representations of "the imaginary relationship of individuals to their real conditions of existence". (Althusser, L. (1971): 152). Similarly, natural or environmental cosmologies are nothing but ideologies themselves. (cf. Ch. 4). When they are the parts of dominant ideology of the time they are very likely to suggest experiences or explanations in accordance with the economic and political requirements of the dominant classes. It is here that constructing a causal link between the class nature of society and the conceptual classifications should be carefully questioned. While Marxist theory would suggest that it is the very process of social division of labour, and of the ownership of means of production which is central to the understanding of other instances and relations in social formations, it would not resort to any generalist determinism of the latter by the former. And while concepts may *express* material reality, they may not *reflect* the forms in which the things exist. Rather, they are the means by which theories are established in order to understand the real. Similarly, and as in the case of M-Nature or M-E; while a class-society may have different ideologies and cosmologies about 'Nature' and 'Environment'; they do not necessarily reflect the material reality as divided into 'M', 'E' or 'N'. Each class *lives* its own conception of the world, or a conception that is imposed on it. It may often be the case that ideologically produced cosmologies (e.g. individual-society, M-E) may be used *to divide the material world for the realization of the dominant interests* more than to 'deceive' the opposing classes.
5 cf. "the Capital-Labour contradiction is never simple, but always specified by the historically concrete forms and circumstances in which it is exercised. It is specified by the forms of the

to be suggesting (a) that there is an "indivisible, original unity" which should not be broken, or (b) that the whole process is a product of mind, and is not in the empirical reality. The theoretical position of this study excludes both of these possibilities: A criticism of a theoretical position is not believed to imply automatically the correctness of an opposite position. As both of these possible suggestions are dealt with in other places it will be sufficient here to state that neither the empirical reality, nor the knowledge process have any 'origin' or 'original unity' from which they evolve. Complexity of any current situation should be understood and analysed *as* complexity, and not as the evolution of a simple or unified origin. The origin of conceptual couples, therefore, is not a single concept, nor the reality which they refer to was *once* free of contradictions, oppositions etc. Any division that is introduced into an object of study should try nothing more than to improve our knowledge of it[1], and should not therefore impose on it a permanent schema produced within ideological discourses.

These theoretical points bring us to the most fundamental characteristics of the conceptual couples:

a) the conceptual couple as a structure is possible *within a problematic* which it helps to constitute, and which, in return, justifies the couple,

b) *each element of the couple presupposes the existence of the other,* and,

c) each element carries with it a particular view of the other which is bound up with the nature of the couple,

d) the problem of their 're-union' is basically an idealist, philosophical, problem which consists of linking them together,

e) in the absence of a clear distinction between the real and the theoretical, the conceptual couples tend to represent these two epistemologically different objects in reified couples of words,

f) the conceptual couples constitute pure principles which are supported by the homogenous field of a *given* phenomena.

Whatever one's philosophical position vis a vis the real/thought or reason/experience controversies is, or whether the result is a realist, positivist, or idealist position, one thing needs to be said about the whole question of the conceptual couples in view of these discussions and doubts may be that *it is the couple itself which needs to be rejected.*[2]

Finally, the relevance of the analysis of conceptual couples to a study of M-E couple is obvious in several ways:

a) 'M-E' is, at least formally, a conceptual couple[3],

---

superstructure . . . by the internal and external historical situation . . . as functions of the existing world context . . . deriving from the 'law of uneven development' . . ." (Althusser, L. (1969): 106 (all emphases deleted)).

1 cf. Canquilhem in Lecourt, D. (1975): 180-3.

2 cf. G. Bachelard, as mentioned in Lecourt, D. (1975): 42.

3 In this context it can be relevant to scrutinize the punctuation that make up the M-E couple. The *hyphen* between M and E has two discursive purposes:

1) it *stands for* the multitude of 'relations' (e.g. 'and', 'determining', 'shaping', 'owning', 'perception') that are claimed to exist *between* M and E;

2) It *combines* M and E as two elements of a significant unity.

These two functions have different, yet often simultaneous places in the ED. The first function of the hyphen is to assist the invariant structure of 'M-E relationship' in its process of variations. In this function it is like a predicate. It accords the invariance some sort of theoretical permanence while, in fact, the 'relationship' between M and E is far from a theoretically specified relationship. Moreover, M-E relationship implies a relation not of two *separate* (See, for ex., Campbell, R.D. & Roark, A.L. (1974): 89) entities, but of *separated* ones (cf. Sec. 4.6.2). Thus, the hyphen is as questionable as other parts of the M-E structure.

The second function is to do with naturalizing the M-E couple as a component of the *language,* as distinct from, but in addition to, the *discourse.* By their frequent use hyphened words become com-

b) The terms of the M-E couples, M' and 'E', singly or together are the epistemological equivalents, homologies, isomorphs, analogies or metaphors, of several other conceptual couples, such as:

Organism-Environment	In-Out	Part-Whole
Man-World	Me-Other-Than-Me	System-Supersystem
Man-Society	Self-Other	Internal E-External E
Man-Nature	Text-Context	Culture-Nature
Society-Environment	Mind-Body	Built E-Natural E
Individual-Society	A- non-A	Building-City
Subject-Object	Private-Public	Subjective-Objective
Knower-Known	Behaviour-Environment	Artificial-Natural
Content-Container	Activity-Space	Designer-Designed

c) Thus, the types of relations that are said to exist between M and E are, in several ways, similar to the relations that are assumed to exist between the other couples listed,
d) The M-E couple as well as some other couples are in fact possible only as a result of these associations: (e.g. Subject-Object/Organism-Environment/Man-Nature/Man-Environment),
e) The existence of the term 'Environment' itself is bound up with its etymology, and conceptual structure: *it exists only in relation to another element which it surrounds (or environs)*[1],
f) The political, ideological or theoretical nature of such associated couples makes it important to investigate the specific ways in which they are situated within the dominant 'practical' and/or 'theoretical' ideologies in a social formation.

3.2.3 Empiricist epistemology as the basis of the structure

After this detour which analysed the major *textual* structure of the ED, it is now necessary to examine the *epistemological* nature of the discourse — as far as it involves the structure of that discourse.

It was said at the beginning of this chapter that the ED is dominated by what could be called an 'empiricist epistemology', and by a M-E problematic which in return is constituted by a 'subject-object' structure. This subject-object structure was then shown to be both a structure serving a particular conception of knowledge, namely the empiricist epistemology, and, secondly, a structure involving the specific division of   reality. Until now only the second feature of the structure was partially tackled. In what follows we will try to see the epistemological and conceptual processes of the ED involving the subject-object structure. To start with, another detour is necessary, this time in the form of a brief discussion on the empiricist conception of knowledge and on the effects of the subject-object structure.

---

pound words, (as it happened to words such as 'landlord', 'playmate', 'waistcoat', 'breakfast', 'sportsman', or as it is happening at present to words like 'wash-basin', 'scrap-book', 'common-sense'). (On these transformations as well as on 'hyphen' in general, see Carey, G.V. (1971): 80-84.)

In the 1970's the frequent use of M-E couple in every conceivable domain and context accorded it a naturalness and legitimacy, and resulted in a lack of questioning as to *what* its structure and elements were. Thus studies on M-E relationship are now called 'M-E studies', 'M-E behaviour' is taken as a system (cf. Tibbetts, P. & Esser, A.H. (1973): 457), a journal is called *'M-E Systems'* (published by the Association for the Study of Man-Environment Relations, Inc., New York) or, posts of 'professor of M-E relations' is officially recognized (for ex., in the Pennsylvania State University, cf. Wohlwill, J.P. (1973): 166). In all these processes the small hyphen has more than ignorable role as a structural mechanism securing the unity of the M-E couple.

1 cf. Sec. 4.4.4 d.

The declared purpose of the process of empiricist epistemology is one of 'attainment' or 'acquisition' of knowledge[1]. This process, according to Althusser, can be outlined like this:[2]

What the empiricists call the 'attainment' of knowledge is, in fact, a question of *abstraction* from the real object (e.g. world, society, events) its *essence*. The possession of this essence by the subject is called 'knowledge'. This abstraction, or extraction process is a result of experiencing the world by a subject. In this conception of the real, the latter is assumed to have two parts:

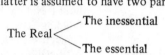

The knowledge is thought to be contained in the real as one of its parts, the inessential part. What the abstraction process does is to purge and eliminate one part of the real in order to isolate the other. These two parts are situated in positions with respect to each other:

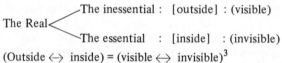

Thus: (Outside $\leftrightarrow$ inside) = (visible $\leftrightarrow$ invisible)[3]

and the essential is *covered*, made invisible, by the inessential. Knowledge process, then, consists of uncovering the essential by removing the inessential from it. That is to say, the knowledge is seen as a *real part* of the real object, and as present in the very 'real object' it has to know — in the form of the respective dispositions of its two real parts. In this way, empiricism declares that the object of knowledge is only a part of the real object, *and* reduces this difference to a mere distinction between the parts of a single object: the real object. This implies that there is, in fact, only *one* object. *This paradox is not solvable in the terms in which it is expressed,* and especially when the distinction between the real object and the object of knowledge is confused and ignored[4]. In fact, in this way, the knowledge becomes an impossibility.

Having outlined the empiricist conception of knowledge, it will now be possible to see the variations in this epistemology. It is particularly relevant to see them if the *mechanism* by which present theoretical ideologies and discourses claim 'scientificity' is to be criticized. Yet, this will not be done in a historicist manner. Instead, the changes in the elements and the internal relations of the invariant structure will be traced through some major philosophical systems. Moreover, the latter will not be taken as empirically given wholes, but as variants of a problematic.

The *materialist* epistemology which provides the basis of this study will not be discussed here. Only some brief criticisms of materialist variants which reproduce the empiricist fallacy will be included. One, rather significant, point to note here is the fact that a criticism of empiricism is *not* the starting point of a materialist epistemology. That is to say, the latter does not take the former as a *negative reference point*. A radical critique, or an 'inversion' of an idealist/empiricist epistemology, does not automatically yield the opposite of these epistemologies. In fact, the question of

1 cf. Hamlyn, D.W. (1971): 5.
2 Althusser, L. (1970): 35-43.
3 $\leftrightarrow$ indicates a 'relationship' the direction of which is not necessarily specified.
4 On this difference see Marx, K. (1971): 206-7.

whether materialist epistemology is the 'opposite' of the idealist one is itself a prob-
lematical matter.

There are some questions which appear in philosophy as 'the fundamental questions', and which usually lead to idealist answers because of the way in which they are
posed. One such question is whether there are *several* 'realities' and, consequently,
a variety of views about them; or whether there is only *one* 'reality' and many different ideas about it. Obviously, both of these alternatives arise out of the conception
of knowledge as a result of the interaction of a subject and an object. The fact that
one of these 'alternatives' assume a multiplicity of subject, and the other a multiplicity of object does not alter their fundamental epistemology. In both cases there is a
couple of 'knowing subject-known object'.

There are several positions in the 'theory of knowledge' and in the 'philosophy of
science' which adhere to, or take as their negative reference point, the variants of this
epistemology. Depending on the differences between the conceptions of subject and
of object variants are produced. For example, in Cartesian philosophy the place of
the subject appears to be doubly determined. Subject is placed in opposition to all
possible objects. "While the existence of the latter may be doubted that of the former
may not; 'I am necessary as the one carrying it out' (Husserl)". Secondly, subject
appears as the subject-matter of psychology. "Thus, the ego appears both to be the
condition of existence of all things and to be a thing that can be known like other
things". Object, thus, is divided into two realms, *matter* and *thought,* and the latter
realm is thought to be the location of the subject which can be known by an 'objective psychology'. Scientific knowledge is then conceived as the result of an abstraction from the experience of the subject, and knowledge of thought as the result of
a corresponding abstraction[1].

One notable diversion from the understanding of subject as an *entity* in the Cartesian system was Pascal's conception of the subject as a *relation*[2]. Hume's empiricism,
on the other hand, resulted in confining the theory of knowledge to the province of
psychology, and especially by the inclusion of scientists and philosophers into the
concept of 'knowing subject' the whole knowledge process became the activity of
individuals. In his 'pre-critical' period Kant, under the influence of Hume's empiricism, has designated the separation between 'logical' and 'real', and favoured experience as opposed to rational thinking[3]. In Kant subject-object opposition is transformed into a 'transcendental subject'-'transcendental object' opposition the first of
which cannot be an object of science while the latter cannot be known in itself. He
represented knowledge "as a combination of *a priori* forms coming from the subject
and of raw experience coming from the 'thing-in-itself' " which is not accessible to
objective knowledge. Only 'phenomena' (i.e. the way through which things *reveal*
themselves in our experience) are knowable. A consequence of this is that the activities of subjects cannot be explained in naturalistic terms, and new physics and
chemistry are excluded as the exemplars for historic and cultural studies of these
activities[4].

1 Hindess, B. (1973 b); 330.
2 cf. "Nature has put us so carefully in the middle (milieu) that if we change one side of the
balance, we also change the other: *Je fesons*: zoa trekei†*. This makes me think that there are
ressorts in our head which are so arranged that whatever touches one touches also the contrary".
(Pascal, B: *Pensees*: 1109, quoted in Wilden, A. (1972): 214n; on Pascal see also L. Goldmann:
  (1956).   (*: Notice the use of a singular subject with a plural verb), and (†: use of a plural
neuter taking a singular verb).
3 cf. Rosenthal, M. & Yudin, P. (eds) (1967): 228-9; Colletti, L. (1975); Hartnack, J. (1968).
4 Hindess, B. (1973 b): 330-1.

Subjective idealists reduce the subject to a unity of the individual's psychic activity, virtually eliminating the object. Objective idealists, on the other hand, see some 'absolute spirit' and 'universal reason' in the absolutized epistemological activity of the subject. Hegel, for example, conceived of the real world as "the result of thinking which causes its own synthesis, its own deepening and its own movement . . ."[1]. His 'autogenesis' of knowledge is in fact identifying thought and being, and consequently putting "the process of the autogenesis of the concept (the abstract) in the place of the process of the autogenesis of the concrete (the real)"[2].

The opposition between subject and object is occasionally said to have been 'superseded'. This, however, is achieved not by refusing such an opposition, but by placing it into consciousness, (e.g. Husserl's anti-objectivism). The distinctions between 'me' and 'other than me', between 'inner' and 'outer', between 'self' and 'world', are made within consciousness[3]. That is, while the distinction is being retained at the epistemological level, it is also shifted into the level of 'consciousness'. Both subjective and objective idealists confine the knowledge process into the 'heads' of the knowing subjects and assume the forms of subject-object interaction as a pre-condition of knowledge about the world.

Some mechanistic and metaphysical materialists, on the other hand, base the relationship between the subject and the object on the action of the object on the subject, and regard the latter as passive and receptive. "Subject was understood to be an individual whose substance was seen only in his natural origin. Subject remained passive not only in the sphere of cognition but also in practical activity . . ."[4]. The similarity between this 'materialism' and Anglo-Saxon empiricism is striking: The latter insists "on a passive organism in which associations are formed by the interplay of processes . . . assuring successful adaptation to the environment."[5] Another variant of this type of materialism is the one which is based on a *reflectionist* theory of knowledge, and which departs from the 'primacy of matter over mind'[6]. This 'materialism' not only reproduces the 'subject-object' schema[7], it also falls into a *dualist* fallacy by resorting to a *primacy* in the first place. Once the primacy of one element within a dualism is 'preferred' there can hardly be an escape from relativism. In fact, there are several implications of this relativism, especially when the sense perception is assumed to be the 'source' of knowledge about the world, and subjective differences are taken to be relevant to the process of knowledge production[8].

There is also a peculiar brand of physicalist materialism which confuses the physical and physiological certainties about the mechanism of sense-perception and mental processes with the process of knowledge production. The way in which, for example, the visual perception takes place (which is explainable in a materialist psychology and in physiology), is not itself an explanation for the question of how the scientific knowledge

1 Marx, K. (1971): 206.
2 Althusser, L. (1969): 189-90.
3 cf. O'Malley, J.B. (1972): 122, 264.
4 Rosenthal, M. & Yudin, P. (eds) (1967): 438.
5 Gray, J.A. (1966): 2.
6 For various positions on this point, see Bonjour, G. (1967); Cornforth, M. (1963); Lenin, V.I. (1970 b); Lecourt, D. (1973).
7 cf. Cutler, A. & Gane, M. (1973): 43.
8 It is relevant here to ask whether scientificity is achievable simply by taking sides of *empirical* human beings, e.g. of the proletariat. This may very well lead to the idea that any theory can be as good as the others. On the contrary, Marx's theory is scientific because it takes as its object the material production, and establishes the exact relationship between the capital and the labour which the classical political economy failed to establish. It is not the psychology or cognition of the proletariat, or the bourgeois, but their structural position in the economic relations that is relevant to a scientific understanding of society.

of the real is possible. Such an understanding would certainly be necessary for quite another reason not altogether unrelated with the question of concept formation and knowledge production which Marx, and recently Althusser, have so much stressed and elaborated. What is *not* correct is to reduce a scientific process to the physiology or consciousness of a subject — whether the latter is an experimenter, a scientist, a designer or an experimental subject.

This second detour was necessary in order to be able to *situate* the subject-object structure into the framework which it belongs, and from which it gets its support. It was also necessary to link what was called the 'textual' (or the apparent) structure with the knowledge process which is conceived in terms of a similar structure. For, the ED was seen as *a practice which establishes a complex conflation of these two types of structures.* It was also identified as a formation which works on *some objects that are the variations of that complex, conflated and confused invariant structure.*

It is, however, not easy to *show* this complexity and confusion simply at one conceptual level. The subject-object structure (carrying with it the supports of M-E problematic and its multiple variations in the ED) should be considered at several interrelated levels. Some of these can be put in question form:

a) are *subject* and *object* the elements of knowledge that is produced?

b) can there be a process without subject?

c) *where* is that structure located: within knowledge, within 'consciousness', in a 'mediation process'?

d) what are the conceptual and empirical status of subject and object in different discourses?

e) are subject-object, organism-environment, M-E couples *schemas, models, principles,* or . . .?

f) are they absolute or relative categories?

g) if they are assumed to be the structure of the real, what (according to *that* epistemology) is the nature of knowledge of that structure? (i.e. what is the 'subject' of the *knowledge of* the 'subject-object' relation? *Who* is it that knows that relationship?) (Hence the controversies of whether the object includes the 'scientist' who studies it, or, whether buildings should be treated as objects or subjects).

h) do they define any *point of view* on the basis of one or the other?

.

.

.

Some of these levels will be considered below, while some will have to wait until they are treated as mechanisms (Ch. 4), discursive relations (Ch. 5) or the questions of status (Ch. 6).

3.3.1 Multiplicity of the structure

The main condition of the complex confusion mentioned above was a mechanism which was said to be closely related with the nature of the invariant structures of subject-object and M-E. In what follows we will try to see this condition. It is possible to describe it as *'multiplicity'.* But, due to its complex nature it is neither possible nor useful to attempt to define it in a simple way. The mechanism of multiplicity involves epistemological, disciplinary, discursive, ideological, professional and linguistic relations.

First of all, the *theoretical* structure of the ED should be identified: It is mainly one which *relates a homogenous field of given phenomena (Environment) and an ideological conception of subject (Man).* However, this relationship is not a simple relationship of two distinct elements. On the contrary, each of the elements is complex (i.e. ideologically *complexified*). Neither the given phenomena, nor its (innocent-looking) counterpart are anything like they seem to be. They carry with them the roots of all sorts of fallacies and effects, some of which will be examined in the following chapters.

3.3.2 Epistemological conditions of multiplicity

Here we will specifically deal with the *conditions* of the multiplicity itself. The epistemological nature of the M-E and subject-object couples lie in *the double status of the subject and of the object.* Although it seems superficial to mention   here, it should still be pointed out that neither this multiplicity, nor any of the elements and structures *identified in this study as belonging to the ED* are ever theorized, ever made explicit and, except in a couple of essays and passing remarks, ever discussed in that discourse.

a) The multiple status of the 'Subject'

The double status of the subject is firmly based on the *humanist problematic.* This concept of *humanism* and its rejection by a 'theoretical anti-humanism' should not be confused with the concern or lack of concern with human beings and with society[1] . What is meant with 'humanism' here is a problematic, (a philosophy and an ideology) which is based on the notion of an abstract 'Man'. The effects of this problematic will be criticized below.

This problematic was first rejected by Marx and Engels in a systematic manner. Feuerbach was shown to have resolved "the religious essence into the *human* essence. But the human essence is no abstraction inherent in each single individual. In its reality it is the ensemble of the social relations. Feuerbach is consequently compelled:
1) To abstract from the historical process and to fix the religious sentiment *(Gemut)* as something by itself, and to presuppose an abstract − *isolated* − human individual.
2) The human essence, therefore, can with him be comprehended only as 'genus', as an internal, dumb generality which merely *naturally* unites the many individuals"[2] .

Engels expressed the same mechanism in another work: "And man, whose image this god is, is therefore also not a real man, but likewise the quintessence of the numerous real men, man in the abstract, therefore himself again a mental image"[3] .[4]

---

1 Besides, it is questionable whether what is commonly called 'humanism' is itself genuinely concerned with human beings. As it is the case, such an ideology seems to be no more genuine than the competitive capitalism preaching the freedom of the individuals while practicing the survival of the fittest; or the imperialist ideology which preaches 'liberty' while conducting genocide, defoliation, forced urbanisation and bombing campaigns.
2 Marx, K. (1969): 285.
3 Engels, F. (1969): 260.
4 Despite all these texts, some 'Marxists' have always reproduced the humanist/essentialist conception of man. Cf. for ex. Lefebvre, H. (1968): 148-52: "Man originates as a humble fragment of Nature, . . . But . . ., he becomes an 'essence' separated from natural existence, at once vulnerable but powerful . . . In the first place the human exists only in and by virtue of the inhuman . . . man's essence is an abstract possibility: an eternal split or separation. Man has not yet been born, he is still in the throes of childbirth . . ." Compare this with 'non-Marxist' positions, for ex. Giedion, S. (1969): 723: "it is time that we become human again and let the human scale rule over all our ventures", or, Brown, N.O. (1966): "We are not yet born: we are dead. The souls of children not yet born are the souls of ancestors dead. The underlying idea is reincarnation" (p.42) . . "To make a world out of himself the dreamer must not only split with the world, but also split himself into both self and world, self and environment, mother and child" . . .(p.49). *Is the resemblance coincidental?*

These can be summarized in this way: For the humanist ideology
1) there is a universal essence of man, and;
2) this essence is the attribute of 'each single individual' who is its real subject.
These postulates then presuppose an empiricist-idealist world outlook:

1) *The 'empiricism of the subject'*   ["If the essence of man is to be a universal attribute, it is essential that *concrete subjects* exist as absolute givens".]

2) *The 'idealism of the essence'*   ["If these empirical individuals are to be men, it is essential that each carries in himself the whole human essence, if not in fact, at least in principle."] [1]

(While criticizing the utilitarianism of Bentham, Marx formulates this fallacy by saying that Bentham first deals "with *human nature in general*, and then with human nature as modified in each historical epoch", and designates a *"normal man"* (an English shopkeeper) as the 'yard-measure' to be applied to past, present and future[2].)

The principle of such a problematic is that empiricism of the subject implies the ideology of the essence while the empiricism of the concept implies the idealism of the subject. It is in such a way that these couples exist and are sustained in a variety of theories and domains (e.g. theories of sociology, economics, ethics, knowledge, etc.).

For example, "the realistic philosophy of the middle ages and of the Greeks was not what today we call realism. It was the belief that behind all specific manifestations of life such as men, trees, dogs, there lies an archetypal, or ideal, form of Man, of Tree, of Dog, so that every particular man is an instance of that archetypal form, and that behind all men is something which can be called Man with a capital M, or the 'substance' of man, of 'human nature'. The nominalists argued that this was a mere abstraction, and that to regard Man (capital M) as possessing any effective existence was to be deluded by concepts. There are only specific individual men".[3] Or, "theoretically, many scientists know that the individual is not a skin encapsulated ego but an organism-environment field. The organism itself is a point at which the field is 'focused', so that each individual is a unique expression of the behaviour of the whole field, which is ultimately the universe itself".[4] In these "the content of the human essence or of the empirical subjects may vary (as can be seen from Descartes to Feuerbach), the subject may change from empiricism to idealism (as can be seen from Locke to Kant): the terms presented and their relations only vary within the invariant type-structure which constitutes this very problematic . . ."[5]. Nor, is a "multiplicity of human natures"[6]   any more than the admission of the built-in multiplicity of the subject at the level of 'essence'. It was in its rejection of these schemas and their terms that Marx's materialism excluded the very conditions of existence of the empiricist epistemology, and the types of 'social analyses' that inevitably follow the former. It is obviously after such a *break* that it was possible to avoid the double subjects (e.g. 'citizen'/'civil man' of Feuerbach), and the myths like *homo economicus;* and get on with the task of establishing a new science of society based on the new concepts of 'relations of production', 'forces of production', 'mode of production', etc.

1 Althusser, L. (1969): 228.
2 Marx, K. (1970) v.I: 371n (italics added).
3 Watts, A.W. (1969): 142.
4 ibid: 140.
5 Althusser, L. (1969): 228.
6 cf. McKinley, D. (1969): 356.

In addition to, and in close association with, the essence/empirical duality of subject, there is the duality of (1) the *'knowing man'*, and (2) the *'acting man'*[1]. While, in the classical philosophy, knowing man was made the subject of the theories of knowledge, the acting man was the basis of economic, moral and political subjects *(homo eco-nomicus, homo moralis* and *homo politicus)*. This *double duality* was reproduced in the ED both in the discussions on how environment is perceived and known, and in those on specific forms of 'physical' environmental interaction.

This complex multiplicity can be illustrated by a diagram – of course, with the awareness of the obvious limitations and distortions that diagrams in theoretical texts may entail. The implications of this structure on M-E problematic will be illustrated by another diagram at the end of this chapter.

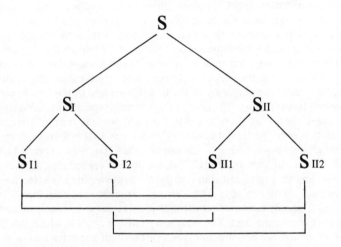

Thus, each 'subject' in the discourse may carry with it the conceptual ingredients of more than one variant. These can be observed in most of the examples cited in this chapter.

b) The multiple status of the 'Object'

A similar multiplicity and a *double duality* exists in the object too. This multiplicity consists of:
I) (1)   There is *a universal essence* of 'Environment',
   (2)   There is an 'Environment' which is *a field of empirical objects* as the realization of that universal essence.
and, the second duality consists of
II) (1)   The object of knowledge or *the known object* (i.e. the counterpart of the knowing subject; the object that is physical, social, and real),[2]

1 cf. Althusser, L. (1976): 199.
2 cf: " 'Stimulus world' 'out there' ", (Proshansky, H.M., *et. al.* (1970): 28).

(2)   The environment that is an experiential, phenomenological, or *'inner' object.*[1]
This double duality can be illustrated in a diagram similar to the one on 'subject' above.

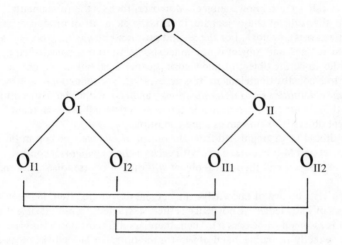

The conditions of this double duality are not too dissimilar to the ones of the subject.
In the essentialist duality the world, nature and then environment and space are the
objects which carry with them both the essences and the properties accorded to them
by several discourses ranging from the religious to the technical. Especially 'space' carries
with it its relatively long history in the classical philosophy, physics, and its present
use in geography and urban planning. For example, for Kant space (and time) was part
of our mental outfit[2] , and rather than being a discursive concept, was a "pure (i.e. a
priori) intuition"[3] . 'Space', just like 'Environment', is used in a very large number of
senses, contexts, statuses and combinations. For example, 'concrete space', 'represen-
tation-space', 'action-space', 'natural space', 'social space', 'geographical space',
'spatial field', 'objective space', 'ego space', 'human space', 'personal space', 'environmental space', 'spatial relations', 'spatial structure', 'outer space', etc.[4]

3.3.3 Multiplicity in the 'subject-object' and 'Man-Environment' structures

The epistemological multiplicity has just been examined. It would be useful to summar-
ize the conclusions of that section:
The ED is based on the multiple (i.e. double and dual) status of its main objects,
M and E,which are themselves the variants of a subject-object couple. The M-E

1 cf. "world transformed into an 'inner world' or psychological environment", 'behavioural
environment' (Koffka), 'life space' (Lewin),(Proshansky, H.M., *et. al.* (1970): ibid).
2 cf. Popper, K. (1963): 179.
3 Hartnack, J. (1968): 19.
4 On the nature of the term 'space', see Harvey, D. (1969): Ch. 14; (1973); 13-14; on the different
uses and variations in different contexts, see Chombart de Lauwe, P.H. (1974): 233-4; Reichenbach,
H. (1957) (physics); Sommer, R. (1969) (personal space); Tekeli, İ. (1973); Rapoport, A. (1973a)
(use of space); Koseki, S. (1972) (physical/social space or natural/artificial space); Lefebvre, H.
(1970) (1974); Lewin, K. (1936) ('Life space').

structure , in accordance with its dependence on the latter, is both an epistemological couple, an invariant structure, and one involving the empiricist knowledge process; it is also an ideological schema for the essentialist view of M-E interaction which is governed by an internal essence. It thus is a couple of knowing subject and known object as well as knowing subject and known subject. Moreover, there is the fundamental question of whether subject and object are, in fact, the elements of produced knowledge (as empiricism assumes), or not[1]. For the second position knowledge process is a process without subject, and object is not an ideal object but one constituted by its *concepts* in order to be the object of knowledge process. Real objects do not need to be referred to a constituting element. It is necessary to see that *concrete is the synthesis of many definitions and determinations*[2] and can neither be reduced to perceived sets of things; nor can it be known in terms of a pure and essential reality which every real object is to contain as a pre-condition.

Real object should be distinguished from the *object of knowledge*. Yet, in the ED subject and object and M-E couples carry with *each* of their elements a confused duality of the real object and theoretical object without, of course, distinguishing them.

In the (empiricist) theory of knowledge subject and object are *given*, i.e. they predate the process of knowledge[3]. Knowledge is then 'extracted' from that object to be known (which is assumed to possess it). Then, there are different positions vis a vis *where* and *how* exactly the subject and object (or me-other, or M-E) division, as well as divisions between objects, is believed to exist. Is it in the physical 'world' or in the perception?[4] Is it within the objects or within consciousness?[5] Is it real,[6] or imaginary?[7] Is it within us,[8] or in an 'interacting system'[9]? Is it social or psychological[10]? Then, there is the question of whether subject is an entity or a relation[11], and whether object is conceivable as a unitary element, or is to be constructed on the basis of its relations to other objects[12].

When the nature of this *relation* is in question, the subject-object and M-E problematics fail to produce a unified notion of the relation. For example, a comparison of differential natures of subject and object in these statements are far from atypical of this confusion.

— "one cannot be a subject of an environment; one can only be a participant",[13]
— "environment . . . includes all material surroundings accessible to sense",[14]

1 cf. Williams, K. (1974): 49f.
2 cf. Marx, K. (1971): 206.
3 cf. Althusser, L. (1970): 35.
4 cf. "This spatial array of objects, which includes myself, . . is possible only on the basis of the presence of each of the others as a potential object of my perception". (Mepham, J. (1973): 123).
5 cf. " . . distinctions between 'me' and 'other than me' are made within consciousness" (O'Malley, J.B. (1972): 122), or cf. (in the Husserlian subjectivization of the world) "the opposition of subject and object is superseded since both are now thought to be contained entirely within consciousness". (Hindess, B. (1973b): 311-2).
6 cf. "Real men and women, and not as objects of knowledge" (Lacoste, Y. (1976): 146).
7 cf. "The line drawn between 'organism' and 'environment' by our conventional model of reality is such a (epistemological) line, and like all such lines it is a fiction. Unfortunately we think that it is real". (Wilden, A. (1972): 219).
8 cf. "For in a very real sense the city is what people think it is — the city of the mind — largely determines the world in which we have our life's experience. . ." (Carr, S. (1967): 199).
9 cf. "The environment is not in the head" (Wohlwill, J.F. (1973)).
10 cf. " . . the concept of spatial boundaries of a social system is an elliptical expression referring to the behavioural rules governing action with reference to physical space" (Klausner, S.Z. (1972): 343).
11 cf. Wilden, A. (1972): 214n on Pascal's conception of subject as a relation against the Cartesian conception of it as an entity.
12 cf. Mepham, J. (1973): 122.
13 Ittelson, W.H. (1973): 12-13.
14 Wagner, P.L. (1972): 66.

(hence to a 'subject'),
– "artifacts . . . constitute a kind of permanent record and guide",[1] (hence, without a 'subject').

All empiricist discourses in general, and the ED in particular, confuse their subject and object by conflating several different variants[2]. For example, the scientific study of society and 'environment' is conceived as a study of society, man and environment by *other 'man'*, i.e. by the scientist or the researcher. Similarly, man the user, man the habitant[3], man the consumer, or man the client are organized, designed or studied by *man the architect,*[4] (or, *man the planner*, or *man the 'environmental scientist')*.

In addition to the multiplicities of the knowing man and known man; the latter is treated by a theory of psychology as the knowing man himself (or herself). S/he is considered as a 'man the scientist', that is, everyman is considered to be a *scientist*[5]:

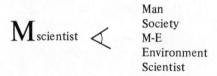

$$\mathbf{M}_{\text{scientist}} < \begin{array}{l} \text{Man} \\ \text{Society} \\ \text{M-E} \\ \text{Environment} \\ \text{Scientist} \end{array}$$

Whatever the sense in which the word 'scientist' is employed, it introduces a new variant into the double duality of epistemological man. It holds the notion of 'subject' in the field of science[6] while eradicating the *specificity of scientific production*. It also involves the question of the dual *conception of 'science'* for *'Man the scientist'*, and that for *'the Scientist'*.

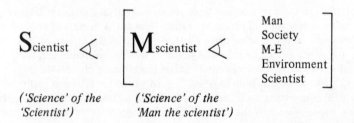

$$\mathbf{S}_{\text{cientist}} < \left[\mathbf{M}_{\text{scientist}} < \begin{array}{l} \text{Man} \\ \text{Society} \\ \text{M-E} \\ \text{Environment} \\ \text{Scientist} \end{array} \right]$$

('Science' of the   *('Science' of the*
'Scientist')   *'Man the scientist')*

Thus, for example, a situation arises whereby it becomes nearly impossible to *identify* even the subject and object of the argument. The statement quoted here is too typical to be ignored:
"And if ECOLOGISTS are merely going to strengthen the GROUP OF EXPERTS giving advice to OTHER EXPERTS so that THEY can structure OTHER PEOPLES' lives more effectively; i.e. interpose THEMSELVES between the ORGANISM and its

1 ibid.
2 Even some Marxist texts are not immune from this type of essentialist and humanistic conflation of subject and object, cf. for ex., Lefebvre, H. (1968): 116: "He is at once a subject and an object . . ."
3 cf. Brabant, J.M. *et. al.* in postface to Lacoste, Y. (1976): 182: "l'homme habitant" and "l'homme producteur-consommateur" as substitutes for the categories of bourgeoisie-proletarian, etc. See also Wolf, L. (1972) for a similar discussion.
4 cf. for ex., Stringer, P. (1970): "Architect is a Man".
5 cf. Kelly, G. (1955), and Bannister, D. & Fransella, F. (1971).
6 cf. Lecourt, D. (1975): 192.

ENVIRONMENT, then how are WE ever going to get a SOCIETY which is responsive to the WORLD in which WE live? . . ."[1] This is mainly because the ED has no scientific conception of the social units it is dealing with, and on the basis of its problematic and structure that the present study is trying to analyse, it cannot have one.

The ED takes ideal and/or empirical individuals as well as ideal societies and/or actual social groups as the substitutes for 'M' a more or less similar relation to the ideal 'E'. While the ideal and/or empirical unity of 'M' is correlated with a unity of the 'E' through the variance of 'M', (e.g. M_1, M_2, M_3, . . .); it is often the case that a unity of the same 'M' is correlated with the variance of the 'E' (e.g. E_1, E_2, E_3, . . .) *at the latters' own limited levels.*

$$M \begin{bmatrix} M_1 \\ M_2 \\ M_3 \\ M_4 \end{bmatrix} \begin{matrix} \longleftrightarrow \\ \longleftrightarrow \\ \longleftrightarrow \\ \longleftrightarrow \end{matrix} E$$

$$M \begin{matrix} \longleftrightarrow \\ \longleftrightarrow \\ \longleftrightarrow \\ \longleftrightarrow \end{matrix} \begin{bmatrix} E_1 \\ E_2 \\ E_3 \\ E_4 \end{bmatrix} E$$

etc.[2]

In the absence of a scientific conception, individuals and social groups are seen as distinct unities, as the subjects of all processes, rather than as the bearers of the complex structure of social formations and of history[3]. One of the effects of this last absence is in the confusion of *singular* and *plural* as well as the *simple* and the *complex.* In social sciences and environmental studies the effect is observable in the dominance of 'methodological individualism'[4] through which all social reality is reduced to individual components, and 'science' is reduced to the study of individual cases or subjects[5]. Especially when the ecological and biological theories on the human body and on other organisms in relation to their surrounding condition are accorded the status of sociological and 'environmental' theories, they not only confuse simple with complex and singular with plural, they also lend support to the notion of M-E relations used in totally diverse contexts and problematics[6]. These 'applications' or

1 Ray, P. (1976) (capitals added): WHO does WHAT to WHOM, or to WHAT?
2 See Sec.3.3.7c below for a complete diagram of these relational fallacies between the variants of M and E.
3 On these questions and on the category 'process without subject' see Althusser, L. (1976): 94-9. See also pp.200-5 where he interprets Marx's declarations that "a society is not composed of individuals" *(Grundrisse)*, and "My analytic method does not start from man but from the economically given period of society" *(Notes on Wagner).*
4 For various views on this position see O'Neill, J. (Ed) (1973); Hirst, P.Q. (1975): 154; Coulson, M.A. & Riddell, D.S. (1970): Ch. 2; Massey, D. (1974): 229-30.
5 For ex., compare the results of a political economy studying 'individual exploiters' with Marx's approach to the 'nature of exploitation' (see Vilar, P. (1973): 101).
6 cf. for ex., statements like this and *the types of ideologies it is bound to support:* "Man then is an organism, a unit in an epiorganism"; "Thus, any functional integration (of individuals in a society) at

'extensions' are often carried into rigorous arguments about *man in general,*[1] and as the
basis of specific cases and subjects, e.g. "man the building user"[2].

But, mainly due to the lack of a conception of social formation and an understanding
of the nature of 'individuals' in that formation, many formulations *speak about
individuals while implying social formations and social processes,* while others *refer to
social phenomena which, in fact, are individual cases that are generalized.* A statement
like "One approach to understanding man's conception of his physical milieu is to
note the natural features which he utilizes and the manner in which he exploits them . ."[3]
is an example to the first confusion. 'Man' here stands for *man in general,* i.e. society
as a whole and producing and owning classes at one and the same time, thus obscuring
the contradictory position of different classes in society[4]. On the other hand, a statement like "The planner sees his model of the projected city as a totality, from above,
the inhabitant sees the present reality, from street level"[5] can be an example to the
second confusion.

Then, there is a similarly vague social theorizing where words like 'people', 'society',
and 'environment' are used as *general* concepts while *referring to no specific social
unity.* In a statement like "how and why people modify and change their environment"[6]
'people' is a generalization of 'man' in anthropology, sociology and psychology, rather
than a social unity definable in terms of concrete social relations.

Moreover, ED is full of statements on "man's perception of man-made environment"[7]
where the *first"man"* refers to an individual, while the *second "man"* to a social whole.
('Environment', *assuming* for a moment that there is such a real object, is made by
society, not by individual man. Moreover, the perception of that real is to be seen in a
determinate relationship to the process and the relations of production).

Just to point out the epistemological and theoretical inconsistencies, one more
question can be raised — this time in a semantic context. In the M-E problematic, the
predicates of M-E relations are variable and multiple in accordance with the variations
and multiplicity of the structure. For example, when a statement says

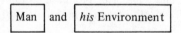

the Man, which is an abstract, ideal and *universal subject* carrying the 'human essence'
is said to be possessing ('his') Environment — another abstract, ideal and universal
term, this time *the object.* The statement thus carries a possessive predicate:

Man (owns) *his* Environment

this level demands the initial differentiation of the units to be integrated . .", or "Man as an organism
is selfish, individualistic, and dominated often by the old brain and its emotional attributes. Man as
a unit in the epiorganism is altruistic, co-operative, and depends on the functioning of his new brain
and its intellectual attributes . . ." (Gerard, R.W. (1942): 82-84.
1 cf. The dual meaning given to the abstract word 'man' to symbolize "a paradox inherent in the
human species — the biological unity of mankind and the experiential diversity of human life"
(Dubos, R.J. (1967): 11).
2 cf. for ex., "These approaches are specified as either treating people as subjects, whose experience
is of interest, or as objects, whose behaviour is of interest. Research carried out into seat selection
in seminar rooms and into individual differences in response to the physical environment is then
described to illustrate the importance of combining both approaches" (Canter, D. (1970): in (Ed)
(1970): 11).
3 Hill, D.A. (1964): 44.
4 cf. Ch. 4 for the mechanisms that produce similar effects.
5 Appleyard, D. (1976): 8.
6 Hillier, B. (1970): 29.
7 cf. for ex., Hesselgren, S. (1971).

when on the other hand, it is said that

> Man is *in his* Environment[1]

the double predicate is spatial and possessive[2]. It is therefore possible to ask whether it is *conceivable* for
— *the man in general* to be *in someone else's* environment?
— *the man in general* to be *outside his* environment?
— *the man in general* not to *own his* environment?
— *the man in general* to *own someone else's* environment?
Obviously these questions are asked not to expect substantive or theoretical answers, but to show the variety of blind-alleys that the ED may lead to if it relies on the unscientific schema of M-E, and on the dubious epistemological and semantic devices.

Multiplicity is present not only in the variants of M and E, but also in the types of *relations* between them. As we have just seen, on the one hand, 'Man' stands for that which is the essence of man; on the other, for the empirical individual who (necessarily) possesses that essence. Similarly, 'Environment' is a homogenous field, a given phenomena as well as a set of (all) objects that are defined by their relations to an 'organism'. Consequently, *'Man-Environment relation'* is conceived both as an *ideal relation* where the 'human nature' and the homogenous given field of environment are realized together; *and* as an *empirical interaction* of men and women with the physical objects surrounding them.

In a close variant of the first case, M stands for an eternal and undifferentiated reality, and E as the totality of pre-existing resources that is equally undifferentiated[3]. Or, the body-mind dichotomy is superimposed on the M-E schema to explain the presumed problems in the latter interaction[4]. Often M and E are conceived in terms of another abstract couple[5].

In the second case, physical reality is organized in terms of the same schema, yet on the basis of empirical data on actual men (and women) or on arbitrarily designated (pieces of) space. Furthermore, the data on M and E are often produced on some aspects of 'him' or 'it'[6]. Of course, in this process, 'M' is taken as individual(s) or group(s) or as abstract unit(s), such as 'public'[7].

But there are more than two possible variants of the M-E schema. It is often the case that either M or E are substituted by variants of different natures. In other words, *M or E may alternately be abstract, psychological, mental, real, physical, architectural.* These aspects include psychological and architectural elements such as attitudes[8],

1 For ex., Klausner, S.Z. (1971); Whitehead, A.N. (1955): 85; Tuan Y-F. (1971): 3; Rapoport, A. (1969): 75-6.
2 For a detailed discussion on these semantic problems and types of methods, such as componential analysis, see Leech, G. (1974) Ch. 7.
3 cf. the discussion in Castells, M. (1975): 238.
4 See, for ex. Koseki, S. (1972) whose conceptual framework is constituted by *'le corps'* and *'la conscience'*.
5 cf for ex.,Clark, W.A.V. & Cadwallader, M. (1972): 'Locational stress and residential mobility'.
6 The question of sexism in the ED is another significant point of interest which cannot be touched upon here. Why is it that 'Man' is 'him' if *it* is a general word for the humanity? (In criticising an ideological discourse it is difficult to avoid using the terms of discourse. The terms in '   ' should therefore be considered as the result of an attempt to indicate where such a danger is avoided, and where it had to be made explicit.)
7 For ex., Wall, G. (1973): 'Public response to air pollution in S. Yorkshire;' or, Amir, S. (1972): 'Highway location and public opposition'.
8 For ex., Tognoli, J. (1973): 'The effect of windowless rooms and unembellished surroundings on attitudes and retention'; or, for ex., Tuan Y-F (1971): 28: " . . . architectural psychologist tries to show how the slope of the ceiling in a room influences the friendliness of its occupants . . ."

sociological and locational ones such as 'status' and 'residential location',[1] or 'quality' in artifacts and in humans.[2]

All these confusions give rise, as well as originate from, some more types of multiplicities. Although these multiplicities themselves are the effects of the epistemological multiplicity that has just been examined, they, however, need to be considered in their specificity.

The fundamental multiplicity of subject and object and M-E can be seen operating in several processes. The variations seen in these processes are the ones of the invariant structure of subject-object and the problematic of organism-environment and M-E. Most of the variants listed can be analysed in terms of double dualities of subject and of object examined above.[3]

	Subject	Object
In the knowledge process:	The epistemological subject	Pure principles of science[4]
	(scientific subject)	(world)
	(knowing subject)	(environment)
	(scientist)[5]	(man)
	(designer, planner)	(experimental subject)
	(man the scientist)[6]	
	(experimental subject)	
In the psychological process:	The empirical subject	Pure forms of perception[4]
	(perceiving consciousness)	(behaviour)
	(homo psychologicus)[7]	(man)
	(behaving man)[8]	(attitudes)
In the philosophical process:	The philosophical subject	Transcendental object[4]
	(philosophising consciousness)	
In the economic process:	The economic subject	Pure principles of economic activity: personal interest
	(homo economicus)	
	(rational man)[9]	(economic activity)
	(consumer)[10]	(environment)[11]
	(producer, homo fabricans)	(commodities)
	(tax-payer)	(private property)
		(profit)
In the political process:	The political subject	Political power
	(citizen)[12]	(society)
	(civil man)	(ownership)
	(individual)	(freedom)
	(electorate)	(control)

1 For ex., Moriarty, B.M (1974).

2 cf. the discussion in Wolf, L. (1972): 133- 6 on industrial design and its discourse.

3 It must, however, be pointed out that the variants of Subject and Object on each line of the list below do not necessarily correspond with each other.

4 Althusser, L. (1970): 54-5.

5 cf. G. Bachelard, discussed in Lecourt, D. (1975).

6 Kelly, A.G. (1955); Bannister, D.G. & Fransella, F. (1971).

7 Cohen, J. (1970).

8 Simon, H.A. (1969): 25, etc.

9 Hollis, M.G. & Nell, E.J. (1975).

10Wolf. L. (1972): 188.

11 K.Polanyi, mentioned in Hindess, B. (1975).

12 L. Feuerbach, as mentioned in Althusser, L. (1969): 226.

In the 'environmental' process: The environmental Subject   The 'environment'

(organism)	(nature)
(Man)	(land)
(user)	(space)
(designer, planner)	(building)
(client)	(city)

In most of these variants subjects are subsumed under a single essence which depends on a persistent identification of the object perceived and the object known on the one hand, and the object of the activities on the other hand. It is this 'parallel distribution of attributes' which disposes Subject and Object face to face, conjuring away the *differences in status* between: the object of knowledge and the real object, philosophical subject and knowing subject, and the knowing subject and the empirical subject.

3.3.4 Disciplinary multiplicities and fragmentations

In all these processes the invariant structures of subject-object and M-E are present not simply as conceptual couples, but as models, as epistemological schemas, as pure principles, as technical guidelines, or as (dependent and/or independent) variables.[1] By means of this variable functioning, the subject-object scheme is reproduced in several disciplines and fields. These disciplines and fields adopt the subject-object scheme or one of its elements in the variants. This, though in very vague and often superficial ways, creates disciplinary boundaries that are usually the products of the *same* problematic (e.g. sociology/social psychology/psychology/environmental psychology). Or, even when a variant like 'M' or 'E' are adopted as the basis of these disciplines, they tend to deal with the *same discursive object defined differently*.[2] Or, disciplinary fragmentations are defined on the basis of differences between some *chosen variants* of M and E, e.g. between 'environment' and architecture[3], between architecture and urban, between physical and human, architecture and building[4], between architecture and art, between architecture and design, between nature and culture, between social and spatial — leading to unclear distinctions between environmental psychology, architectural psychology, architecture, urban design, urban planning, architectural engineering, art, industrial design, ecology, landscape design, anthropology, geography, etc. Similarly, on the basis of whether discourses define subject and/or object in this or that way they diverge into different theoretical positions such as subjectivism, objectivism, determinism, idealism, empiricism, experientialism, behaviourism, phenomenology, . . . Despite these differences, however, they remain within the same problematic defined by subject-object schema.

subject $\longrightarrow$ object : subjectivism, idealism, relativism, phenomenology . . .

object $\longrightarrow$ subject : determinism, behaviourism, positivism, . . .

While the former group absolutizes the epistemological activity of the subject and sees object as the product of the epistemological activity of subject[5], the latter sees the subject as the dependent variable under the determination of object. In the particular context of M-E problematic, these positions appear to be.

M $\longrightarrow$ E

E $\longrightarrow$ M

which involve designation of 'points of view' from which the *other* is viewed.

1 cf. Ch. 4 for these mechanisms.
2 cf. Sec. 2.2 on the unity of the object of ED and the diagrams in that section.
3 cf. [My advocacy] "is addressed to environmental [psychologists] as distinct from architectural psychologist because in my view the emergent laws of the former will be inclusive of the latter." (Lee, T.R. (1970): 18).
4 cf. Pevsner, N. (1964): 15; Lewis, A. (1970).
5 cf. Rosenthal, M & Yudin, P. (eds) (1967): 438.

3.3.5 Relative and multiple points of view

Each discourse, discipline or theory tends to take either the subject or the object; hence, either the organism or the environment, either M or E as its *point of view*. As it was mentioned in the object formation [1] these points of view are often arbitrary but appear to be founded on one of the elements.

The epistemological point of view consists either of the subject 'looking at' the object, or the object 'looking at' the subject. In the case of the organism-environment schema this is reproduced to such an extent that the so-called human sciences are divided between those that take the position of the subject, and those that take the position of the object or environment[2]

Moreover, concepts of social reality, such as those that the ED utilizes, tend to ignore these levels and the *historicity* of the phenomena. Thus, problems are discussed as if they have no determinations, no contexts, no social and historical specificity; or, as if they are static. Also in this way, political and economical problems are presented as if they are 'environmental'[3], 'urban', 'experiential', etc. New concepts (or rather notions) are introduced or transformed from other domains, which are abstract, trans-historical, and universal. For example, 'urban', 'city', 'environmental setting', 'experience', 'modern', 'industrial society', 'values', 'territoriality', 'crowding', etc.[4]

3.3.6 Multiplicity and confusion of different levels and instances

Another type of multiplicity is the one the effects of which are observable in the confusion or reduction of the various *levels,* or *instances* at which the real is situated. In other words the multiplicity in the structure of the ED confuses, reduces, or ignores, the specific complexity of the real which is structured in terms of various determinate levels (e.g. economy, politics, ideology, theoretical). How this actually happens will be examined in Ch. 4 on mechanisms. Suffice it to say here that each level and instance of a social whole is *related*, yet, often *relatively autonomous*. Moreover, each instance, element or level may have a different historical existence. Their histories are not linear and continuous, but staggered, and uneven.[5] In environmental disciplines such as geography the point of view becomes a physical one and it functions in the geographical representations and analysis[6], or in the political designation of territorial divisions in terms of *interior* x *exterior* points of view.[7] Or, points of view are prescribed, as in the touristic ideology of architecture and cities, to determine the way objects are *wanted to be seen* (and photographed!).

In ecology an *'outward'*, whereas in physiology and anatomy an *'inward'*, point of view appears to be dominant.[8] These directional points of view are reproduced in environmental psychological studies or in the changing fashions of architecture. Some trends emphasize the inward, while others the outward point of view in advocating new design principles. Also in ecology, an inward view is proposed as a possible principle at theorizing 'organism' − environment relationship. For example, the concept of environment is defined as "organism-directed, organism-timed, organism-ordered and organism-spaced"[9]

1 cf. Sec. 2.3.
2 cf. Hillier, B & Leaman, A. (1973): 508.
3 cf Sec.s 4.5.6 and 2.4 on the impossibility of a purely *environmental* phenomena.
4 These and similar notions are too common to be specified by sources. As to their critical analysis there are very few attempts. See, for ex., Castells, M. (1975); Massey, D. (1974). See also Sec. 4.2.3 for the nature of these trans- and a-historic notions.
5 cf. Althusser, L. (1970): Ch.4 for a detailed discussion on the concepts of history, levels and instancees in a materialist epistemology.
6 cf. Lacoste, Y. (1976): 23.
7 cf. Raffestin, C. (1976): 186-87.
8 cf. Rowe, J.S. (1961): 423-4.
9 Mason, H.L. & Langenheim J.H. (1957): 339.

Of course, all these points of view are objectified and made 'natural' by means of graphical representations such as

that will be examined in detail later on.[1]

3.3.7 The variants

It must be obvious by now that the structural properties of the ED are extremely *difficult to analyse.* This is mainly due to its immense scope, complex discursive and non-discursive relations and many built-in confusions. On the basis of the theoretical tools utilized these difficulties are overcome to a great extent, and the structure of the discourse has been analysed with significant   results. The *multiplicity* that is due to the variations in the invariant structure has been shown to be at the root of many problems examined in other chapters.

In the course of these discussions numerous examples are given as *illustrations.* These examples varied from long statements to phrases or words. In what follows we will try to finalise this chapter by giving larger lists of variants and a diagrammatical representation of *how* an infinite number of variations is not a surprising result.

In this form, the quotations and lists that follow can be considered partly as the summary, partly the conclusion , and partly an appendix, of the chapter.

The inclusion here of these *discursive examples* is governed by the principles of discursive analysis explained in the *General Introduction.*

There will be three sub-sections:

a) Some quotations (some of which may have already been included elsewhere in the study) to illustrate the multiplicity of terms and relations in the discourse,

b) Lists of variations of M,E and their 'relations',

c) A schematization of how the infinite number of variations are made possible. (In fact, this will be a *review* and will lead to the conclusions of the chapter.)

a) Some statements

The following quotations are selected not because they carry with them any 'truth' which other illustrative examples given elsewhere lack, nor are they the only or the most 'typical' ones that could be cited. There cannot be 'typical' statements in a discursive analysis. They simply prepare the ground for the (astonishing) lists of variations that will be given in (b) and that were in most part abstracted from such texts.[2]

"CREATION OF THE IDEAL ENVIRONMENT is expressed through the specific ORGANISATION OF SPACE, which is more fundamental than the ARCHITECTURAL FORM and is closely related to the CONCEPT OF THE ETHNIC DOMAIN. This can be defined as the IDEAL ENVIRONMENT made visible; it is basically NONPHYSICAL in inception and is given manifest form through BUILDINGS." [3]

---

1 Sec. 4.6.7. See also Sec. 4.6.3 for the relativist fallacies that the multiple points of view produce.
2 All capitals in these statements are added to emphasize the variant terms and relations.
3 Rapoport, A. (1969): 49.

"MAN may build to control HIS ENVIRONMENT, but it is as much the INNER, SOCIAL and RELIGIOUS ENVIRONMENT as the PHYSICAL one that HE is controlling − the IDEAL ENVIRONMENT IN CULTURAL TERMS"
". . . the HOUSES constitute the bulk of the BUILT ENVIRONMENT"[1]

"Different LEVELS of the ENVIRONMENT are emphasised by PEOPLE on different LEVELS of SOCIAL CLASS HIERARCHY. Among the LOWER CLASS, it has been claimed, a SAFE HOME is an ultimate end. Rainwater argues that SAFETY and SECURITY are the chief requirements of the LOWER CLASSES in their HOMES.[2] *THEY must provide safety from 'both NONHUMAN and HUMAN THREATS' and a SENSE of AUTONOMY from EXTERNAL EXIGENCIES. Among these threats, he lists the following: NONHUMAN: RATS and OTHER VERMIN, POISONS, FIRE, . . . COST OF DWELLING. HUMAN: VIOLENCE to SELF and POSSESSIONS, ASSAULT, FIGHTING and BEATING, RAPE, . . . OWN FAMILY, NEIGHBOURS, CARETAKERS, OUTSIDERS, attractive ALTERNATIVES that wean ONESELF or valued OTHERS away from a stable LIFE."*[3]

"elementary scheme to represent the Environment - Behavior Interaction Cycle:

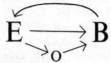

. . . E and B . . . refer to ENVIRONMENTAL and BEHAVIORAL variables, respectively, defined in molar terms. On the "E" side they may refer to geographically or topograph-ically defined SETTINGS, CHARACTERISTICS OF INTERIOR OR EXTERIOR SPACE, or GENETIC ATTRIBUTES of the environment such as NOISE LEVELS, amount and intensity of STIMULATION, etc. On the "B" side they may refer to a variety of OVERT BEHAVIORS directed at specified features OF THE ENVIRONMENT (e.g., ENVIRON-MENTAL EXPLORATION, MOVEMENTS OF APPROACH OR AVOIDANCE, MODES OR PATTERNS OF SPACE USE) or otherwise placed into relationship with the environ-ment (e.g., TASK-PERFORMANCE, SEXUAL ACTIVITY, COMMUNICATIVE BEHAVIOR, etc.), as well as more dispositional variables such as ATTITUDES, PREFERENCES, PERCEPTS, COGNITIVE MAPS, etc. As for the "O" element, it is intended to include such variables as EXPECTATIONS, ADAPTATION LEVELS, MOTIVATIONAL STATES, SOCIAL AND CULTURAL ATTITUDES OR VALUES, etc., which MAY modulate the INDIVIDUAL'S response to HIS ENVIRONMENT".
"This schema comprises three kinds of relations: First, DIRECT, DETERMINATE RELATIONSHIPS . . . Second, INDIRECT RELATIONSHIPS . . . Third, EFFECTS OF BEHAVIOR ON THE ENVIRONMENT"[4]

"Current RESEARCH on environmental psychology is largely limited to the impact of the ENVIRONMENT, conceived as a CONGLOMERATE OF VARIABLES, on a PASSIVE ORGANISM, conceived as a BUNDLE OF DISCRETE RESPONSES or RESPONSE DISPOSITIONS. This paper presents the contrasting organismic-developmental perspective on TRANSACTIONS of MEN with THEIR ENVIRONMENTS. From this perspective, MEN are GOAL-DIRECTED, their actions aiming to realize ENDS or VALUES; MEN'S actions take place in a SOCIAL and HISTORICAL CONTEXT; and the

1 Rapoport, A. (1969): 60,127.
2 Rainwater, L. (1966): 27.
3 Michelson, W. (1970): 115-6.
4 Wohlwill, J.F. (1973): 168-9.

SITUATIONS in which MEN act are partly defined by this CONTEXT. Finally, the TRANSACTIONS of LIVING BEINGS, including MEN, with their ENVIRONMENTS are not all of a piece, but vary in their organization; these VARIATIONS are susceptible to genetic-structural ordering. In short, a conception of environmental psychology is called for that emphasizes the way HUMAN BEINGS actually EXPERIENCE THEIR ENVIRONMENTS, the way they CONSTRUE THEIR WORLDS, and the way they UNDERTAKE ACTION on that basis. MEN STRUCTURE THEIR ENVIRONMENTS – try to MAKE SENSE OF, GIVE ORDER TO, or LEND MEANING to THEIR ENVIRONMENTS; and MEN ORIENT THEMSELVES, FIND THEIR PLACES, in the WORLDS so structured." [1]

"At Stockholm, the DEVELOPED NATIONS were somewhat vague on just what they meant by the ENVIRONMENT. But they all agreed it had something to do with POLLUTION; Everybody except Japan agreed it could be stretched to include WHALES; and all but the French agreed it meant NOT LETTING OFF ATOM BOMBS IN THE PACIFIC. The developing nations, on the other hand, . . . , said that POVERTY was the worst form of POLLUTION and that the ENVIRONMENT was all bound up in . . . WORLD TRADE and VIETNAM. . . . the Swedes . . . spoilt the whole thing by saying that VIETNAM was ENVIRONMENT, and YOU-KNOW-WHO ought to stop DROPPING BOMBS on IT. The DEVELOPED NATIONS resigned themselves to the ENVIRONMENT involving EVERYTHING from MULTI-NATIONAL CORPORATIONS to ECOCIDE IN INDOCHINA, and comforted one another with the thought that if the subject was really as broad as all that nobody would ever be able to do anything about it. . . . . So the U.N. Environment Programme, disappeared into darkest Africa, the RICH NATIONS went back to explaining to THE POOR ones that ENVIRONMENT meant SMOKELESS ZONES and SALMON IN THE THAMES, . . . " [2]

"One was conscious as the day wore on of how many conferences within conferences the SOCIAL ENVIRONMENT encouraged and spawned. If YOU were bored with the endless reading of papers in the ACOUSTICAL ENVIRONMENT, you could retreat to a VISUAL ENVIRONMENT . . . or you could go to Synfoam Two and extract . . . some knowhow about making SYNTHETIC ENVIRONMENTS; or . . . "
"That evening there was a SPECIAL ENVIRONMENTAL EXPERIENCE put on by the Hans-Rucker Corporation. A GIANT AIR-FILLED MATRESS, was the site of squirming, awkward but happy, playful BODIES bouncing up and down while their sensory receptors were inundated with sounds and sights"
"Tuesday found the morning heavy with rain and moisture that seemed not to dampen the spirit of the 280 students and 280 pros who once again assembled in such places as "Squires Small Ballroom" or "CES Auditorium" to hear about ENVIRONMENTS FOR THE AMERICAN INDIAN, for WOLVES, for CHILDREN, for the ELDERLY (or even elderly females,) etc.; to PARTICIPATE in ACOUSTICAL ENVIRONMENTS, VISUAL ENVIRONMENTS, MAN-MADE ENVIRONMENTS, within NATURAL ENVIRONMENTS that exists within POLITICAL ENVIRONMENTS that are a part of the SOCIAL ENVIRONMENT . . . WE had finally discovered that all of our lives WE have lived in the ENVIRONMENT" [3]

1 Wapner, S. et al. (1973).
2 Tinker, J. (1975): 600.
3 Eberhard, J.P. (1973): 515-16

b) Variations of 'Man', 'Environment' and their 'Relations'

The lists below are constituted by the variants of the terms 'Man', 'Environment' and those of the (supposed) 'Relations' of M and E. They are selected from a large range of texts and domains. Thus, each of them may have been defined in those texts and domains differently. Yet, as emphasised several times, their inclusion in this section is due to the *problematic* that most of them share, or, in some occasions, criticize. There has been no attempt to evaluate, classify or order these variants according to a pre-existing schema other than that *given by their problematic*. This, of course, does not imply their *recognition* as legitimate 'objects'. The size and the variety of the contents of these lists prohibited the inclusion of bibliographical references. Besides, such a long list of references would do little service to an understanding of the ED. Many of them are already quoted or referred to in other sections of the study. Furthermore, a mere listing of names and sources would create misconceptions as to *who* said *what* in *what context* and *why*. As pointed out above, these variants appear in several sources not always approvingly, but often for the purposes of criticism, analysis, or simply as marginal references. These lists are expected to provide sources for this study as well as for further research.

LIST I: Variants of 'Man' (M)

man	ego	*homo economicus*
people	society	*homo luden*
voter	*M the scientist*	*homo faber*
electorate	*M the tool-maker*	*homo sapien*
architect	*M the symbol-maker*	*homo psychologicus*
designer	*natural M*	*homo eleator*
planner	*physiological M*	*l'homme revolte*
values	*psychological M*	*l'homme-habitant*
culture	*industrial M*	*animal loguax*
scientist	*urban M*	*animal ridens*
actor	*civilized M*	*animal laborans*
citizen	*prim itive M*	*zoon politikon*
consumer	*modern M*	*human animal*
producer	*civil man*	*rational man*
knower	*client*	*one-dimensional M*
subject	*user*	*technological M*
agent	*member*	*behaving M*
individual	*owner*	*inquiring M*
organism	*tenant*	*total M*
me, I	*inhabitant*	*radical M*
self	*homo fabricans*	*transcendental M*
us		

LIST II: Variants of 'Environment' (E)

environment	spaceship earth	*religious E*
space	community	*urban E*
habitat	society	*rural E*
field	out	*meso - E*
medium	other	*macro - E*
building	world	*micro - E*

city	milieu	geographic E
Vietnam	them	phenomenal E
sea	other	non-behavioural E
water	body	biological E
air	total E	organic E
land	built E	inorganic E
house	physical E	derived E
room	social E	socio-psychological E
forest	psychological E	socio-physical E
ambiance	behavioural E	socio-biological E
biosphere	ecological E	non-human E
lifespace (Lebensraum)	natural E	human E
object	spatial E	economic E
food	ideal E	visual E
sound	political E	interior E
noise	acoustic E	exterior E
landscape	mental E	designed E
setting	inner E	housing E
conditioner	outer E	

LIST III: Variants of 'Relations' (R)

[What follows is a list of *'relations'* that are *supposed to* exist between M and E. Most of them are not specifiable or definable. Nor are they defined in the very statements they are taken from.

A relation, in the *theoretical* (and not necessarily in the Environmental Discursive) sense, is not an empirical entity. It is a structural element or a property that constitutes the fundamental condition of existence of real or theoretical objects. In fact, objects can only be known and become intelligible in terms of their relationships to other objects. Yet, relations cannot be experienced or perceived as empirical givens, but are present in *wholes* where elements are connected in complex and determinate ways. Phenomena is a 'tissue of relations".[1] Its properties manifest themselves in its relations to other things or to other relations.[2] A discourse, on the other hand, is established as a practice by a complex group of relations.[3]

'Relations' cannot be fully understood without also an analysis of *those* that are actually related. Similarly, a radical transformation of the relationship is possible not simply by changing the relations but also the *terms* that are related. Furthermore, the types of relations that maintain the M-E couple are the relations of the *M-E problematic*. As has already been stressed before, it is precisely this problematic to which both the *terms* and their *relations* owe their existence.

Thus, a listing of types of relations abstracted from the ED should not and cannot be taken to explain anything by itself. It is expected that the list, together with the lists of variants given above, will provide one more evidence for the complex *and* confused state of the ED, and will therefore be *considered in view of the whole analysis* .]

1   Bachelard, G. (1975): 152.
2   cf. Marx, K. (1970) v.I: 63.
3   Foucault, M. (1972): 45-6

abstraction
analog
adaptation
and
alienation
abuse
appropriation
appearing together
appearance
association
analogy
attitude
acting on/in
assessment
articulation
access
antithesis
avowal
assimilation
anthropophilic
anthropozenic
availability
against
boundary
both/and
binary
break
barrier
building
buying
balance
behaviour
correlation
correspondence
complementarity
contradiction
causality
cause - effect
consciousness
  (within)
coordinatory,
  coordinary
continuous
communication
contiguity
competition
culture - nature
combination
control
cognition
connotation

conceptualize
coexistence
conflict
contradiction
catalysis
constraining
conditioning
create
contact
connection
coupled
communion
community
confusion
construe
complexification
consumption
constructivism
contrariness
contingency
cooperation
cognitive dissonance
centroversion
classification
categorical difference
condensation
conceptual coupling
contribution
completion
coincidences
contemporaneity
chronology
comprehension
contain(ment)
conquest
collaboration
crystallization
dedifferentiation
different
distinction
determinism
determination
dialectical R
dialectically
  contradictory unity
discontinuous
denotation
differential,
  differentiation
dualism
dyadic

dependency
destruction
division
dialogue
dissonance
demarcation
displacement
distance
direct R
design
deduction
direct
domination
distribution
digital
despoilation
disruption
disturbance
develop
extraction
either - or
exchange
extention
exploitation
expressive totality
ecosystemic
exclusion
externality
exclusivity
effect
externalization
epistemological R
explanation
expression
entailment
explore
expectation
experience
engulf
enfold
fit
feedback
fission
fusion
friction
forming
fixity
filtering
feel
generalization
genetic

harmony
homology
hierarchy
hostility
headship
hyphen (−)
holistic
interaction
interdependence
interrelationship
integration
identity
identify (with)
imaginary
independency
interface
impossible contrariness
isomorphism
internality
insensitivity
influence
inclusion
internalization
indirect R
inference (causal)
ideal R
induction
ignorance
indifference
in
inhibit
inflect
in/out
involvement
impose
intervention
imbalance
impact
indirect R
interest
join
knowledge R
knowing
kinship
logical R
level
learning
limiting (effect)
lordship
learn
meaning

mediation	*overcoming*	*reaction*	*surround*
metaphor	*outwitting*	*response*	*spectator*
metonymy	*orientation*	*reading*	*stamp*
metabolic	*opaque*	*relate with*	*support*
mutual functioning	*point of view*	*rupture*	*superiority*
misuse	*practice*	*renting*	*sovereignty*
misfit	*part (of each other)*	*revelation*	*simplification*
match	*part - whole R*	*(of self)*	*synergy*
mismatch	*perception*	*retreat (into)*	*study*
mutual exclusivity	*plus (and)*	*representation*	*syncretism*
morphogenesis	*paradox*	*rhythm*	*totality*
morphism	*possession*	*relocation*	*totality (expressive)*
morphology	*production*	*revenge*	*totality (structural)*
mutuality	*parallel*	*research*	*transformation*
mapping	*predication*	*reduction*	*transaction*
manipulation	*presupposition*	*structuring*	*turbulance*
mirroring	*participation*	*structural causality*	*transparent*
model	*participation*	*structural*	*taking for*
manifestation	*mystique*	*determinism*	*granted*
mastery	*precision*	*stimulus-response*	*theorizing*
modification	*primacy*	*causality*	*tangency*
making sense of -	*proximity*	*stimulation*	*think*
millefeuille	*projection*	*size*	*transcend*
measure	*partnership*	*scale*	*teaching*
message	*permit*	*symbiosis*	*transmit*
making	*parasitism*	*simultaneity*	*togetherness*
negation	*praxis*	*symmetry*	*triadic*
necessity	*pollute*	*symbolic,*	*unity*
non-differentiation	*questioning*	*symbolization*	*use*
non-correspondence	*quest*	*separation*	*unrelatedness*
opposition	*reflection*	*split*	*understanding*
originate in	*reference*	*satisfaction*	*undifferentiation*
one-many	*real*	*similarity*	*unnatural*
oppression	*relativity*	*succession*	*treatment*
ownership	*reproduction*	*shift*	*utilize*
otherness	*rivalry*	*stable*	*variation of*
outline	*reciprocity*	*shaping*	*violence*
ontological R	*regulation*	*signification*	*whole*
order	*reciprocal*	*settlement*	*whole - part R*
omission	*determination*	*supply - demand*	
observation	*reduction*	*selling*	
oneness	*regularity*	*sympathy*	

c)   A diagrammatic representation of the M-E structure

[However difficult it may be to 'visualise' and to 'represent' a complex discourse in a schematic way, and however paradoxical it may seem on the part of the criticism made in this study of the schematism in the ED, it is still worthwhile to conclude this chapter by a comprehensive diagram. It is expected that this diagram will be studied with these inherent difficulties in mind, and under the light of the whole analysis. This caution is especially important in view of the fact that the ED itself owes much of its confusions and, not paradoxically, its unity, to schematization and simplified representations of its arguments.[1] In this respect, the diagram below should be seen as a representation of the structure of the ED as it is analysed by the present study.]

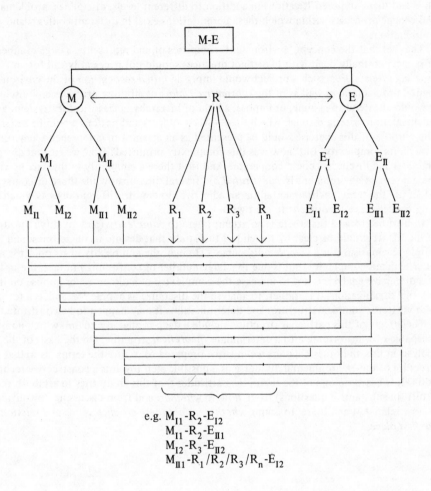

e.g. M_{I1}-R_2-E_{I2}
M_{I1}-R_2-E_{II1}
M_{I2}-R_3-E_{II2}
M_{II1}-R_1/R_2/R_3/R_n-E_{I2}

(All these different variants of elements that are analysed according to their epistemological status as well as to their multiple relations have *further variations* within different discourses, disciplines, domains and problematics. Thus, further permutations can be identified: For example, M_{I2}-R_3-E_{II2} in Discipline A may well be different from M_{I2}-R_3-E_{II2} in Discipline B or in Discipline C ...)

___

1   See Ch. 4 for the diverse mechanisms that produce these results, and in particular Sec. 4.6.7 on graphical representations.

3.4 Concluding remarks

What this chapter and the diagram above intended to show is that the structure of the multiplicity *in* the ED consists of a complex permutation of the multiple status of M, E and their supposed Relations in addition to different levels, disciplines, problematics and change processes within which these permutations exist in different contexts and combinations.

The fact that the concept 'environment' comprises of, and represents, a large number of objects normally dealt with in distinct practices should not necessarily call for an ordering process. For, such a project would imply an *initial recognition* of the environmental problematic as well as of the *substantive claims* of all those practices and disciplines. It would also tend to assume, or impose, a kind of hierarchy, a classificatory system, and a demarcation criteria through which these diverse objects and notions would be ordered.[1] The purpose of this exercise would be presented as an attempt to comprehend 'environment' with all its complexity. But, how was this complexity produced? How was it that diverse practices and discourses could cooperate? And isn't there a circularity in the way in which the concept of environment is *constituted by* several discourses while those discourses infact *use* the term 'environmental' (as an adjective) to denote different objects which they conceive as *environment* to start with.

It must be stressed that there is no attempt here to *complexify* (and mystify) the structure of the ED. It should be clear by the end of this study that despite its obviousness and simple schematism it is a *complex* discourse. (Though, the complexity of its object is not an articulated complexity, but is due to a large number of confusions.) In fact, the tasks of a discursive analysis is not to increase the complexity of a discourse, or impose on it an external organization. It is, rather, to analyse the discourse as a practice, and as a formation with whatever complex structures and determinations it may happen to be constituted by.

The *effects* of this particular structure include a deep-rooted *relativism* which no reform is capable of transforming into a determinate *theoretical* structure. On the basis of the analysis in this and other chapters we must be prepared to *refuse* the terms as well as the structure of the environmental discourse as a possible step towards a constructive reconstitution. It is based on one of the theoretical attitudes that this study tries to establish, that is, a shift (in substantive questions) from *how* to *whether*; and from discussing how divided or how related M and E are to asking *whether in fact there are such terms and relations in the first place.*

---

1 See, for ex., Spizzichino, R. (1971) who suggests to understand the system 'environment' by a set of sections ('decoupages') and sub-systems according to some scales, topologic segmentation or perception of globality and psycho-social notion of 'territory': (pp 4-5). See also a Parsonian systematization of 'environmental sub-system' in Tekeli, I. (1969).

4 The Mechanisms of the Environmental Discourse

"What they had regarded as a solution,
he considered but a problem"[1]

4.1 The question 'how' *(Introduction)*

The questions of *how* 'Environmental Discourse' exists as a discourse, *how* it functions, and *how* it produces its effects have partly been examined in earlier sections. In this chapter we will continue investigating the question *'how'* still further, by identifying the *mechanisms by which the whole discourse functions.*

To mention a few, the set of mechanisms includes the 'shifts' of domains, terms and problems; the reduction of levels, complexities and unities, and the relativism of terms and concepts. While these 'mechanisms' are not exclusive to the ED, they perform certain functions in that discourse that make them specific to it; but, before tackling these specific mechanisms, a close look at the *epistomological bases* of these mechanisms should be useful. Thus, the chapter will start with a detailed (and, hopefully, not over-emphasised) set of discussions on the 'givenness' of a 'homogenous field' defining the discursive objects and operations, on the idealist bases of the discourse in terms of 'essences', 'origins' and 'pure principles', and on the 'division of reality' that ED maintains in order for the reductions, shifts and other mechanisms to be possible.

4.2.1 Givenness of the 'environmental'

It is easily observable that there exist, in the ED, numerous 'facts' about so-called 'environment', and about the assumed relationship between 'environment' and 'man' (as the examples included in the present analysis would illustrate). But these facts and relations are not presented by *that* discourse as a result of an explicit process of theoretical production. Despite the amount of facts and abundance of assumptions, why is it that the theoretical construction of this discourse is not made explicit? How is it that there can be a silent 'consensus' on what constitutes an

---

1 F. Engels, in Preface to Marx's *Capital,* v.II (1970):16.

'environmental problem', what type of relations can be considered as M-E relations, or what are specifically *'environmental facts'?*

It would be in vain to look for a clear answer to these questions within the discourse itself. It is simply written, or said, that E is the totality of what is outside 'us'. M and E interact in many ways, and we can measure, collect data on, and record, 'environmental facts'. But these are all presupposed conceptions. They are not produced, but, simply *assumed.* They are assumed as *'given';* and what is given, by definition, pre-exists any statement about it. It is assumed to be "accessible to direct observation and attention: their apprehension does not depend on the prior theoretical construction of their concepts".[1] Thus, any theoretical or empirical work that is conducted is done so on the basis of this givenness precluding the possibility of questioning the basis of so-called 'environmental facts', 'data', and 'relations'.

4.2.2   Homogenous field of reference

But, rather paradoxically, this givenness itself does not exist in a vacuum. All these objects, facts and relations are given within a *homogenous field.* It is in this 'field' that they are assumed to interact and to be measured. The main function of this field is that it enables the discourse to be assured of legitimacy, and it provides an unquestioned *field of reference that is itself a given.*

This field replaces the need to have a theoretical construction of concepts to think, to organize, to pose questions, and, most important of all, to be accountable to theoretical scrutiny. Instead, the 'facts', objects, or events are made accountable to, or verifiable by, experiences,[2] 'styles of existence'[3] or statistical procedures. Yet, neither the subjectivism of existential perspective, nor the statistical precision of an empiricist approach touches the question of a homogenous field which enables them to operate so easily. While the former needs no assurance but the subject (transcendental or otherwise), the latter ignores the fact that "statistical procedures themselves are not open to any kind of empirical verification or falsification, and consequently can be safely supported by appeal to authority"[4] or to the products of the homogenous field such as 'pure principles' and 'original unity' as we will be seeing later in this chapter.

The homogenous field of problems becomes visible by *projecting* their abstractness, uniformity and pure principles *upon* some objects which are supposed to be positioned in that field. In other words, (1) either some problems are first defined in abstract and then identified as belonging to some physical objects or relations, or (2) some problems in observable phenomena are accorded the status of the 'environmental'. In either case the reference is to a homogenous field of 'environmental': in the first case to a given set of empirical objects, in the second, to a circular definition of specificity.[5] Furthermore, in the first case, in order for the relations between M and E (or society and environment, or society and space) to exist as the relations between *given* objects, it is necessary that all elements of E, M (and society) must be assumed to be uniformly distributed on a plain. (Many theories and concepts in geography are

---

1 Althusser, L. (1970): 161.
2 cf. "true statements, alternatively called 'facts', are, for the scientist, propositions about phenomena verifiable by reference to publicly replicable and communicable experiences" (Nettler, G. (1970): 87).
3 cf. "the existential perspective regards all perceived facts as organised by my style of existence ..." (Hampden-T.,C. (1970): 32).
4 Willer, D. & J. (1973): 99.
5 cf. Sec. 2.4.

based on this assumption, for example the concept of 'region',[1] or theories such as Central Place theory, or Industrial Location Theory[2]. This assumption, however, carries with it a set of others. It implies an epistemology of 'subject-object', and of 'individual' – all assumed as homogenous givens. It excludes contradictions, unevenness, and struggle. It also excludes the concepts of 'restricted entry'[3] and property relations.)

It can here be asked whether the abundant variety, in so-called 'environmental studies', of objects of study and of types of empirical data on them is paradoxical in view of this homogeneity. The answer is that it is far from paradoxical as far as the ED is concerned. The homogeneity of the environmental field and the variety of the environmental elements is a result of the *invariant* structure of the M-E problematic which persists in all its *variants*.[4]

4.2.3   Temporality and 'essential section' of the M-E problematic

Homogeneity of the given environmental phenomena is the dominant mechanism not only in the *spatial* or physical arguments of the discourse, it also dominates the latter's *temporality*. The question of temporality as far as a discursive analysis is concerned should be that which concerns the historical context as well as the history of the specific discursive objects. In the case of the ED, the discursive objects are constituted by a peculiar confusion of the 'real' with the 'theoretical'. First of all, this confusion itself must be seen in relation to a wider historical context (i.e. ideological, political, economic . . . determinations). Secondly, the real and the theoretical objects have their own senses of temporality. To start with, the real is not a static entity. It is continuously transformed by some 'natural' processes as well as by activities under definite modes of production. Whether the real is spatial and physical objects, or institutional, political or professional formations, *it can only be understood in the context of its material conditions of existence which themselves continuously change;* and as it often happens, are transformed through *breaks* (i.e. not necessarily through a smooth evolution). When ED reduces this determinate context into a homogenous field where there is no *time* (except in the sense of descriptive histories of architecture and urbanism), and no *contradiction,* the obvious givenness of all 'environmental' phenomena is expressed in a-historical and trans-historical terms, (e.g. 'Architecture', 'user', 'urban society', 'region', 'community', 'cosmos').

Also due to this homogeneity, the conception of history, if ever invoked, comes very close to the conception of unilinear time in idealist histories. According to this conception history is a continuous and unilinear chronology of events, personalities and objects which can be abstracted and studied as identifiable realities. This involves a mechanism of *'essential section'* which attempts to analyse historical totality as a contemporaneity. This section is assumed to make the events, persons and objects of that totality visible.[5]

In reality, essential section is possible by conflating and collapsing diverse instances, distinct levels and spatial differences into homogeneity and pure principles. Yet, *each object and level of the social whole has different temporality.* They are related with

---

1 However, there is a school of *'heterogeneity'* initiated by Vidal de la Blanche (cf. his (1926)) though this position commits the fallacy of 'anthropomorphism' in its emphasis on the 'character' or 'personality' of regions. For a criticism of the latter, see Sec. 4.6.5.

2 For a critique of Industrial Location Theory, see Massey, D. (1973); and Wagner, P.L. (1976).

3 cf. Denike, K.G. & Parr, J.C. (1970): 49f.

4 cf. Ch. 3.

5 For a detailed discussion of linear and historical time as well as essential section, see Althusser, L. (1970): Ch. 4.

each other in a *staggered* way; each changing, transforming, effecting at different levels and times. Thus, for example, even accepting for a moment that there exists specifiable objects of 'man' and 'environment', they should not be correlated at the same historical 'present', nor should they be reduced to the ideal and a-historical entities of 'man' and 'environment'. In fact, even when they are recognized as such, it should not be possible to reduce complex and multiple existence of empirical men, women and physical objects (that E refers to) into homogenous givens, simply because when a piece of 'environment', or a notable characteristic of one of the men or women is changed or transformed, the pure principle inherent in the M-E problematic can no longer be maintained. Therefore, even if the (assumed) M-E relationship is valid at one stage, it does not follow that it will be valid in the transformed stage. In other words, the 'original' M-E schema can not hold once at least one of its elements is transformed into another object. But it is assumed in the ED that whatever happens to 'environment' its relation with 'man' is subject to the same M-E schema with which the analysis started. Thus,

$$E_1 - M = E_2 - M = E_3 - M = \ldots = E - M$$
$$E - M_1 = E - M_2 = E - M_3 = \ldots = E - M^1$$

Of course, there are other complex problems regarding the question of change, temporality and stability of M and E. Moreover, in different branches of the ED, as well as in different environmental problematics, the nature of M and of E are seen differently. The question of whether M is stable while E is changeable, or whether it is the other way round, or, in fact, whether both are static or active is answerable in as many different ways as the number of different conceptions of M and E.

Now, there is no need to go any further in this illustrative discussion that is on *hypothetically real* M and E. What is more relevant to look at is the *discursive* reality of M and E that is sufficiently full of problems to justify a full investigation. The second domain in which the effects of homogeneity and givenness can be seen is the nature of the concepts themselves as discursive objects. As it is shown elsewhere, the terms M and E are imaginary, ideal, generalistic and vague.[2] They are also *trans-historical* and *a-historical.* Even when they are seen as ideal originals (in the past?), or as goals to be achieved (in the future?) what dominates their existence is a timeless and universal principle.   This provides the basis for a universal and ubiquitous use of the terms and their variants in every conceivable context.

But there is another historicity which concerns the present analysis. It is not the (lack of) historical content of the discourse or its objects, but the historicity of the discourse itself. In other words, we are concerned with *the actual historical existence of the discourse and its elements as the objects of the present analysis.* As such, it is asked why is it that the ED exists in the present historical conjuncture? Why and how did it emerge and develop in the 1960's and 70's. What is the relationship between its emergence and the actual material (i.e. scientific, political, professional, ideological) conditions prevalent in a certain period? All these questions which *cannot* be posed, let alone be examined, within the M-E problematic will be the subject-matter of the section on the relations of the ED and non-discursive domains.[3]
Suffice it to say here that it is of utmost importance to see at what stages of socio-economic development, and what precise conjuncture certain discourses and certain

1 These are simplified illustrations on (hypothetically real) M and E. For the mechanisms of their variations in the discourse itself, see Sec. 3.3.
2 cf. Sec. 2.5.
3 Sec. 5.3.

terms emerge and gain currency. However, this should be done without invoking any
historical determinism or simplistic one-to-one correspondences. It should also be noted that the timeless universality of environmental discourse and of its categories constitute what we can call an *'environmental ideology'*.[1]

4.2.4   Original unity

It was argued above that the ED could function only on the basis of a homogenous
field and the givenness of its objects. It was also said that the latter mechanisms imply
an *'original unity'* which is 'given' to the 'knowing subject', and which is supposed to
be accessible to analysis. This complex set of mechanisms is completed by the inevitable counterpart of 'the origin': *'the goal'*. All these in return contribute to the constitution of some 'pure principles' according to which the whole discourse is structured[2].

The concept of 'origin' is part of an idealist problematic. It is closely tied up with
the essentialist as well as the teleological positions. According to this problematic every
object (whether real or theoretical) has an origin from which it developed, and at which
it had its essence constituted. This essence, in return, is supposed to be revealed in the
multiplicity of phenomena[3]. Depending on the discourse and problematic in which the
'origin' is present, it takes on different functions, serves as a discursive mechanism,
and contributes to the effects that that discourse produces.

Basically, the idea of 'origin' is possible as a discursive mechanism when a theoretical analysis of the real is absent. For, in a theoretical analysis what determines the
knowledge of the real is not its 'origin' or its 'essence', but its *present* as a complex,
overdetermined whole. Neither the world, space and nature have specifiable beginnings[4] or origin, nor their 'knowledge' can be traced back to an origin. Then, especially in discourses which are *not* dominated by scientific concepts and procedures, the
concept of origin is bound to serve as a substitute for analysis.

In the religious discourse 'oneness' of the world, its unity with 'God' (or, with itself) and the 'original, natural harmony', are all *given* as the only means available to
understand (or, rather, *to accept*) the belief system imposed upon the world views of
individuals:[5] These belief systems and world views constitute *cosmologies* which
supposedly carry with them the *'universal truth'*. This'universal truth' starts with,
and is 'proven' by, God. The argument goes like this: "In the beginning life was complete, man was in contact with God:

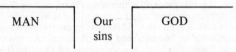

... But now it is different, life is incomplete, man is out of contact with God."[6]

What makes this original unity so pervasive is another concept which concerns the

---

1   cf. Ch. 5.

2   cf. Sec. 4.3.

3   For this last point, see Foucault, M.(1973): 26. On the question of 'essence', see Althusser, L.
(1970): 35 ff, and Sec.4.2.3 in this study.

4   For the Kantian assertion on this point, see Hartnack, J. (1968): 114-5.

5   "Following Augustine, Thomas Aquinas affirms that God, instead of creating actual plants and
trees, fishes and birds, created only potential ones, i.e. only their origins and causes". (Weiss, P.A.
(1947): 121).

6   Victory Tract Club (1974): 1-2.

present: *'split'* (or *separation*)[1]. It is thought in religious, mystic and several other idealist discourses that the present state of things is *imperfect, incomplete, alienated,* and *pathologic.*[2] An extension of this basically religious conception is present in several discourses, from social, scientific to the ecological, from epistemological to the architectural. The split of the present is seen in these discourses between mind and body, between man and nature, knowledge and world, subject and object, inhabitant and city, or between the reality and its 'essence'.

There are two basic assertions implicit in all these conceptions:

1) that the original unity was the mode of existence of the real 'once upon a time',
2) that the origin of knowledge is the central question of theories of knowledge.

The first is what most environmental and ecological mysticism assumes to be the universal truth about nature, environment, space and man. The second, on the other hand, is the basis of empiricism, transcendentalism and even of genetic epistemology[3]. Both assertions, however, support the historicist, evolutionist and almost invariably, idealistic positions.

In the ED the first assertion operates in the claim that M and E are at present in conflict with each other whereas they *were* originally in harmony.[4] Or, in more specific contexts, it is often said that cities and buildings have become out of 'human scale' (that is, they *were* originally in human scale), or that buildings are 'depersonaliz-ed'[5] (that is, they *were* originally personal and humane). The same assertion is present in the definition of environment as a 'total environment' which is believed to be not merely physical, but to include "a substantial psycho-social component"[6] and that man's essence is alienated from 'him'.[7] There are also more subtle positions according to which architecture *once* reflected society and social values[8], primitive people lived in close harmony with nature, or undeveloped societies build their houses in the understanding that their houses are in unity with 'environment'.

As to the assertion on knowledge, it is simply one which is in search of the origin of knowledge: whether it is the object itself (e.g. empiricism), subject (e.g. subjectivism), transcendental subject (e.g. transcendentalism), behaviour (e.g. genetic epistomology), or scientist or architect (e.g. sociologism of science). In all these positions knowledge is referred to an *origin* from which the former is extracted and obtained.

In the ED there is very little concern with the question of knowledge. It is often assumed that the designer, planner, speaker or writer *knows* the object (e.g. environment, city, building, theory) which s/he is dealing with. The assumption on the object

1 cf. "ontologically, there is only one world, one divine being. But the fall of being shattered and divided it, the world came into a diseased state'. (Berdyaev,N. (1955): 143)

2 As in all notions that are used in these discourses, there is a vagueness and all-embracing generality in the definitions of these terms. It is this property which makes them easily utilizable in many discourses, including the ED. The debates on them are of only marginal relevance to the present analysis. However, it is significant to note that it is not an accident that by employing these notions even those who call themselves 'materialists' or 'Marxists' end up with disastrous consequences in theory and in politics; or in the least, let themselves be abused and misplaced. (For the first case, see the debate between J. Lewis and L. Althusser in *Marxism Today:* Jan., Feb., Oct., Nov. 1972 which represents, though very roughly and in a polemical style, the problems with 'alienation' trend in Marxism. For the second case, see Colletti, L. (1975): 27-8: "Modern society is a society characteriz-ed by division (alienation, contradiction). What was at one time united, has now been split and separated. The 'original unity' of man with nature and of man with man has been broken . . . ."

3 of .Althusser, L. (1970): 62-3; Hindess, B. (1973 b): 336 f.

4 cf. "In the beginning man lived as part of nature . . . In the Neolithic period man began the long process of separation from nature, to take possession of the world, to identify and name places". (Rykwert, J. (1973) : 13).

5 cf. for ex., Perin, C. (1970): 30.

6 Wells, B.W.P. (1965a): 164.   7 cf. Sec. 3.3.2.a.

8 cf. for ex. Tafuri, M. (1976)'s presentation in MIT Press catalogue, Spring 1976, p.6.

embodied in the first assertion is present in the second one as a precondition for making a selection between *given* schemas, prescriptions, explanations, styles or fashions. In the absence of an explicit conception of how knowledge is produced, reference is made either to suitable theories of knowledge in other domains, e.g. in psychology (for example, to constructivist psychology[1]),or in majority of cases to idealist and mystic formulations in philosophy (for example, to Buddhism,[2] to sacred geometry[3], mythology[4], biblical metaphors[5], dubious historical assumptions[6]).

It is also significant that this urge to relate one's conception of reality to an origin or to a 'beginning' has a counterpart within the same problematic. As mentioned earlier, this counterpart consists of a teleological conception of an 'end' or a 'goal state'. In fact, a logical and necessary consequence of origin is that the reality has an end. The differences of opinion is then confined to the question of whether this end is a desirable one or one that should be avoided. As in the case of 'harmonious origin', the inevitable 'end' is desired to be (or, rather *believed* to be) a *return to the origin*[7]. While in religious discourses it is the God or the Jerusalem[8] that the soul of the man is to return to, in the ED   it is rather more down to earth: It is a return either to man[9] or to the harmonious relation between M and E: an adaptation or a return to land. (As a step towards this end ruralism, naturalism, or communal living are suggested or practiced.) In effect, this movement can be seen as an attempt towards the realization of a practical utopia[10]. The undesirable end, on the other hand, is the catastrophe or chaos that the present situation is believed to be leading up to. This 'catastrophe' is presented both as an inevitability *and* as something which 'we' can avoid only if we came to 'our' senses[11].

Concluding the discussion in this section it can be said that in all these positions related with or based on the notion of original unity the mechanism is one in which:
1) the original unity is asserted as given,
2) the present is claimed to be the opposite of that original unity,
3) the goal of human activity (material or cognitive) is said or implied to be a *return* to, or re-integration and re-unification of, what is at present split. This can be shown by the diagram that follows.

The mechanism of original unity can thus be seen as a tautological reference to an ideal origin. It is this tautological mechanism which the ED needs more than any other in order to be able to function. Further mechanisms which lend support to this mechanism, and which at the same time need its arguments, are 'pure principles' and 'models' which will now be examined.

---

1 cf. Moore, G.T. (1973).
2 cf. Tuan, Y.-F. (1968) (1971).
3 cf. Critchlow, K. *et al* (1973); Stewart, T.C. (1970); Tyng, A.G. (1969).
4 cf. " 'Origin' means two things in mythology. As the content of a story or mythologem it is the 'given of grounds' (Begruendung); as the content of an act it is 'founding' (Gruendung) of a city or the world. In either case it means man's return to his own origins and consequently the emergence of something original, so far as accessible to him, in the form of primordial images, mythologems, ceremonies. All three manifestations may be manifestations of the same thing" (Eliade, M., quoted in Stewart, T.C. (1970): 15).
5 cf. "then once again we shall see Jerusalem . . ." (Seymour, J. (1974): 5).
6 cf. "I know architecture as a spirit rising out of the presence of architecture. Greek architecture is foremost in my mind. In the beginning, architecture took hold because it was true to man. Once felt and expressed it always was to be" (Kahn, L., quoted in Stewart, T.C. (1970): 63).
7 cf. "An adult cannot become a child again, or he becomes childish" (Marx, K.(1971): 217).
8 cf. Seymour, J. (1974): 5, (in note above).
9 cf. "to become human again" (Giedion, S. (1969): 723).
10 cf. Sec. 4.3.4 below for a related discussion on 'Utopianism'.
11 For a critique of this paradoxical position, see Enzensberger, H.M. (1974): 25-6.

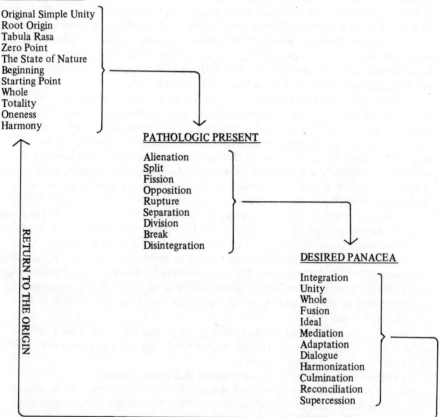

MODE OF ORIGIN

Original Simple Unity
Root Origin
Tabula Rasa
Zero Point
The State of Nature
Beginning
Starting Point
Whole
Totality
Oneness
Harmony

RETURN TO THE ORIGIN

PATHOLOGIC PRESENT

Alienation
Split
Fission
Opposition
Rupture
Separation
Division
Break
Disintegration

DESIRED PANACEA

Integration
Unity
Whole
Fusion
Ideal
Mediation
Adaptation
Dialogue
Harmonization
Culmination
Reconciliation
Supercession

4.3.1   Pure principles

One of the central mechanisms of the ED which represents an 'authority' to which frequent appeal is made is what can be called 'pure principle'. A pure principle is a *pseudo-theoretical* structure defined by a homogenous field. It is assumed to be the property of the 'essence' of the phenomena. As such, it is a 'unique internal principle'[1]. This unique 'internal principle' is then recognized as the truth of all its determinations reflected in its variants. The totality which a pure principle refers to is an *expressive totality*[2].

Not that principles are inpermissible in a theoretical field. On the contrary, they are one of the necessary tools of theoretical practice on the one hand, and one of the guides for action[3] and critique on the other. Yet, a pure principle which is constructed in the way described here and which serves to justify pre- and un-scientific explanations is not to stand for scientific principles. Moreover, it is important to distinguish an 'organising principle' from an 'explanatory' one. What a pure principle does is in fact

1   c.f. Althusser, L. (1969): 102-3.
2   A totality *each element* of which is endowed with its internal principles. More will be said about this concept in the section on complexity below, (Sec.4.5.2). On 'expressive totality' and its criticism in favour of a 'complex structured whole', see Althusser, L. (1970): 96 ff; (1969): 202-4.
3   O'Malley, J.B. (1972): 97

a conflation of these two distinct principles into one as in the case of 'conceptual couples'[1] . More will be said about this and about the related mechanisms mainly because *a pure principle not only requires the support of a more or less fixed conception of reality and a certain understanding of totality, it is also a constituent of those conceptions.* In other words, a pure principle is both the basis and the structural form of the concepts such as 'original unity', 'genesis', or 'essence'.

As in the case of these concepts a pure principle is an internal principle through which several *operations* are carried out in the discourse. Some of these can be mentioned here briefly as they will be examined later under different headings:

— A pure principle (such as 'M-E relationship', 'total environment', 'man as the centre of the world', or 'human scale') is a simplification of what in reality is a complex and overdetermined whole.

— It is a *reduction* of that whole to a single aspect, or to one of its constituents.

— A pure principle is an abstract schema, yet it *objectivizes* that schema and helps its visualization as *the* reality.

— By conflating and reducing different levels, domains and practices of a social whole into a simple principle it *distorts* and *displaces* the conception of that social whole.

— It is the source and locus of 'conceptual couples', analogies, metaphors, imaginary and idealist explanations, circular reasonings, trans-historical principles, false universalities, normative procedures, as well as the justification of ideological systems such as ethnocentrism[2] .

— The concept of *'ideal type'* is basically a pure principle which is based on an abstraction of "outstanding features from some (more or less clearly demarcated) historical complex".[3] It is "formed by one-sided accentuation of one or more points of views and by the synthesis of a great many diffuse, discrete, or more or less present and occasionally absent concrete individual phenomena, which are arranged according to those one-sidedly emphasized viewpoints into a unified analytical construct".[4] Like other pure principles, 'ideal types' are neither derived from empirical generalizations, nor are they rational hypotheses. They are defined by 'values' which are subjective and relativist. Yet, once selected, they guide research, and effectively pre-determine their results. This is because it is the *problematic* of an inquiry which determines not only its methods, concepts and procedures, but also the results obtained.

The ED's use of pure principles is of fundamental importance for the functioning of that discourse. First of all, the 'M-E' schema owes its very existence to its being a pure principle. In other words, *the assumption that there exists a relationship between two presupposed unities*[5] *is carried all the way to the end of the argument where each variant of these elements as well as their 'relationship' is to carry that mental pure principle.* Explanations based on 'M-E' schema tries to answer a large number of questions and solve a large number of problems *in terms of* that principle. Thus, articulation of the differences between these questions and problems are limited by the terms of the pure principle. This limitation has often been due to the imposition upon the problems of built-forms, settlements or objects an *abstract model of reality,* in other words, an ideology, which was dominant in a particular social formation.

In earlier ages when sciences were still undeveloped logical classes and number systems were projected into the physical universe (as Aristotle and Pythagoras did respectively[6]). These were pre-scientific attempts which were valuable contributions in

---

1 c f. Sec. 3.2.2.

2 All these mechanisms have either been discussed elsewhere, or will be discussed in the following sections of this chapter.

3 Watkins, J.W.N. (1973): 144

4 M. Weber, quoted in Shils, E.A. & Finch, H.A. (1949): 90.

5 c f. Sec.2.2   on the unity of the discursive objects.   6 cf. Piaget, J. (1972): 73.

their own theoretical and social conjunctures. Then, there developed several cosmologies, religious systems, and pseudo-scientific conceptions of the 'world' and 'nature'. These were neither abstract (in the sense that mathematics is abstract), nor were they concrete (in the sense that a scientific analysis of social phenomena is concrete). They were (and still are) *self-justifying belief systems which are closed in their very beginning*. It is these pre-scientific belief systems that are now dominant in the ED at several levels.

One form of pure principle is the *'Golden Rule'*[1] . 'Golden Rule' (or 'Golden Section') is a proportion system in ancient architectural practice. It is constituted by a 'perfect number'. Buildings and their components were expected to carry this rule in their design and organization. In a way, this rule was the implicit mathematical principle of *how a building should be like, or it should look like.* Moreover, it was also recognized as the proportion of perfect human measurements which was then used as the criterion of beauty.   With the industrialization and the consequent developments of housing architecture and the 'Modern Movement', such quasi-sacred 'rules' were replaced by the rules of the industrial production and materials, but also by the ideology of scepticism and experimentation[2]. Yet all these material developments themselves were dominated by two main problematics: 1) a pervasive, yet untheorized *pragmatism* which was accentuated by the classical ideology of Art on the one hand, and commercialism on the other; 2) a worldview or cosmology which changed from one of 'divine order', patronage, aspirations of artistic creations and industrial realism to *a pseudo-moralistic concern* with 'human comfort', 'ecologic balance', 'individual expression', and *a pseudo-scientific framework* of 'human behaviour' – all finding their expressions in the M-E problematic.

These trans-historical, formalistic and moralistic elements constituted what we can now identify as the 'Environmental Discourse'. The complex and varied principles which evolved by, and guided, all these developments seem now to be culminated in *a discursive formation which owes part of its cohesion to a small number of pure-principles.* These pure principles not only guided (that is, seemingly guided) the production process of built forms; they also provided justification for the specific features of that production. Histories of art, architecture, and urbanism are full of such examples, "historical problems in art and architecture were seen in terms of fundamental categories and typified schemes on a comparative basis",[3] (cf. for example, the categories used by H. Wolfflin: linear x painterly, plane x recession, closed x open form, clearness x unclearness, multiplicity x unity, which seemed to differ from analytic systems of B. Fletcher, or from mysticism of S. Gideon (e.g. 'the eternal', 'the absolute'), and which was 'modernised' by R. Venturi.) It was on the basis of such frameworks and pure principles that every phenomena from public housing to the Parthenon, or from street furniture to the Utopian towns came to be conceived.

The two main problematics mentioned above continue to make possible the remnants of all past approaches. For example, settlements and built forms are still 'explained' in terms of the *supposed* guiding principles of ancient architecture[4]. The

1   It must, however, be pointed out that at a more precise analysis, 'principles' and 'rules' are different constructs, at least as far as a 'rule' is formalized and is *an external directive* for extra-theoretical practices, and a 'principle' is *internal to the practices* and are formed in the constitution of the latter. (cf. O'Malley, J.B. (1972): 97f, and (1970): 8). In view of these differences the term 'principle' is used here only in the context of 'pure principles', and 'rule' only as the description of the proportion system referred to. For 'Golden Rule' (or, 'Divine Proportion'), see Tyng, A.G. (1969):141f.
2   Though, of course, a scheme like *'Modulor'* of Le Corbusier can be interpreted as a modernized 'Golden Rule', (cf. Le Corbusier (1954)).
3   Knight, S. (1972): 34.
4   cf. for ex., "When man becomes conscious of his VERTICALITY the world around him takes on measurable direction". "Sacred places, the ordered microcosms of the whole of nature, were

most common of these 'principles' is 'circle' and 'centre'. These will be dealt with
while discussing the graphical representations and ethnocentrism. It would therefore
be sufficient here to consider those aspects of 'circle' and 'centre' that involve pure
principles and 'ideal unity'.

4.3.2 'Centre' and 'circle'

In the quasi-religious discourse *'centre'* "represents an ideal point which belongs not
to profane geometrical space, but to *sacred space,* a point in which communication
with 'Heaven' or 'Hell' may be realised, in other words, a 'centre' is the paradoxical
place where the planes interact, the point at which the sensuous world can be transcended. But by transcending the universe, the created world, one also transcends
time and achieves stasis – the eternal non-temporal present"[1].

In the ED, on the other hand, it is assumed that "man's space is 'subjectively
centred'[2], and that there *is* a centre of the world[3]. Both the *reference to a 'centre'*
and the *definition by means of a (closed!) 'circle'* are the mechanisms of a discourse
which operates on a scientifically unspecified, and often imaginary, object: *'Environment'.* In a scientific practice neither an imaginary centre or circle, nor an empirical
object which has the form of a circle or which has a centre would be needed to
explain or to appropriate the objects of that practice. This is so even when a multiplicity replaces the singularity of centre[4] or centre is diffused to 'everywhere'[5].

The fundamental epistemological characteristic of all these positions is that there
is a total absence of differentiation of the *real* and the *concept.* In other words, there
is a constant confusion or blurring of differences between symbolic, physical, psychological, . . . 'centres' and 'circles'. These positions cannot see that *the* whole *which the
theoretical analysis takes as its object is 'centreless'.* It is a *decentred* structure in
dominance[6]. It has no essence, no ideal unity and no pure principle to refer to.
Finally, while it is possible to establish a discourse around such notions, it is not
equally possible to claim the status of 'truth' or 'scientificity' for that discourse[7].

---

raised on mounds or platforms: the concept of ELEVATION. Man's effort in understanding himself
and the world, which set him apart from the world, was frequently re-enacted in long, elaborate,
and expensive ceremonies. Those led to the creation of ceremonial centres related both to geometry, man's essential tool for understanding space, and those forces dealt with through ritual and
social action. The Ziggurat, a sacred mountain representing the model of the world, was ORIEN-
TATED in relation to the cardinal points. In Egypt the pyramids and their related courts and
chapeis were related AXIALLY to the cardinal points. Temple plans were tightly organized into
sequences of spaces, based on the RIGHT ANGLE". (Rykwert, J. (1973): 13-15). See also (1976).
Or, for ex., "those aiming to define by their buildings man's total position in the world, throughout the centuries returned to centralization and longitudinality as their main themes". (Norberg-
Schulz, C. (1971): 62). Cf. also "the geomantic theories that govern the foundation of towns, the
conceptions that justify the rites accompanying their building". (Eliade, M: *The Myth of the
Eternal Return,* quoted in Stewart, T.C. (1970): 25).

1 Eliade, M.: *Images and Symbols,* quoted in Stewart, T.C. (1970): 45.

2 Norberg-Schulz, C. (1971): 18.

3 cf. "If the 'centre of the world' thus designates an ideal public goal, or 'lost paradise', the word
'home' also has a closer and more concrete meaning. It simply tells us that any man's personal
world has its centre" (Norberg-Schulz, C. (1971): 19): See also, Tuan, Y-F (1971): 18-32.

4 cf. Eliade, M. (1959), discussed in Cooper, C. (1971): 28f.

5 cf. "Neither centralized nor decentralized, but centered in every place and at every stage of
multiplication with the interior horizon of space as constant comparison – that, surely is our real
home". (Aldo Van Eyck, in Smithson, A. (ed) (1968): 104).

6 cf. Althusser, L. (1970): 104, 319.

7 cf. Ch. 6 on the question of 'status'. See Sec.4.6.7 below for the graphical representations
of circle and centre in the ED.

4.3.3 Models

A *'model'* is a tool that operates not only in the ED, but also *within* other mechanisms of that discourse. While the relation between M and E is expressed in terms of a model of (environmental) reality, mechanisms such as origin, ideal, pure principle or conceptual couple are all constituted by, and within, a *'theory of model'*. The dubious status of such a 'theory' (as far as the ED is concerned) has to wait until we examine the status of the discourse as a whole. What should be said here is that the models that are examined in this section are neither architectural models (i.e. small scale representations of buildings in three dimensions), nor technical ones (such as the ones used in traffic planning, or structural calculations). They are, rather, *quasi-epistemological frameworks which guide, regulate and often condition, the relationship between the terms and between the terms and the mechanisms of the ED*. In other words, they underlie the operations of the discursive practice as *the means of connection,* and if necessary, as *the means of explanation.* They serve as 'theory' though they often have nothing to do with theoretical modes of operation.

Model, as understood in sciences, is an analogue or computational device which behaves in an 'as-if' kind of procedure. It neither proves nor disproves any reality. It must remain within the empirical domain (e.g. technical, architectural, models) or within theory (e.g. theoretical models which relate one theory to another). Thus, its functioning as a connection device between the empirical and theoretical, and as an explanation of the real is totally devoid of theoretical content. A theory works on a real which is other than the real object[1]. In other words, *a model is not a substitute for theoretical analysis.* In ED models exist in several forms: as technical tools, they are used as descriptive, predictive and prescriptive abstractions of the real object. As explanatory tools, *they impose upon the real a conception* that limits the chances of producing scientific conception of ('environmental') problems. They prepare the ground for several other mechanisms such as cause-effect relationship, reductionism, definition of artificial points of view or false correlations and correspondences. Ecological models[2] and eco-urban models[3] *reduce* the complexity of global and urban problems to operationalized variables which either ignore or misplace their contradictory structures[4]. Moreover, several models of 'environment', 'environmental behaviour'[5], 'man'[6], or 'environmental preference'[7] are constituted as guides for empirical research.

There is no intention here to survey or to criticize the question of models as a whole. It is beyond the limits and the objectives of the present study[8]. What, however, needs to be stressed here is the way in which the M-E schema is accorded the status of a universal model without, or in place of, a theory). This is achieved by simply accepting 'M' and 'E', 'M-E' and 'Behaviour-Environment' as *given, natural* and *universal models* in terms of which diverse problems are formulated.

---

1 On this question see Althusser, L. (1970): 117-8, 39n.
2 for ex. those developed by Club of Rome, by *The Ecologist* or by Forester.
3 for ex., those of Park-Burgess, (cf. Park, R.E. *et.al.* (1925)).
4 cf.Sec.4.5   on reductionism, and Sec. 5.3 on the relations of the ED and non-discursive domains
5 for ex., Sonnenfeld, J. (1972b).
6 for ex., Altman, J. (1973): 105 ff.
7 for ex., Richardson, H.W. *et.al.* (1974).
8 For a detailed and general examination of models, see Harvey, D. (1969): Ch. 10; Badiou, A.(1969); Hindess, B. (1973 a). For models in geography, see Harvey, D. (1969): Ch. 11, Chorley, R.J. & Haggett, P. (eds.) (1967); Medvedkov, Y. (1976). For models in architecture, see *Architectural Design,* May 1971 issue; Hawkes, D. (ed.) (1975).

4.3.4   Utopianism

There are several discursive effects of the mechanisms of homogenous field, givenness, timeless/ideal/original unity,   pure principle and model. Some of these will be examined under specific headings, or in later chapters. One direct effect, however, can appropriately be mentioned here: *utopianism.* Utopianism in ED is a mechanism by which many of the effects of that discourse are produced. Like several other mechanisms, utopianism is not specific to the ED alone. It is a very common component of several discourses (e.g. political, artistic, religious).

The general characteristic of utopianism is its opposition to, and substitution of, scientific analysis of concrete problems. It operates on the idea of an 'ideal', a 'goal', and a timeless nostalgia of an 'original' past. It is *a-historical* in that instead of basing its statements on an analysis of the real, it constructs totally idealist schemes out of some ideological worldviews. Specifically in the ED, it proposes a *'utopian space'* which is in part symbolic[1], and in part descriptive. In its descriptive form, utopian discourse consists of discontinuous images and fixed states of *finished* objects[2]. The space in utopia is both discontinuous and finished, because it is constituted by a process of abstraction in the mind on the one hand, and modelling a pure reality on the other. The idealist abstraction prepares the ground for a formalist universe in which models replace analysis. While this universe is one of 'ideal essence', the model is bound to carry that essence according to the empiricism of the object[3].

The religious and cosmological overtones of the environmental discourse carried out through utopianism is not coincidental. As we will see in the analysis of the relations between discourses[4] there are profound theoretical and epistemological reasons behind such similarities. As with religions and cosmologies, utopian discourse is *closed, abstract,* and *irrational.* Since it is closed, that is, *finished,* it is not possible to expect change and development in it. If often turns out to be regressive, conservative, and mystificatory in the face of revolutionary changes in society, in technology and in sciences.

In the ecologism of the 60's and the 70's this regressiveness is distinctly dominant. While rightly criticizing the adverse effects of capitalism on physical and natural resources as well as on the health and well-being of people, that movement falls into an ideology of anti-technology, anti-progress, anti-science, and often, anti-politics. Instead of trying to identify the sources of problems in relation to the nature of capitalist mode of production, and instead of seeking solutions in the transformation of that mode of production, it turns to *moralistic, cosmological* and *quasi-religious* problematics. Social problems are explained in psychological, individualistic and mystic fashions. 'New models' and 'states of mind' are proposed. When the failure of capitalism in securing the basic protection of natural resources, and in providing the basic care of human health is recognized, environmentalism and ecologism turns to partly correct but essentially regressive modes of living and health care (e.g. communes, back-to-land, guru following, yoga, bio-feedback, etc.). Diverse ideological backings are provided in popularized eco-cosmologies[5] e.g. the monopoly capitalist system is confronted with 'Buddhist economics'[6].

1 For an analysis of the geographical symbolism of Thomas More's *Utopie,* see Marin, L. (1971), and Goodey, B. (1970).
2 On the discursive specificity of utopianism, see Choay, F. (1973): 300-8.
3 cf.Sec.3.3.2   on 'idealism of essence' and 'empiricism of subject and object'.
4 Sec. 5.2.
5 see, for ex., *The Ecologist*; Watts, A.W. (1969), (1973); Tuan, Y-F (1968), (1971).
6 see, Schumacher, E.F. (1968).

This whole mechanism both requires and produces a *mystification of the past and 'primitive' modes of living and thinking.* In another way, it is thought that there *was* an original harmony and unity of M and E, which was broken by 'man'[1]. Utopia, then becomes the realization of that *past* harmony.

In *architectural discourse,* utopianism operates at several levels: a major part of architectural ideologies according to which architecture is an art which gives form to permanent values, which is a humanitarian production of spaces and structures, which is the 'liberator of man', which can prevent social revolutions, or, at its most modest, which can satisfy human needs and aspiration.[2]

Obviously, these positions are based on more than just a misconception of architecture as a social practice. Neither architectural ideology nor utopianism are themselves autonomous entities. They are part of the dominant socio-political ideology in specific social formations. What is common to all utopian positions, propositions and projects in architecture is itself common to other utopian propositions examined earlier.

Architectural utopias seem to belong to the future only because they do not belong to the present.[3] In fact, it is doubtful whether they ever want to change the present.[4] They describe modes and models without processes. They propose architectural projects *built on imagination*, and often, imagination alone.[5] They construct technological fantasies, formal solutions and representations for undefined (or, ill-defined) problems.[6] They reduce complexity to simple and pure principles. And, as with other utopias, they mystify and aspire the architectural and urban forms produced by pre-capitalist societies (cf. vernacular movement) and misinterpret the struggle for shelter in underdeveloped capitalist societies (cf. self-build movement).[7]

Finally, it is significant to remember that however anti-establishment and however critical such utopias and movements seem to be, *they fail to see the economic determination* in the realization of their projects. In this context it is suggestive to quote a criticism of 19. century utopian socialism:
"They still dream of experimental realization of their social utopias, of founding isolated phalansteres, of establishing 'Home Colonies', or setting up a 'Little Icaria' — pocket editions of the New Jerusalem — and to realise all these castles in the air, they are compelled to appeal to the feelings and purses of the bourgeois".[8]

4.4.1   The division of 'reality' *(Introduction)*

In chapter 2 on the object of the ED, the questions of specificity, singularity and unity of the object were briefly discussed. In chapter 3 on the structure of the ED, it was shown how the invariant structure of the discourse was giving rise to a multiplicity of objects, subjects and relations, and how this multiplicity was the basis of further variations due to different points of view, disciplines and problematics.

1 cf. *'participation mystique'* according to which individual cannot distinguish himself/herself from the object, proposed by Levy-Bruhl, L. (1912); on this, see Whorf, B.L. (1963): 79-80, 79n. Cf. also: "One of the major elements in Aboriginal tradition and culture is land. In their legends it is part of them and they are part of it . . ." (Knewstub, N. (1974)).

2 For an historical analysis of these ideologies, especially in the context of the development of capitalism, see, Tafuri, M. (1976). See also Sec.5.3.8 on the false expectations and inflated self-image of architecture.

3 Özkan, S. (1973): 29.

4 cf. Heumann, B. (1973): 24 on the nature of utopian ideologies of the bourgeoisie.

5 See for ex., P. Soleri's **Arcology,** (1969).

6 cf. for ex. the Archigram.

7 For different and more detailed discussions on architectural utopias see, Tafuri, M. (1976); Battisti, E. (1975): 182-7; Bauer, E. (1971): 63f.

8 Marx, K. (quoted in *A Handbook of Marxism,* N.York, Int. Publ. Co, 1935, p.57).

One of the fundamental issues that an understanding of this multiplicity would unveil is *the way in which so-called 'reality'*[1] *is divided, only to be related again*. In the following sub-section we will look at this question in some detail.

First of all, it must be said that the classical philosophy's preoccupation with the 'unity and wholeness of reality' is perhaps the central constituent of many pervasive problematics in several discourses. Like all such 'fundamental' questions the question of reality involves much more than a limited and closed discussion on preconceived positions. It is necessary to understand that *the way in which the division of that 'reality' takes place determines the modes of coupling and unification that follow.* An object, whether real-concrete or concrete-in-thought, is to be defined and distinguished from other objects in order to be identified as a *specific* object. This obvious-looking requirement, however, is what the object(s) of the ED consistently fail to meet. As with most non-scientifically specified objects, the objects of the ED carry implicit meanings, imaginary contents and, often, a confusing status.

The mechanisms that are involved in any process of distinction and specification include classification, typology, choice and demarcation. As preliminaries of identifying these mechanisms some fundamental problems should be clarified:

1) Is the distinction (or specification, or classification) done at the *level* of real-concrete, or concrete-in-thought?

2) What type of *criterion* is used to achieve the distinction or specification?

3) What is the *type* and *degree* of distinction: e.g. separation, discrimination, or difference?

4) How is the *singularity* (or multiplicity) of each element specified?

1) First of all, it is the distinction between *real object* (or real-concrete) and *thought object* (or concrete-in-thought) which is basic to the question of specifying an object.

It is basic because without such a distinction, other types of specification cannot even be conceived of. And, for the same token, their confusion or conflation would impede the development of a scientific understanding of real problems. Thus, for example, it is hard to find discursive processes on 'environment' which do not make this confusion. When 'environment' is referred to, it is often taken both/either as a set of objects in space and/or as a relation and/or as a concept. Similarly, it is hardly clear whether 'man' is a concrete empirical man, or a concept, or an ideal, imaginary being. Consequently, the supposed relation between E and M appear to be both/ either/neither a physical interaction and/or/nor a theoretical or discursive relation.

Central to this mechanism is the blurring of the difference between the *physical boundaries between physical objects* and *theoretical specificity of thought objects.* This confusion leads to some simple applications of theories of communication, culture or language to architecture or urban practices[2]. This is possible as much by an analogical use of theories as by a failure to distinguish real object from thought-object, and empirical reality from conceptual structures. What follows is a confusion between the analysis of objects (such as cities, and buildings) as economic objects in particular, social formations, on the one hand, and idealist conceptions of environment or 'space' within the dominant ideologies on the other hand.

Similarly, in the discourse on art a confusion of 'artistic production' or 'art objects' with 'art'[3] (as a discursive/theoretical object) leads to analyses which fail to answer the

1 The reason for the 'so-called' will be clear in the discussion below.
2 For this mechanism see, Sec.4.5.4 below.
3 On this distinction, see Swenarton, M. (1974).

questions on the effects of artistic ideology, and on the material existence of artistic production in particular social formations.

It must be emphasized that systems of classification, typology and demarcation are *not* the intrinsic properties of the real-concrete (as empiricism or some systems theories suppose) but are abstract systems which are to be seen as tools for an analytic understanding of (real or theoretical) reality. Thus, it must be seen that even if there may occasionally be apparent overlaps of divisions in the real and in the classificatory system, these arise mainly due to the confusions mentioned above. Most important problem, however, is the *effect* of such systems of division. They are not simply explanatory tools. *They tend to dictate the mode of explanation; and impose upon the real a conceptual system.*

For example, the notions of 'built environment-natural environment', 'in-out' or 'region's[1] impose upon the physical world a system of classification. They are the results either of uncritical transfers from everyday or ideological discourses, or of discursive productions that are then presented as belonging to the reality.

2) The criteria of distinction or specification used in classifying or demarcating elements are usually *external.* They are brought in from other domains and discourses to organize the internal mechanism of objects. These may be epistemological, ideological, political, aesthetic, physical, legal, perceptual, economic and temporal[2] criteria to classify or demarcate real and/or thought objects.

For example, 'environment' or 'space' are specified according to, and in terms of, physical barriers, ideological conceptions, taboos, legal norms, perceptual limits, positions of the (knowing) subject, personal experiences, conception of society, disposition of material objects[3], political preferences, architectural considerations, etc. It is thus said, for example, that "a bicycle shed is a building; Lincoln Cathedral is a piece of architecture"[4] or that objects can be classified in terms of their being 'Pieces of Art' or 'artifacts'[5] or 'public' space may be distinguished from 'private'[6]; sacred from profane[7], built environment from natural environment[8], urban from rural[9], town from country[10], or 'building' from 'environment'[11].

Similarly, 'man' is specified and classified in terms of user, client, designer, owner decision-maker, subject of research, researcher; or 'society' in terms of rural/urban, industrial/non-industrial, primitive/modern, contemporary/historic, small/large, etc. As with all subjects which have double status, these terms implicitly carry the 'ideal essence' of 'man' or 'society' while conceiving them in terms of empirical subjects.

3) In the absence of a scientific rule to specify objects and to distinguish them from each other, there is nothing to stop discourses from under- or over-stating, ignoring or exaggerating differences between their objects[12]. Ignoring differences may result in grouping together objects which are distinct from each other. Exaggerating differences on the other hand may complete the *separation* of objects

---

1 On the status of the notion of 'region' see, Lacoste, Y. (1976): 61.
2 For the inclusion of time, see Mason, H.L. & Langenheim, J.H. (1957): 331.
3 Chombart de Lauwe,P-H. (1974): 234.
4 Pevsner, N. (1964): 15.
5 cf. R. Erskine in a BBC2 'Open University' film, 18.12.1976.
6 Lorenzer, A. (1968): 63-4: *"offentlicher Raum/privaten Raum";* or Norberg-Schulz, C. (1971):38; Joedicke, J. (ed) (1968): Ch.4.
7 cf. Chombart de Lauwe, P.-H. (1974): 239.
8 cf. Rapoport, A. (1969): 127; Brown, H. (1973): 14f; Wohlwill, J.F. (1973): 170.
9 cf. Medvedkov, Y. (1976): 80f.
10 cf. Raymond, M-G. (1968).
11 cf. Broady, M. (1968).
12 For the mechanism of ignoring instances see Sec. 4.5.11.

which are only *distinct* from each other[1]. In fact, labelling the parts (or levels) *for convenience*[2]should not imply assuming their separateness. Thus, the boundaries of (and between) 'thought objects' are either blurred, or firmly established, or distorted in such a way that a *conceptual precision*[3] becomes a requirement that is difficult to achieve. This difficulty is further increased as the ED relies on certain vague and imprecise conceptions such as split, alienation, struggle, on the one hand, and unity, integration, totality or harmony on the other[4].

4) Along with other, above-mentioned, problems pertaining to the conditions of specificity there is a feature that is particularly common in the ED it is the *singularity* and *multiplicity* of objects. As this question has already been analyzed in detail[5] it would be sufficient to say that an object should possess a clarity as to whether it is a real or a thought object, whether it is specified as a general notion of a large number of diverse phenomena, or as a precise and universally recognisable one, and whether it refers to the same thing or to a phenomena that is relativistic.

As mentioned above, conceptual precision is an absolutely essential condition for a concrete analysis. While precision does not exclude flexibility and potentiality of terms, it, however, is incompatible with ambiguity and vagueness. The amazing variation in which the terms 'environment' and 'region' are used and interpreted is a case in point[6]. This may invoke the question of whether there is a *'line'* which determines and defines terms. But, the question should not be diverted to a *generalist* question of "where to draw the line"[7] as there is no single line that can define *all* terms and concepts in all situations. Furthermore, most lines are *imaginary*[8] and not real, and they are *drawn* and not *given*[9]. There will be other occasions to show that the relativism that originates in this kind of imaginary identification has grave consequences in the ED.

4.4.2   Classification and typification

We can   now see the mechanisms which are operative in the constitution of the specificity (or pseudo-specificity) of the objects. *Classification* is a "formalizing process"[10]which generates analytic terms or concepts. The classes which classification produces are reductive and generalised objects. The counterpart of classification at the empirical level is *typification*. Typologies attempt to group objects of similar properties according to a criterion that is specified by the problematic of the inquiry. They are one of the analytic tools that enable experimental/scientific studies to tackle specialized objects. Unlike less disputable typologies in natural and physical sciences typologies or typification in the ED are dictated by ideological, institutional or personal requirements rather than by theoretical or technical ones. The standards, regulations and codes of practice are full of typifications *which could easily be different given different points of view or problematics.* For example, why and how is it that a 'public' space is distinguished from a 'private' one, or housing is typified as 'low-income', 'middle-income' and 'high-income' housing, or why is it that settle-

1 On 'difference' see, Wilden, A. (1972): 220.
2 cf. Hampden-Turner, C. (1970): 33.
3 For different views on the question of theoretical and conceptual precision, see Althusser, L. (1969): 172, 199; Harvey, D. (1969): 304-7; O'Malley, J.B. (1972): 14.
4 cf. Sec.4.2.4   above.   5 cf. Ch. 2.
6 cf. Harvey, D. (1969): 304-5.
7 Kaplan, A.: *The Conduct of Inquiry,* San Francisco, 1964, p.66, quoted in Harvey, D. (1969): 305.
8 cf. Wilden, A. (1972): 219-20.
9 cf. Kaplan, A., ibid.
10 O'Malley, J.B. (1972): 56, 58f.

ments are typified according to the size of their populations, or how is it that the typology of countries, regions and areas are produced?

4.4.3　Choice of problems and objects

Choice, on the other hand, is a mechanism with built-in assumptions of knowledge, interest, ideology or purpose. Choice also *implies* a classification, typology or demarcation according to which it operates. Although it is the locus of theoretical diversions or emphases, the latter are seldom explicitly declared. In other words, *all choices in discourse are presented as the* only *correct and 'natural' ones.* This, in fact, is where relativist positions are most likely to emerge.

The ED is full of unspecified choices: choices of objects, domains, problems, points of view and theoretical frameworks. To start with, there isn't an explicit set of rules to specify what is and is not 'environment', thus, what object is *'environmental'*, and what is not[1]. Secondly, the choice of problems to be studied is dictated not by theoretical necessity but often by social determinations, personal interests or by institutional preferences[2].

4.4.4　Demarcation

Determining the specificity of objects involves one basic process, that of *demarcation*. It is a process which is part of all classification, differentiation and typification processes. Each definition requires an initial demarcation. In ideological discourses this process is often implicit, intentional and/or governed by extra-theoretical concerns. In scientific discourse, on the other hand, specification of objects is a theoretical and/or demonstrative problem. In view of the un-scientific nature of the ED it should be no surprise to find that there is hardly any precise criteria of demarcation. Moreover, the set of problems discussed above have a direct bearing on the mechanism of demarcation as far as the ED is concerned.

First of all, if 'environment' is the *name* given to some physical objects or relations which are alternatively referred to as milieu, surrounding, space, world, nature, city or building, it must be seen that the universe constituted by those physical objects is not arranged in accordance with such mutually exclusive and/or relatively defined alternatives. The world (or 'environment', or nature) is not "given to us in classified form"[3]. It is the *language* which "divides reality"[4]. Yet, there isn't a direct correspondence between 'things' and 'words'. 'Words' refer to things which are themselves abstractions from the complex unity of the real-concrete. Thus, there are specific things, objects, artifacts; and *not* a general 'environment' — which is practically everything that can be conceived of in the world. Moreover, *any conception which is required to go beyond the simple recognition of objects and things is bound to be constructed within sciences and in terms of scientifically specifiable concepts.* Thus, unless it is specific enough to be specifiable, a real object can not be the object of a scientific practice, and cannot constitute a *theoretical object.*

To return to the ED it can be said that nearly all its objects that are spoken of, written about, or actually designed and organized, are *ideologically given generalities.* They neither stand the scrutiny of a critical observation as *physical* objects, nor can they be regarded as precise *theoretical* objects to facilitate theoretical inquiry. The demarcation that is made between the objects of the ED displays a profound lack of

1　cf. Sec. 2.4　　on the specificity of 'environment'. See, also, Sec.s 4.5.11 and 4.5.12.
2　cf. Ch. 5 for the material determinants of the ED.
3　Watts, A.W. (1973): 33.
4　Barthes, R. (1967): 64.

precision and many confusions: it confuses epistemological status of its objects as well as their material specificity. Consequently, objects of different functions, different properties[1] and different determinations are brought together to construct (non-) theoretical structures such as 'M-E' or 'S-E' relationships.

Of various types of demarcations that operate in the ED four can be seen as the most pervasive ones:

a) Epistemological demarcation,
b) Social demarcation,
c) Temporal demarcation,
d) Spatial demarcation.

a) Epistemological demarcation

The presumed schema of M and E is based on a demarcation between a subject (Man) and an object (Environment). Thus, it is basically an empiricist schema[2]. Secondly, as it has just been stressed, it is not clear whether the objects that are related are real objects or theoretical objects. Thirdly, due mainly to the *double status* of the subject and the object, and on the basis of the above-mentioned confusion, an empirical individual is related to an ideal 'environment', or, for example, the 'ideal essence' of 'man' is put into interaction with the 'built environment'. Consequently, an abstract differentiation is asserted as the basis of a 'functional integration'[3]. Fourthly, the status of the *'boundary'* that is supposed to exist between M and E, between Organism and E, or between S and E is a dubious one . In the absence of a clear distinction between real and thought objects, the epistemological status of that boundary becomes difficult to identify. It therefore becomes quite possible to use spatial metaphors as real objects, real boundaries as theoretical specifications, or psychological conceptions of 'ego-boundaries' as justifications for economic/legal/ ideological appropriation of territories. Similarly, uncritical *applications* to the architectural domain[4] of theories on communication is achieved basically by such an impression and with an assumed homology between diverse phenomena.

Boundary, in environmental psychological studies, is taken in its subjective and psychological sense, i.e. as 'body boundary', 'non-human environment' or 'territory'. Inspired by psychiatric conceptions on the one hand[5], and by ethology on the other[6] explanations of 'territoriality'[7], 'personal space' or 'privacy' are made on the assumption of the existence of territories and boundaries in space or in mind[8].

The 'boundary' between M and E, or between S and E is an imaginary boundary: it either does not exist in the real, or it exists only in the imagination (cf. Lacan). "The line drawn between 'organism' and 'environment' by our conventional model of

1 cf. H. Lefebvre mentioned by C. Leroy in Bresson, F. *et al* (1974): 270.
2 See, Sec. 3.2.3 for a detailed examination of the empiricist conception of knowledge, and Ch. 3 for the structure of the ED. See also Sec. 2.5 for the status of these terms themselves.
3 cf. Gerard, R.W. (1942): 82: "Thus, any functional integration at this level demands the initial differentiation of the units to be integrated . . .".
4 cf. for ex., Russell, B. (1973), or Clarke, L. (1974) for applications of B. Bernstein's theories on 'classification and framing' of educational knowledge', (1973).
5 cf. Searles, H.F. (1960); Cooper, C. (1971).
6 See, for ex. the environmental psychological works (based on K. Lorenz's and R. Ardrey's studies) by J.B. Calhoun, R. Sommer, E.T. Hall, O. Newman. See, also, the bibliographical survey by Evans, G.T. (1973).
7 cf. Rapoport, A. (1973a); Esser, A.H. (ed) (1971); Newman, O. (1973). For a critique of the latter's attempt to derive social engineering by spatial means see Hillier, B. (1973).
8 A detailed examination of these approaches is necessary and relevant especially with reference to their political, ideological as well as spatial implications. Yet, tackling such a subject in a rigorous manner would go beyond the limits and objectives of the present study. However, without the type

reality is. . . a fiction. Unfortunately, we think that it is real"[1]. It is assumed to exist in the skinbound biological individuality"[2], or in cultures whose structures are understood in terms of 'binary oppositions' (cf. Levi-Strauss). "To speak of man's behaviour in relation to the physical environment — or for that matter any kind of environment — implies that a dichotomy can be made between the person on the one hand and the environment on the other. Theoretically, however, such distinction is untenable"[3]. Even an anthropologistic distinction between those parts that belong to 'Nature' and those to 'Culture' does not free itself from the relativistic, ideological and anthropomorphic tendencies implicit in such dichotomies. (As also apparent in animal/man, natural environment/built environment, rural/urban dichotomies.)

   Epistemological demarcations are produced and supported by several other mechanisms some of which have already been discussed. For example, the original unity of the world situated around a 'centre' or an 'axis' (according to geometric conceptions)[4] is accorded the status of fundamental, internal, principle of environmental phenomena. An effect of this demarcation can be seen in the mechanism by which the order in which real relations exist is distorted. While this order (whether hierarchic, determinant, homogenous or uneven) is based, in the capitalist mode of production, on the relations of production with specific modes of distribution and exchange[5]; it is taken, in the ED, as a *natural* state of affairs organized by the principles of nature, aesthetics, illusory qualities, M-E relationship or patterns of perception.

b)   Social demarcation

To start with, social demarcation should not be confused with the theoretical identification of determinant elements and instances of a social whole (as, for example, the Marxist social theory does). Secondly, the definitions of other types of demarcation should not be seen to be exclusive of the *'social'*. On the contrary, whether it is epistemological, temporal or spatial, they are all *socially constituted and determined.* But these are not the precise accounts of what can be called 'social demarcation of space' or 'social determination of epistemology' as these questions need to be considered in a much more substantial manner[6]. What the present discussion tries to analyse, then, is the particular *conceptions of social whole and social relations of production in the ED.*

   'Social demarcation' involves first and foremost the way in which these conceptions are internally divided, defined and classified. The ED is, basically, an individualistic discourse, that is, its structure is   based on individual subjects, events and phenomena considered in a self-contained singularity, or an evolutionist complexity[7]. Society (rather than 'social formation') is thought to be the complex sum of individuals, or groups of individuals, given in a unity. In this conception society is first divided into two: 'Man' and 'Society' which are then counterposed to each other[8]. The individualism and individual-society relationship is represented in terms of structures such as a 'tree'[9] or a

---

of discourse analysis pursued here, it is difficult to make a rigorous critique of those implications. Discourse is a field where all practices (consciously or unconsciously) express and display their natures.

1 Wilden, A. (1972): 219.   2 Wilden, A. (1972): 220.
3 Proshansky, H.M., *et al* (1970): 33.
4 cf. Sec.4.3.2 above. See, for ex., Eliada, M. in Stewart, T.C. (1970): 43.
5 For a specific critique of this distortion in the industrial design discourse, see Wolf, L. (1972): 164-5.
6 These questions will be dealt with, though briefly, while examining the relations of the ED in Ch. 5.
7 These conceptions will be examined in Sec. 4.5.2 on reductionism.
8 On this peculiar mechanism see Marx, K. (1969): 3rd thesis: "This doctrine must, therefore, divide society into two parts, one of which is superior to society".
9 See, for ex., Friedman, Y. (1975): 150f.

semi-lattice'[1] which are then related to different 'environments'. The *ideological divisions* into public-private[2] or us-them[3], *relativist divisions* into nations[4], regions[5], neighbourhoods, or lifespace[6], *arbitrary divisions* in terms of size or quantity such as "man-room-dwelling group-small neighbourhood-neighbourhood-small town- . . . ecumenopolis", or populations of 1,000-2.000-4.000-40.000 – . . . -30.000.000.000[7], or *sociological divisions* into communities, social classes[8], ethnic groups or 'housing classes'[9] all carry with them:

a) the individualistic, linear and functionalist conception of social phenomena,

b) the implicit spatiality of supposedly 'social'divisions[10] that are later correlated with the spatial aspects of the same phenomena.

Moreover, on the basis of these conceptions the structural division of social whole into classes according to the relations of ownership (that are specific to particular modes of production) are distorted, and presented as psychological or cultural variables (as in the cases of 'localism' and territoriality)[11]. Thus, ambiguous and relativistic notions such as 'man', 'users', 'clients', 'pedestrians', 'housewives', 'participants' are used as the human subjects of problems that are *basically* economic, political or technical. Or, they constitute the terms of *non-problems* that are produced in the course of empirical researches. By solely concentrating on the consumable products and subjects' attitudes towards, or use of,them environmental discourse becomes a 'consumptionist' (or 'consumerist') one wholly ignoring the *production* aspect of the products in question (except in technical studies of building activity). By a deliberate *separation of production and consumption* aspects of products in architectural, urban and industrial design[12] activities, 'society' is transformed into a curious entity of users and clients who only consume finished products. These products are conceived in terms of their functions, comfort, properties and prices, and in terms of subjective preferences of the consumers. In such a mechanism it is not only the consumption which is separated from the production processes. The production process itself, if ever tackled, is reduced to technical, administrative or bureaucratic problems in isolation from the political/economic nature of the whole process. This effectively obscures the fundamental status of production, and social relations of production which determine and define not only the way in which the society is *structured* and *divided* (into classes and stratas), but also, through particular modes of ownership and distribution, *determine the mode of consumption itself.*[13]

c) Temporal demarcation

Temporal demarcation of 'organism' and 'environment'[14] involves the initial question of how specific sets of 'environmental facts' are related with specific 'O's': If *a different* E

1 See, for ex., Alexander, C. (1966): 51f.

2 See, for ex., Giedion S. (1969): 72; Lorenzer, A. (1968) 63-4.

3 See, for ex., Goodey, B. (1974): 49-50.

4 For a critique of the domination of *nationalist division* of territory, see Soja, E.W. (1971): 9ff.

5 For this concept, see Juillard, E. (1962); Tekeli, I. (1972): 46-59. For the critiques of the problematic of region, see Lacoste, Y. (1976).

6 See, for ex., Seablom, S.H. (1970): 611 (after M. Webber).

7 as in 'Ekistic Logarithmic Scale', cf. Bell, G. & Tyrwhitt, J. (eds) (1972): 27.

8 See, for ex.; Fried, M. & Gleicher, P. (1961); Rainwater, L. (1966).

9 For this pseudo-Marxist term, see Rex, J. & Moore, R. (1967).

10 For this question see (c) below.   11 cf. Fried, M. & Gleicher, P. (1961).

12 cf. Wolf, L. (1972): 188.

13 On this point, it would be useful to remember that,
(a) "Consumption is . . . a phase of production", and
(b) "production . . . produces not only the object of consumption but also the mode of consumption".
(Marx, K. (1971): 199 and 197 respectively).

14 Hereafter referred to as 'O' and 'E' respectively.

is defined relative to each O^1, can an 'essential section' reveal the 'typical' pattern of an O-E relationship in view of the fact that the life-cycle of each 'environmental fact' and each O is necessarily different? Moreover, can an event be specified in terms of its *duration*, and the life span of an O in terms of the 'duration time' of its E?

We know that 'environment' is not only a relational and relativistic notion, it is also a confused one as far as its specificity and status are concerned. It is both a relation, a set of constraints or conditions, *and* a set of physical objects (e.g. a building is a physical object (i.e. an O) *and* an E for the persons and functions in it.) Secondly, events are timed though undirectly spaced, and objects are spaced though undirectly timed[2]. This timing however is *linear,* and spacing *relative.* Thus, the dimensioning of O and E can not be reduced to a linear timing or to a relational spacing alone.

Now, before commenting on this question further, it must be reminded that these arguments do not aim to produce an 'alternative' conception of O-E relationship, but to try to show *the internal inconsistencies of 'environmental theories' in their own terms.* For, as we have shown earlier the scientific study of a reality cannot be based upon an 'essential section', or upon the self-contemporaneity of structure[3]. Reality can not be divided into separate events that are distinctly ordered on a uni-linear time, and conception of phenomena (especially social phenomena) can not be relativistic, i.e. depend upon points of view, or time scales.

In this sense, attempts to produce a temporal demarcation of spatial objects are to be replaced by *a conception of different levels at which each structure is articulated and each level has different temporality and different spatiality.* This point is particularly relevant to a critique of theories on socio-spatial phenomena which tend to relate objects, events, locations, periods, abstract qualities and ideological structures to each other as if they were all autonomous elements on a unilinear time scale, or on a plane, homogenous, field.

d) Spatial demarcation

In a relativist conception of environment which assigns definite 'environments' to each object, the question of *spatial demarcation* arises in three senses:
1) How are these 'E's' *defined* and classified?
2) What is it that *distinguishes* O from E?
3) What is it that defines the E of a particular O, in other words, *"how much* of any given environmental phenomenon is to be considered the environment of the organism"[4].

1) Definition, division and classification of 'space' is bound up with the problematic of environment which ensures the *unity* of the object of ED in the first place. As an effect of the multiple status and confusions that dominate this problematic, divisions and classifications cannot but reflect these multiplicities and confusions: all of which are assumed to be 'objectively determined'[5]. For example, 'space' and 'environment' are classified in terms of points of view, internal-external[6], domains-places-paths[7], 'anthropophilic-anthropozenic'[8], size (e.g. mezo-, macro-, micro-environments)[9] or subjective perception[10]. These and other types of division of 'environment' are funda-

1 cf. for ex., Tekeli, İ. (1973); Mason, H.L. & Langenheim, J.H. (1957): 330-1.
2 O'Malley, J.B. (1974): 3, ('undirectly' is O'Malley's category).
3 cf.Sec. 4.2.3. See, also, Althusser, L. (1970): 321-2.
4 Mason, H.L. & Langenheim, J.H. (1957): 333, emphasis added.
5 cf. Soja, E.W. (1971): 9.
6 cf. Raffestin, C. (1976): 186.
7 cf. Norberg-Schulz, C. (1971): 18, 23.
8 standing for 'suitable for man-alien to man', mentioned in *Progressive Architecture,* April 1975 .
9 cf. Fitch, J.M., mentioned in Turan, M. (1974): 186.
10 cf. Ittelson, W.H. (1973): 18.

mental to the demarcation of the real, whether it is social and/or physical.

2) The second question can only be answered by another relativistic procedure: that of taking a *point of view*. Depending on what one considers as the O, its E differs considerably. That consideration, on the other hand, is a function of the point of view of the O to 'view' the E, and the reverse to 'view' the O^1.

3) The third question, on the other hand, is more of an operational demarcation than a quantitative one, though the latter property also came into the picture. In the ecological context of plants or micro-organisms it may be possible to define an 'operational environment' which is absolutely essential to their survival, and which impinges upon the O during its life cycle^2. Yet, when a complex O like a 'region', a city or even a building is concerned, it becomes difficult to see what exactly the O and its 'operational E' are, and how they are specified for analysis and design purposes. Whether spatial connotations of the term 'environment' is denied^3 or emphasized^4, it remains to be one of the multiple senses in which it is used in the ED^5. This is, in fact, only one of the reasons why biological analogies and O-E problematic are bound to fail in tackling spatial problems of particular social formations.

'*Boundary*' is a *spatial* concept too. It is used, and produced in the empirical world to describe, designate and produce spatial operations. It defines 'sides', and in doing so, it is supported by, and it collaborates with, equally relativistic concepts of 'circle', 'centre' or 'in-out'. For example, a wall^6, a fence, a plot-line, or a national border^7 are all boundaries, or, 'territorial markers'. As such, they are physical or legal boundaries, and are *means of exclusion*. They prevent free movement between the designated, or pre-supposed, 'sides'.

In urban sociological discourse 'boundaries' are charged with expressing or defining spatial relationships, freedom, accessibility, permeability, class characteristics, 'sense of belonging', property relations, etc^8 or the 'uniqueness' or social characteristics of zones, regions^9. In all these functions the concept of 'boundary' is asked to express (and, inevitably confuse) the sociological in epistemological terms, and the epistemological in sociological terms.

'Boundaries'also carry symbolic, cultural and ideological meanings whether made explicit or not. These meanings are the products of material/social conditions. They express the ideology of a social order some of whose physical requirements they meet. That is, they define the legal ideology of '*private property*', and provide tangible affirmations of *possession*^{10}. They define the limits and extent of the appropriation of surplus value, provide physical or metaphysical separation between peoples, and consolidate the existing social divisions.

But, *physical* boundaries are objects of a specific order: they are 'real objects'. They do not necessarily have epistemological corrolaries. There may be walls in different socio-economic systems and they may have completely different social functions. They may function as property boundaries in one system, while they only define areas of use or

1 See Sec. 3.3.5 and 4.6.3 for a more detailed examination of this question.
2 cf. Mason, H.L. & Langenheim, J.H. (1957): 333.
3 as Mason, H.L. & Langenheim, J.H. (1957): 333 does.
4 cf. Rapoport, A. (1973a): 30.
5 For, a 'bracketing' is only possible in *writing* (e.g."environment" as distinct from environment).
A *discourse*, on the other hand involves all types of statements whether written, spoken or only thought.
6 On the symbolic and design aspects of walls, see Hillier, B. & Leaman, A. (1974); Evans, R. (1971).
7 cf. Soja, E.W. (1971).
8 See, for ex., Fried, M. & Gleicher, P. (1961): 312-4; Young, M. & Willmot, P. (1962).
9 cf. Lacoste, Y. (1976).
10 For the fundamental and significant distinction between 'property' and 'possession' see, Marx, K. (1971), (1970) v.1 ; also, Althusser, L. (1970): 176-77.

function in another. Some may not even have any *social* specificity, (e.g. a fence to keep cattle in is more of a functional device than a definition of ownership of cows or of the grazing field). Thus, not all demarcations of spatial nature between M and E have social and economic definitions, nor can an imaginary boundary be charged with the task of demarcating elements that are ideologically defined, and are imaginary, in the first place.

Even when E is conceptualized not as the 'surrounding'[1], the 'encircling'[2], or as a container[3] of the O but as a set of conditions, the implicit 'otherness' of the E with respect to O remains to be neutralized if the M-E schema is intended as a scientific conception. For, even at the biological level "there is no sharp line between what is felt inside or at the body, and what is left at a distance. No being can be sure of just where its body ends and the rest of the world begins. We have difficulty in determining whether the heat we feel is in our bodies or in the world about . . ."[4]. On the other hand, and as shown during the discussion on epistemological demarcation, the locus of epistemological boundary is not clear either, i.e. does the boundary belong to the M or E?[5] And, it is not possible to think of " 'an environment' and 'an organism' without abstraction, there exists between these two, . . . a complexus of relations of changes and reactions which implies complete physiological continuity".[6] Similarly, neither the conceptions of O and E can be connected by a kind of mediating substance (e.g. Newtonian 'ether'), nor can the mediation of "cognitive representations" that the people "have of the environment"[7] avoid the initial *'separatedness-in-mutual-existence'* of the M-E schema. Thus the question of demarcation is either avoided without solving it, or is uncritically reproduced.This spatial separateness of O and E (or M and E) coupled with this or that type of relationship is not confined to contemporary environmental discourse alone: when the natural ideology was the dominant mode of amphibological displacements[8], people spoke of "the 'antithesis in nature and history' as though they were two separate 'things'."[9]

Furthermore, it is not possible to demarcate social formations[10], individuals or groups of people in basically *spatial* terms by establishing physical, symbolic and often arbitrary boundaries. The fact that everyday as well as geographical, anthropological and historic discourses are full of entities with unquestioned boundaries does not necessarily justify their status. In fact, a social formation is not an empirically given and physically observable entity, but is an articulated structure of several instances. As such it can have no *boundary* which demarcates it from other entities, such as from 'environment'. But, if both are seen as *internal* to each other (i.e. not as separable phenomena), then, *the question of the 'spatiality' of social formation needs to be answered not with reference to a superimposition of two separate entities, but in terms of the complex and overdetermined articulation of different and contradictory elements.* The individual person is not a *'unit'* of social structure, and social phenomena cannot be reduced to the summation, or interaction, of individuals in them. It

1 cf. Tekeli, İ. (1973): 6-7.
2 cf. Mason, H.L. & Langenheim, J.C. (1957): 333.
3 cf. Harvey, D. (1969): 208.
4 Weiss, P.A. (1947): 115.
5 cf. Wilden, A. (1972): 185.
6 J. Piaget, paraphrased in Searles, H.F. (1960): 17-18.
7 Moore, G.T. (1973): 232.
8 cf. Sec. 4.5.8.
9 Marx, K. & Engels, F. (1970): 62 while commenting on Bruno Bauer.
10 cf. (b) above on social demarcation.

would be a relativistic tautology to suggest that any functional integration of individuals in a society would demand the initial differentiation of the units to be integrated"[1], or that society is an 'epiorganism'[2]. Let's assume for a moment that social formations can, *hypothetically,* be demarcated in spatial, physical, or demographic terms on the one hand, and symbolic, cultural, historical, or political terms, on the other. In all these cases, however, a *unit* of collectivity, rather than a structure, is assumed to define the whole operation. Moreover, even in non-physical demarcations, such as in cultural or political ones, spatiality of boundary is implicit or inevitable. Thus, demarcation of a social formation is not reducible to a presupposed empirical given. It is a theoretical construction of a scientific analysis.

That 'facts' and data are used in most of the empiricist studies on space, 'environment' and society does not alter their fundamental positions *vis-a-vis* the question of demarcation. The very act of collecting data on a pre-determined area or 'region'[3] implies an implicit demarcation. Same is true for distinctions like natural/built environment, human/non-human environment, etc.[4] The relativism/subjectivism of such pre-determinations is only one more point of obvious weakness of these positions which we need not go into here. In fact, most positions on the question of *reflection* of social structure in space commit the mistake of assuming the existence of *two* distinct elements which reflect, and interact with, each other. This mistake may persist even when a materialist conception of spatial organization asserts that space is organized as a function of dominance, contradictions, tensions and discordances[5].

4.5.1 Reductionism and shifts *(Introduction)*

Reductionism is one of the most pervasive and effective mechanisms of the ED. It operates wherever there is a multi-levelled and complex whole having several instances and elements. In other words, it is not an integral mechanism (like 'homogenous field' or 'pure principle'), but an *inter-level* one. It belongs to the discourse proper rather than to the objects themselves. Thus, it can best be observed in the course of a discursive analysis. For the same token, it cannot be deduced from a study of those empirical objects which the ED refers to. Like most other mechanisms of the ED reductionism is present in various other discourses, sciences and disciplines — especially in the process of developing their 'general theories'[6]. It occurs mainly in the course of constituting or establishing the objects of a discourse or theory.

Reduction, as has just been said, *is an interlevel mechanism which reduces the complex to the simple, new problems to the terms of older ones, one discipline or practice to the techniques and problematics of another one, social phenomena to individual behaviour, and multitude of factors to a simple schema or to a pure principle.* While a single reduction may suffice to constitute a 'theory' or a 'problematic', the same cannot be said for a discourse — especially for one as diverse and complex as the ED, which is constituted by a large number of mechanisms, including an equally varied range of reductions. In fact, it has already been shown that it is characterized by the very *multiplicity* in its fields of operation, its objects and its structure[7]. Reductions will therefore be analysed in terms of these operations, fields of operation, problematics, etc. With 'operations' we understand the specific types of *inter-level movements*

1 cf. Gerard, R.W. (1942): 82.
2 ibid.
3 cf. Lacoste, Y. (1976).
4 cf. Rapoport, A. (1973a): 30; or Searles, H.F. (1960).
5 cf. for ex., Chombart de Lauwe , P-H. (1974): 236.
6 cf. Harvey, D. (1969): 95 for a survey of different positions on this process.
7 cf. Sec. 3.3.

that a particular type of reduction performs amongst various concepts and conceptual systems. For example, shifts of concepts from one domain to another, or correlating two or more 'variables' are specific types of movements. In a second mode of analysis the reduction is seen to be present as the *organizing principle* of a particular problematic, or of an ideology or method. For example, what are known as 'functionalism' and as 'methodological individualism' are possible only because of their reliance on reductionist principles.

As pointed out earlier[1], the ED is constituted as the 'cross-roads' of a large number of disciplines, ideologies and practices. It not only borrows, but also adopts and distorts, the mechanisms and methods of all these domains. Thus, none of the reductions that are examined here is exclusively 'environmental'.

As far as the ED is concerned, one of the most effective mechanisms is the *'shift'* which functions between levels and instances, and often, simultaneously with other mechanisms such as 'confusions', 'conflations', 'substitutions' or 'amphibologies'. Moreover, its field of operation can be semantic, metaphoric or literal[2].

As a whole, the mechanisms of reduction can be observed in a large number of other mechanisms and domains which can be listed here for reference purposes as they are examined in this chapter:

| reductions
shifts
confusions
conflations
interchanges
amphibologies
ignoring
correlations
correspondences
assimilations
substitutions | of/
between/
in/ | practices
domains
subjects
objects
discourses
disciplines
fields
styles
representations
levels
instances | forms
facts
points of view
concepts
categories
terms
notions
theories
relations
problematics
magnitudes | differences
complexity
determinations
elements
functions
unities |

Of course, not *all* mechanisms function on *all* objects listed against them. Neither is there any one-to-one or one-to-all correspondences between them. Therefore it is not possible to proceed with a 'reading' of all discursive statements as if there were such a 'universal grid'. The following analysis will attempt to tackle some major mechanisms of the ED that are reductionist in one way or another.

Before starting to examine these reductionist mechanisms, a note on the modes of analysing discourses is thought to be relevant. In the ED, as in 'social sciences', the conception of the real is usually based on some empirical generalizations (which are then called 'theories'). Observational 'facts' abstracted from the complexity of the phenomena are classified according to a preconceived (yet, *untheorized*) schema, and processed statistically, to test some hypotheses. So-called 'theories' are then said to have been established. In such a process reduction of theory to facts, or derivation of theory from facts are the bases of several relativist and subjectivist approaches to 'environmental' problems. An examination of these approaches would be beyond the objectives of the present study. However, it is possible to suggest that even the conception of 'reductionism' is far from universal, and is subject to various effects of differing positions in the philosophy of science. Yet, most of these would analyse a discursive mechanism as if they were analysing some observable physical objects. The most pervasive mode of

1 in Ch. 1 while examining the unity of the ED, as well as at the beginning of this section.

2 The author owes his *initial* insight into conceptual mechanisms such as 'shifts' to the late Dr. J.B. O'Malley — though the present conception of these mechanisms as developed in this study differs considerably from those of Dr. O'Malley. The mechanism of 'shift' should also be distinguished from the linguistic concept of 'shifters' as developed by R. Jacobson, (cf. Barthes, R. (1967): 22-3).

analysis is what is commonly called the *'history of ideas'*. It is characterized by its
taking texts, authors, movements of ideas, schools of thought, as empirical givens to
be listed, interrelated with, or opposed to, each other. In this mode of analysis
reductionism could be seen as one of the ways of labelling some of these *literary*
objects. The present analysis tries to avoid the trappings of both empirical generalizations and those of 'history of ideas' in favour of a *discourse analysis* whose
principles have been described at the very beginning of the study.

4.5.2 Reduction of the complex

One of the common types of mechanism is the *reduction of the complex to the simple*.
Needless to say, depending on the different conceptions of complexity, different types
of reductions take place. For example, the reduction of a whole to its parts, the
multiple to the singular, complex connexions to one-to-one relations are all distinct
forms of reductions.

The process of reduction is internal to the very conception of complexity an
understanding of which requires posing some questions such as:
− Is complexity a feature of observable phenomena or/and of underlying structure?[1]
− Is it a feature of 'organism' or/and of 'environment'?[2]
− Is it a relational or an objective category (of 'parts' and 'wholes')?[3]
− Is it merely a quantitative or a proportional measure in the 'part-whole' relationship?[4]

But, all these questions and the problematics in which they are formulated imply an
essential unity, an original state and a binary scheme. As we have already seen it is these
very mechanisms which lend support to the other mechanisms in the ED[5].

The conception of complexity in the ED is one that is evolutionist, linear, dualist,
analytic, expressive, relativist, and most significantly, simplistic. As this rather brief
description would suggest, according to this conception what is 'now' complex is thought
to have evolved from a simple origin following a linear process. Furthermore, this linear
process is *relative* to the 'knowing subject' who conceives of the phenomena. The
phenomena in question carries with it parts each of which expresses and reflects the
whole universe (i.e. Leibnizian *pars totalis*)[6]. ED's conception of complexity is integral
not only to its treatment of its objects, but also to its own constitution. It is a complex
discursive practice with many determinations, yet, it is at the same time a discourse
that functions on the basis of 'essences' and pure principles, and works on objects whose
complex connexions and contents are reduced to simple schemas and correlations[7].
Overdetermined, articulated and uneven complexity[8] of socio-physical phenomena is
reduced to the descriptive accounts of isolated elements.

Simplicity is not the *origin* but the *product* of complex processes[9] both at the real

1 cf. Mepham, J. (1973): 107.
2 cf. Simon, H.A. (1969): "A man viewed as a behaving system is quite simple. The apparent complexity
of his behaviour over time is largely a reflection of the complexity of the environment in which he finds
himself" (p.25).
3 cf. Piaget, J. (1971): 8-9.
4 cf. Odum, H.T. & Peterson, L.L. (1972): "Generally, complexity is proportional to the square of the
number of parts involved that are of different type and function" (p.625).
5 cf. Sec. 4.2.4.
6 cf. for ex., "the individual is not a skin capsulated ego but an organism-environment field. The organism itself is a point of which the field is 'focused', so that each individual is a unique expression of the
behaviour of the whole field, which is ultimately the universe itself". (Watts, A.W. (1969): 140).
7 cf. Ch.3.
8 For a detailed formulation of the conception of 'complex structured whole', see Althusser, L. (1969):
Ch.3, Ch. 6.
9 cf. Marx, K. (1971): 209.

and at the theoretical domains. In fact, there is *no* 'simple' phenomena to speak of as a unity. "Phenomena is a tissue of relations. There is no simple nature, simple substance, the substance is a contexture of attributes. There is no simple idea, because a simple idea . . . ought to be inserted, to be comprised, in a complex system of thought and experiences . . . The simple ideas do not point the definitive base of knowledge."[1]
An understanding of the complex *as* complex is necessary to an understanding of other, simpler, levels or elements[2]. Reduction of complex phenomena to visible relations, or to hierarchies does not fulfil this requirement, but, rather, attempts to achieve the understanding by first constructing hierarchies by empirical generalizations, then using them as the basis of explaining what was earlier generalized[3]. Another notion in the ED that ignores the question of complexity (by *confining it to a term*) is 'Total Environment'. It is a tautological notion in that *its 'totality' is explained by assuming the globality implicit in the term 'Environment'*.[4] One final, yet fundamental, point regarding the connexions between reductionism and ED's conception's of complexity is that *most of the mechanisms of that discourse depend upon the existence of a 'whole' which is understood in a simplistic manner.*

What has already been said can be illustrated in specific types of reductions that are commonly found in the ED:
– Complex structured wholes are reduced to pure-principles, or to 'root-causes' such as 'competition', 'moral state', 'cultural pattern', 'civilization'. These reductions provide the bases for fallacious positions and spurious correlations[5].
– Complex reality is reduced to a single framework, such as 'ecosystem'[6] 'ecological viewpoint'[7], 'behaviour', or 'total environment'[8].
– Contradictory and uneven wholes are reduced to one of their aspects[9].
– Even the recognized object of the ED, 'Environment', is reduced to some of its elements, for example, to 'rooms', to 'built environment', to 'city', to 'nature', or to artificially created units such as "environment of 'Them' " and "environment of 'Us'[10].
– Some complex activities, policies and decisions are reduced to the behaviour or performance of one subject (or group of subjects) who is then held responsible for the effects of those activities. For example, architects are blamed for the ill-effects of high-rise blocks, or planners for the motorways[11].
– Physical objects, products and spatial orders are reduced to easily conceivable things; for example, houses to machines, or cities and traffic to rivers[12].

1 Bachelard, G. (1975): 152-53.
2 cf. "The anatomy of man is a key to the anatomy of the ape". (Marx, K. (1971): 211).
3 also by an "atomistic compounding of prior elements" (Piaget, J. (1971): 7). See, for ex., Simon, H.A. (1969) who tries to explain complexity in terms of hierarchy, and hierarchy in terms of complexity, (pp.87, 108). (For a critique of Simon's position, see Teymur, N. & E. (1974)).
4 For different views on 'Total E', see Proshansky, H.M., *et, al.* (1970): 33; Wells, B.W.P. (1965a): 165; Klausner, S.Z. (1972): 334; Broady, M. (1968): 20-1.
5 See, for ex. Hollingshead, A.B. (1940) for an attempt to associate ecological order with competition, and social order with communication. A similar ecologism of competition is the basis of the Chicago school of geography.
6 cf. for ex., Stoddart, D.R. (1965): 243.
7 cf. for ex., Esser, A.H. (1972): 72f; Willems, E.P. (1973): 79, 88.
8 See above for this notion.
9 For ex., urban sociology reduces the complex urban systems to one or two of its aspects, such as to 'mode of life', 'economic mechanisms', 'behaviour of individuals' (cf. Wolf, L. (1972): 13f. See Castells, M. (1975) for a general critique of urban sociology).
10 For the last terms, see Goodey, B.R. (1974): 49-50.
11 cf. Sec. 5.3.8 for examples of such claims. See Mugnaioni, P. (1976) for a critique of attributing failures of planning to the incompetence of planners rather than to the structural incompatibility of planners' objectives and the demands of the capitalist system.
12 The former is Le Corbusier's, the latter L. Kahn's. See Sec. 4.6.6 below on analogies and metaphors

— Every object is reduced to a *representation*, if not always to a form especially in technical practices like architecture[1] or industrial design[2]. This reduction then limits the mode of perception to a *figurative* one. Moreover, a similar reduction of real and/ or theoretical objects to graphical representations is a commonly employed mechanism in the ED — often, as a substitute for theoretical analysis[3].

— Complex properties, forces and factors in socio-spatial reality are reduced to some of the latter's physical aspects (*physicalism*), or to a notion of 'physical environment' with which "to explain human and institutional traits by the properties of the physical environment"[4] (*environmentalism*) In a rather different version of physicalism physical systems or objects, such as architecture, are accorded the status of the *symbols* of society, world and 'value systems' or, still further, certain social patterns and behaviour are correlated with physical forms (as in the case of high-rise blocks of flats where crime is said to be concentrated[5].

— The biological phenomena are reduced to the sociological, or the sociological to the biological[6], which obscures the real domain of problems (with, of course, many ideological, political and technical implications)[7].

— Shift of ecological crises to the 'natural' domain (*naturalization*), tends to represent socio-political nature of the 'crises' as 'natural catastrophes'[8], and reduces urban problems to the natural[9], or to ecology[10], often in a metaphorical way. The mechanism of naturalization ultimately leads to substituting the *social* with the *natural*[11]. The naturalization process has another aspect. Due mainly to the double status of the word 'nature' in environmental as well as other discourses, shifts and reductions in this process take place *within* the term 'nature' just as much as between natural and non-natural ones. The double status of 'nature' are (1) the reality of all non-man-made objects and phenomena, (2) the 'true essence' of things (i.e. their 'nature'). Following the second sense of the term, certain problems and phenomena are conceived as 'natural', that is, normal, internal, or 'how they are supposed to be'. These two versions of naturalization, when confused and collapsed, lend a substantial support to the conservative ideology of environmentalism[12].

— Structural social conflicts are reduced to superficial issues[13] which are then thought to be solved by minor technical re-arrangements or administrative measures. But, when reduction takes place in substantial problems, the danger of *technicism* is likely

---

for a more detailed discussion on this type of reductions. For an opposite view which, however, idealizes the same object, cf. "The house is not an object, a 'machine to live in', it is the universe that man constructs for himself by imitating the paradigmatic creation of the gods, the cosmogony". (Eliade,M. (1959): 57; see also Cooper, C. (1971): 29).

1 cf. Battisti, E. (1975): 161.

2 cf. Wolf, L. (1972).

3 See Sec. 4.6.7 below.

4 Tuan, Y-F. (1971): 26.

5 cf. Sec. 4.6.2 for a critique of such correlations.

6 cf. Odum, H.T. (1971) who expresses "both social and natural events in a common biophysical language" (Klausner, S.Z. (1972): 337n; see, also pp. 346-7).

7 cf. Morin, E. (1974): 5 who calls such a reduction as 'imperialistic'.

8 cf. Remøren, E. & T.I. (1975): 8; Galtung, J. (1973): 102.

9 cf. Tafuri, M. (1976): 3-4.

10 cf. for ex., Park, R.E. *et. al.* (1925).

11 for ex. "Like the challenge posed by war, the ecological challenge effects all classes . . . when the enemy is nature, rather than another social class, it is at least imaginable that adjustments could be made . . ." (Heilbroner, R. (1970)).

12 cf. Ch. 5 on this ideology. For the conflation of different senses of 'nature', see, for ex., the assertion that city is a "product of *nature*, and particularly *human nature*". (Park, R.E. *et. al.* (1925); also, Perin, C. (1970): 18-9, (emphases added).

13 On this, see Kade, G. (1970): 571.

to follow. In substantial and complex problems the 'technical' instance is isolated from other instances (e.g. economic, political, cultural, artistic), and is elevated to a self-standing framework by itself. This is one of the bases, also, of a fallacious position that can be called *'technical determinism'*. The latter is a common discursive mechanism in architectural, planning and engineering practices. According to the technicist problematic, what always matters is *finding suitable explanations and/or solutions to already defined problems*. Once confined to the domain of technical problem solving, other aspects of problems are effectively ignored. It involves a curious position in professional practices as well as in their education whereby any criticism of technicism meets with claims such as "one's got to do one's job", or "I am not a sociologist, I am only an architect"[1]. Transformation of economic and political questions into the realm of the technical produces *incomplete* and *distorted* conceptions of problems which have little or no value even for technical solutions[2]. In still another respect, technicism performs an *ideological* function by displacing problems, and by neutralizing contradictions in many commercial, political or military undertakings. For example, to what extent do the anti-public housing, or anti-public transport policies of British Toryism involve *architectural* and *urban* techniques? Or,we may remember that millions of people starved in Africa in 1973 as a result of the consistent colonialist policies of France to reclaim 2.5 ml. hectares of forests in order to plant peanuts. It caused an unprecedented deprivation of land which turned it into a desert, and caused   widespread starvation[3]. To what extent was this an essentially *ecological* problem, and what ecological techniques could revitalize the land and the people on it? Or, for example, to what extent were 'Force Draft Urbanization' or 'Strategic Hamlet Programme'[4] in Vietnam (masterminded by 'experts' and perpetrated by the US government) were *urban* operations that could be criticised or, be put right, by alternative urban planning techniques?
− All socio-physical problems are reduced to their *economic* dimensions, and a macroeconomics is built out of microeconomic considerations[5], and world resources are reduced to some 'budget approaches'[6].

4.5.3 Psychologism

Perhaps the most pervasive type of reductionism in the ED of 1970's is *psychologism*. Simply stated, it is the reduction of various phenomena to the psychological, in other words, their shift from the domain where they belong to the boundaries of psychology. In fact, this mechanism is present in many other disciplines and discourses such as economics[7], and historiography. On the other hand, within psychology itself there is a significant place of reductionism, as in the transfer of methods and concepts from physical sciences (i.e. methodological reductionism) or, reduction of psychological

1 Arne Jacobsen, reported in *Politiken,* 28.2.1971, p.13.
2 For such cases in geography, see Lacoste, Y. (1976): 85f.
3 cf. *L'Express:* 'Famine en Afrique', 28.5.-3.6.1973, p.40.
4 'Force Draft Urbanization' and 'Strategic Hamlet Programme' were new types of concentration camps (similar to the ones in S. Africa and Rhodesia) designed by the US administration to contain Vietnamese peasants who were forced to move from country to town, or into fortified areas. Their aims were to avoid the peasants' alliance with National Liberation Front whose 'rural-revolution' was expected to be reversed by the American idea of 'urban-revolution' (See, *The Sunday Times,* 17.6.1973), or *The Guardian,* 20.6.1973 for these and other methods of 'ecological warfare' used in Indochina, see Weisberg, B. (Ed.) (1970): especially see, Rank, D.: "How not to keep them down on the farm", pp.159-62; and Chomsky, N. 'From After Pinkville', pp.126ff.)
5 cf. Sachs, I. (1972): 47-8   6 cf. Galtung, J. (1973): 101.
7 For ex., "At the heart of his *General Theory* Keynes placed "three fundamental *psychological* factors, namely, the psychological propensity to consume, the psychological attitude to liquidity and the psychological expectation of future yield from capital assets". (F.H. Knight; *The Ethics of Competition,* London, 1935, p.158, quoted in Watkins, J.W.N. (1973): 159; emphases added).

propositions to propositions of other sciences (i.e. theoretical reductionism)[1].

In practices such as architecture, urban planning and design it is rather a new development. What happens is that either problems that have already been defined by these practices are *rephrased* in psychological terms to fit one of several psychological models and frameworks (such as to Stimulus-Response, motivation, or attitude); or *new* (and often, non-) problems are defined by looking at physical, architectural and urban phenomena from the viewpoint of psychology. In the first strategy, non-scientific nature of said practices dominate the scientific pretensions of psychology, while in the latter, non-psychological issues are explained as psychological problems[2]. However, a growing amount of empirical as well as theoretical work is presently trying to establish an independent discipline of 'environmental psychology' with strong academic support[3].

The effects of psychological reductionism, however, extends well beyond the academic domain. By *displacing* vaguely and only marginally psychological questions from the domain to which they belong, such reductions lead to false explanations and even to justifications for wrong policies. For example, urban problems, housing shortage, deterioration of residential quality, are all represented as factors of 'crowding'[4], 'choice'[5], 'preference', 'satisfaction'[6], 'class differences in environmental perception'[7], 'territoriality' or 'privacy'[8]. In this way, the political nature of the decisions and the choices concerning these problems are effectively distorted and displaced.

4.5.4 Linguistic reductionism

In another form of reductionist mechanism structure of theoretical discourses and their 'concepts' are reduced to everyday language, and 'words'. This mechanism is based on the fallacious assumption that ordinary language can express all human thought, as well as all activities and phenomena. It is on this basis that empirical researches are conducted within psychological or sociological problematics that solely rely on the resources of 'subjects', and in order to manage the unlimited variety and flexibility inherent in everyday speech several methods such as 'adjective lists', or 'semantic differentials' are devised. This may often lead to a *non-theoretical* research practice in which subjectivism and positivism dominate the procedures as well as the 'findings'[9].

1 cf. Wolman, B.B. (ed) (1965): 18-19.
2 Several illustrative examples to psychological approaches have been given in nearly all sections of this study. However, a couple of examples would be useful here:
− 'Bedroom size and social interaction of the psychiatric ward', (Ittelson, W.H .*et. al.* (1970)),
− 'The effects of windowless rooms and unembellished surroundings on attitudes and retention', (Tognoli, J. (1973)),
− 'Design of a programmed environment for the experimental analysis of social behaviour', (Brady, J.V. *et. al.* (1974)),
− 'A better sociopsychological climate in our housing estates', (Olivegren, J. (1971)),
− 'Belief and behaviour as determinants of environmental attitude', (Bruvold, W.H. (1973)).
3 For some of the conditions of this development, see Ch. 5.
4 cf. for ex., "Crowding was conceptualized as an experiential state, involving the individual's perception of spatial restriction, which results from a disparity in his supply of and demand for space . . . Three experimental factors were manipulated: room size, task set, and sex of subject". (Stokols, D. *et. al.* (1973)). For a review of 'crowding' literature (which itself commits a reductionism by discreetly excluding *economy* from the range of instances), see Fischer, C.S. *et. al.*(1975).
5 cf. for ex.,'Socioeconomic status and residential locational choice', (Moriarty, B.M. (1974)).
6 cf. for ex., 'Locational stress and residential mobility', (Clark, W.A.V. & Cadwallader, M. (1972)): "The decision to move is presented as a function of the difference between the household's present level of satisfaction and the level of satisfaction it believes can be attained elsewhere".
7 cf. for ex., Goodchild, B. (1974).
8 cf. for ex. Sommer, R. (1969); Pastalan, L.A. & Carson, D.H. (eds) (1970); Esser, A.H. (ed) (1971).
9 For further discussion on the questions of individualism, subjectivism and relativism, see Sec. 4.6.3.

4.5.5   Superstructuralism

The process of psychological reduction, moralism, technicism, etc. that have already been considered constitute another, general, type of displacement or shift: one we can provisionally call *superstructuralization*. It is the process of displacing physical objects and phenomena to the realms of culture[1], 'imagery'[2], perception, or everyday life[3]. Thus, for example, "the city is considered in terms of a superstructure . . . The contradictions of the contemporary city are resolved in multivalent images, and by figuratively exalting that formal complexity they are dissimulated"[4]. Not that these objects and phenomena, such as 'city' or 'building', have nothing to do with culture, perception, etc. What is at stake is a wholesale transfer of the whole phenomena into the ideological instances of social existence. Furthermore, while this in itself is not totally irrelevant to an understanding of social reality in general, and city and buildings in particular, it cannot still be a substitute for a detailed analysis of complex interrelationships that constitute the physical, as well as the conceptual, structure of these phenomena. In fact, this position often extends to the study of certain phenomena whose complexity is initially recognized. But due mainly to the fundamental subjectivism and psychologism, inquiries are pursued in terms of what the subjects (e.g. inhabitants, users, 'people') *think about* the phenomena. It is this neo-humanist subjectivism that is the main component of the contemporary 'environmental' ideology.

4.5.6   Environmentalist reduction

While most of the reductions found in the ED can be found in other discourses, one type of reduction is more or less identifiable with the ED itself. It is the reduction of many phenomena to the *'environmental'*. As argued in the chapter on the unity and specificity of the object, *environmentalist reduction is a circular mechanism by which sum total of a large number of things is designated as 'environment', while (and, because) those things are believed to be 'environment'.* This leads to (a) transferring a large range of objects into the imaginary domain of 'environment'[5], and (b) dismissing, ignoring, shifting or, at best, correlating, those phenomena which do not come under that domain.

The major effect of this type of reduction is *the constitution of the ED itself as a discourse.* A large number of objects from many disciplines and practices do establish a discourse with the notion of 'environment' as the central discursive object. One further effect, on the other hand, is the production of reductions, such as, *technicism,* as the practical counterparts of environmental reduction. As the reduction of a large variety of problems to a single, all-embracing, phenomena of 'environment' is not the sufficient condition of solving them; or no 'environmental' problem can be solved in the domain of 'environment' (which, after all, is an *imaginary* object) problems are either left at the discursive level, or are reduced to manageable domains such as technology, design, decision-making, etc. As a result, some absurd claims are made whereby problems such as housing shortage is 'solved' by design quality, pollution by better knowledge of substances that pollute the air, water or streets, hunger, energy, and housing by new developments in plastics, or

1 cf. for ex., Oakley, D. (1970); Skolimowski, H. in *Building Design,* 23.7.76.
2 cf. for ex., Lynch, K. (1964); Lee, T.R. (1968).
3 cf. "Urbanism as a way of life" (Wirth, L. (1968))
4 Tafuri, M. (1976): 137.
5 cf. for ex., "the Swedes . . . spoilt the whole thing by saying that Vietnam *was* environment, and You-Know-Who ought to stop dropping bombs on it" (Tinker, J. (1975): 600).

'environment' itself is protected by this or that product[1].

4.5.7   Shifts *(Introduction)*

Shifts between disciplines and discourses is a type of mechanism which involves an analysis of what we can call *'discursive traffic'*. This will be done in Chapter 5 while examining the relations between discourses. However, it must be stressed that such shifts are not always, and necessarily, reductionist. They can be indicative of the ability of a problematic to *exist* in several disciplines[2]. This ability is a *theoretical* one, and has very little to do with the simple question of shifts in attention, or research interests[3].

Shifts in ED are done not only at the level of disciplines and discourses (i.e. 'discursive traffic'), or at the level of objects (e.g. naturalization, environmentalism, psychologisation), but also in the *terms* and *words* (which are not necessarily concepts) of these discourses. Thus, terms used in one context is transferred to another without any theoretical specification of such a transfer. This is particularly apparent in (so-called) 'architectural theory'. In the absence of a theoretical procedure to ensure what can and cannot be borrowed, any word or term that seems to fit into the literary structure, or the subject-matter, of statements and texts are imported. Similarly in new sub-disciplines such as environmental psychology as well as in more established ones such as histories of art, architecture, urbanism and in urban sociology terms that are imported from philosophy, historiography, everyday and technical discourses, folklore, social sciences, literature . . . are absorbed easily and often without any critical scrutiny. The type of *eclecticism* this leads to is already apparent in the examples mentioned in the context of multiplicities, division of reality and the relations of the ED[4].

4.5.8   Amphibologies

One version of this mechanism is *amphibology* which is quite common in theoretical discourses. It is a kind of "terminological round trip that never leaves its conceptual starting-point", or "an empty transposition"[5] of concepts into another domain with all that these concepts carry with them, but not necessarily yielding a *new* knowledge[6].

It is by such amphibological shifts that the socio-political determinations of technical problems are displaced through an intellectualization process, and become social or psychological ones.

1 All these are commonly held positions in everyday, as well as academic,discourses. Thus, it is quite un-necessary to give extensive examples here except,perhaps, a few just to set the 'tone' of such, often commercialized, claims:
− "Protim Prevac protects both timber and the environment". (Advertisement in *Building Design*, 18.7.1975, p.7),
− " . . . paper production is not increased for environmental reasons". (BBC Radio News, 21.11.74),
− "Artist G. Stinton is compaigning to brighten up London by sticking light, bright, flexible glass reinforced plastic sculptures . . . [which] could help boost public morale in these gloomy laden days of recession . . ." *(Building Design,* 6.2.1976, p.3),
− "Peabody: the environment company", (Advertisement in *The Guardian*, 15.4.1976).
2 cf. Ch. 1.
3 as, for ex., the *'sociological imagination'* which is "the capacity to shift from one perspective to another − from the political to the psychological; from examination of a single family to comparative assessment of the national budgets of the world; from the theological school to the military establishment; from considerations of an oil industry to studies of contemporary poetry". (Mills, C.W. (1970): 13-4).
4 cf. Ch. 3, Sec.s 4.4.1, 4.4.4, Ch. 5, respectively. For the eclecticism inherent in architecture, see Horton, F. (1974): 55-6.
5 NLR (1972): 65.
6 For an example see J. Ranciere's analysis of Marx's *1844 Manuscripts* in which anthropological words such as 'man', 'object', 'alien being' are transposed on political and economic laws of production, value, and contradiction between labour and capital ((1973): 19ff.).

4.5.9 Intellectualization

One of the effects of the shift of terms can be seen in another mechanism, that of *intellectualization* of the ED. It is a mechanism whereby inherently speculative nature of the ED is reinforced by terms and concepts *that give the impression* of a theoretical discourse while what is being said is essentially a-theoretical or obvious[1]. What actually happens is a mystificatory practice through which ordinary and obvious facts or statements become 'respectable' components of a discourse. It is worth quoting at length the abstracts of some 'studies' that exemplify the point:

"It was hypothesized that the presence of architectural constructs which reduce the impact of one individual on another would moderate reaction to invasion of personal space. Examination of this hypothesis in a field study designed to place the burden of activity on the subject yielded data which generally confirmed the expectations of the study: subjects drank more often from a screened water fountain than from a water fountain without such barrier. The importance of this finding is also discussed"[2], or,

"Multivariate testing of aggregate crime statistics has added limited incisiveness to an understanding of the geography of crime. An alternative perspective is proposed, emphasising the individual crime site as a behaviour setting. Generic macro-scale settings conducive to crime are investigated using data on stripped abandoned cars in inner-city Philadelphia. The local social system of territorial control is interpreted as a central explanatory variable . . ."[3].

A similar mode of *intellectualization* is observable in statements that turn into *theoretical* what in fact is *technical*. This is a reverse process of technicism, and is equally pervasive in the ED. In another variation of this process, transportation of complex problems into the confines of a single discipline produces 'new', but displaced, problems and problematics.[4] In still another process a practice as a whole is transferred into 'intellectual', 'conceptual', 'mental', as well as 'cultural', realms. For example, architecture is said to be a "construct of the mind . . .", a process that "does not replace the experiential basis . . ."[5].

4.5.10 Philosophizing

Environmental discourse is both constituted by, and produces, a spectrum of arguments which are often dominated by pre- or non-scientific processes. *Philosophizing* is one of such processes. This form of argument substitutes moral, subjective and vague ideas for the *precision* needed in concrete analysis. A few exemplary statements can be cited here:

"I think that in spite of suffering, there is a great deal of grandeur [in poverty] that if we were rich we wouldn't possess. We need to achieve the condition of society

1 See, also, Sec. 4.5.12 below for the question of 'trivialization'.
2 Baum, A., *et. al.* (1974).
3 Ley, D. & Cybriwsky, R. (1974).
4 A section of a song by a Puerto Rican in the USA is quite a biting criticism of this mechanism:

"Mira que soy problema!	(Look at me, *I'm a problem*
Ay mi compae, pero que dilemma!	Oh what a miserable life
Me dicen una minoria	*They call me a 'minority'*
Problema en sociologia	*A sociological problem*
Quiero solo ganar unos 'bolos'	But I just want to earn a little
Pa 'la defensa, del humilda hogar".	To look after my family.)

(From *Protestleider aus Aller Welt*, Frankfurt, 1967, p.80, quoted in Castles, S. & Kosack, G. (1973): 318n (emphases added)).
5 M. Graves, an American architect, interviewed by J.M. McKean in *Building Design*, 10.10.1975, p.8: 'The architect as intellectual artist'.

exhorted by T. de Chardin; then 'Being' and 'Knowing' will be more important than simply 'Having'."[1]

"All people are builders, creators, moulders of shapes of the environment; we are the environment".[2]

"Indeed, the truly 'great' city is characterised by a particularly pronounced *genius loci.* I want to point to this fact to stress that existential space cannot be understood in terms of man's *needs* alone, but only as a result of his *interaction* with an environment, which he has to understand and accept. In this way we return to Piaget's double concept of assimilation and accommodation. Existential space, therefore, symbolizes man's being in the world . . . "[3]

These statements *repeat* some idealist conceptions, without producing any knowledge of them, and subject them to displacements.[4]

Philosophical arguments are used in the ED either to *explain* what, in fact, is *not* philosophical, or to justify what has already been produced without a constitutive contribution of philosophy. For example, architectural production is realized within the terms of that practice, and a philosophical system is attached to it afterwards[5]. On a reverse order, arguments are put forward to defend the idea that philosophies or systems of ideas are *reflected* or *embodied* in physical forms such as buildings or cities. This form of reflection or embodiment is often used to justify the idealized past, or to criticise the empirical present[6].

4.5.11 Ignoring and obscuring problems

Ignoring parts of the whole, therefore, confining problems to the limits of the rest of the parts, is one of the mechanisms that facilitate and justify reductions and shifts. For, it is always easier (theoretically as well as ideologically) to *ignore* and *proceed as if certain elements did not exist* than to find reasons for reductions or procedural omissions. Many an empirical research could not be possible without such an elimination, or abstraction, of instances, determinants, relations, areas, persons or contradictions. It is not an exaggeration to claim theoretical validity for the dictum: "Ignorance, like knowledge, is purposefully directed"[7]. Paternalism in appreciating (so-called) 'vernacular' or 'primitive' buildings, moralism in participation ideology and mystification of squatter settlements all owe their coherence to an *initial omission* or *ignorance* of the global nature of social relations, historic specificity of each social formation, complex political and economic determinations of physical settlement patterns, or subordinate position of culture, taste or aesthetics in situations of acute shortage and misery. For example, 'urban phenomena' is often studied without reference to the *rest* of the social formation in question, namely the 'rural' or non-urban settlements.

1 Architect Oscar Niemeyer, interviewed in *L'Architecture d'Aujourdhui,* No. 171, 1974, p.LXXXII.

2 Sommer, R. (1969).

3 Norberg-Schulz, C.(1971): 27.

4 cf. Lecourt, D. (1975): 47.

5 cf. for ex., " . . . J.P. Sartre's concepts of 'existential freedom' and 'existentialist responsibility' have been the basis of architectural values approached", and Educational and General Buildings of the Turkish Bank of Agriculture have been designed "starting with these concepts" (Güran, A. (1976): 136). For the so-called 'existentialist approach' see also Norberg-Schulz, C. (1971).

6 cf. for ex., "Throughout history, from Carnac to today's new towns, men have moulded their environment to convey ideas: social or religious or political or even philosophical . . . (From the advertisements of S. Jellico's book *The Landscape of Man,*(1975),or "The city grows outward, and its past is always buried within it like a kernel. The form of the town is a metaphor of memory". (Rykwert, J. (1973): 12). See also, Sec.5.3.6 on the question of reflectionism and projectionism.

7 G. Myrdal, (source unknown).

At best, the latter areas are left to other specializations to deal with. Similarly, squatter housing draws all attention while equally large numbers of people live in much worse housing conditions (such as in caves) in non-urban areas. Whole types of buildings are ignored in studies of building types — for elitist and ideological reasons. History of architecture *is* about monuments, palaces and places of culture and worship. The buildings where majority of people live is often left outside the field of attention, and not even included in typology of buildings[1]. Most 'architectural criticism' is also about 'selected' types of buildings which ED finds it easy to cope with and with much 'literary potential'[2]. They tend to shift the real problems inherent in the ignored building and settlement types to obscurity. Many 'environmental studies' follow this line and ignore whole sets of problems[3].

At the level of political and social practices such discursive processes are realized in decisions, often reinforcing and purifying the discursive omissions in a more concrete way. The 'public' building programmes in most countries reflect this bias. In 'development' (i.e. demolition) programmes, the situation is quite similar: the principles in these processes can be summed up in two Turkish sayings: "gözden ırak, gönülden ırak" (= far from eye, far from heart), or "bana (sana) değmiyen yılan bin yaşasın" (= let that snake live thousand years as long as it doesn't touch me (you).) These are exemplified in demolitions of squatter dwellings, or clearing the unemployed or the lumpen from towns[4].

All such processes of 'ignoring' 'omitting' or 'sweeping under the carpet' cannot be explained in a psychological way (as the two proverbial principles quoted may seem to suggest). Neither can they be explained solely by the insularity of administrators, failure of architects and planners[5], lack of concern of the rich[6], or by recourse to the question of differential 'environmental perception'[7]. It is the very basis of these social formations and the specific types of social relations that determine how each individual, group or class behaves in specific situations. Neither pinpointing the psychological specificity or professional competence of technicians[8], nor uncovering the 'betrayal' by politicians,can stand for a scientific analysis of particular social formations in which the basis of problems and real solutions should be sought.

1 One recent example is N. Pevsner's *A History of Building Types*, (1976).

2 cf. for ex., A.L. Huxtable, the architectural critic, who "misses whole classes of buildings". (Kay, J.H. (1976)).

3 "as if a study is made more scientific by ignoring problems". (Worsley, P. (1973)).

4 Three examples:
— 18.000 black Africans settled around Salisbury in shelters made of nylon sheets were driven off, and their shelters were demolished. The reason given was that it was "against *public* health" and that "they must go back to their villages" (BBC TV film, 4.4.1972 . See also *The Guardian*, 5 & 6.4.1972).
— "Ugandan administrative officials, district commissioners and chiefs have been ordered to round up the unemployed and vagrants in their areas, Uganda Radio reported yesterday. The broadcast monitored here, said the Ministry of Provincial Administration has instructed the officials to take "immediate and appropriate action" based on a recent decree by President Amin. The decree is aimed at clearing the jobless from Uganda's towns". *(The Guardian,* 16.4.1977).
— Gaziantep City Council has decided to compulsorily purchase Keleşhoca (a neighbourhood of 80 households in a cave-like ground across a prestigious neighbourhood, Bahçelievler), by paying TL 80.000 per household (where average price of a 2-room flat is at least TL 300.000) on the grounds that "the neighbourhood spoils the appearance of the town". *(Cumhuriyet,* 11.3.1977).

5 cf. for ex., "Urban renewal and highway planners in particular seem unaware of or indifferent to the textures and complexities of life in such areas" (Fellman, G. & Brandt, B. (1970)).

6 cf. Teymur, N. (1973).

7 cf. for ex., Goodchild, B. (1974): 'Class differences in environmental perception'.

8 cf. for ex., "In a system which almost perfectly insulated him from the needs of lower class families the social content of housing is the least of the designer's worries". (Montgomery, R. (1966): 31). For a detailed critique of false accusations of ignorance or incompetence of planners, see Mugnaioni, P. (1976). On this question, see also Ch. 5 and *Conclusion*.

4.5.12   Problem definition: absences, constrictions, trivializations

The mechanism of ignoring invokes the question of how exactly certain 'problems'
that are studied and/or practically dealt with, appear, disappear, are defined or ignored.
As in the examples given above, certain issues are simply ignored while others are reduced, shifted or displaced. But, in all these operations the guiding principles are contained
in often extra-scientific problematics. 'Problem' is a *theoretical* object that needs a
problematic to exist, to be defined, and tackled. Neither empirical observations, nor
ideological schemas such as 'M-E' relationship', can suffice to explain the operations
referred to above.

ED takes as its subject-matter certain 'problems' such as pollution, migration, shanties,
psychology of users, regional disparities, role of professional bodies on education, etc.
But, in majority of cases these 'problems' are recognized *as* problems only after the
extra-scientific discourses recognize them as such. In other words, they are *given* to the
ED, and to the studies within that discourse, by empirical or ideological recognitions
rather than by theoretical analyses. Thus, there is good reason to suspect the validity of
such problems (i.e. 'environmental problems') and to work for the establishment of a
problematic that will adequately deal with real and theoretically defined problems.
This, in fact, is what the present study aims to direct its possible contributions to.
Secondly, environmental studies come to recognize real and scientifically specifiable
problems only if the latter are formulated in empirical and fragmented terms on the
one hand, and neologistic and intellectualized manners on the other. For example,
'crowding' or 'density' (instead of 'distribution'), groups and individuals (instead of
classes), houses and rooms (instead of housing), objects (instead of products[1]) . . . are
recognized as the loci or types of problems in the ED.

Another characteristic of 'environmental problems', whose theoretical status has
just been questioned, is their minimized content, obviousness, trivial concerns, and
often, non-problematicity. Partly due to the *technical* nature of environmental (e.g.
architectural, urban and design) practices, and partly to the inherent limitations of
other disciplines and practices whose methods and concepts were introduced into these
practices, there is a dominant mode of fragmentation with consequences of minimiza-
tions or trivializations. (It must be noted that by 'trivialization' or 'minimization',as
with 'reductions',we do *not* imply the existence of an original truth of higher order. We
do not make a subjective value judgement as to what is and is not trivial — though this
is possible in the context of social, political and theoretical conjunctures. What we are
concerned with and are critical of here is the artificial elevations of certain obvious
statements to the status of 'scientific findings'.)

Technical practices necessarily deal with detailed and often small-scale 'problems'.
Yet, they should be seen in their proper status, context and level, and not as the
expressive parts of a universal M-E schema. On the other hand, it is not necessary and
useful to transfer into the environmental practices the fragmented approaches of
social sciences. The methodological individualism, essentialism, functionalism,
behaviourism and a fundamental *absence* of the conception of complex social whole
exert several negative effects on architectural and urban discourses which the latter
cannot criticize and correct within themselves. ('Findings' such as:
"among high-income respondents there is a propensity to spend significantly more
time on social interaction and participation activities and significantly less time on the
rest and relaxation than the low-income respondents"[2], or,

1 cf. Wolf, L. (1972): 188, 152.
2 Brail, R.K. & Chapin, F.S. Jr. (1973).

"The psychological benefits people derive from gardening, a leisure activity intimately involved with the natural environment, were examined through a questionnaire completed by 96 Ss ranging widely in age, background, and type of gardening. Three areas of benefits were identified and related to the kind of garden, attitudinal, and role variables. The importance of *Tangible Outcomes* was strongest among vegetable growers who also were more likely to be the least experienced gardeners. The *Primary Gardening Experiences* were most satisfying to the housewives in the sample and to home gardeners who derive greatest satisfaction from nature experiences, as a whole. The third benefit, *Sustained Interest,* deals with the kinds of fascination that gardening as well as other activities strong in intrinsic interest have in common. This source of psychological value is predicted by several *environmental attitude variables*, independent of the individual's role and of the kind of gardening he participates in"[1], or "This experiment showed that the propensity to litter is critically affected by the characteristics of the individual (young people litter more) and environmental factors (people litter less when litter cans are present and also litter less when the area is clean and well-maintained)" [2], are far from a-typical.)

In addition to the reasons given for the poverty and obviousness that pervades the ED, there is the initial *constriction of the field of problems while extending still further the global and multiple nature of the M-E problematic*. This, in return, is due to the misconception of 'complex reality' as discussed earlier in this chapter. Moreover, one of the theoretically inevitable consequences of this misconception is *the absolute validity that is accorded to isolated, trivial and inconsequential research*[3].

4.6.1 Confusions

One mechanism that cuts across the whole range of reductions and shifts is that of *confusion.* Confusion as a mechanism is difficult to define as there exists no theory to specify how exactly such a mechanism operates. We can know its effects from which the types and procedures of confusions can be identified. The confusions in the ED constitute what we can provisionally call a *'field of confusions',* that is, a field defined by those mechanisms that have the effects of confusion. A brief list of such confusions can be those of:

− *different types of phenomena:* (such as spatial forms, social structure, culture, psychology of 'users' . . . yet, almost always within the simple schema of M-E relationship);

− *different types of knowledges:* (e.g., the everyday common knowledge with scientifically produced ones, or technical knowledge *(savoir)* with scientific knowledge *(connaissance)*);[4]

− *the domains:* (for example, 'the urban' and 'architectural' domains with their built-in difficulty of differentiation)[5];

− *the levels:* (through the relativism of the 'organism-environment' problematic, nearly every object at a certain level is both an 'organism' and an 'environment' depending on its relationship to other levels[6].)

1 Kaplan, R. (1973).
2 Finnie, W.C. (1973).
3 On this last point, cf. Enzensberger, H.M. (1974): 6f.
4 cf. Ch. 6 for the status of knowledges in architectural and planning practices. See, also Foucault, M. (1972): 15n, Ch. 6, etc.
5 On this point, see Choay, F. (1973): 300.
6 For ex., "The object of study of whatever level must contain, volumetrically and structurally, the objects of the lower levels, and must therefore be itself a part of the levels above. Each object will then constitute the immediate environment of the object at the level below while forming a structural-functional part of the object at the level above". (Rowe, J.S. (1961): 421).

— *'the real' and 'the theoretical';*
— *the metaphors with what is meant*[1];
— *the visual and the structural:* (due, mainly, to the specific mode of perception in 'environmental practices', namely, figurative, formalistic, stylistic and pragmatic, the ED very often confuses the visual and physical aspects of phenomena with their structural and theoretical explanations);
— *the representation and what is represented*: (for basically the same reason as in the confusions of the real and the theoretical, and that of the visual and the structural, complex structure of the phenomena that is dealt with (e.g. discussed, studied, designed, planned, criticized) is reduced to a representation, if not always to a form)[2];
— *the points of view*[3];
— *the interfering in, dominating, supporting, constituting or conflating,* often incompatible, or incommensurable disciplines, discourses and problematics;[4]
— *the interference of different non-discursive domains and forces with discursive ones*[5];
— *the epistemological structures of different discourses, disciplines and practices*[6];
— *the multiple status of 'subject' and of 'object':* (namely, the idealism and empiricism of the subject and of the object)[7];
— *the singular and the plural:* (as in most of the central objects of the discourse, namely in 'man' which has multiple status both epistemologically, and quantitatively (i.e. man, men/women, group, society, individual(s), M-E, subject(s) (of research), etc);[8]
— *different variations of the same invariant element:* (all the variations of the M and E listed earlier[9] (such as, Environment, Nature, Space, World, Cosmos, Milieu, Built-environment) are used interchangeably, and without any principle of contextual relevance)[10].

4.6.2   Correlations, correspondences and causality *(Introduction)*

While examining the structure of the ED we have noted that the basic elements of the discourse, namely M and E are *related* with each other in hundreds of variant forms. Among those 'relations' were included *'correlations', 'correspondences'* and *'causality'*. In what follows these three types of relations will be considered as *discursive mechanisms*. What is fundamental to all these mechanisms is their internal, procedural specificity. *They relate what the same problematic separates in the first place.* Thus, the elements that are somehow related are not totally separate[11] entities or phenomena,

1 cf. Sec. 4.6.6.
2 cf. Sec. 4.6.7 below on representations. On the figurative mode of architectural perception, see Battisti, E. (1975): 161.
3 cf. Sec. 3.3.5 and Sec. 4.6.3.
4 cf. Sec. 5.2.
5 cf. Sec. 5.3.
6 cf; Ch. 1 on the unity of the discourse.
7 cf. Sec. 3.3.
8 cf. Sec. 3.3.
9 cf. Sec. 3.3.7.
10 cf. for ex., "We are *Man,* and *Man* is a part of the *scheme of things,* but *we* do not have to destroy the *soil,* wreck the *landscape,* pollute the *air, rivers* and *seas* (. . .) And if the *ecologists* are merely going to strengthen the *group of experts* giving advice to *other experts* so that *they* can structure *other people's* lives more effectively, i.e. interpose *themselves* between the *organism* and *its environment,* then how are *we* ever going to get a *society* which is responsible to the *world* in which *we* live? . ." (Ray, P. (1976), (author's emphases deleted, present emphases added).
11 *not,* for ex., as suggested by Campbell, R.D. & Roark, A.L. (1974): "the words 'man' and 'environment' are linked with a hyphen. This means that they are separate entities which are somehow related to each other in such a way as to create a new entity". (p.89).

and their very definitions imply each other[1].

ED, like social sciences[2], tries to correlate, correspond, or put into a causal relationship, artificially separated elements. But this separation itself is based on a unity that is constituted on the basis of some ideal entities in the first place. This circular process interests the present discussion insofar as it produces certain effects or mechanisms (e.g. determinisms, confusions), and insofar as the separation involves an artificial division of reality − a question that has already been dealt with.

a) Correlations and correspondences

Most common type of correlation in the ED is the one between two variables that are, in fact, the variants of the M-E structure. The types of variables are often designated as 'dependent' and 'independent'[3]. According to the conclusion that is desired to be produced and according to the problematic that dominates the operation several empirical studies are constructed on the basis of correlations.
The following examples would illustrate the variety of such 'relations':

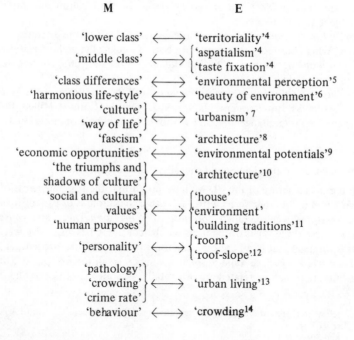

1 cf. Ch. 2 and Ch. 3.
2 cf. Hampden-Turner, C. (1970): 30.
3 cf. for ex., Wohlwill, J.F. (1973): 177f; Tekeli, İ. (1969):31f;(1973).
4 Montgomery, R. (1966): 37.   5 Goodchild, B. (1974). See also Keller, S. (1966).
6 Attributed to the 'Western man', Tuan, Y-F (1971): 38.
7 Wirth, L. (1968).
8 cf. for ex., the debate between L. Hellman and D. Wild in *Building Design,* Nov. 1976; or 'Architecture: Le temps du fascisme . . . a Venise', in *Le Monde,* 11.8.1976,p.11.
9 Porter, P.W. (1965).
10 H. Skolimowski, reported in *Building Design,* 23.7.1976, pp.8-9.
11 Oakley, D. (1970).
12 Maguire & Murray, Architects' exhibition notes on their design, ICA, Jan. 1976.
13 Newman, O. (1973); see also the discussion below on causality.
14 On this see Freedman, J.L. (1975), and Mercer, C. (1976).

'social interaction'	$\longleftrightarrow$	'bedroom size'[1]
'locational stress'	$\longleftrightarrow$	'residential mobility'[2]
'social ritual'	$\longleftrightarrow$	'architectural space'[3]
'social structure'	$\longleftrightarrow$	'urbanization process'[4]
'vandals'	$\longleftrightarrow$	'lighting fittings'[5]
'unemployment'	$\longleftrightarrow$	'city size'[6]

The variables designated by the ED *vary* not only quantitatively and internally, but also in kind. There are problems not only at discursive and epistemological, but also at methodological, levels. For example, in studies that are based on empirical surveys and data (consisting of 'responses') there are several problems which do not fundamentally concern the present analysis (for example, straightforward correlations between two 'responses' or two 'variables' do not, firstly by intent, secondly by design, tell us the *reasons* behind the responses, and behind the variables)[7]. Essentially, what happens is that for the 'M' variable 'individual', 'psychological', 'economic', 'organizational' or 'cultural' whereas for the 'E' variable all sorts of physical, spatial, visual objects or phenomena are *substituted*. This substitution mechanism is greatly assisted by the epistemological structure of the M-E couple[8], and is itself instrumental in securing correlation of the theoretical with the physical, the object of one domain with the subject of another, the element of one problematic with the real object of another practice, etc.

These confused constructions are further assisted by the inherently *figurative* nature of perception in design and planning practices as has already been pointed out. In other words, by the way in which the objects of these practices are seen, perceived (in a general, and not simply psychological, sense), and known (in the sense of *savoir*[9]), most other objects and phenomena are reduced to the physical, visual, figurative and formal. Even so-called 'architectural semiotics' reproduces this mode of perception and consequent reductions. 'Meaning' is reduced to the meaning of what is *visible*.

Similarly, social problems (such as 'crime') are represented in terms of physical and figurative variables whose solutions, then, *appear to be* necessarily physical and formal. This type of mechanism is central to the reductions such as 'environmentalism' and 'physicalism', to the 'reverse causality', and to the ideology of environment and architecture.

Correlations are constructed not only between the *elements* of the discourse but also between the *problematics* or theories. In fact, the correlation of M and E (as two elements of the discourse) can be traced to the level of two problematics (those of M and of E). The problematic of M and that of E have already been shown to exist in discourses other than the ED. It is also shown repeatedly that as far as the ED is concerned, these two problematics *presuppose* each other.

What is worth pointing out here is a question that will be discussed in the chapter on status, as well as in the *Conclusions*. As the relation between M and E is not one

1 Ittelson, W.H., *et. al.* (1970).

2 Clark, W.A.V. & Cadwallader, M. (1972).

3 Joiner, D. (1971).

4 On this, see Castells,M. (1975); Harvey, D. (1973).

5 Advertisement for Coughtrie polycarbonate exterior luminaries, *(Building Design* literature request cards).

6 Vipond, J. (1974).

7 cf. Locke, E.A. (1969).

8 cf. Ch. 3.

9 cf. Sec. 4.6.1 and Ch. 6 for the difference between *savoir* and *connaissance;* and Teymur, N. & E. (1978).

between real and/or scientifically specifiable objects, or between scientific concepts, but, rather, between ideologically given discursive objects,[1] the correlation or correspondence between M and E is bound to be ideological and cosmological. And, it is not possible to construct non-ideological explanations within ideological schemas. Moreover, such a scientific specification may require a *break* from the past status of the concept and problematic with the possible consequence of *abandoning* the 'environmental problematic' altogether. In this respect, *a M-E correlation is unlikely to have a validity in the scientific study of these phenomena that the notions of 'M' and 'E' seem to be representing in the contemporary ED.*

b) Causality

While correlations constitute a general type of mechanism, each type of correlation may function in specific ways and produce specific effects. Causality and determinism are two such mechanisms. Basically, causality involves the search for a cause for each effect observed. It is either an external universal mechanism which is assumed to be applicable to all phenomena, or one which is internal to the very problematic of the domain in question.[2]

This search for causality (as well as for correspondences and correlations) rules out the possibility of structural non-correspondences, non-simultaneity or determinations *('Determination',* however, should not be confused with *'determinism'*. While determinism is the concept of mechanical and linear effects of one element over another, determination is the specific, complex and uneven effectivity of a structure at its several levels[3]). In fact, the search for causality is only possible when there is an absence of a conception of *structure.* 'Causes' do not produce events but determine the outcome of processes[4]. Seen as a structural mechanism, it is *internal* to the organization of the phenomena[5]. It may be absent, for, a structure whose causality is in question is present only in its *effects.* This is contrary to the positivist claims of producing knowledge by accumulation and interpretation of facts which are believed to have objective existence.

In fact, it is this 'obviousness of facts' that is the objective condition of the search for empirical causes, and the component of the problematic of a given, homogenous field. It is a dangerous and fallacious starting point for a knowledge process as the scientific knowledge cannot be produced on the basis, simply, of given and obvious facts, but on the *theoretical* conception of structures[6]. Thus, an understanding of structure would replace the need to look for 'causes'. For the same token, it is quite

1 See, Ch. 2.
2 Causation or causality is one of the fundamental issues of epistemology and philosophy of science, and it is impossible even to summarize the controversies and arguments on such a question. For a brief summary, see Harvey, D. (1969): Ch. 20.
3 cf. for ex., the difference between environmental, economic or ideological determinisms that dominate social sciences, 'environmental studies' and histories of art and architecture, and the explanation of multiple, unlinear and historical determinism in the social whole exemplified by Marx's theory: "It is the mode in which they gained a livelihood that explains why here politics and there catholicism played the chief part". (1970) v.I: 86n.
4 O'Malley, J.B. (1974): 7.
5 Glucksmann, M. (1974): 149.
6 "The relations of production are structures and the ordinary economist may scrutinize economic 'facts': prices, exchanges, wages, profits, rents, etc., all those 'measurable' facts, as much as he likes; he will no more 'see' any *structure* at that level than the pre-Newtonian 'physicist' could 'see' the law of attraction in falling bodies, or the pre-Lavoisierian chemist could 'see' oxygen in 'dephlogisticated' air." (Althusser, L. (1970): 181).

dangerous, theoretically, to isolate events, objects or phenomena (such as so-called 'environments' or 'environmental problems'), and to correlate them with some 'causes'. After all, in social phenomena there is no *'single cause'*, no 'reason', and no 'goal', but complex, uneven and contradictory structures with overdeterminant relations[1]. This is not the appropriate occasion to go into this question in greater detail. What is relevant to the present discussion, however, is the way in which the whole ED is organized around mechanisms such as causality and behaviourism[2]. As already mentioned, the ED not only relates causally its objects (i.e. M and E), but also the problematics that constitute the discourse.

As exemplified by the correlations listed earlier, search for determinism and causes is the underlying mechanism of many studies and arguments. For example, one of the most striking arguments is that there is a close correlation between the rate of certain 'pathological' behaviour, such as crime, and the type and density of housing in urban areas. It would be sufficient to give only a couple of examples from popular as well as academic media to demonstrate the pervasiveness of the argument:
- C.R. Jeffery: *Crime Prevention Through Environmental Design*,(1971),
- P. Watson: 'The crime-proof city', *(The Sunday Times,* 14.10.1973),
- O. Newman: *Defensible Space,* (1973),
- O. Newman: 'Defensible Space', *(The   Listener,* 7.3.1974, the text of a BBC TV-film devoted to this question),
- 'Teach-in on how Architects can help in fight against crime', *(Building Design,* 13.12.1974);
- 'Crime-rate rises with height of buildings', *(The Guardian,* 9.12.1974),
- 'Architecture can cut openings for crime', *(The Guardian,* 21.5.1975),
- 'Newman gets backing in vandalism report', *(Building Design,* 14.5.1976).
Despite the criticisms that are directed against the fallacies of this argument[3], due mainly to its *sensational* and *ideological* value it is already popularized and recognized as the 'explanation' for the failure of high-rise, high-density working-class housing in western capitalist societies.

While the causal mechanism is itself full of problems, a further mistake is committed in constructing *reverse causalities*, i.e. *identifying effects as causes,* (or 'putting the cart in front of the horse'). One typical example is blaming urban (or international) migrants as the causes of urban overcrowding, pollution, or shortage of certain social services. Note, for example, this (allegedly) 'scientific' observation:
"The urban immigrants sequestrated land, built tin and cardboard shacks, established narrow pathways to the few water spigots, and moved in with their chickens and their goats. They brought with them disease, hunger, and illiteracy beyond any immediate social remedy. Benevolent governments moved, at length, to correct the problems according to their understanding"[4].
Or, according to another example (that is derived from a 10-year review of the *Reader's Guide to Periodical Literature* to uncover 'expert' opinions) "the effects of crowding on human behaviour" are grouped into three:

1 For the latter conception see Althusser, L. (1969): Ch. 3 & 6.
2 cf. for ex., Steward, J.H. (1955) and Studer, R. (1969).
3 Notably, though from quite different points of view, see, Brown H. (1973): 32-9; Hillier, B. (1973); Freedman, J. (1975); Mercer, C. (1976); Cooperman, D. (1974).
4 Agron, G. (1974): 242. Besides the reverse causality, note also the paternalism that is quite typical of statements on working people as a sharp contrast to those on 'human behaviour', 'man in his milieu', etc. There is good reason to suggest that the 'man' whose 'milieu' and 'habitat' that the ED so sympathetically talks about is *not* a universal being, but one designated by the type of dominant social relations.

"1. *Physical effects:* starvation, pollution, slums, disease, physical malfunctions,

2. *Social effects:* poor education, poor physical and mental health facilities, crime, riots, war,

3. *Interpersonal and psychological effects:* drug addiction, alcoholism, family disorganization, withdrawal, aggression, decreased quality of life"[1]

And, finally, "the belief that poverty, delinquency, prostitution, and alcoholism magically inhere in the buildings of slums and will die with the demolition of the slum has a curious persistence"[2] . . .

Due mainly to its rather different concern, the present analysis cannot undertake to examine the whole question at practical   or statistical levels, or to disprove arguments whose very *problematic* should be rejected in the first place. However, what is possible to say briefly is that *such a deterministic problematic is not only shallow and fallacious, it also ignores the overdetermination, i.e. what actually determines the 'structures' within which both the particular forms of settlements and the types of (so-called) 'pathologic behaviour' exist simultaneously.* A rejection of deterministic problematics requires a *discursive analysis* which the present study attempts to pursue. It also requires a theory of social phenomena (such as the Marxist theory) to relate the ideological, technical and discursive instances to the political and economic ones[3].

4.6.3   Individualism, subjectivism and relativism

If 'reduction' is a mechanism that operates *between* levels, instances and discourses, *'relativism'* is another which operates *at all* levels, or, rather, on the precondition of the *irrelevance* of levels. Depending on the epistemological peculiarities of the discourse involved, relativism is based on several structures and mechanisms. The epistemological peculiarities mentioned are already discussed as far as the ED is concerned. These can be summarized as:

1) ED has a subject-object epistemology. Subject-object structure is invariant in the variations of subject and of object,(cf. the chapter on structure).

2) The multiple status of subject and object imposes on the discourse a series of multiplicities not only in the variants of subject and object, but also at several other levels,(cf. the chapter on structure).

3) Notions of 'Man' and 'Environment' carry a large variety of contents and connotations, and are defined in many different ways, (cf. the chapter on object).

4) These definitions take as their starting point the 'individual' who is supposed to *know* 'environment', as well as *live* and *behave* in it, (cf. chapter on object).

Thus, it is possible to analyse the question of relativism in terms of

1) multiplicity of terms, status,

2) individualism and subjectivism,

3) multiplicity of points of view.

Multiplicity has already been identified as one of the structural bases of theoretical confusions. Different types of multiplicities (namely, epistemological, disciplinary, terminological, temporal and semantic)[4] are instrumental in the production of a diversity which could only be contained by equally diverse mechanisms. Relativism is, therefore, a necessary consequence of these multiplicities. As far as the variants of the 'subject' is concerned ED has 'man', 'user', 'designer', 'planner', 'inhabitant', 'people'

---

1 Reported by Zlutnick, S. & Altman, I. (1972): 48-9.

2 Fried, M. & Gleicher, P. (1961): 305-6.

3 See Ch. 5 for a detailed examination of the relationship between these different instances.

4 cf. Ch. 3.

on the one hand, and 'empirical individual' and 'ideal essence of man' on the other, which are substituted for each other. Secondly, the variants of the 'object' such as 'environment', 'space', 'milieu', 'world', 'nature' . . . are themselves substituted for each other. It is through this *double multiplicity* that the presumed M-E relationship is *infinitely relativized.* In other words, each variant of the subject is the potential counterpart of most of the variants of object[1]. Here two distinct, but related, relativisms are produced:

1) An inbuilt relativism is realized by each variant of the subject becoming the 'knowing subject' (or, perceiving, building, designing, using, or producing . . . subjects);

2) Another, theoretical/discursive relativism is produced when the (knowing, designing, planning) subject perceives the M-E relationship in terms of one of these multiple relations.

The first type of relativism constitutes *everybody* as 'Man', and *everything* as 'Environment'[2].The second type of relativism, on the other hand, assigns to, and expects from, every conceivable discipline the task of studying M-E relationship. The first one produces epistemological, as well as ideological, effects[3], while the second, a *disciplinary relativism* in which same real problem is defined differently by different disciplines and is made the object of inconsequential researches with little or no theoretical validity, and often negligible or misleading practical relevance[4]. Moreover, the first type of relativism is the underlying mechanism, as well as the effect, of what is known as *subjectivism* and *individualism.*

These epistemological positions arise out of adopting the 'individual' both as the *source* and the *object* of knowledge and as the locus of knowing process. Yet, as the individual is necessarily unspecifiable, **ubiquitous**, and *relative* to the scientist, researcher, designer or planner as well as to the disciplines and problematics involved individualism and subjectivism become the positions from which many theoretical fallacies originate. (The discussion above on types of reductionism were full of examples to these fallacies). Basically, **the psychological conception of individual** is the precondition of these positions. It is that conception which asserts the relativity of both the knowing subject and the known object[5] while reducing the theoretical processes to psychological and social determinants to individual ones (such as to perception, cognition, motivation, interest, etc.). In such a conception migration, for example, becomes a result of individual or group decision over the potentialities of an 'environment'[6] or the ideology of housing becomes an 'individual self-image'[7]. This is supplemented and supported by a *'cultural relativism'* according to which each 'culture' has its own conception of 'Environment' and 'M-E relationship'[8].

1 See, the diagram of relations in Sec.3.3.7.
2 cf. Ch. 2 for the structure and the mechanism of this generality. There are also several illustrative examples in that chapter.
3 For ex., in such a relativistic   framework, the labour-capital contradiction cannot exist: 'Need' of a worker (= a 'man') and that of a capitalist (= a 'man') are considered as the same (cf. Biolat, G. (1973): 47).
4 cf. the definitions of 'Environment' in Ch. 2. On disciplinary relativism of 'environment', see, for ex., Baladier, C. (1976): 42.
5 cf. " . . . each of us has many different 'worlds inside our heads', and that these notions of the world are constructed in the context of a series of ongoing transactions between ourselves and the environment". (Moore, G.T. (1974): 184); or, ". . . environment is experienced the way it is because one chooses to see it that way. In this sense the environment is an artifact created in man's own image" (Ittelson, W.H. (ed) (1973): 18).
6 cf. Wolpert, J. (1965): 161.
7 cf. Cooper, C. (1971): 14.
8 cf. Rapoport, A. (1973): 31; Lowenthal, D. (1975): 112; Hurley, J. (1972): 22-3. For an opposite view, i.e. *'cultural constancy'* of M-E relationship in different societies, see Wagner, P.L. (1972):58.

Finally, there is another structural mechanism that produces relativism and individualism, and gives them a certain epistemological effectivity. As has already been discussed
in detail[1], each discourse, discipline or practice adopts a *point of view* on the basis
either of subject (organism) or object (environment). Even disciplines are divided
according to such an arbitrary criteria. Discourses and practices of geography,
architecture, urban sociology, ecology, environmental psychology are partly constituted on this basis. It is therefore not accidental that *physical* as well as *theoretical*
points of view are used interchangeably to designate territorial divisions, to define
'environments', and to identify 'environmental problems'. Moreover, it is a determinate version of this very mechanism which is instrumental in bringing about the
ideological mechanisms of ethnocentrism, sociocentrism, ecocentrism and, to a certain
extent, anthromorphism. Some of these will now be examined.

4.6.4 Ethnocentrism

The two main objects of the ED, M and E, have differential, yet mutual, existence in
the discourse. Their mutuality is a condition imposed on them by the M-E (or Organism-Environment) problematic. Their differential existence, on the other hand, is a
result of several epistemological, semantic and ideological mechanisms, some of which
have already been examined.

The most significant mechanism of this differentiation is the type of relativism
that is incurred by the *privileged position accorded to the subject, namely, 'Man'*, compared to that which is accorded to the object, 'Environment'. This privileged position
is pervasive not only in the theoretical discourse. It can be traced back to some
religious and classical cosmologies. The ancient notion of *'animal laborans'* (labouring
animal who is the servant of Nature) gave way in modern religions to the notion of
'homo faber' (lord and master of the earth)[2].

In Judeo-Christian as well as Muslim philosophy, 'man' is the *master* as well as the
centre of the world, or is superior to all other creatures and objects[3]. Christianity
systematically asserts the belief that man is created in God's image. In this respect it
is perhaps the most *anthropocentric* religion[4]. The thought that man (that is, 'western
man') is the "nature's head and lord"[5] gave way to the humanist ideology according
to which it is the power of man's 'essence' that is capable of constituting the identity
of subject and object out of the latter's alienation[6]. Despite the secular claims of
the humanist ideology, its close resemblance to the religious cosmologies is due mainly to *the problematic they share.* 'Human essence' opposed to the 'inhuman', A to
non-A, Man to Nature (or Environment) are all structures that underlie the discourse
on man.

In (so-called) human sciences, however, 'man' has been adopted as the object of
study quite recently[7]. This emergence can be seen on the background of the emerg-

1 Sec. 2.3.c and Sec. 3.3.5.
2 cf. Arendt, H. (1958): 139.
3 "And olsun ki biz Adem oğullarını üstün bir izzet ve şerefe mazhar kılmışızdır . . . onları
yarattıklarımızın bir çoğundan cidden üstün kıldık". ("Surely, we accorded the Mankind a high(er)
value and honour . . . [we] made them superior over [and compared to] most of what we have
created"), *Kur'an-ı Kerim,* El-Isra: 70); or, "man is the master of all living creatures". *(Old
Testament).*
4 cf. White, L. Jr. (1969): 347.
5 Watts, A.W. (1973): 5.
6 cf. Althusser, L. (1969): (especially) Ch. 7, and (1976): 196ff.
7 cf. Foucault, M. (1970): 344f, 348, 386-7, according to whom it appeared after the end of the
18th century.

ence of the bourgeoisie as the dominant class. The free, rational and 'economic man' is the concept of how bourgeoisie wanted to represent itself. It can also be seen as the logical conclusion of the notion of man as the lord and master of nature which justified the way in which that very 'nature' was appropriated[1] and all working peoples were exploited.

Man in the ED is conceptualized in a variety of ways in both epistemological and semantic senses. Despite the multiplicity of its meanings[2] and its alternating position in the ever-changing points of view, *it*[3] is an object of architectural, artistic, urban, and ecological discourses just as much as it is the object of economics, sociology and psychology. 'Human' is used in the ED as a privileged adjective to designate all that is 'good', 'natural' and 'desirable' in man[4]. The M-E problematic is based on a conception of 'Environment' that *surrounds* man, but is itself *viewed, known, owned, perceived* and *built* by man. It is in man's mind and deeds that 'Environment' exists. Man is in the *centre* of the 'Environment' in conceptual, verbal as well as graphical modes of representation[5].

Furthermore, contemporary environmentalism and ecologism assert this centrality as the source of solutions to so-called 'ecologic crisis'[6]. It is suggested either that the crisis is the result of man's alienation from 'his' essence, humanity and centrality; or, rather paradoxically, that it is due, as already mentioned, to the positioning of man at the centre and mastership of earth. This paradox, in fact, is an inevitable consequence of both positions being within the *same* problematic. As to the solution of this paradox, it may be necessary to take up a radically different position, and even, to *refuse* the problematic altogether.

On this occasion, it is relevant to mention another type of centrism; it is neither the centrism of man nor of environment, but of the *'environmental' disciplines* and *practices*. In the absence of a scientific conception of what exactly these disciplines and practices, and what their objects and domains of operation are, each practice takes *itself* as the centre of a large number of problems which it claims to be able to tackle best. This mechanism leads either to the fragmentation of complex problems, or, as is the case recently, to the disciplinary reductionism such as ecologism, environmentalism, aestheticism, sociologism etc. These have already been examined above. However, what is necessary to say here is the impossibility of producing a radically new problematic on the basis of existing fragmentary, reductionist and anthropologistic disciplinary structures[7].

1 cf. Tuan, Y-F. (1970): 244f.
2 cf. Sec. 3.3.7.
3 'Man' is an 'it', that is, an object of discourse; rather than 'he', that is, a sexist designation with several ideological connotations. (Similarly, why is the God 'he'?).
4 cf. Perin, C. (1970): 16.
5 cf. Sec.s 4.3.2 and 4.6.7.
6 cf. for ex., Krieger, M.H. (1970): 323-4.
7 For a more detailed account of this proposition, see Sec. 5.2.

4.6.5 Anthropomorphism

The humanist ideology dominates not only the status of the subject, but also that of the object[1]. It not only confuses the 'ideal essence of man' with the 'empirical individual', but also accords 'human qualities' to physical objects, or to their relations. This mechanism, which we can call *anthropomorphism*, is distinct from, though closely associated with, analogies and metaphors which will be examined below.

As the basis of the 'human qualities' itself is of *double* status, (i.e. 'ideal essence of man': S1, and 'empirical individual': S2) the anthropomorphic mechanism carries with it this duality. It resembles an *analogy* when a physical property of the individual man (S2) is associated with physical objects such as cities, buildings or parts of buildings. It resembles a *metaphor* when the meaning and the symbolism carried by the content of the 'S1' is the ideal essence or 'human qualities' of man. In the first type of anthropomorphism, physical measurements or proportions of the human body are used to inspire, or to organize, architectural solutions and even the proportion systems have been devised for that purpose[2].

While *ergonomic* considerations are perfectly legitimate in studying the measurements of the human body and in systematically relating them to the objects and spaces that human beings use, these should not be extended to *qualify* those objects and spaces, as in the case of 'human scale'. When extended still further, such relations produce idealist and ethnocentric conceptions such as 'man as the measure' in physical[3] as well as quasi-physical[4] senses. In its colloquial usage 'human scale' can · hardly be conceived without reducing the urban phenomena to the lives and interactions of individual subjects *and* to the undefinable feelings of cosiness, intimacy, and smallness (often associated with the opposite of what the American cities generally represent).

The physical properties of human beings (or in fact, of organic bodies) such as the capacity to live and die are transformed into the urban processes at an analogical/metaphorical sense[5]. Similarly, society and architecture are likened to organisms with all the latter's growth and structural patterns[6]. Or, the physical universe is qualified in human terms in expressions such as "mother earth"[7]. *'Humanness'* is raised to the level of a criteria by which all that does not fit is labelled as *'inhuman'*[8]. Thus, nature[9], cities, buildings or institutions become 'inhuman' on the basis of their sizes, shapes and forms. Such objects are also labelled negatively as in "depersonalized building"[10], "human zoo"[11] or "anti-human spaces"[12]. Humanness as a positive attribute is psychologically reinforced, and then applied to objects from household utensils[13] to regions[14] or environments[15].

1 cf. Ch.2; Ch. 4.
2 cf. for ex., the systems of proportion by Leonardo da Vinci and Le Corbusier. For the 'Golden Section' and 'Modular' as pure principles, see Sec. 4.3.1.
3 cf. Gurevich, A. (1977): 8, on such conception in the Middle Ages.
4 cf. Dubos, R.J. (1967): 11, according to whom " 'Man as the Measure' implies that human beings prize their individuality above everything else".
5 cf. *The Death and Life of Great American Cities,* by J. Jacobs,(1965).
6 cf. W. Gropius's *'Gesellschaft als Organismus'* (see, Lorenzer, A. (1968): 115); or F.L. Wright's *'Organic architecture'* or *'The Living City'* (see, Wright, F.L. (1958),(1970)).
7 cf. Seymour, J. (1974).
8 On the arbitrariness of this distinction in design discourse, see Perin, C. (1970): 16.
9 cf. Watts, A.W. (1973): 6f.
10 cf. Perin, C. (1970): 30.
11 cf. Morris, D. (1969) .
12 Sommer, R. (1972): 68.
13 cf. Wolf, L. (1972): 133-36 for anthropomorphism in industrial design.
14 cf. Lacoste, Y. (1976): 169.
15 cf. "Menschlicher Umwelt" (Lorenzer, A. (1968): 59).

Thus, *personality* or *'individuality'* of Hi-Fi equipment, rooms[1], cities, housing estates[2], neighbourhoods[3], geographic regions[4], urban/rural phenomena[5] are established *as if* they were some inherent properties that could be specified.

Furthermore, once such qualifications are seen fit for objects, their *absence* is thought to be compensated by policy, design, planning and expertise; such as by "implanting of positive human values"[6] or by building rooms that "respond well to the student's own personality"[7], or by "policy and objectives aimed at producing a philosophy and ethic for the production of fully resolved socially responsible environments"[8].

4.6.6 Analogies and metaphors

Establishment of *similarity* between objects on the basis of similarities in their properties and aspects is not peculiar to the ED alone. Nor is it a special 'environmental' mechanism. *Analogies* and *metaphors* are mechanisms that are the bases of many theoretical and discursive constructions in most sciences and discourses.

Analogy is made by an operation (or assumption) that relates the properties a, b, c, d, e of object B to the properties b, c, d, e of object C, and asserts the similarity of objects B and C. This is made possible on the assumption that object C also possesses the property a[9].

Metaphor, on the other hand, is a mechanism in which the meaning of one thing or realm is appropriated to designate it to another. It carries with it the images, ideas, sensations as well as modes of discourse and representation that normally belong to the domains from which metaphors have originated (For example, psychological metaphors carry with them the individualist principles and behavioural or psychic frames of references). Similarly, the problematic and rationale of the original domain take up determinant positions in the second domain.

Both analogy and metaphor are the bases of model-building, and like models, they become dubious and dangerous discursive mechanisms when their nominal, partial and provisional natures are transformed into complete, exhaustive and permanent 'truths'. Yet, models are not to be reduced to analogies and metaphors. Moreover, scientific use of all these mechanisms in different disciplines differs considerably. The above-mentioned transformations and reductions are more prone to ideological conceptualizations in 'social' disciplines than in 'physical' ones (accepting for a moment the existing disciplinary divisions). Thus, the present discussion does not attempt to cover these three modes of theoretical and discursive mechanisms, nor does it claim the final word on their status and effects in all domains. It tries to show briefly the types of possible discursive forms that they produce in the ED.

The *similarity* that analogies are said to establish are between not only properties of certain objects, and the (so-called) 'environment', but also between whole disciplines. While in the first type of analogies similarities are sought between isolated phenomena and their properties, in the second, fundamental problematics of disciplines are transferred into the field of 'environmental' practices.

1 As in "personalized dormitory room door" and "individualized student work space" (Zeisel, J. (1975): 37).
2 cf. Lund, N-O (1970): 76 on O. Hansen's 'Open Form'.
3 ibid.
4 cf. Vidal de la Blanche, P. (1926); Lacoste, Y. (1976): 169.
5 cf. Koseki, S. (1972): 64.
6 cf. Blair, T.L. (1970): 1085.
7 Maguire & Murray, Architects, (exhibition note, ICA, January 1976).
8 From 'Messages from a sinking ship', in *Architects' News* (GLC), No. 41, 3.11.1976, p.4.
9 cf. Rosenthal, M. & Yudin, P. (eds) (1967): 17.

Whatever the type of analogy, it is used to *explain* conveniently what is difficult or impossible to explain, or to *prove* what, in fact, is untenable in the first place. Furthermore, by visual and graphical representations of analogical positions, a scientific understanding of social and physical problems are substituted by schemas which are easy to construct and 'attractive' to look at.[1] This mechanism is partly due to, and partly responsible for, the visually dominated mode of perception (in architecture, town planning and design practices) that reduces the understanding of physical/social organization to the *visible* properties and patterns of settlements. This reduction is also a function of an epistemological fallacy examined earlier: 'the obviousness' of perceptual experience and visible objects as the basis of knowledge and explanation. But, "appeal to analogy cannot function as a principle of explanation in the absence of a theory justifying the analogy by reference to similarity of internal coherence"[2]. The practices mentioned are characterized precisely by such absences[3]. Thus, analogies in the ED function in a *pseudo-heuristic* manner. They refer to certain visible objects or patterns as the source of explanation, or even of proof. In fact, this mechanism is possible only by an isolation and hypostatization of those empirically observed objects.

Often, analogies are the *only* basis of discussion and justification. They are used not only as explanatory devices, but as *evidences*. It is worth quoting in full a paragraph from the presentation of a lecture:
"Traditional cities are sprawls. The megalopolis can be characterised as an explosion of the scattered parts of the same organism. Traditional cities are flattened giants. As with the dinosaurs, they have lost their capacity for survival because of their sheer size. Traditional cities cannot work and will not work because they are the outcome of a false order and they can only perpetuate false orders. 'The exponential savagery of chaos is the outcome of false order, an order-deprived structure'. Our endeavours as architects and city planners within this order 'are doodles on the back of a cosmic phenomenon . . . unlimited doodling produces squalor'."[4]

Analogies and metaphors are so common in the figurative and descriptive discourses of architecture and urbanism that they often turn out to be the dominant mode of expression[5]. There is also a close similarity in the modes of academic and popular discourses on buildings. If the *absence of theory* is obviously one of the reasons for this similarity; the very specificity of *architecture as a complex practice* is perhaps the main one. Compare, for example, these descriptions:
"Look at those extractor fans sucking out all the cigar smoke, bad breath and hot air from this enormous building, keeping the place clean and healthy, and puffing more fog out into the haze. The haze that hangs around Manhattan and the East River. All those buildings are breathing mechanically like this one. Each one a concrete iron lung"[6].
"The light that shimmers through the tubes is of a marvellous quality. The impression of the hall is magic. We look up into the light like fish from the bottom of a pond, and the plates seem to swim in the flowing glass"[7].

1 cf. for ex., the attempts to explain or interpret the urban structure by patterns of ice-molecules, or geometric patterns of stars, polycentric networks, tapestries, (as, for ex. by K. Lynch, reproduced in Battisti, E. (1975): Fig. 95).
2 Mepham, J. (1973): 111.
3 cf. Ch. 6.
4 From a handout presenting a lecture on P. Soleri's "City of the Future, Arcology", by H. Skolimowski, 28.6.1975, London (emphasis deleted).
5 cf. "We experience and classify architecture roughly in terms of metaphors . . ." (Jencks, C. (1974) : 13).
6 Johnny Morris: BBC2, 1967, quoted in *The Listener*, 10.6.1976: 727.
7 Giedion, S. (1960): 423.

"And so these incredible battered and cobbled wooden shackeries have grown up and up all over the hillsides of Rio. Like great colonies of sea birds perched high on the cliffs and, like seabirds, they nest and breed and have no alternative but to endure in the filth they make themselves . . ."[1]

At   more doctrinaire (though equally *untheorized* and *ideological*) statements, architecture is equated with 'frozen music' (Bacon), houses are likened to " 'machines' to live in" (Le Corbusier), urban life to a 'theatre' (R. Sennett, L. Halprin), or the earth to a 'spaceship' or mother (B. Fuller, B. Ward). Similarly, town-centres are referred to as 'hearts', parks as 'lungs', roads as 'arteries', or 'undesirable' areas such as slums and shanties, as 'tumour'[2]. Moreover, buildings are 'explained' as 'organisms', while their surroundings and interiors as 'environments' — in biological and ecological senses. The evolution of building types and technology are paralleled to the evolution of societies, species and cultures[3].

Not all analogies, in particular 'natural analogies', function as analogies. Some are simply imitations of natural forms and structures. Especially when such forms or structures are used as *design principles* what actually happens is the transfer of some natural forms or patterns into the geometric or engineering operations as alternative solutions. It must also be noted that these alternatives are occasionally innovative, i.e. they only come to realization on the basis of such transfers[4]. Yet, such obvious usefulness should not be extended to provide a 'scientific truth' about design, planning and production[5]. Similarly, architectural objects should not be seen as *reflecting* or resembling the 'world-order'[6]. Nor, can a 'circular analogy' be a substitute for a general theory. A circular analogy is an analogy in which a hypothesis stemming from a conception of the real is reapplied to that real after being transferred to another realm[7].

It was said at the beginning of this section that analogies are established not only between objects and their properties but also between disciplines. In the course of examining certain types of analogies, the relations between disciplines and between practices (such as biology and architecture, social theory and biology) have already been discussed. To these can be added the 'linguistic analogies' which either use the tools and concepts of linguistic and semiotics to explain architectural objects, or see architecture *as a language*. As the figurative mode of architectural and urban perceptions dominates the conception of the real in the ED linguistic analogies are based on the visibility of objects and spatiality of relations[8].

As we have already seen, the term 'environment' *itself* is a metaphor[9]. It desig-

---

1 Johnny Morris: Radio 4, 1970, quoted in *The Listener,* 10.6.1976: 727.
2 This type of metaphorical statements can be found in architect L. Kahn's 'poems' about cities. For a criticism of such organicism, see Derks, H. (1974): 11. See also, Morin, E. (1974): 3-5; Klausner, S.Z. (1972): 346-7.
3 For an overview of biological analogies in architecture and design, see Yeang, K. (1974).
4 For ex., the research and the structures by Frei Otto.
5 For ex., "Atomism, in its broadest meaning, or mass production as practiced by nature, is the deepest scientific truth". (J. Tjompson, *Previews of the Future,* p.37: quoted in Gutnov, A. *et. al.* (1975): 143-4).
6 cf. S. Langer, mentioned in Lorenzer, A. (1968): 91. Or, "Chartres Maze: a model of the universe?" (Critchlow, K., *et. al.* (1973): 11).
7 For example, Social Darwinism of Sumner and Spencer that, according to Marx, is a circular analogy, i.e. "an analogy on top of an analogy in which the selection hypothesis orginally stemming from capitalist society was reapplied to capitalist society after being transferred to the biological realm". (Willer, D.E. (1967): 65n).
8 On this type of analogy see, Collins, P. (1965); Daru, M. (1973). On the relation between linguistics and architecture or planning see Sec. 5.2 on relations between discourses.
9 cf. H. Lefebvre, as a response to a question by the author, London, 19.3.1973. See also, Lefebvre, H. (1970): 245-6.

nates several types of real and conceptual objects while at the same time constituting itself as a unity (though with a dubious status)[1] . Moreover, the ED uses psychological, sociological, ecological, literary, mystic metaphors. But, what is most important is the *spatiality* of most of these metaphors. The terms that refer to physical objects or spatial relations. are *themselves* spatial, that is, they literally carry spatial meaning. This is most peculiar in graphical representations which we will examine below. For example, the 'surrounding' capacity of environment is implicit in the M-E schema that is constructed by two (seemingly legitimate) notions. Yet, it is tautological conception in that, it is not only the fact of M being 'surrounded' by E that makes up such a relationship, but *E is defined and represented as an object that surrounds*. Moreover, it implies relations or properties of in/out, boundary, opening or area. As. a metaphor for a large number of objects (cities, forests, buildings, rooms, society, . .), relations (surrounding, feeding, expressing, enveloping, . . .) and other metaphoric notions (milieu, lifespace, setting, . . .), 'environment'is actually *meant* in discourse: *it is a 'metaphor which is meant'.*[2] The term 'environment' represents an 'essence',[3] and unlike other representations, it *represents* things, but also *resembles* what it represents.

4.6.7 Graphical representations

The supposed relationship of M and E in the ED has just been shown to be *explained by metaphors* and *visualized by analogies*. It has also.been mentioned in passing that it is *represented by graphical means*. Before attempting to examine the mechanisms and effects of such means, we can see some examples of these representations.

Basically, there are two types of representations in the ED:
1) The graphical representations of M or E (or their variants),
2) The graphical representations of M-E *relationship*.
The first type of representations are not necessarily the products of the ED while the second ones are. Yet, as argued earlier,[4] M and E are not accidentally or deliberately brought together to form the M-E couple. *They imply each other*. Thus, in what follows these two *types* of representations are referred to only as a convenient way of ordering the examples, and not as the elements of an absolute typology.

1) *The representations of 'Man' and 'Environment'*
(a) *'Man':*
The ethnocentric, anthropocentric and anthropomorphic conceptions of social and physical world are responsible for most of the (mis)conceptions of 'Man'. These have already been examined in other chapters and sections. As far as *representations* are concerned they tend, in a majority of cases, to originate from the images of 'Man' that religions, cosmologies and certain theoretical ideologies carry with them. Most of these systems of thought confuse the empiricism and idealism of subject, i.e. 'Man',in their representations. They talk about a 'universal essence of Man' while conceiving of 'Man' in the body either of a prophet (e.g. Jesus Christ) or a 'perfect man' in terms of 'his' measurements (e.g. Leonardo da Vinci's drawing).

1 cf. Ch. 2 on the unity and the status of the term 'environment'.
2 cf. the schizophrenic situation whereby through a homophony the 'literal' and 'figurative' coalesce; the symbolic is confused with the real, and metaphor with what is meant. (G. Bateson, referred to in Wilden, A. (1972): 59-60, 227).
3 cf. Sec.s 4.2.3, 4.2.4, and 3.3.
4 cf. Sec. 3.2.2 on conceptual couples.

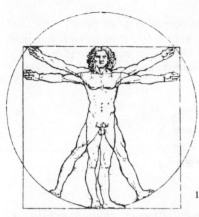

1

Of course, depending on the type of variant that is recognized or desired to be expressed graphical representation of 'Man' varies. In one it becomes a scale, in another a collectivity.

3

5

6

7

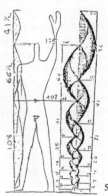

1 Leonardo da Vinci's 'Man', used in a large number of places as symbols, trademarks or representations of 'Man'. (For ex., in Manpower agency, *New Society, Design Activity Conference* (London, 1973), or its variant in *ODTÜ Mimarlik Bilimleri Bölümü Önerisi* (Ankara, 1975).).

2 An American poster depicting a crucified man among the industrial wastes polluting the 'Environment', (source: Yanker, G. (ed) (1972): 203).

3 Cover design for DRS/DMG *Design Activity Conference,* London, 1973.

4 "Welcome to the human race . . .", design for USA Environmental Defense Fund, 1970, (Source: Yanker, G. (ed) (1972): 205).

5 Le Corbusier's 'Modulor Man', cf. his (1954), or Hatje, G. (ed) (1963): 201.

6 Perspective drawing of Arne Jacobsen's design of Mainz Town Hall, Copenhagen, 1969.

7 'Scale Man' in instant lettering.

(b) *'Environment':*

'Environment', defined almost always in a relativistic manner is one thing for one, and another thing for another person or analysis. It is *everything*. Thus, its representations can be expected to be as varied as its definitions. Usually, its 'surrounding' function[1] subordinates its other functions. Thus, it is represented either as a circle, or a circle with an 'organism' *in* it.

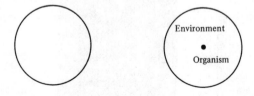

As 'environment' is the all-purpose name for all sorts of natural, physical, architectural, urban or psychological objects or frameworks, it designates all such objects often at one and the same time. (For example "Environment is where you live and where you work. It is intolerable housing conditions, where noise from the TV upstairs or the children next door can be worse than Concorde. It is unacceptable factories and pits and workshops all over the world. Environment is a big word and we must accept all that it means to all people. It is a word with many levels. It leads some of our friends to campaign for world wild life, to protest against factory farming, to be vegetarian and not wear furs. Others translate their concern in demonstrating against chemical defoliation in Vietnam. For some it is not having an airport or a motorway too near; demonstrating against planners who want to pull down old houses. To others environmental progress is having an indoor lavatory and being put on main drainage; or having somewhere to park their car, without necessarily wanting everybody else to have a car. The spectrum of concern ranges from the person who drops his picnic papers on the ground to the factory owner who hopes that the local river can drink up all his problems".[2])It is therefore no accident that 'environment' (or its variants such as 'World', 'Earth', 'Cities", 'Trees') is the object (or, often, the *intention*) of many graphical or pictorial representations.

1 cf. Sec. 2.4. and Appendix.
2 Labour Party (1973): 3 .
3 Environment, 119 Fifth Av., N. York, 1970, (Source: Yanker, G. (ed) (1972): 204).
4 Environment, USA, 1970, (Source: Yanker, G. (ed) (1972): 204).
5 Advertisement, *The Guardian,* 15.4.1976.

2) *The representations of M-E relationship:*

The relationship that is assumed by the ED to exist between M and E is *implicit* in the conceptions of M, and especially in that of E. Graphical representation of such a relationship thus carries with it the principles that guide the emergence of certain geometric or figurative conceptions of M and E. The dominant form in such representations is a combination of those of M and E as exemplified above. Basically, M is *surrounded* by 'Environment' (or, an 'organism' by a milieu) often in the form of a circle.

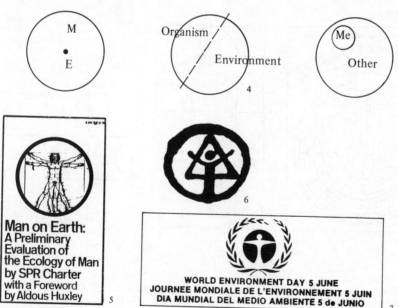

1 Publicity illustration for 'World Environment Day', 1976, by E. Lutczyn .
2 *Harper's Magazine,* May 1970.
3 Safeway Supermarkets bag.
4 cf. Wilden, A. (1972): 221.
5 Cover design of Charter, S.P.R. (1972).
6 Symbol of the UN Human Settlements Conf., Habitat, Vancouver, 1976.
7 World Environment Day, The UN Environment Programme.

The variants of 'Environment' are graphically related not only to 'Man', but to Man's culture, belief systems, world-views and ideologies. For example, cities, settlements or buildings are represented in complex, and often totally symbolic, ways. *Pure principles,* and *correlations* (between geometric form and belief system) are constructed out of the geometric analyses of ancient settlements. These pure principles and correlations then provide the *bases of explanation* of the same settlements – this time as the design and planning principles of harmonious and 'ideal' objects, or as models of universe.[1]

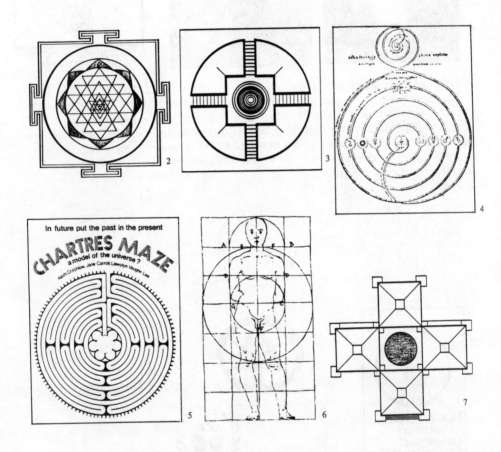

1 cf. Sec.s 4.2. and 4.3. For examples, see Jung, C.G. *et al.* (ed) (1968): 266-75; Stewart, T.C. (1970); Rykwert, J. (1973); Critchlow, K. *et al* (1973); Tuan, Y-F. (1971).
2 The Shri Cakra yantra (a form of mandala) . . . symbolising 'wholeness'. (cf. Jaffe, A. (1968): 268).
3 "The Dogon Model for a World System", (Source: Stewart, T.C. (1970): 32).
4 Spiral as the symbol of the universe, (Source: J. Purse, lectures at the ICA and AA).
5 cf. Critchlow, K. *et al* (1973).
6 "A plan for a circular church or basilica based on the body's proportions, drawn by the 15th C. Italian artist and architect F. di Giorgio". (Jaffe, A. (1968): 275).
7 Plan of the Bath House at Trenton, N. Jersey, by Louis Kahn. (Source: Stewart, T.C. (1970): 62).

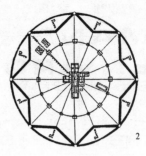

2

Environment and Man are also represented in less symbolic and more *figurative* manners.

3

4

5

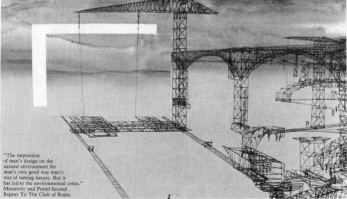

6

1 Fortress town of **Palmanova**, **Italy**, (built 1593), (Jaffe, A. (1968): 271; or Crosby, T. (ed) (1973): 23).

2 "The Sforza of Milan commissioned the architect Filarete in 1457 to construct 'an ideal city for the tyrant', . . . The two superimposed squares form an eight-cornered star, signifying planetary constellations. The palace stronghold has the plan of a gnomon, above which would have risen a stepped tower, a world mountain". (Moholy-Nagy, S. (1969): 69).

3 Publicity illustration for World Environment Day, 1976, (by **B**. **T**ag El Din).

4 Cover design, *New Scientist*, 12.6.1975.

5 Environment , 119 Fifth Av., N. York, 12.6.1975.

6 "The imposition of man's design on the natural environment for man's own good was man's way of

¹

However, it is not only the E which is depicted to be *surrounding* and *encompassing* M, it is also assumed, this time in a psychological sense, that through perception and behaviour, M *conceives, construes* and *constructs* E (that is, schools, homes, streets, . . . the world) *in* 'his' (or 'its')[2] head.

Finally, M-E, S-E or organism-environment relationships are conceived in terms of, and represented by, *diagrams,* that is, by *schemas* through which categories and notions are connected. As will be argued below, these diagrams impose upon these categories and notions preconceived types of conceptions. For example,

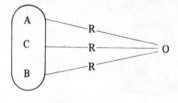

(O: Organism
R: Relation
A, B, C: Environmental phenomena
ARO, BRO, CRO: Environmental relations of O
The ellipse is the class 'operational environment'
of O)[5]

taming nature. But it has led to the environmental crisis" (Mesarovic and Pestel, Second Report to the Club of Rome), (Publicity illustration for World Environment Day, 1976) (by H.G. Rauch).
1 Poster for a British Psychological Society Conference, Oxford, 1973.
2 cf. Sec. 3.3.3: footnote for the *sexist* conception of M in the ED.
3 Cover design, Bycroft, P. (1973).
4 Cover design, Porteous, J.D. (1977).
5 Mason, H.L. & Langenheim, J.H. (1957): 331

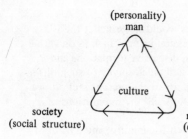

(personality)
man

culture

society
(social structure)

nature
(environment)[1]

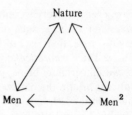

Nature

Men ⟷ Men[2]

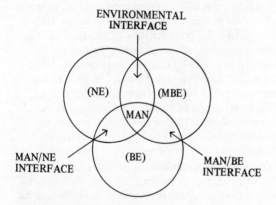

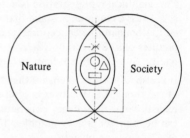

(Model of a territorial ecologic complex)[4]

**ENVIRONMENTAL
INTERFACE**

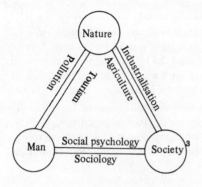

MAN/NE
INTERFACE

MAN/BE
INTERFACE

(NE: Natural Environment
MBE: **Man-Built** Environment
BE: Behavioural Environment)[5]

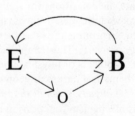

(Environment - Behaviour
Interaction Cycle)[6]

1 Adam, M.Y. (1973): 48.
2 Biolat, G. (1973): 12.
3 Moles, A. (1971): 31.
4 Marinov, H. (1974): 292.
5 Simplified from Morrison, B.M. (1974): 176.
6 Wohlwill, J.F. (1973): 168.

Now, even a cursory examination of these examples would suggest that the ED *includes* and *relies on,* such non-verbal means of expression just as much as on verbal ones. Of course, their uses differ in different contexts, discursive formations and practices. Their *theoretical* contents differ too. While a detailed survey of such differences would certainly be beyond the objectives and limits of the present section, we can discuss briefly the nature of graphical representations and their conditions of existence in the ED.

Graphical representations are one of the *tools* of scientific inquiry, and a *form* of discursive activity. Without appropriate symbols most ideas and concepts could not be *expressed* or even *thought of.* Basically, they signify "a coordination of the system *a* to the system *b, c, . . .* of other physical objects [or categories] which is possible only because all these systems are realizations of the same conceptual system A".[1] Yet, graphical representation is not a *visualization.* Just as *a* is visualisable, so are *b, c, . . .* It is a common mistake that once a representation is devised (e.g. *a*), it is allowed to dominate the conceptual relations of *A,* and the latter is represented by visual pictures of *a.* But, *a* is only a 'preferred system', not an absolute representation of reality. Symbols do not have to (and, should not) look İike that which they symbolize.[2]

It is also important to ensure that the chosen symbol is *not* essential for the content of the thought.[3] Moreover, a symbolic representation does not need to have a direct realistic value in ordinary experience[4]. In short, every object does not have to be, nor can be, representable in graphical forms. There cannot be such a condition or prerequisite put on objects.

Particularly in the spatial context graphical representations and metaphors present serious problems. Most of the spatial concepts that are in current use are *spatial,* that is, they are concepts of spatial objects while, especially in everyday discourse, these concepts have their metaphors in space. They are *present* in space (as in the terms, such as, 'urban society', 'village life')[5]. Their graphical representations, or symbols, such as 'circle', *are* spatial symbols. They define enclosures, spaces and areas. Thus, they create the conditions for a confusion of the *real* with its *concept* and *symbol.*

As we have seen in the analysis of the confusions[6] and metaphors[7] in the ED the term 'environment' is itself a *metaphor.* It is also a *name* describing *a* real object, i.e. 'environment'. Thus, graphical symbols represent certain images or cosmologies as well as objects or physical relations. In the course of this representation process the mathematical nature of geometry is reduced to the ideological task of *representing what is already given in the imagination of the subject:* the world as experienced.[8] This mechanism functions in another level too: as metaphors cannot stand in for notions[9] or for concepts, the necessity of concepts for a scientific discourse is bypassed in the ED simply by reinstating *images* from everyday discourse or from ideological systems (e.g. religions) into concrete socio-physical relations; and by conflating metaphors by what is meant.[10]

1 Reichenbach, H. (1957): 106.
2 cf. N. Hızır, (in a lecture in Ankara, April 1968).
3 cf. Reichenbach, H. (1957): 107.
4 cf. G. Bachelard, in Lecourt, D. (1975): 53.
5 cf. B. Hillier, in a seminar in London, 18.3.1974.
6 cf. Sec. 4.6.1.
7 cf. Sec. 4.6.6.
8 On this question see, Hindess, B. (1973b): 324-5.
9 cf. G. Bachelard, in Lecourt, D. (1975): 106-7.
10 cf. Sec. 4.6.6, and Wilden, A. (1972): 59-60.

In short, representations of M-E relationship reproduce the empiricist problematic by serving as the *models* of the real. As we have already discussed, models tend to correlate empirical givens with theories, or real objects with images[1]. Especially when models are themselves graphical, i.e. visual, they tend not only to abstract, to simplify, and to correlate, but also to help 'visualize' a real that is given in images. Some features of empirical reality are first transformed into models, and then visualized *in terms of* these models[2]. In the absence of a theory, all these models, representations, metaphors and analogies function as *explanations* of an 'environmental reality' with a presumed validity.

'Environmental practices' do, in fact, use graphical means and representations for purposes other than the cosmological and epistemological. They produce their proposals, plans, projects and designs in *drawings*. Drawings can vary from perspectives to working drawings, from maps of countries and regions to street elevations, or from geometric and topological representations of the world to the graphs and figures of industrial production, land use, traffic pattern, or heat-loss in buildings[3]. These models of representations are as necessary to the practices involved as writing is to literature. Therefore, the present critique of graphical representations in the ED does not imply a wholesale dismissal of such modes of representations. However, it is here that we can link the powerful domination of graphical representations of 'M-E relationships' or 'environment' to the *nature of the practices* that give them currency and support. It is not accidental that the ED finds it convenient to represent its conceptual and cosmological schemas in graphical medium. As pointed out earlier, architecture (like other environmental practices) bases most of its knowledge (i.e. *savoir,* or know-how[4]) on its *figurative mode of perception*[5].

Once dominated by this mode of perception, environmental practices tend to give form to, and convey, not only the information and proposals that they normally produce, but also some *non-technical ideologies*. On the one hand, quite *functional,* and *primarily technical* representations are produced (such as military maps, political definitions of territory, or designs to satisfy the demands of 'clients'[6]) – a role which basically technical practices in a class-society can hardly avoid taking on. On the other hand, this capacity to produce and to communicate with visual means enables these practices to *read* and *represent* the world, objects and society in graphical terms. In other words, it is a *philosophy made visual.*[7]

In various ways, this mode of recognition and representation provides the only 'evidence' of the validity of the M-E conception which provides the framework for the recognition in the first place. This tautological process is further demonstrable in a specific shape that is used very frequently: *Circle* is a shape which has a direct, realistic and experiential nature, and which commonly represents an enclosed space. Most significantly, it has a geometrically defined *centre*. It is this centre (alongside the circle itself) which carries many metaphorical, cosmological and mystical

---

1 cf. Sec. 4.3.3.

2 On this function of models see Althusser, L. (1969): 120-1; (1970): 39n.

3 For detailed discussions on different modes of representations, see, for ex., Harvey, D. (1969); Ch. 14; Lacoste, Y. (1976): 23, 155f, 163-74.

4 For the specific differences between scientific knowledge *(connaissance)* and, technical knowledge and know-how *(savoir)*, see Ch. 6 on the status.

5 cf. Battisti, E. (1975): 161.

6 On these, see, for ex., Lacoste, Y. (1976); Soja, E.W. (1971); Wolf, L. (1972).

7 There are several 'trends' in Western capitalist societies interested in cosmological geometries. These geometries are usually derived from studies of Oriental or Medieval belief systems, religious architecture or superstitious symbolism. Even a 'philosophical geometry' is proposed. (Vandenbroeck, A. (1972)).

connotations.[1] Thus, as with most of the spatial terms 'circle' is both the *name* of the shape just referred to *and* an idea, a notion or a *concept.* Moreover, it is mathematically definable. It can thus exist in the form of a formula, or in the memory of a computer. On the whole, it is both a *real* object and a *theoretical* object.

It is in its metaphorical function that most problems arise. The 'real' that it is assumed to represent is *not* a physical object, with any fixed shape, or form. The circularity of 'World', 'Environment' and 'Space' are all *symbolic,* and it is this very symbolism that is in question here. For, the latter is the locus of a *relativism:* For example, one of the most common areas of use is in designating in-out relationship. It is assumed that circle defines an 'inside' and an 'outside':

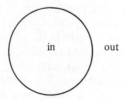

Yet, in a *large and undefinable* universe (such as 'Nature', 'World', 'Environment' or 'Space') 'in' and 'out' are relativistic depending on
(a) whether such a boundary is conceivable and perceivable at all,

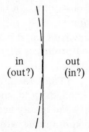

and,
(b) where the 'knowing subject' is located (i.e. the relative *point of view*).[2]

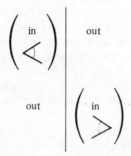

In order to sustain such a fallacious conception, *external* supports are needed. Legal ideology (property rights), political division of territory (artificial boundaries between countries) or physical barriers (walls, fences) are examples of such supports[3]. Thus, the discourse on 'environment' is bound to reproduce at least one such support in order

1 cf. Sec. 4.3.2.
2 cf. Sec.s 3.3.5 and 4.6.3.
3 cf. Sec. 4.4. on division of reality.

to adopt 'circle' as one of its representational objects.

The M-E relationships, when represented by a circle, carries with it all the problems associated with that shape.

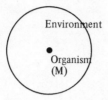

As already argued, the boundary between the thought objects 'M' and 'E' are nothing but imaginary[1]. And, depending on whether a particular discipline or knowing subject takes the position of the organism (M) or that of E, *different* in-out, or boundary relations are defined. Hence, the relativism just referred to.

Finally, the graphical representations in general, and circle in particular, must be seen as the products of attempts to reduce the complex structured whole of physical and social phenomena to simple and recognizable symbols. They carry with them several theoretical problems that the ED is hardly able to foresee and to tackle in its inherent (in)capacities – especially when the discourse is partly *constituted* by such problems.[2]

1 cf. Sec.s 4.4.1 and 4.4.4, and Wilden, A. (1972): 219-20.
2 cf. Sec.s 2.3; 2.5 and Ch. 6.

5 The Relations of the Environmental Discourse

"Turkish TV has stopped broadcasting
the BBC's production of Dr Jacob
Bronowski's The Ascent of Man
because authorities found the
Darwin theory of evolution expounded
in the series objectionable, . . . "[1]

5.1 'Relations' *(Introduction)*

It must be clear by now that no meaningful statement, let alone a theory or
a discourse can exist by itself. As a formation, *discourse is a network of*
relations – both internal and external. The *'internal'* relations are what
constitute the structure and mechanisms of a discourse. These have already been
examined in previous chapters, and there is no need here to repeat or summarize
them. The *'external'* relations, on the other hand, are those relations that a
discourse is bound to establish, or that it finds itself in. They are the relations
between discourses and between discourses and non-discursive formations.[2]

The following discussion will attempt to analyse this second type of relations
without in any way invoking a hierarchy of importance or pertinence *vis-a-vis*
the relations between the ED and the present analysis. In other words, for the
present analysis there is no question of discriminating the types of relations for
the purpose of raising the status of one at the expense of the others. This caution
is essential if the danger of claiming the determinant primacy of one particular
type of relation is to be avoided.

Perhaps the preliminary condition of the existence of relations is the fact that
there *are* distinct discourses and disciplines. A discussion on the reasons and
conditions of such divisions is beyond the objectives of the present study. Yet,
as far as the relations of the ED is concerned it is possible to identify some of
the significant conditions of their existence. The objects around which the ED is
constituted ('Man', 'Environment', 'Space') are the objects of *other* discourses and
disciplines too. This is partly due to the multiple status of its objects and partly
to the system of concepts (problematics) that they share. Thus, seemingly artificial
divisions are related with each other at the level of the objects and concepts they

---

1 *The Guardian,* 24.1.1976.
2 See Sec. 3.1 for the clarification of the distinction 'internal/external'.

deal with in their own ways. *This unity, however, is a unity around an imprecise object and an incoherent problematic.* It is on this background that we can see the conditions under which the relations of discourses are established.

5.2 Relations between the Environmental Discourse and other discourses

While examining the unity of the ED[1] it was said that the ED was situated within a discursive field which crosses, and is crossed by, several disciplines and practices. It is not a pure and independent discourse. The problematic around which it is constituted, namely that of M-E relationship, is the problematic of several other discourses as well as disciplines and practices. In other words, the relationship between these discourses and practices must primarily be seen not in terms of their institutional definitions — though they are also relevant to our analysis here,[2] but, rather, in terms of the problematics they share or recognize. Moreover, they share not only the same problematic, but often the same terms. In order to see *how* exactly these relations or connexions are possible we must look at some mechanisms which operate in the ED, and some structural conditions. As these have already been shown in detail and with illustrations, the following discussion will be a brief one.

There is no precise object 'environment'. The discourse on that object is not precise either. ED is a generalist discourse situated in a generalist field. Through its problematic and terms the ED operates in a large number of disciplines and practices, for example, in planning, architecture, ecology, biology, sociology, economics, psychology, as well as in everyday discourse. Through so-called 'environmental education' an already *vague field* is established as a *discipline*.[3] This is expected to compensate the traditional insularity and detachment of architecture and design from all sorts of theoretical and scientific developments taking place in other fields.

The field (that is comprised of all those activities, practices, terms, techniques, discourses, institutions that are called 'environmental') is defined as a disciplinary unity. This is followed by the assumption that this new 'discipline' is capable of getting into contact with other disciplines. While the field itself is a questionable unity, its legitimization, and the relations that are based on this assumed legitimacy, is bound to be regarded with utmost caution. In the course of establishing relations the ED becomes impregnated, and occasionally dominated, by one or more of these domains through their notions, frameworks, images, modes of expressions or techniques. There develops a kind of *'discursive traffic'*, to coin a metaphorical term, between these domains. Shifts, reproductions, analogies and substitutions take place in the marked *absence of a theory to specify the rules* of the 'traffic'.

Everyday discourse, for example, not only dominates the ED by providing it with notions and images, it even incorporates that discourse into its practices. 'Everybody', in every conceivable context, talks or writes about 'environment' and 'M-E relationship' for an infinite variety of objectives. Certain geographic,[4] architectural,

1 in Ch. 1
2 See Sec. 5.3 below on the relations between discourses and non-discursive formations.
3 cf. Perin. C. (1970); Gutman, R. (1968); Broady, M. (1968), (1973); Hurley, J. (1972); Martin, L. (1958) for different positions on the question of education that relates social sciences and architecture.
4 cf. Lacoste, Y. (1976): 24. See also "The universe of geographical discourse, in particular, is not confined to geographers it is shared by billions of amateurs all over the globe" (Lowenthal, D. (1975): 105); or "The lay image of architectural production is nourished in mass-media which forms the references of social imagery for architectural production." (Aubert, J. et. al. (1968): CXXXIX).

ecologic or design[1] images are imposed and sustained by mass-media, quasi-scientific publications and consumerist policies. By an unquestioned assumption that social sciences provide relevant frameworks, concepts and techniques, 'environmental problems' are defined and tackled in sociological or psychological terms.[2] This is done either by one social science[3] taking as its object a given problem initially defined as 'environmental'; or 'environmental practices' adopting the techniques, concepts or explanations of social sciences. It is not accidental that a general schema such as 'M-E relationship' could find prominent places in most 'social sciences' as well as in several other discourses. For example, it found itself easily at home in sociology which is based on the individualistic study of human groups, and in economics which is a study of 'rational economic behaviour'. Psychology was a natural ground for such a generalist cosmology as it is in fact a discipline centered around individual behaviour and individual - environment relationship in the first place. Political discourse, with the object of defending class interests of the bourgeoisie, took it immediately upon itself *to defend 'environment' in word while destroying it in reality* for the last three centuries. Moreover, evolutionist positions in social sciences found a close affinity between their ideas on 'environment' and the environmental ideology which they came into contact with, or contributed to. In the course of these adoptions, however, each discipline and discourse transformed and shaped the ideological notion of 'environment' into their own particular objects. Although most of them *kept the term,* they *changed the content* to suit their 'needs'. Yet, some have been effected by the developing ideology of environment, and their objects started to include, or reflect, this ideology. Sociology found it natural to see *'Society' as an environment* of individuals, groups or institutions.[4] Economics placed economic behaviour, organizations (firms and clients) in their 'environment', and attributed all constraints on them to the environment.[5] Psychology was quick to turn its concern with 'environment' (of individuals) into one with 'built environment', and initiate the sub-discipline of 'environmental psychology'.[6]
There are various other approaches that develop out of applications of disciplines, discourses or systems of thought to one another. For example, semiotics to architecture[7] (which regards space and buildings as symbolic systems), games theory to geography,[8] or systems theory to geography,[9] and to architecture.[10]
As a result of such interactions either environmental problematic is incorporated into, or remoulded by, basically 'non-environmentalist' domains, or new disciplines or sub-disciplines are established as already mentioned.

1   cf. Wolf, L. (1972).
2   cf. for ex. "The behavioural sciences hold great significance for the architecture of the future" (H. Horowitz, quoted in Sommer, R. (1972): 20).
3   The questions of to what extent such disciplines can be called 'sciences' and whether they are adequate to their *own* tasks are open to discussion which we cannot pursue here.
4   On relations established between sociology and 'environment', see, for ex. Klausner, S.Z. (1971); Perin, C. (1970); Broady, M. (1968).
5   On the application of the problematic of economics to architecture, see, Oishi, I. (1970); on the relation between economics and geography, see Chisholm, M. (1970); Harvey, D. (1973).
6   On environmental psychology, see, for ex. Proshansky, H.M. *et al* (eds) (1970); Canter, D.V. (ed) (1970), (1974).
7   cf. Eco, U. (1967); Lefebvre, H. (1974): 19-20; Jencks, C. & Baird, G. (eds.) (1969); Castells, M. (1975): 273 f.
8   cf. Gould, P.R. (1963).
9   cf. Stoddart, D.R. (1965); Mabogunje, A.L. (1970); Eisenschitz, A. (1973).
10 cf. Handler, A.B. (1970); Seablom, S.H. (1970).

In the absence, as just pointed out, of a theoretical mode of relating disciplines and discourses, problematics or approaches are often confused.   For example, sociological approaches are easily confused with epistemological ones. As a consequence, generalist and multiple arguments on 'M-E relationship' are developed, and the individualist and empiricist conceptions of man, society and physical phenomena are uncritically accepted as *given*. Not only in discourses and disciplines, but also in *discursive analyses* confusions may arise when, for example, the status of the internal structures and mechanisms of a discourse is   confused with its utilization in non-discursive practices. (Thus, for example, it is often argued whether there can/ cannot be 'socialist science', 'bourgeois planning', 'Fascist architecture' , etc.)[1]

As the ED often goes beyond the limits of single practices that it dominates, it leads to mistakes as to *what each practice can or cannot do.* The realization of M-E relationship, (that is seen as the realization of *ideal*   and *essential* relations), is assigned the tasks of many concrete problems. For example, physical space is seen as the expression of culture, planning is conceived as the creator of social order, while architectural forms are seen as the determinants of human behaviour.[2] Art is identified as the source of happiness, or ecology as containing the wisdom to correct the 'environmental imbalance'. Similarly, correlations, many of which are impossible, are produced between the elements of different practices and between their different levels.[3]

With all these confusions and correlations, the specificity of each domain is effectively obscured and problems are *misidentified* or *misplaced.* For example, it is concluded that the ecological crisis is due, mainly, to our ignorance of ecology and natural balance, that undesirable housing designs are due to our lack of environmental psychological knowledge, or that ill-consequences of plans are caused by the planners' incompetence. Similarly, mystical explanations are offered for all such problems and crises. Whilst originating in different religious discourses and ideologies, these modes of explanation reduce the complex social problems to factors such as 'spiritual bancruptcy', 'sins', 'alienation', 'desecration of environment', etc.[4]

Often what is correlated or exchanged between discourses are their *conclusions* – *without reference to their premises, contexts, specific levels and scales.* For example, statements on biological systems such as cells or species are carried into a discussion on social evolution or functioning of a building,[5] or observations on animal behaviour are first accorded the status of a 'science', namely ethology, and then generalized into social behaviour of human beings. (such as, concepts of and studies on 'proximity', 'territoriality', 'crowding'.)[6]

1   In this context it would be useful to examine the ambivalent relations of Marxist theory and the ideology of environment. The former has either ignored or dismissed the debate on 'environment', or adopted it *in its own terms* with, of course, serious mistakes. This question is left out of the present study as a brief discussion would not do justice to its complexify and political implications.
2 that "a particular architectural form justified by a muddled social philosophy, will make people behave in approved ways" (Hurley, J. (1972): 21). On this question, see also Lee. T.R. (1971); Broady, M. (1968).
3 cf. Sec. 4.6.2.
4 cf. Sec. 4.2.4; see, also, White, L. (1969); Blackstone, W.T. (ed)(1975); Tuan, Y-F. (1968)(1970)(1971); Cooper, C. (1971); Ritterbush, P.C. (1968) for different positions on the relations between religious and environmental discourses.
5 cf. sec. 4.6.6 on analogies. See, also, Willer, D.E. (1967): 65; Enzensberger, H.M. (1974): 8.
6 Cf. for ex., a study on 'boundaries' and 'invasion': "A field observation investigated the hypotheses that dyads resist penetration of their social boundaries and that the strength of this boundary varies with the sex composition of the dyad. On a city sidewalk, an experimenter positioned himself so that penetration of an oncoming dyad was imminent. Both hypotheses were supported; 61% of the dyads avoided penetration of their social boundary by moving the social unit. This effect was strongest for cross-sex dyads and weakest for male-male dyads." (Knowles, E.S. (1972)).

These discursive relations result in several spurious correlations and 'theories'. For example, 'stress' in the psychological sense is associated with urban crowding, or 'stress' and 'strain' in physics is associated with migration and squatter housing[1].

As has already been argued in the context of reductions, these inter-discourse shifts often end up *obscuring the fundamental nature of problems* by favouring one definition or approach in a total disregard of others. For example, consider a research programme studying people's perception and reaction to a proposed new motorway which is due to pass through a working class district. Such a study often yields a mass of psychological data on individual responses, reactions and aspirations with no knowledge relevant to (a) the conditions of existence of the motorway, (b) the concrete modes of opposing it. A *different* approach, for example, an *economic-political* one, would conclude that the motorway was planned in that particular way, (a) because of low property values[2], and (b) because the people living there were not represented in the decision making process in the first place. In both approaches the (a) implies a predominantly economic, and the (b) a political, determination. Now, what does psychology have to do with this problem and with its solution?

In a different way discursive elements and terms of 'environmental' disciplines are *used* in (non-environmental) practices, such as politics, to promote the latter's arguments. Geography and planning, for example, are the most common sources of political assertions, specifically in the popularly followed issues on border disputes, national and racial questions, regional disparities, colonialism, underdevelopment, political alliances, etc.[3] It is at this very point that discourses in general, and the ED in particular, *should* be seen as one of the social practices. An understanding of this question, however, would involve an examination of the relationship between the ED and *non-discursive* domains.

5.3.1 Relations between the Environmental Discourse and non-discursive domains (Introduction)

By its very definition, a 'relation' is not visible, or easily observable. As with the internal relations of the ED, and the latter's relations with other discursive formations, the relations between the ED and non-discursive domains is difficult to pinpoint. It is not a physical or empirical relation but one which is *itself constituted within a discourse. This* discourse on the relationship between the ED and non-discursive domains is what the present analysis deals with in this section. But unlike this study's deliberate *refusal* to take up a position within the 'environmental' debate,[4] (which would imply a *recognition* of the 'environment' as a legitimate object of discourse), the present section takes as its object *both* the relations between the ED and non-discursive domains, *and* various positions on this relationship.

To start with it is quite legitimate to ask how exactly these two domains are *distinguished.* Yet, in order not to fall into the mistake of artificially separating two empirical objects to be related again (as in the case of 'Man' and 'Environment', or 'Society' and 'Space'), the *Environmental Discourse* whose unity has already been identified[5] is seen in its relationship to *all non-discursive* domains that are identifiable as such. Thus there is no attempt to relate a discourse to 'everything' other than itself, but to see its unity, its objects, its

---

1 cf. for ex. Turan, M. (1973).
2 cf. Eisenschitz, A. (1973): 55.
3 On this specific relationship between geography and political discourse see Lacoste, Y. (1976): 85-93, 155-161. See also, Soja, E.W. (1971), and issues of the journals *Hérodote, Espaces et Société , Antipode.*
4 See Sec. 2.4 for the reasons for this refusal.
5 cf. Ch. 1.

mechanisms and effects in a *context* larger and other than that the ED itself can conceive of.

But, how can the so-called *'non-discursive'* be identified? As with all objects that can even be talked or written about, 'non-discursive' domains themselves are *specified* and *described in* discourses. Here, at this point, it is possible to identify different strategies vis-a-vis this question:

1) The non-discursive domains may be taken as objects that the ED deals with only *indirectly*, (for example, when it discusses a question such as the 'environmental' aspects of migration, it has to presume, ignore, or touch, the *'non-environmental'*[1] determinates of migration. ED either reduces the latter to 'environmental' factors such as climate, livelihood, survival, resources etc., or borrows from other discourses or disciplines (such as from sociology or psychology) the explanations of the phenomena: In either case, however, the 'non-environmental' (hence, non-environmental discursive) phenomena is expressed *in* a discourse, i.e. in the ED.)

2) Thus, on the basis of (1) the non-discursive domains may be taken as the *direct* objects of certain discourses other than the ED,

3) The non-discursive domains may be taken as objects that the present analysis deals with *besides* the ED, (for example, the present analysis *defines* several professional, political, artistic. . . domains as 'practices' or as 'formations' that are somehow related with the ED).

Whatever strategy is chosen two pitfalls should be avoided:

1) that of *'discursive reductionism'*, i.e. reducing every mode of conceptualization to discursive forms, (for example, how can the existence and multiple effects of repressive/mystificatory political regimes be reduced to the *discursive* aspects of their repression/mystification?)

2) that of *correspondance* between non-discursive objects as real objects (independent of discourses) on the one hand, and as discursive objects on the other. In other words, the analysis of the relations between the ED and non-discursive domains should not be confused with the establishment of correlations between the ED and some real objects that are assumed to be the objects of the discourse.

As a whole, the question posed in this way and pursued in terms of the strategies defined is full of critical problems that are basically *epistemological.* This implies taking up an epistemological position and applying it to the definition of 'non-discursive'. Yet, for the reasons that cannot be dwelt upon here, it will be more fruitful for the purposes of the present study to *re-pose* the question in the following way:

1) A discussion (on those non-discursive objects and domains) that is counterposed to the ED must be saved from the determination of that discourse. They must *not* be defined as those objects that the ED seems to exclude while defining them as its other-than-itself, in other words, keeping them within its problematic.

2) As most of these 'non-discursive' objects and domains themselves are conceived in some sort of discourses, they are non-discursive not in the sense of having nothing to do with a discourse, but in the sense that their discourses are not within the field defined by the ED. As such they are the objects of 'non-environmental discourses'.

3) As these 'non-environmental discourses' are in fact discourses, and as they may constitute other formations such as disciplines and ideologies, their relations with the ED can be analysed as *'relations between discourses'*, i.e. the subject matter of the preceding section.

4) Yet, as for the differential effectivity of each object or domain (whether expressed in a discourse or not), we have to look to the concept of 'social formation' and to the concept

1 Of course, this very term is within the environmental problematic: *what is 'non-environmental'?* (cf. Sec. 2.4).

of 'discourse' understood as a practice. This last point can then be considered in two distinct discussions:

a) *The effects of the ED* : This involves the discursive effects of the ED, as, for example, in creating a discourse on 'Society - Environment relationship', or constituting the substance of an 'environmental ideology'. These questions are discussed on various occasions in this study.

b) *The materiality of the ED* : This involves the social existence of the ED as a practice.[1] This will be examined here.

Before starting to examine this question one point should be made sufficiently clear. Neither in the relations between discourses, nor **those**   between discourses and non-discursive domains should there be a necessary *determinism*. A discourse or a domain can not be assumed to determine others prior to the theoretical examination of the whole relationship involved. This is particularly important in the following analysis of the social existence of the ED. To consider the latter as a practice in society does not need to entail a social determinism, nor, in fact, a discursive determinism.

Another significant pitfall to avoid is the tendency to establish a correspondence or symmetry between the ED and non-discursive phenomena (as has already been pointed out). Each of these unities has different 'time', different determinants and different structures. Their relationship may, or can, be one or more of reproduction, support, homology, incorporation, subordination, repression, sanctioning, deformation, regulation, control, relative autonomy, effectivity, mediation, promotion, approximation, resemblance, representation, omission, *etc.* This 'etc.' is not an indication of an a-theoretical approximation; but a warning that most of the relations between the domains in question have never been theorized, and that they should not be reduced to simple and singular explanations. In this sense, the following analysis is *provisional*. It does not pretend to be anything more than a step forward with respect to the contributions of the previous analyses.

5.3.2 Environmental Discourse as a 'practice'

The ED, as other discourses, is a *practice*. Like other practices it does not fall from the sky, or is invented out of nothing. It is constituted, modified and articulated within/in spite of/ together with/against, *other* practices.[2] It is a *formation*. As such, it has an articulated structure which can, and should, be analyzed. An analysis of this practice and this formation that we call 'ED' involves an identification of what exactly gives that discourse its *status*, its *legitimacy*, its *function*, its *currency;* and what exactly *derives, organizes, institution-alizes, transforms, ignores* or *promotes,* it.

Similarly, it involves what the ED can do, or in fact, does, in spheres *other than those* that it includes within the field of 'environment': Why, and how, does it effect the *functioning, distortion, division, legitimation, mystification, understanding, shift* or *substitution,* of questions.

Once posed in this way the ED loses its uniqueness and can be seen in the same way as other discursive formations and practices can be. For example, we know that the terms 'justice', 'freedom', 'individuality', 'free-will' . . . are the historically produced expressions of the bourgeois. And, we know that they are contradictory expressions, yet, are more than simple lies or deceptions; and are necessary for the functioning[3] of the capitalist mode of production especially during its pre-monopoly stage. More will be said about this in a

---

1 The term 'materiality' can be provisional for want of a better concept. It should not be taken to sufficiently express the 'social existence' referred to here, or to imply a materialist reductionism.
2 On this question see Foucault, M. (1972): 162-5.
3 cf. Therborn, G. (1971): 75.

moment. For the time being we must pursue the question of 'practices' further.

First of all, there can be no practice *in general* (as is usually assumed in a variety of discourses including, partly, in the Marxist one), but only *distinct practices*.[1] Discourse, and in particular, the ED, is such a distinct practice with its specific structure and relations. This practice is constituted at the point where the power of knowledge (*connaissance*) and information (*savoir*) is instituted at the very structure of social relations of production. The assumed 'knowledge' (which is not necessarily *connaissance*) that the established power recognizes and promotes, is shown to be as 'natural' and legitimate as the epistemology of 'subject - object', and sociology of 'individual - society'. The ED as a practice is governed by all the rules that other practices in the same social order are subject to: *exclusion, prohibition, naturalization, division, rejection, prosecution, praise, ritualization, realization,* and, especially, *institutionalization.*

While, on the surface, discourses on planning and   design are neutral and universal activities of a technical nature, their functioning in socio-economic practices, and the latters' use of the ED are far from 'neutral' and 'universal'. We will see below the specific effectivities and functioning of these activities. Similarly, education seems to be a process of training, or an activity of disseminating knowledge and information that are necessary for the activities just mentioned. Yet, as we will see in a moment, the concept of practice does not allow us to ignore the institutional, ideological and practical nature of the education process.

5.3.3 Appearance and disappearance of discourses

When a discourse is produced as a practice, how and why is it that it is produced, or it disappears, at a particular moment in time? Without invoking the kind of determinism already mentioned it can be suggested that the appearance and disappearance of discourses and objects of discourses are closely related with the particular stage reached by the society in its appropriation of the forces of production, and the forms of its relations of production.[2] In other words, there are (discursive as well as non-discursive) conditions necessary for the appearance of an object of discourse. *"One cannot speak of anything at any time."*[3]

When the individualist-humanist problematic of   liberal capitalism appeared, the latter was already establishing itself as a mode of production. It was not only 'convenient' for the bourgeois class *to understand itself in these terms,*[4] but that was *how the economic system had actually operated.* 'Free and rational man' was the unit, master, and the ideal agent of the capitalistic mode of appropriating other'men's labour and resources.

The contradictory nature of the term 'man' as it exists in the ED has similar implications. The fact that the ED still uses the rhetoric of the competitive capitalism and liberalism in the era of monopoly capitalism is only one of the signs of its reactionary nature.[5]

Here, we may attempt to exemplify the conditions of emergence of objects of discourses, by making a detour, and looking at the mechanism by which the term 'Environment' has

---

1 On this, see, Althusser, L. (1970): 58ff.
2 cf. for ex., the concept of 'nature' and its appropriation, (Schmidt, A. (1971): 167-8).
3 Foucault, M. (1972): 44f, (emphasis added).
4 cf. T. Adorno, mentioned by D. Silverman in *Times Higher Education Supplement,* 1.3.1974; also see Althusser, L. (1969) that men 'live' their ideologies, and that "the bourgeoise has to believe its own myth . . . it lives in its ideology . . . which allows it simultaneously to act on itself . . . and others . . ." (p.234).
5 This should not however be confused with the possibility (in theory) of taking as initial the categories which may historically arise later (as in the case of Marx's study of commercial and banking capital and rent after industrial capital) (cf. Rosenthal, M. & Yudin, P. (eds) (1967): 64-5).

emerged to take up part of the place previously occupied by the term 'God'. Like the term 'God', 'Environment' implies, without differentiating, *both* a grand conception which is necessarily beyond human comprehension, *and* a real object which is practically *inclusive of everything, and exclusive of nothing.* Yet, this is a point of more than analogical interest. It carries with it the mechanisms and places of grand ideologies in societies. We know that while early religions were only tribal or national, and while they arose rather spontaneously, "they lost all their power of resistance as soon as the independence of the tribe or people was lost".[1] They were replaced by universal religions with 'almighty', 'omnipotent', 'omnipresent' god(s). Instead of a spontaneous conception of man's own nature and external nature, world religions were imposed on societies as the ideologies of dominant classes. In the Middle Ages the dominant ideology was religion and theology. Only after the bourgeoisie started to rise that other ideas — judicial, political, etc. became alternative ideologies.

That the Christian idea of God was 'a mirror image of man' (Feuerbach), or, more specifically, a "copy of the single oriental despot"[2] is significant in understanding the formation of the bourgeois legal ideology based on the 'individual man' with 'his' free will, rights and choices. Instead of the omnipresent/omnipotent God (which is 'ever-never' 'everywhere-nowhere') came the abstract Man which is supposed to be the image that real 'men' have of themselves in ideal.[3]

The theological ideology of the middle ages was so overwhelmingly dominant that nearly all social and political movements took on a theological form.[4] It was the only frame of reference. Even physical sciences could not ignore this frame of reference. Any dissent against the cosmology was a dissent against the God (and against the Church). It was not accidental that the dominant ideology, cosmology and the world view and the nature of socio-political developments were in 'harmony' with one another. (It would not be wrong, therefore, to suggest that each social formation tries to maintain itself and its basic mode of production by specific articulations of its instances.) As pointed out at the beginning of this detour the conceptions of 'God' and 'Environment' (or World, or Nature) are not simply analogical in their scope, but have some similarities in their places within the complex structure of the social whole. In constituting the basic 'elements' of dominant ideologies, they form the ingredients of the present M-E ideology.

While the God's gradual fall into irrelevance was clearly functional in the development of capitalist production, and while the formation of legal ideology was necessary for the bourgeoisie; the blame for the 'undesired' consequences of the capitalist mode of production (pollution, poverty, wars, slums, waste) could not be put on the very *liberalism* which legitimized them in the first place. Nor could they any longer be attributed to the curse of God with whom man is said to have lost contact through his sins.[5] The inherent anarchy of capitalist production, the contradiction between the forces and the relations of production, the growing awareness of the exploitative and destructive practices, and the rising struggles for social ownership of resources at a global scale could no longer be repressed by force or by ideology. It was necessary for the bourgeois ideology to shift the emphasis from society to nature, from omnipresent-omnipotent God to the "grand open book of Nature",[6] and to present economic and political conflicts as the 'struggle with Nature'.

In the first, a pervasive ideology was necessary to *naturalize*; in the second, to *neutralize*,

1 Engels, F. (1969): 258-9.
2 F. Engels, mentioned in Rosenthal, M. & Yudin, P. (eds) (1967): 178.
3 cf. Ch. 3 for 'man' as the *subject*, and for the multiple status of the subject.
4 Engels, F., *ibid*: 279.
5 cf. Victory Tract Club (1974): 2. (Mentioned in Sec. 4.2.4).
6 cf. Lacoste, Y. (1976): 61, 73 in the context of geographic discourse.

social contradictions, and in both cases, to *displace* problems.[1] Thus, a general, all-
embracing concept of 'environment' was already in existence in the form of an ecological
concept on the one hand; and a cosmological substitute for Nature and World on the
other. As to the psychology, or sociology, the 'environment' was that which was external,
but sometimes inclusive of, 'man'. However, its transfer into the discourses which are
about physical reality (i.e. architecture, urbanism, design), and its sudden acceptance in
popular discourse made it a 'notion' which is presently becoming as pervasive and as
mysificatory as 'God' was in the Middle Ages.

5.3.4 Relations with non-Environmental practices

The ED was said to be a *tool* and a *form* by which technical practices operate and certain
social relations are secured. The degree of its effectivity, however, is a question that needs
to be examined. It will be done in the context of the effectivities of design and planning.
Outside the field of the ED, however, the effectivity of that discourse is a function of the
relationship between the modes of appropriation. Arguments on 'environment', geographic
borders, cities, resources, air and water, housing,regional planning, 'environmental impact'
of investments, aesthetic effects of particular built-form, . . . impregnate the discourses
on politics, diplomacy, health, education, behaviour, social, aesthetic and class differences,
or social development in general. The ED provides these intrusions, borrowings or amphibologies in several ways. These have already been examined as the *mechanisms* of the ED.

It is necessary and possible to understand the *relationship* between the ED and the theory
of social formation (or, "the operative relation between the theory of narrative systems and
the theory of class struggle"[2]). This cannot be done at the level of the ED for the specific
reasons of its status and structure. It can, however, be done in terms of a conception of
*discourse as a practice the articulation of which is closely bound up with that of the non-
discursive practices.*[3] The relationship is, then, to be sought both at the level of concepts
and **problematic,***and* at institutional and professional levels.

Professions such as architecture, planning and design are linked up with other 'non-
environmental' practices at disciplinary, discursive, physical, political, technical, artistic,
economic, . . . levels. While the theoretical compatibility of these relations can be observed
at the conceptual and discursive levels, their operational effectivity should be analysed at
the institutional level. Moreover, the multiplicity, vagueness and theoretical poverty of
the ED and its objects is directly instrumental in the degree of its operational effectivity.[4]
Yet, effectivity is not measurable in terms either of the pervasiveness of the discourse, or
of the official recognition it may seem to have obtained. We know that it is not always
the 'truths' of sciences that inspire decision-making. We have already argued that it is not
the 'justice' or 'freedom' that the dominant ideology *claims* to be about that counts; it
is, rather, how that ideology actually *functions* that is important.

1 At this point it must be noted that this explanation should not be seen as paradoxical in a study which
refuses to explain ideologies or theories with reference to their origins or originators, and which does not
explain them teleologically. Instead, it tries to show (a) the material   condition   of the existence of
ideologies, (b) their internal structures, (c) their relative autonomy and relations within the complex
unity of specific social formations.
2 Faye, J.P. (1976): 59.
3 cf. Sec.s 5.3.1 and 5.3.2 above.
4 Of course, this discrepant relationship is seldom admitted in non-environmental discourses. Therefore
an 'admission', such as the following, is quoted merely for its exceptional value rather than its theoretical
rigour. (In the 1972 United Nations Human Environment Conference at Stockholm) "The developed
nations resigned themselves to the environment involving everything from multi-national corporations
to ecoside in Indo-China, and comforted one another with the thought that if the subject was really as
broad as all that nobody would ever be able to do anything about it." (Tinker, J. (1975): 600).

Moreover, it is not the popular terms of the discourse that we should look at but the nature of the positions (theoretical, class, etc.). 'Environmental policies' that are declared to cure the 'environmental problems' benefit those who are already in control of the problem areas and who already benefit from a mode of production with whose undesirable effects people live. So-called 'environmental movements' are basically *conservative* rather than revolutionary, *mystic* rather than rational and technical.[1] When such movements become part of the established mechanism they retain their theoretical naivety while attaining a more profound ideological effectivity. Establishment of *'Ecology Parties'* and their relative electoral successes in France are significant examples of this process. [2]

These movements, policies and parties exemplify the fact that the same ideology may be crossed by different problematics, or the same problematic may be crossed by different ideologies as   has   been stressed in another context.[3] What is relevant to the present discussion is the claims of different political parties and groups on 'environmental problems' which is partly due to their uncritical acceptance of the dubious *orthodoxy* (or the *'paradigm'*) on environment, and partly to their own conditions of existence.

5.3.5 Modes of appropriation in Environmental Discourse and in the economy

Appropriation of a discourse is certainly different from that of land, resources, or labour. Yet, as a form by which the survival of certain social relations are secured, a discourse is a potential *tool*, whose utility the dominant power cannot ignore. Whole sets of institutions as we will see later, are established *to maintain or modify the appropriation of discourses,* "with the knowledge and the powers it carries with it".[4]

Established 'sciences', particularly those that are of direct relevance to technology and production are "as much annexed by capital as the labour of others".[5] While the 'physical sciences' are obvious examples to this process, the appearance and development of economics is perhaps the best case as far as (so-called) social sciences are concerned. While 'rational man' became the subject of economics, the artificial and ideological separation of 'man' into 'producer' and 'consumer' is one of the effective mechanisms borrowed by the ED to constitute its own multiple subject.[6] While the fact that even a question such as the capitalist division of labour (e.g. the separation of conception and execution, education and production, theory and object of theory) fails to deserve attention in the ED, the 'producer/consumer separation can be indicative of its status as an ideological discourse.

This separation is *implicit*, mainly because the ED and its regional discourses (such as the ones that are current in architectural or industrial design[7]) are involved more with the 'satisfaction of the consumer needs' (i.e. users, inhabitants, clients, housewifes, . . .) than the 'sweat-and-blood' mechanism by which the marketable products are actually produced. While the colour of the curtain, or the design of the kitchen are the subject matters of researches that could get grants from government agencies, a problem like the high rate of accidents in the building industry is left to 'others' to worry about. It is here that *consumerism* shows its pervasiveness in the ED both as an economic *and* an ideological form of functioning. A house is no longer a structure in which to make a home but is a

1 cf. Krieger, M.H. (1970): 322; Galtung, J. (1973); Mandel, W.M. (1973): 413; Enzensberger, H.M. (1974): 10.
2 cf. *Le Monde,* No. 9991, 15.3.1977; *The Guardian,* 10.3.1977; and in the English context, the establishment of the Ecology Party, *The Guardian,* 19.4.1977.
3 cf. Ch. 1.
4 Foucault, M. (1971): 19.
5 Marx, K. (1970), v.I; 365n.
6 cf. Sec.s 4.4.4.b, and 3.3.
7 cf. Wolf, L. (1972): 189.

commodity.[1] (It is not accidental that the techniques of market research are suggested and used to find out what the prospective residents, i.e. the consumers, want.) *The mode of appropriation of the labour* and that of other resources determine, if not directly and exclusively, the statements, researches and the education on 'environment'. Conversely, the dominant discursive 'truths' disseminated by the media and institutions are instrumental in the maintenance of the (mis)conceptions about the nature of social relations of production as well as of the modes of exclusion.

5.3.6 Reflectionism and projectionism

Reflectionism, as an epistemological position, is sufficiently problematic to require some critical analysis especially if its claim to be an explanatory tool is to be investigated. It is often used as one of the multitude of *relations* that are assumed to exist between 'M' and 'E'.[2] As such it is the basis of many speculative arguments on how 'built environment', or 'space', *reflects* the social or cultural structure.[3] Such arguments in the ED were already shown to be an effect of the subject - object epistemology and M-E problematic.[4] What the present section is concerned with is the reflectionist positions in the conceptualization of discourse – non-discursive   relations. Simply stated, this position asserts that concepts, notions, ideas, ideologies, philosophies, discourses are *projected in the 'environment'*.[5]

This argument can be taken to imply both a materialist view of discourses (similar to the one expounded in the present section) or a simplistic search for correspondences. It is reasonable to assume that a *view* of nature, space or society could be based on the *knowledge* of those objects. In that case it is not the reflection or projection of a discourse on 'environment' but a *theoretical discourse on those ('environmental'?) objects* that should be of our concern, and it is precisely what the present study tries to provoke by its critique of the ED. One thing that needs to be said here is that it is not the *view* on nature and society that is responsible for the specific modes of appropriating them. Those *views and discourses develop in relation to the modes of appropriation* which in fact needs those views and discourses for their effective functioning.[6]

1 This is best summed up in the building society symbols emphasizing 'savings', 'gains', 'investments' (rather than usual qualities that are so much researched and speculated on):

The house is no longer a 'roof over one's head', but a 'roof over one's assets'.(cf. Pawley, M.(1976) on the changing pattern of building society andmortgageadvertisement.).
2 cf. Ch. 3 on structure of the ED, and the list of relations in Sec. 3.3.7 b . For the epistemology of reflectionism see Lecourt, D. (1973).
3 cf. for ex.Rapoport,. A. (1969): 49, 127; Rykwert, J. (1973): 20f; Ural, S. (1974): 7; *Mimarlık Haberleri:* 16.6.1976, p.4.; Gropius, W. in Gabor, L. (1975): 3; Cooper, C. (1971): 7,15.
4 cf. Ch. 3.
5 cf. for ex., ". . . in Medieval Europe, Gothic architecture was the direct expression of society's hopes and beliefs". (S. Gavin, in *Building Design,* 7.5.1976.)
6 It is not therefore a question either of 'naturalistic immediacy, or of a 'mediated generalization'. (cf. for ex., Leiss, W. (1972): 185 who remarks on F. Bacon's argument that the dominant philosophy of his time unwittingly projected false notions into nature, and that human concerns were being read into the order of nature in a wholly abstract manner. So, Leiss concludes, Bacon proposed to replace this immediacy with a mediated consciousness; with the effect of transforming Nature from the domain of naturalistic categories to a   universality as the generalized object of investigation, experimentation and technological applications – as the basis for a conception of Nature as a field or object to be dominated.

Other attempts of projection include semiotic and linguistic approaches to architectural and urban phenomena[1] where semiotic schemas and concepts are projected over the elements of buildings, cities or other objects. On the other hand, systems approach, especially when applied simplistically, tends to impose upon the physical world, and especially on complex and overdetermined aspects of it, a closed pattern of the discourse.[2] This, as in the case of semiotic projection, is an *explanatory* mechanism with certain implications on other practices. As such, it is an operation that is the reverse of the search for discursive pattern in non-discursive domains pointed out earlier on.

One specific mode of projectionism can be seen in architectural and urban design practices. The designs and plans are *conceived* partly in drawings and partly in imagination, and *expressed*, in return, partly in drawings and partly in architectural and urban discourses, but,finally, in physical forms and organizations. Mainly due to this traditional method of production as well as to the figurative mode of perception and representation[3] in these practices, it is usually assumed,

a) that these practices are involved in projecting the physical, economic, cultural, psychological . . . characteristics of a society over space, and

b) that an observation of physical forms would yield an understanding of how society sees itself.

Once again, these positions are basically reflectionist. They reduce the complexity of producing physical objects (artifacts) to an interaction between two distinct and exclusive elements. It is these elements which then reflect, project, build, design, observe, or understand . . . each other. The basic fallacies of these positions have already been sufficiently stressed not tò need repetition here. However it is useful to remember that though design and planning activities *organize* the forms of consumption and distribution of surplus - value[4], and as such, they may carry part of the responsibility for the prevailing pattern of 'collective consumption'[5], *understanding* of none of these functions can be reduced to a projection or reflection in the built domain.

5.3.7 Effectivity of the Environmental Discourse: some (mis)conceptions

Perhaps the most justified question concerning the analysis in the present section might be that of the *effectivities* of the ED in non-discursive domains. This, however, must be distinguished from the *effects* that it produces. What is meant with 'effectivity' is the degree to which the ED and the so-called 'environmental practices' are capable of producing effects. This question is very much tied up with some other, more specific, questions. As the ED is operative in various practices and activities, it is reasonable that these questions are directed to them. However, there will be no attempt here to answer all these questions. The rest of the study contains sufficient answers and examples for them. Instead, the questions will try to produce *further questions*. It is hoped that the complex and difficult enterprise of the present analysis will not be reduced to these deliberately simple, yet provocative, questions.

The first and the central question is: *what exactly is it that design activity* designs *or planning activity* plans? In other words, *What is their object?* Is it 'environment', 'space', 'brick-and-mortar', human behaviour, social interaction, or something else? Consequently, *where does the ED produce its effects?* We have already seen that all these 'objects' are

1 For comments on this mode of projection, see Choay, F. (1973): 294.
2 For a critique of this position see Wilden, A. (1972): 216 etc.
3 cf. Battisti, E. (1975): 161.
4 for ex., the conceptualization of city as a place where surplus-value is concentrated and distributed, (cf. Harvey, D. (1973): 216f).
5 cf. Castells, M. (1975):502f. etc., and Lojkine, J. (1976) for this concept.

vague, multiple, relativistic and often undefinable. We have already disclosed some possible objects or relations that may actually be the objects of these activities, and the actual loci of problems that the ED talks about. For example, it was already suggested that it could be the distribution of the surplus-value that is actually being planned and organized.[1] It can also be suggested that it is to the ideological demands of the dominant classes that design activity gives form and utility[2]. Thus, the ED cannot be seen as a simple tool of 'environmental' practices, but also as an (ideological) expression of dominant social relations that determine those practices.

What is the discursive and non-discursive nature of physical planning? Physical planning and design are activities that organize certain physical as well as cognitive, financial as well as cultural, resources. They do not *produce* but *utilize* knowledge and information. They express their schemes in drawings, in technical specifications, in statistical tables and in words. Thus, the effectivity of the ED in these practices depends upon the modes of functioning in specific socio-economic contexts as well as upon their modes of perception and representation.

Who precisely is it that benefits from design and planning activities? 'Domination' that is frequently referred to in this chapter is not an abstract notion, but a theoretical concept. It denotes, among other things, the specific forms in which a particular relation of production thrives to function and to be maintained. The domination is thus one of the means of production of goods as well as ideas, physical objects as well as discursive formations. It is in the context of this mechanism that the question of "who benefits from a particular discourse" can be answered — though with some caution, as it must avoid reducing the whole discursive practice to simple utility.

What rentability do   design and planning have? Design is *integral* to the enterprise that produces industrial objects and buildings. Yet, it is *marginal* with respect to the relations of production dominant in the social formation.[3] For planning it is rather different, as no contemporary social formation, whether capitalist or socialist, can function without some sort of planning. Thus, the question of effectivity that concerns the present section should be answered in connection with specific social formations, and specific areas of design (industrial, architectural, graphic) or planning (economic, physical, urban, agricultural). The service and the function of the ED in these specific cases should thus be examined in relation to each case though general guidelines on the relationship between discourses and non-discursive domains mentioned above could apply to these examinations too.

How correct is the distinction 'theory/practice'? What effects do the (mis)conceptions on this distinction have on the practices involved? The simplistic correlation established between a *general* 'Theory' and a *general* 'Practice', though pervasive in every conceivable discourse, inevitably implies a conception of discourse — non-discursive relationship. In this conception, there is a body of 'Theory' (presumably consisting of speculative speeches and writings in architecture, planning and other 'environmental' professions), and a 'Practice' (presumably what these professions and activities *do* — as if this would not include speeches and writings referred to). There is no intention here to dwell upon this question. Suffice it to say that this misconception displaces the form and locus of effects that the ED produces on other practices and domains. It also tries to 'judge' a theory or suggestion on the basis of some ubiquitous criteria of 'Practice'. This attitude, which we can call 'theoretical pragmatism', is dangerously misleading especially in discussing the problems of education and research.[4]

1 For the interpretation of the intervention of dominant forces in these processes, see, Castells, M. (1975); Barel, Y. (1972): 208; Lintoft, Y. (1970); Harvey, D. (1973); McLeish, H. (1976).
2 cf. Teymur, N. & E. (1973).
3 cf. Wolf, L. (1972): 185 .
4 cf. Teymur, N.& E.(1978) for a detailed examination of·this question.

What are the discursive bases of misconceptions, illusions, wishful thinkings, unjustified
expectations and accusations about professions? A commonly held assumption in everyday
discourse is that planners and architects are the ones who are responsible for the mistakes,
problems or inadequacies in the 'environment'.[1] This assumption inevitably leads
a) to blaming professional cadres for the undesirable products of economic and political
decisions usually determining and overriding the local ones made by said professionals,
b) to absolving the prevailing relations of production for these problems,
c) to calling for 'changes' in local government organization, in education, in 'our attitudes',
etc, hence, setting up of institutional models, 'alternative courses of action', decentralized/
self-built participationist modes of building, etc.[2] while effectively keeping the *basis of*
power intact. This is not the proper context in which to examine the epistemological,
ideological and technical status of these positions. Nevertheless, it can be said that at
theoretical levels such conceptions arise either by a misunderstanding of the role and nature
of *technical* practices, or/and by the implicit belief in the possibility of *social engineering*
by physical forms. Both of these positions will be examined below.

5.3.8 Professional ideologies, their determinants and effectivities

The question of the role and function of professions depends very much upon the conception
of the latters' nature. Professions and disciplines emerge, develop and function in close
relation with prevailing socio-economic systems. This has already been repeatedly stressed.
    What is to be said here is that each professional practice has *different* links with the
socio-economic-political system in question. Those that are most closely concerned with
the   reproduction of labour power (such as medicine) have different links than those that
are essentially concerned with the advance of the productive forces (such as engineering).
Their relations with sciences are also effected by these links. For example, medicine's link
with biology is different from engineering's link with physics.[3] The ideologies of these
professions are thus linked with the *applications* that they make, of various sciences. As
to the practices dealing with physical and spatial organization (geography, town planning,
architecture, landscape design), their nature and function have to be seen in the context
of their material determinants, namely *the specific modes of transformation of territories.*[4]
The effectivities of these practices are often misunderstood due either to their self-image,
(i.e. their belief that they can function as the chief organizers of the universe), or to the
dual role assigned to them by dominant powers. On the one hand, the traditional respect
for professional persons and self-image of architects as special persons, elites and 'Artists'[5]
and the self-image of planners as decision-makers backfire on these professions in everyday
discourse *when they fail to fulfil the ideological roles assigned to them.* They are accused
of being incompetent, ignorant, 'middle class', etc. as has been observed above. On the
other hand, the dominant mode of production, i.e. *the monopoly capitalism, is not*
interested in tackling the tasks proposed by   *professional idealism* (compared with
the 'progressive' and patronizing attitude towards architectural and planning proposals

1 For a detailed critique of this assumption see Mugnaioni, P. (1976). See also Sec. 4.5.2.
2 cf. for ex., setting up of an institutional model for "a course of action resting on cognitively right
knowledge applied to morally right social policy" (Klausner, S.Z. (1971) in *Man-Environment*
Systems : (3)3: 179; or, 'Do-it-yourself new town', 'anarchist new town' proposals of C. Ward
cf. *ICA Quarterly,* January – March 1976, and the issues of BEE.
3 For these differences see Brewster,B. (1971): 32 commenting on M. Pecheux and E. Balibar. On
medicine's place in industrial development and the changes in medical discourse, see Foucault, M. (1973).
4 On this question see, for ex., Strum Group (1971).
5 These images are glamorized, reinforced and reflected most clearly in some popular journals and

during the rise of capitalism).[1] These two discrepancies (or 'realities') point to the fact
that *professions cannot be 'useful' above, and in spite of, the prevailing political -
economic system.* They cannot *also* be (fully) blamed for the consequences of decisions
they do not make and appropriations they do not determine. It would however be a
gross mistake to either absolve them completely of their responsibilities, or to claim that
they are of no *use* to   monopoly capitalism. Even the 'uselessness' of most of the
discourse has *functions*, namely, those of mystification, trivialization, distortion,
depolitization, etc.[2] Nor, is it correct to dismiss the central role that the ED itself
occupies in this whole question.

It is in the ED that these discrepancies are either distorted or obscured. It is also in
that discourse that further arguments (such as M-E relationship, harmony, unity, change
of values, reflection of social order, environmental determinism, pseudo-scientific explanations, ideological justifications) are produced for political, popular as well as professional
consumption. As in the case of all ideologies, *the professionals* (whose object is presented
in the ED as 'the Environment') *believe and live in their own ideologies.*

We will see below how the material and institutional status of these practices and the
ED are determinant in what these cadres can and cannot do. One thing that should not
be underestimated however is that there are, in Western capitalist societies, several 'conjunctural struggles'[3] which closely involve professional people. Besides, there are specific modes
of intellectual and professional interventions that *can* at times be polemical or even naive,
but can also be creative, provocative and effective. These range from *refusing* to serve
certain anti-social interests to declining to provide technical solutions to social problems.
It is also possible to facilitate awareness and understanding by *producing knowledge* about
the complex determinations of technical/professional activities, or by pointing out the

---

newspapers where architects are chosen as the 'special' people to promote often 'nonarchitectural'
products.This is partly due to their above-average purchasing power, and partly to their socially recognized
image. (compare this with airline pilots, rally drivers and managers who smoke the 'best' cigarettes!)
On the other hand, architects unlike many other producers of artifacts or services in society, are singled
out as the distinctive 'creators' of prestigeous symbols of social-ideological-economic systems (such as
temples, palaces, banks . . .)

(The first two examples are from *Der Spiegel,* No. 48, 1970; p.35 and p.45; and the third one
(depicting architect Arne Jacobsen monumentalized in front of his Danish National Bank) is
from *Politiken,* 26.2.1971, p.1.)

1 On this attitude and its relation to the Modern Movement, see Tafuri, M. (1976): 170.
2 On this double view of effectivity, see Lacoste, Y. (1976): 10.
3 cf. Foucault, M. (1977b): 12-13.

'logic' of a system by making polemical suggestions and (even) gestures.[1] These struggles, when situated in relation to political struggles and specific ideological critiques they achieve, are significant signposts for social change. Changing class alliances in these struggles *include* the changes in the positions of professional groups within the production process.[2]

5.3.9 'Truth' and Power

Whether it is knowledge *(connaissance)* or information *(savoir)* that a practice produces or deals with, it involves an exercise of *power*. This, in return, provides the conditions of emergence of new objects of knowledge, new problems, new information. Thus, the exercise of power perpetually creates knowledge while "knowledge constantly induces effects of power".[3] In fact, it is not possible to exercise power without knowledge.[4] In the course of this exercise the practices, among them discourses, are organized, instituted, constituted and forced, to carry the recognized 'truth' (and 'falsity') of the dominant power. This mechanism is neither extraneous nor superfluous, nor can it be avoided by simply ignoring its existence and effects. What is necessary is to understand the conditions and rules of the mechanism. In fact, this study in general and the present section in particular tries to do that.

Production, constitution and exercise of power through knowledge and information is made possible both at the level of the conceptual/ideological structures of the disciplines and discourses and at the level of institutional systems.This includes *inclusion* or *exclusion* of certain problems, *distortion* or *ignorance* of certain issues, *division* and sub-division of disciplines, *facilitating* or *denying* access,and *determining* the modes of communication.

Most important of all, this exercise of power is not an abstract and voluntary act, but is inseparable from the modes of appropriation specific to each social formation. Though scientific, professional or technical disciplines and discourses have a certain autonomy, they are nevertheless defined and determined by the specific type of social relations of production and by the development of the forces of production.

These interventions or determinations are the loci of various theoretical debates and controversies; and specifically for the ED and related practices the debate is far from settled. For the reasons outlined in the *Preface* and *Introduction* as well as at the beginning of this section, it is not possible here to go into the details of these debates. The present discussion is therefore meant to function as a generator of questions at a field which is dominated by *unquestioned assumptions* about the relationship between 'environmental practices' and social structure. Now, while disciplines and practices are under the effect of social/political/ideological factors, the former themselves constitute a specific system of control in the production of discourses.[5] Again, as already argued, this control is exerted both at theoretical/conceptual, *and* at institutional levels. The latter, nevertheless, is the *material basis* on which the former level operates.

5.3.10 Institutional materiality of the Environmental Discourse

Institutional power is only one of the forms of domination. It operates through certain *apparatuses* established as part of the political-legal system called *state*. The state apparatus

---

1 For ex., "The architect/planner must exercise all his expertise, on being asked for artifactual conditioning, on the relevance of or necessity for doing anything at all. *(The best technical advice may be that rather than build a house your client should leave his wife)*"(Price, C. (1966): 483). Or, "*A square-wheeled canon is the artist's protest against war*" (Architect L. Kahn to A. Jacobsen, source unknown).

2 For a comprehensive analysis of these changes with special reference to the division of manual and mental labour, see Poulantzas, N. (1975): Part 3.

3 Foucault, M. (1977a):15.

4 ibid.

5 cf. Foucault, M. (1971):17.

is constituted by a large set of institutions (ministerial departments, universities, institutes, professional bodies, mass-media, offices, hospitals, service centres, financial and industrial organizations, repressive apparatus such as army and police, legal system, etc.). These institutions (and the 'persons' in charge of them, though they should not be reduced to the latter) define either statutorily, or by other means, what *can* or *cannot* be said, written, studied, sought for, implemented, financed, developed, popularized, or repressed. These 'persons' include experts, specialists, professional and skilled workers as well as managers. However, it is not the sheer knowledge and information possessed by these 'persons' that put them in control of discourses. There are also some secondary tools that the dominant social relations of production employs to control both the information and those who produce and use it: Regulations, laws, rules, norms, standards, channels of communication, classification of data, codes of practice, quantitative techniques are some of the effective means by which discourses, and among them the ED, are produced, manipulated and institutionalized.

The legality of professions, the official and social status of sciences, the professionalism and the 'codes' used by specialists are all complex factors themselves situated within the determinant relations of production in particular societies. While certain specific patterns and rules of discursive formations may have common characteristics vis-a-vis non-discursive domains, each particular discourse in specific social formations may have different types of relations. For example, knowledge produced and possessed by the specialist may be an asset *and* a threat (of differing degrees and kinds) for dominant politico – economic powers. The level of the development of productive forces and the mode of production that determines that level put on different requirements on the sources of discourses.

Popular discourse is no exception to this. What *can* and *cannot* be popularly discussed, *and in what terms*, is not independent of what goes on in the state apparatuses and in their various branches. Mass-media as well as publishing system favour or censor certain terms or objects of discourses, or whole discourses, for ideological as well as financial, for political as well as scientific, reasons.

It is becoming obvious that all capitalist countries (or their rulers) are now 'aware of' the 'ecological disasters' that their 'development' faces. But, this is almost invariably *communicated in terms of* 'moral concern with one's milieu', 'understanding of the environmental balance', and 'harmony in M-E relations', etc., thus *obscuring* the systemic determinants of problems and *mystifying* the concrete possibilities of solution. As there have already been ample discussions and examples to these mechanisms in earlier chapters there is no need here to go into details. Suffice it to say, however, that whether in the 'hands' of selfish professionals or of their 'public' institutes, and whether in repressive states or in United Nation conferences, the epistemological and discursive mistakes of the ED are continuously perpetuated and reproduced.[1]

As to the *educational* apparatus, it is necessary to stress one or two points: Education in 'environmental' fields occupies a direct position vis a vis the production of those objects that are called (in the ED) the 'built environment'. In fact, education is an institution which functions precisely where *certain technical, economic, ideological and symbolic requirements of the dominant social system are to be satisfied* – though this can never be fully done. (The reasons for this relative autonomy and specificity of environmental practices are partly in the differential effectivities of the practices that the education in question tries to serve).

The discourse that provides the substance of a particular education creates a closed circle by which that discourse is reproduced and new variants are produced. It is also meaningful

---

1 cf. for ex., a reeent 'contribution' to this process: "A prize of $ 50,000 is to be awarded annually by the UN for the most outstanding contribution in the field of the environment. The awards, to be presented each year on June 5, World Environment Day, are being contributed by Iran. . . . " *(Building Design*, 26.3.1976, p. 20).

to consider the relationship between a certain system of education and the dominant economic and political system. The former is almost always dominated (though, obviously, with certain autonomy, and not always fully successfully,) by the latter. Among the forms of this domination two are most distinctly observable:

1) the domination of the content of the education, i.e. the problems and the problematics that are recognized, developed, and taught ;

2) the domination, on the basis of the first one, by means of institutional recognition. But as a whole, the recognition is formulated in *curricula*   in the former, and the *educational policies* in the latter forms of domination.[1]

This domination, however, should not be reduced to a direct management, but be seen as a complex and overdetermined rule in a particular social formation with a definite and determinate mode of production. For example, the demands of the survival of a particular formation, or mode, may show themselves in education through the domination by the ruling classes of professional bodies, government   departments, research institutes. Consequently, contents and forms of teaching, and what is and is not researched and published, are effectively controlled. This, for example, may show itself in often negative attitudes towards theoretical work in the name of 'the needs of the profession', while what is really at stake is the *undesirability* (for professional bodies) of the development of critical and theoretical debates with inevitable political implications.

There are notable exceptions to this type of domination by professional bodies. In countries with developing political consciousness professional bodies become directly *political*. They try to serve their members' interests only in so far as the latter are in accordance with progressive and democratic principles, thus *countering the structural tendency of such professions to ally with the ruling classes*. This implies that such bodies voice progressive and critical suggestions for the education of the professionals, initiate their unionization, introduce new elements into the discourse on sociophysical problems such as housing, transportation, urbanization, pollution, and act as significant pressure groups.[2] If universities and other educational establishments are the places where the dominant discourses are reproduced and disseminated, they are also places where ideas and knowledge that are *not* officially sanctioned are also produced. This is due, partly, to the *relative autonomy* of theoretical, scientific and technical practices, and partly to the fact that in nearly all areas a structural analysis would inevitably yield insight into the nature of social relations of production involved and dominant in that area. This insight is bound to be *political*. It is for this reason that in societies where repressive, reactionary, colonial, dependent or fascistic political forces are in power, universities and their discursive outlets are among the first to be silenced and censored.[3] In situations like these education itself may be used to reverse its own progressive and inquiring capacities. As education is

1 The detailed examples for these observations would be misleading if not backed by some description of their contents; but this is not possible in the present context. However, on the environmental education policies in the U.K., see Watts, D.G. (1969): 1f. (on Plowden Report of 1967); various issues of the *RIBA Journal*, *ARse*, *J. of Architectural Research*, *BEE*, and Project Environment (1975). See Sommer, R. (1972) and Perin, C. (1970), and the issues of *Man-Environment-Systems* for the U.S.; Hekstra, G.P. (1973) for the Dutch; and *Mimarlık* 1976/3 for the Turkish cases — though, of course, from differing points of view. The institutional recognition of the *M-E problematic* in the U.S. can be seen in the number of 'Associations'. 'Departments' and 'Institutes' of the 'M-E studies', or of academic posts such as "Professor of M-E. Relations", J.F. Wohlwill (cf. Preiser, W.F.E. (ed) (1973): v.II: 166). Similarly, most departments of architecture and planning as well as those of geography, art and design, biology and engineering in the UK and elsewhere have now been changed to 'departments of environmental studies'.

2 A good example to this type of professional organization is the Turkish Chamber of Architects (TMO), and the Federation of Turkish Chambers of Architects and Engineers (TMMOB).

3 For different analyses of such cases in geography, see, Santos, M. (1974), Lacoste, Y. (1976) and issues of *Antipode* and *Herodote*; in architecture, see issues of *Mimarlık*; in industrial design, see Bonsiepe, G. (1975).

an instrument whereby every individual in a society can gain access to nearly any kind of discourse,[1] (a) by controlling the mode of distribution of this access, and (b) by manipulating the discourses themselves, the dominant power can disseminate *its* discursive choices as'*universal* knowledge'.

As has already been argued above, educational institutions provide the means by which conditions of reproduction of (scientific) knowledges have their effects on the forms of their production.[2] It was also argued that the analysis of the relations between discourses and non-discursive domains are reducible neither to discursive or institutional causality nor to economic determinism. The relationship is a complex one that cannot also be dealt with in terms of a simplified base-superstructure couple. A discourse is neither simply a superstructure or an ideology, nor are all non-discursive domains necessarily economic. Economy and politics operate *at all levels* as determinant instances. Based on a misconception of education which fails to see it in this complexity, several 'approaches' are experimented One such approach is the *individualistic* one which supposedly opposes 'indoctrination' without taking into consideration the determinate relationship in which so-called 'environmental education' is situated.[3]

Finally, there is the question of establishing relations between education and so-called '*real world situations*' or 'real conditions'. We have already shown the epistemological fallacy of correspondence between real and discursive, or 'Theory' and 'Practice'[4]. What is relevant to the present section is the practical failure of such a *realist* education at discursive as well as technical levels. The desire to take 'real conditions' as the object of education may seem to be consistent with the domination of education by the class interests of those who have the economic - political powers — as it may seem natural for these powers to make practical use of the education. But what is at stake is the nature of the *question* itself. The desire to tackle 'real world situations' or 'real conditions' cannot start with a *given* conception of the real — which is often bound up with the dominant ideology, itself. Thus, if the 'realist' desire is to be any '*progressive*' *it must ask and answer what precisely those 'real' conditions are.* It is not an advance over what already exists if it limits itself to a study of site conditions, climate , availability of materials, etc. as these are the most basic objects of professional activities for which the 'environmental education' is there to train people. It is not also enough to mention 'social-economic-political factors' if what is meant by these are the simple data on income groups, number of children, or cultural expectations. *A desire to provide real solutions to real problems presupposes the need to define and know the real conditions with all their complexities, preconditions and determinants.* Unless the education is geared (and this has to be achieved despite the limitations set by the dominant ideology and power) to providing these definitions and knowledge (even in a seemingly technical education) the latter cannot tackle real problems any more than any *tool* does the task that is demanded from it, that is, without *questioning the task itself* and the discursive forms in which it is presented.

5.3.11 Historicity, conjuncture and determinations

Institutional connexions of the ED were shown to be as relevant to its understanding as the epistemological and discursive properties that constitute the discourse. While examining

1 cf. Foucault, M. (1971): 19.
2 cf Lecourt. D. (1975): 139-40.
3 cf. for ex., "Formal indocrination about attitudes and exhortation to be more environmentally conscious are unlikely to achieve anything . . . There is seldom a simple right or wrong solution to the problems; each individual must weigh the evidence and identify his own position . . . " (Project Environment (1975): 6.)
4 cf. Sec. 5.3.7.

institutional connexions as well as effectivities and modes of appropriation it was stressed that the ED, as a practice, was a product and part of social practice as a whole. In what follows these points will not be repeated. It will only be argued that, as a practice, ED is conceivable as *a formation that has a historical and conjunctural exis- tence.* As a discourse is constituted not only by its objects, not only by its connexions, and not only by its mechanisms, the question of historicity should be posed to all these elements that constitute the discourse. The objects, mechanisms and connexions of the ED are either part of, or related with, an ideology which can be called *'ideology of environment'.* It is through this ideology that the ED is related with the dominant ideology in specific social formations.

Basically, the materiality of a discourse involves the question of the link that exists between the *transformation of reality* as well as the discourse that talks about that reality. Yet, this should not mean to say that there is a correspondence between these seemingly separate processes. What we intend to see in this section is the real nature of the link mentioned, not a pre-established type of it.

The dominant class, and specifically the bourgeois, believes and lives its own ideology[1]. Not only does it believe and live in it, it also imposes it as *'the* worldview' i.e. 'the correct and universal conception of society and the world'. Moreover, in order to maintain its economic, political and ideological dominance, it needs to suppress alternative views and ideologies. Thus, the apparent set of mechanisms can be listed as
1. belief in its own ideology,
2. living in its own ideology,
3. imposing its ideology,
4. suppressing other ideologies.
The key to understanding the materiality of the ED lies in an understanding of these mechanisms. Various sections of the present analysis have already tried to examine some significant aspects of these mechanisms.Here we will look at certain unexplored questions that are relevant to a section leading to the conclusion of the study.

The mechanisms of imposition and suppression are based mainly on class interests (certainly in societies where there are classes). Yet, *'class* interests' cannot be the sole criteria of 'correctness' and 'falsity' of statements. They do not legislate every aspect of a discourse – especially when the discourse in question is only partly concerned with directly political questions. Neither are all class positions as 'correct' as each other (i.e. a class relativism). The present study is concerned *not* with a question of 'correctness' but with that of *effectivity.* The latter is not a question of legislation, but of *analysis.*

The class struggle is not an easily observable object as it takes place at many levels and at different times. Among them are the discursive/narrative/theoretical[2] level(s) with their own specific and determinant structures and mechanisms. (For example, as in a discursive mechanism like 'amphibology'[3] the bases of class struggle are often *presented* in terms most suitable for a particular class position: e.g. 'man' instead of 'labourer', 'wealth' instead of 'surplus-value'. Or, dominant classes may see it more appropriate to avert the class struggle by reducing it to negotiated settlements)[4].

1 cf. Althusser, L. (1970): 149ff.
2 As far as the discursive aspects of class struggle is concerned, see, for ex., Foucault *(discursive),* Faye *(narrative),* Althusser *(theoretical),* and Marx (for all three).
3 cf. Sec. 4.5.8.
4 cf. for ex., the 'debate' between so-called 'rich' and 'poor' countries: the terms themselves are domesticated and distorted to allow mystificatory solutions. cf. also the admission by the president Echeverria of Mexico:"The accumulation of poverty is leading to a dead end. If we do not make these changes through negotiation and understanding, we shall inevitably be led to violence" *(The Guardian,* 2.6.1976).

Imposition/suppression mechanisms try to (mis)represent/hide the way in which the resources (including those labelled as 'environment' and 'space') are appropriated. Hence the link between the economic and the cognitive. The imposition mechanism tries to present some *models* of reality (including those of 'man' and 'environment') that enable the dominant powers to make decisions.

There is an inherent *unevenness* in the development of social phenomena and instances. This entails that each instance may have its own *time* and there may not be correspond-ences between types and loci of changes in different domains. Thus, for example, economy, politics, technology, art, architecture, physical and biological sciences and language may present different patterns and speeds of change in different social forma-tions. Consequently, no discourse and no theory can be called for to take an *'essential section'* (i.e. a section through *all* instances) representing corresponding patterns and forms. A developed economic system may have a regressive conception of nature (as in contemporary capitalism),or a slave society such as the ancient Greek society was able to produce most refined works of art[1].

There is also the question of the *needs* of a mode of production. As a mode of produc-tion does not have to correspond fully to a particular geographic location, a concept of nature or a type of culture it may appropriate the physical resources of a location where the peoples of that location may be believing and living in a *different* ideology. This was and still is the case with colonialist, neo-colonialist and imperialist domination of peoples all over the world. And, this is where the imposition/suppression mechanisms are most operative, alongside,of course, a more subtle one — that of 'freedom of belief'. This last type of mechanism has the *appearance* of a liberal humanitarianism, while the *effect* of a continued mystification. In so-called 'underdeveloped' countries, the hard-ware and relations of production of monopoly capitalism dominate the society while a mixture of metropolitan culture and preserved regressive ideologies are deliberately promoted. The former component of this 'dependent culture' is necessary for the monopoly capitalism to promote its *mode of consumption* while the latter component helps to mystify, distort and misrepresent,the contemporary reality, hence averting and delaying possible struggles for independence and social justice[2].

As to the statements of more specific professional domains which can be made in particular contexts, the materiality is in the order of the institution rather than of the spatio-temporal localization[3]. The same ideology or the same problematic may dominate different institutions of the same practice in different social contexts. Physical planners speak the same 'language', and are educated in the same curriculum in London as in Lima, or New York as in Ankara. This is due partly to the domination of what is called 'cultural imperialism' that has just been mentioned, and partly to the specificity of the discourse and institutions of each practice. But, the common mechanism of these two determinations lie in the material base that is defined and provided by the dominant class for the architect or planner to *represent* or to *translate* into empirical practice. (One result of this process can be seen in the personal development of these professional cadres. They either become technicians, i.e. mere executioners of certain interests and demands, or try to be critical and

1 On this case, see, Marx, K. (1971): 216-7.
2 A very telling example is the discrepancy between the Western mode of capitalist appropriation and oriental mysticism as in the case of 'geomancy' (i.e."the art of adapting the residences of the living and the dead so as to co-operate and harmonize with the local currents of the cosmic breath", (H. Chatley: 'Feng Shui' in *Encyclopedia Sinica*, (ed) Couiling, S., Shanghai, 1917, p.175, quoted in Tuan, Y-F (1970): 247)). "The Chinese were always very amused by the English in Hong Kong. They pretended to know nothing about geomancy, but they always bagged the best sites". (J. Cox, talking to J. Sale, *The Guardian*, 3.4.1976).
3 cf. Foucault, M. (1972).

creative – which the former result denies them. Yet, in order to excel as intellectuals, they are forced to become part of the power structure, either acting as bureaucrats or as ideologists of the dominant class[1]. To become 'intellectuals' by transcending the limitations of technicism or academism often denies them the institutional and ideological recognition of the existing power structure, and may lead to a divorce from the production process of the 'built form')[2].

These determinations at institutional and personal levels should be seen as the consequences of the requirements of the monopoly capitalism. They include the tendency to *integrate* all levels, domains and instances though in different ways[3]. This tendency (or what can be called 'totalizing tendency'[4]) to integrate economic as well as other instances goes hand-in-hand with the tendency to *exclude* the 'undesirable' alternatives expressed in discursive forms as well as political action, (cf. the *imposition/suppression* couple mentioned earlier).

In order to integrate certain discursive forms and to exclude certain others, monopoly capitalism has many ways and means at its disposal. One of these is containing opposition by 'domesticating' or by *'detournement*'[5]. Thus, established institutions (e.g. ministries) and agents of production (e.g. capitalists) started to involve themselves with 'environment' *after* the latter became a public concern. The *'environmental concern'* became a fashionable, and benevolent area for businessmen to speculate about. This 'concern' has been publicized *while the so-called 'environment' is being exploited and destroyed by the same establishments*[6]. In this process common traits are *pessimism*[7], trivialization[8], obvious contradictions made manifest in many occasions[9].

These distorted positions in the institutional existence of the ED are in no way paradoxical vis a vis the general arguments on materiality. It is *not* necessary for a discourse to be *consistent* with the non-discursive domains it refers to. It does not even

1 On these processes, see Battisti, E. (1975): 161; see also Tafuri, M. (1976).
2 It is *not* an escapism or paying lip-service when 'radical' theoretical texts on planning are concluded by remarks such as: "An urbanism founded upon exploitation is a legacy of history. A genuinely humanizing urbanism has yet to be brought into being . . . And it remains for revolutionary practice to accomplish such a transformation" (Harvey, D. (1973): 314); or "The long theoretical detours, [that are] the mediations that are necessary to unblock concrete research in an ideologically dominated field, must not move off from the ultimate target of the tasks undertaken: to smash the technocratic and/or utopist myths about 'the urban' and to show the precise ways in which the practices thus connoted are articulated with social relations, that is to say, with the class struggle". (Castells, M. (1975): 481).
3 cf. "Science, generally speaking, costs the capitalist nothing, a fact that by no means hinders him from exploiting it. The science of others is as much annexed by capital as the labour of others. Capitalistic appropriation and personal appropriation, whether of science or of material wealth, are, however, totally different things . . ." (Marx, K. (1970), v.I: 365n).
4 cf. O'Malley, J.B. (1972), or Alberoni, F. (1972) – though they interpret these tendencies in a phenomenological sense.
5 *'detournement'* is a French term used after 1968 by the Situationists to refer to the tactical process by which opposite arguments or forms of representations are contained by assimilation and diversion.
6 cf. for ex., the constitution of the Club of Rome by leading international businessmen; the 'Limits to Growth' conference and publication supported by Ford, Fiat, Vokswagen foundations; and a Philips advertisement in *Time:* "Another innovation: our air pollution measuring system. It's the key to cleaner air". cf. also the emerging fact that corporations start owning, producing, marketing not only depollution devices, but also clean water, even clean air. (cf. Galtung, J. (1973): 101, 112-3n. For the last observation see A. Gorz in *Le Nouvel Observateur*, no. 397, 1972. For the relationship between *Limits to Growth* ideology and dependent countries, see Yavuz, F. (1975): 8, Sec. 25).
7 "as a rule, classes outliving their age turn to pessimism" (Rosenthal, M. & Yudin, E. (eds) (1967): 326).
8 cf. Sec. 4.5.12, and an example: *"Birds and Ecology"*: a conference in Gaziantep, a provincial Turkish town beset by many social and physical problems and with no tree left for birds to survive · due to so-called 'urban *development'*. (cf. the news in *Kurtuluş*, 24.5.1975, p.1.).
9 for ex., 'The death of thousands of fish floating in Vigo harbour in Spain has probably been caused

have to have a referent. The form of inconsistency, discrepancy or paradox is a function of the ideology of   capitalism. It is an ideology which *serves its purpose* by its *contradictoriness*, its *inconsistencies* and its frequent *incompetence* to explain the 'reality' of capitalism[1]. If, for the capitalist, housing is just another field of investment, forests, a source to be exploited, towns, a place to speculate on land, or Switzerland, a country where tax and banking is made convenient, the architectural, ecological, planning and geographic views on certain 'problems' can neither be the relative truths, nor can they be easily isolated from the effects of the former. *Neither the ideology of environment nor the 'environmental practices' can be understood without a clear understanding of the dominant ideology of the prevailing mode(s) of production.*

If, for example, designers propose 'disposable', 'throw-away', 'one-off', 'exchangeable' products (whether it is milk bottles or housing units), it is not so much a *technological* question as a result of the *commercial* demands of capitalist mode of production. Yet, what the ED does here is to displace such problems from their institutional settings, and pose them as *technical* or *technological.* One effect of this displacement is the emphasis on technical perfection guided by marketability. The criticism of these products is   confined to details rather than to their economic, social and ecological nature[2]. When, on the other hand, 'radical' and 'democratic' proposals find the chance of being experimented or implemented they can hardly override the political (and economic) powers that *dominate* the very field that is attempted to be 'radicalized' and 'democratized'.[3]

5.4 Concluding remarks

All that this section tried to emphasize is that the ED is *not* an autonomous practice. It is analysable as a discourse, yet its non-discursive relations can and should be analysed in order to situate the theoretical problems associated with the field of 'environment', and expressed in the ED. This is to be prior to any discussion on a referent (e.g. 'environment') which is *given* by a questionable discourse in the first place.

The channels by which a discourse is practised and an ideology is disseminated are as important to analyse as the concepts and mechanisms that make up the discourse. Social distribution of knowledges is as significant an object of study as the processes of their production. Class relativism of arguments is   as relevant as the theoretical relativism and subjectivism of the ED. A knowledge of the system of education, or forms of cultural imperialism, is as necessary as the contents of teaching or the mass-media.

However, there is no single, simple and general explanation for all ideological/political/ technical problems — as most of so-called 'environmental' issues are. Constitution of each problem has to be analysed to see the determinations, effects and other connexions.

---

by detergents used to clean up the nearby grounds of the recent world fishing exhibition, the city authorities said yesterday". (M. Walker, *The Guardian,* 19.10.1973)

1 As was the pre-Marxian political economy vis-a-vis the competitive capitalism.

2 For example, the fact that Concorde is an irrelevant 'achievement' in view of so much inefficiencies and inequities in public services is *distorted* and *blurred* by a discussion on its noise level. The controversy on high-rise/low-rise blurs the fact that *cheap* housing is being built as a logical consequence of the capitalist mode of ownership of, and access to, resources. The ED is not alone in this type of displacement, however. (When, for ex., the question of monarchy is reduced to the salary that the members of a of royal family get, it is largely depoliticized and distorted).

3 A very suggestive case is the fate of an attempt to involve residents in the design of housing during the building process:
"A housing estate using PSSHAK, the flexible internal partitioning system with tenant involvement over layout, [. . .] could now be sold off by the council. [. . .] any delay or a decision to sell could mean the end of the flexible plans. [. . .] GLC housing chairman G.T., under the new Tory administration, has instructed his officers to prepare a report to suggest a number of alternatives in line with the Tory's stated objectives of selling new housing" *(Building Design,* 1.8.1977, no. 357, p.1).

This is necessary not as an 'academic exercise', or as a 'purely'(?) theoretical activity. *All problems are complex* in some way. No problem is 'purely' theoretical, 'purely' architectural, or 'purely' political. Refusal to face these complexities would inevitably condemn simple answers to failure or redundancy. This failure or redundancy would be the result not only of a *discursive* dogmatism or reluctance to tackle complexity, but, perhaps, of some *non-discursive* determinants which are denied recognition in the first place.

6 The Status of the Environmental Discourse

" . . . it is this initial object which commands both the transparency of the problem and the impossibility of its solution."[1]

6.1 'Status' of discourses *(Introduction)*

The preceding chapters have tried to answer one fundamental, if implicit, question: *"What kind of discourse is the Environmental Discourse?"* In doing that they tackled the question in terms of its different, but closely related, aspects. This was essential in the *analysis* of a discourse as complex as the ED. But, can it be assumed that the question itself has been answered? Or, does it still need to be scrutinized? Are there further points of inquiry as far as the question is concerned?

The present chapter will be concerned with answering these *procedural* questions. In doing that it expects to discuss certain issues that might not have been sufficiently emphasized earlier on regarding the initial question itself. In this respect, this is a concluding chapter. And, due, mainly, to this specificity its mode of writing may be somehow different from the preceding chapters. To start with, the present chapter will try not to *repeat,* but will be content with *referring to,* those issues that have already been examined elsewhere in the study. It will therefore be brief. It will also try to *isolate* certain theoretical problems, draw out conclusions, and make brief statements concerning the question "what kind of discourse is the ED?"

The whole question can be summed up in the term *'status'.* This term is not meant to pre-establish, presume, or impose, any universal criteria of judgement. Nor does it mean that every discourse is classified according to some order containing *privileged* levels and points of view. It is not also the 'codename' for a science/ideology (or bourgeois/proletarian, good/bad, useful/useless) type of opposition, for the simple reason that *a discourse cannot be labelled as a whole.* Even the limited analysis of the ED presented in this study should be the sufficient evidence for this principle. Thus, 'status' should be taken as nothing more than a rough sum total of the *conclusions* of a discursive analysis.

It must also be stressed that the *status of a discourse* is not necessarily the same as the *status of the practices* it refers to, and it operates within. For example, though

---

1 Althusser, L. (1969): 124.

architectural practice finds part of its expression in the ED, or the ecology movement
solely relies on it, it does not follow that the status of architectural practice or that
of ecology movement fully correspond to the status of the ED.[1] Each practice,
whether discursive or not, is constituted by a large number of objects, instances,
levels and relationships. So, the status of a practice is observable in the effects of the
complex structure of these elements. Discourse, on the other hand, is a practice in
itself. Yet, its objects, mechanisms and effects exist at nearly *all* levels of the practices
in question. (For example, the ED operates, and its effects are present, in the *research,
conception, design, detailing, building, marketing* and *use* stages of building production
– though in different forms, and intensity.) Thus, it becomes essential to consider the
status of so-called 'environmental practices' in relation to the status of the ED while
keeping in mind their specific differences. The present study only marginally deals
with the former as it is a complex problem that deserves a study of its own and in as
much detail as the ED is studied here.

Finally, it can be observed that as the ED undertakes to solve, to talk about, or to
legislate so many diverse questions and problems, one expects it *to be able to answer
the questions about its own status*. In other words, it is expected of the ED to tell
the nature of its phenomena, its objects, the basis on which it can talk about them,
the differences and oppositions between several discourses in their claims to the same
objects, the adequacy of its statements, its divergences, multiplicities, compatibilities,
its criteria for inclusion and exclusion of problems, and its conception of the non-
discursive domains and their problems; but, it is impossible to find this discourse to
be aware of, or at least to be explicit about, its own nature. That is part of the reason
why the present analysis is done *from without* that discourse following the observations of the above-mentioned incapacity.

6.2.1 The status of the Environmental Discourse

The status of the ED can be considered in terms of
– its object,
– its structure,
– its mechanisms,
– its relations and effects,
which have already been analysed in detail in the preceding chapters, and as has been
said above there is no need to repeat what has already been discussed. Instead, a
relevant question will be discussed: it is that of whether or not status of a discourse
can be expressed in terms of a *'criterion of scientificity'*. In other words, it is a
question of whether the ED can, as a whole, or in its various elements and aspects,
be identified as, say, 'scientific', 'pre-scientific', 'pseudo-scientific', 'ideological', etc.

At the basis of this whole question lies two conjunctural observations – each one
regarding the arguments in different domains:
1) In the domains of theory, epistemology and philosophy of science there have long
been discussions on the possible *demarcation criteria* to determine what is and is not
'scientific'. This is an ongoing statement and will be referred to below only when
necessary.
2) In the domain which we provisionally designated in the beginning of the study as
architecture and planning practices, and which we showed to be dominated by the
ED, there were several arguments until recently. Yet, they were hardly ever concerned with a question of Science-non-Science; but, with those of Art-non-Art (or Art-
Artifact), Architecture-non-Architecture (or Architecture-Building), Urban-Rural,

---

1 For the conditions of relations between these practices and domains see Ch. 5.

Modern-Historical (or Modern-Vernacular) . . . that were of significance to the discourse. It was on these lines that not only discursive products (e.g. theories, courses, ideas, texts) but also non-discursive products (e.g. buildings, industrial objects, works of art, settlements) were *classified*.

It is regarding the second domain that we will now consider the question of status. We will relate the two domains, as it is in their *recent* positions that the present analysis takes their arguments and their relations as its object of study.

6.2.2 'Scientificity' and 'scientification' of the field of Environment

Following the growing awareness of the built-in incapacity of the 'environmental' practices to deal with many complex and urgent problems several 'diagnoses' and 'remedies' have been suggested especially during the last two decades. Each of these discursive suggestions and statements was inevitably influenced by the current mode of thought in popular as well as academic discourses and by the state of particular modes of production, particularly in Western social formations.

In the case of design and planning it was 'science' to which the appeal was made. When the source of incapacity and observed failures was identified as the *'lack of scientificity'*, the remedy that was suggested was bound to be to bring 'science' into design and into planning. These attempts can provisionally be called *'scientification'*. Consequently, scientific methods, approaches, techniques as well as 'jargon', were imported into the ED. Parallel to this process was the emergence of *'Environment'* as the central object of inquiry. Yet, due partly to the nature of the activities in question, and partly to the conceptions and misconceptions of 'Science' adopted by these activities, this 'scientification' process has brought in several confusions and pseudo-solutions[1].

But regardless of these confusions and misconceptions, the term 'Science' was already a (respectable) addition to the description of the 'environmental field'. An 'environmental science' was constructed out of the fuzzy combination of various disciplines, practices, discourses and techniques:
— climatology, engineering, acoustics, optics, psychology, systems theory, computer science,
— traditional techniques of design and planning,
— the vague, multiple, ideological and humanistic objects and structure of the ED.
The curious intermingling of these disciplinary and discursive inputs resulted in a *field* which is hard to define and operationalize — despite the fact that it is already widely recognized in institutions (e.g. departments of environmental science), in professional literature and in the ED as a whole.

It is on this background that the science/ideology debate has to be seen. To put it simply: posed *within* the ED itself it is not possible to conduct this debate mainly because:
a) the ED's conception of 'Science' is faulty, misleading and reductionist, or at best, questionable,
b) the ED lacks a conception of 'ideology',
c) the unsettled debate on science/ideology (taking place *outside* the ED) cannot be imported into an already confused and *a-theoretical* field. Thus, the present analysis of the status of the ED does certainly stay *outside* these positions, and tries to suggest a more cautious and analytical attitude towards the question of status.

---

1 Some of these have already been examined in Ch. 4.

It is useful to remember that it was for good reason that the present study refused
to answer the question "What is environment?" Instead, the question was transformed
into "What is 'Environment'?" (i.e. what is the nature and status of the discursive
object 'Environment'?).[1] Similarly; it was observed that the question of "What is
the status of the ED?" was itself debatable and problematic — as it might induce an
answer that would end up identifying a discourse as a 'thing' that could in return
be categorized as 'A', or 'B', or 'C' . . . (i.e. a pre-established and untheorized
categorization). In earlier discussions, it was often said that the ED was 'ideological',
'a-theoretical', 'pseudo-theoretical', 'anti-theoretical', 'vague', 'complex', etc. It may
now be asked why it is that the ED is identified in these terms, and what it is that
defines *its position vis-a-vis the sciences.*

If the ED is said in this study to be *'ideological'*, if its objects or mechanisms are
identified as ideological or a-theoretical, and if it is shown to be dominated by the
humanist/technicist/artistic . . . ideologies, it does *not* necessarily follow that this is
so because the ED is totally 'unscientific'. Regardless of the diversity of positions
vis-a-vis the question of 'Science' (in general)/'Ideology' (in general)[2] it is still possible
to suggest that *every conceivable discourse does not have to be either scientific or
ideological.* Thus, by stating that the ED is ideological, this study does not intend to
invoke the argument that "because ED is ideological, it is *therefore* unscientific",
or that "it is ideological *because* it is not scientific". The fact of being 'ideological'
does not necessarily entail being the specific opposite of 'scientific'. In other words,
a discourse can be ideological not solely because it is *not* scientific, but because of
its specific structure, mechanisms, relations and effects. The ED is ideological in the
same way as a discourse can be technical, political, scientific or artistic. This
identification originates neither from an absolute criterion of scientificity, nor from
a subjective choice between several designations. In short, *a complex and widespread
discourse,* such as the ED, *cannot and should not be compartmentalized, labelled,
criticized or discussed, in a simple and wholesale manner.*

Moreover, the answer to the question "what kind of discourse is the ED?" extends
far beyond the limits specified by the term 'ideological'. First of all, the ED has
several aspects that are, or can be, considered as *science-based.* It has several state-
ments/objects/problematics that are *neither* ideological *nor* scientific, but, for
example, *technical, artistic, observational, experiential, behavioural, climatological,
literary,* . . . The practices such as architecture and planning involve informations
('savoir'), as well as knowledges *('connaissance').*[3] In other words, they operate by

1 cf. Ch. 2.
2 Positions in this matter can roughly be summarized as such (without any intention of writing a
'history of ideas', thus, without giving extensive references as to who occupies what position, etc.):
— Science is different from Ideology,
— Science is the opposite of Ideology,
— Science excludes Ideology,
— There is a 'rupture' (a 'break') between Ideology and Science,
— Ideology is the pre-history of Science,
— Science and Ideology are the instances of social formations,
— Science *is* ideological,
— Science is not exclusive of Ideology,
— A certain Science (e.g. Marxism) is the ideology of a class.
— 'Science/Ideology demarcation is not possible:
   (as it implies a separation of knowledge,
   (as there cannot be (and there is not) any demarcation criteria,
   (as it does not exist in the first place,
   (as the question is posed 'incorrectly').
— . . .
— . . .

3 This distinction is a useful one. It avoids the confusion in English between *knowledge* and *information* both of which are used in everyday and theoretical discourses in a variety of ways, and often

means of many tools which *include* experience, know-how, catalogued information, public standards, by-laws, codes of practice, building regulations just as much as knowledge and principles produced within sciences, such as physics, chemisty, geology, geography, political economy. They employ techniques of measurement, representation, calculation, communication — most of which are the techniques of other disciplines and practices, though architecture and planning develop their own techniques too. Some of these techniques, whether they are borrowed or developed within practices, may be the techniques of sciences while some others may be auxiliary to them. Due to the specific character of each discipline or practice, and that of their techniques, methods and modes of perception and representation their 'contributions' to the 'environmental practices' and to the ED are different both in kind and in degree. Consequently, if the ED cannot be precise in its use of the terms and techniques of, say, physics, or political economy, it is partly due to the inherent nature of that discourse, and partly to the mismatch between the objects and structures of the ED and those of other domains for which (and in which) those terms and techniques were originally produced.

Now, a question may be asked as to whether these critical and somehow sceptical observations imply an abandonment of efforts to *improve* the discourse and practices that operate in the field of environment. Leaving aside the general question of *what to do with the ED following the present analysis* (which will be discussed in the *Conclusion*) some preliminary suggestions can be made: while there are good reasons for questioning the *status* of the ED and the 'scientification' processes, this does *not* mean that the *objects and problems which the ED refers to* cannot be studied, appropriated, or dealt with in terms of sciences or their techniques. These objects and problems which are *presently designated and defined by the ED* should be seen not as specified objects, but as the *indications of the loci of problems* (some of which could indeed be false, or non-problems). This question is significant not only because it is of discursive interest but also because it is one which involves the very activities of design and planning. It is a question of *"what* actually, and what exactly, does design activity design?"* and, *"what* actually does the planning activity plan?"*[1] . To answer these questions and to be able to identify the *objects* of design and planning it is absolutely essential that the nature of these activities as *practices* should be identified.

As was said at the beginning, the status of (environmental) practices and that of the ED are not to be confused, though, it was added, they are closely related. This relationship is most apparent in the types of objects and problems that each practice deals with, and the techniques that each one uses. Usually it is through a specialized discourse that these objects, problems and techniques are coordinated with each other. And, it is also in this context that the material conditions of existence of the ED can be studied.[2] It is therefore relevant to ask whether the objects that are dealt with in design and planning activities are actually constituted and defined *within* these practices. If so, the argument becomes circular:
— The ED dominates these practices, *(and/therefore)*
— It dominates the definition of objects that these practices deal with, and that, in fact,

interchangably. The French distinction, stressed by Foucault, avoids this confusion. (See, Foucault, M. (1972): 15n, Ch. 6, etc.). (The inability of the English *language* to distinguish scientific knowledge from other(everyday, technical) types of knowledges can be related to the insistence of British *philosophy* on everyday language as the basis of philosophic discourse. This connexion, however, is too specific and marginal to be the concern of the present study.) For an analysis of architectural and planning discourses and education on the basis of these distinctions, see Teymur, N.& E. (1978).
1 These questions have already been asked and discussed in a different context; see Sec. 2.4.
2 For the last point, see Ch. 5.

constitute the practices.

Avoiding this circularity requires not simply getting out of it, or refusing to recognize its existence. It requires a radical reconstitution of the conceptions of 'Environmental Discourse' and 'Environmental practices'. This, in return, implies an *analysis* of these fields and phenomena as complex wholes with determinate interrelationships. It is only on the basis of such an analysis that these fields and phenomena as well as the 'problems' they refer to can be *redefined, reorganized* or, if necessary, *transformed.*

7 Conclusion

*"Since it is not for us to create
a plan for the future that will
hold for all time, all the more
surely what we contemporaries
have to do is the uncompromising
critical evaluation of all that exists. . ."*[1]

There can be no finality in theory. No analysis and no critique can ever be closed. Where and when a particular *inquiry* begins and ends cannot absolutely be determined. Yet, a *text* must be concluded within particular conjunctural limitations. The *'Conclusion'* therefore marks the momentary 'end' of a study. It therefore is an appropriate place where the conditions of this 'end', and of what may follow it, can be discussed. That is why, instead of repeating and summarizing the content of the study, this section will point out some key questions briefly and without much diversions, distractions and examples.

These questions will basically be concerned with the type of the attempted *intervention* of the study and its possible *contributions*. In the *General Introduction* the conjuncture in which the study was initiated, formulated and developed has already been discussed. It was stressed that the study took as its object not the given problems of a discourse, but *that discourse itself.* Therefore, its intervention is primarily aimed at the discourse and the practices using that discourse. In other words, the initial production of the study is a unity that it proposed to call *'Environmental Discourse'.* Having identified this unity, the study went on to analyse it. Yet, as there was no adequate method or mode of analysis within the ED and within the so-called 'environmental' practices, it had to develop one. In the end, the study produced not only an *analysis of the ED,* but also a *mode of analysis* that can further be developed and used in similar projects. Finally, it is relevant to the purposes of this *Conclusion* to discuss the possible *effects* that the above-mentioned intervention is likely to produce.

First of all, the precise nature of the intervention should be identified. It was said that the intervention of the study was to the 'ED' and 'environmental' practices. Yet, as there was no *unity defined as 'ED' prior to the present analysis, it had to be constituted* (only to be *deconstituted).* Thus the intervention, in fact, was
a) to the practices themselves where the ED was operative at various levels, and
b) to the dominant ideology one of whose components is the 'ideology of environment.'

1. K. Marx, (From a letter to Ruge, Sept. 1843).

Now, as explained in the *General Introduction,* the reason for developing a mode of analysis was mainly the absence of one adequate to the task in hand. Without repeating what has already been said about the specificity of this (discursive) mode of analysis, we may examine *what* it had achieved and *how.*

The question of *what* the analysis has achieved is bound up with those of
– the state and the effects of the ED prior to the analysis,
– what the analysis did, or made possible,
– what it did *not* do, or did *not* allow to happen,
– its effects on its object (i.e. the ED), or on the questions which are presently expressed in the ED,
– its effects on the general field of theory.

On the other hand, the question of *how* it achieved the analysis, the critique and the effects mentioned is implicit both in the description of the discourse analysis as attemptedin the *Introduction* and in the discussion on *what* that follows.

The ED was shown in the study to be a widespread discourse that is constituted basically by a 'man-environment' problematic. The elements of that problematic, namely 'Man' and 'Environment' were surveyed through the specific discourses in architecture, planning, ecology, industrial design, social sciences and everyday life. They were shown to belong to an ideology of humanism the epistemological structure of which was constituted essentially by the subject-object couple. Thus, the analysis has identified the *objects* and the *structure* of the ED. It was then shown that that discourse was producing its effects by means of a set of *mechanisms.* These mechanisms were not readily and explicitly given in the discourse, but had to be seen in their operations and effects. Mechanisms such as 'shifts', 'reductions', 'anthropomorphism', 'amphibologies', 'ignoring the obvious', 'division of reality' . . . were all identified, analysed, and their relations to each other have been demonstrated. This was followed by an examination of the *relations* of the ED with other discourses and with non-discursive domains.

In the course of these analyses a large number of discursive effects were observed. Some of these were recorded, illustrated and discussed. For example, it was argued that the ED's claim to 'scientificity' was impossible to maintain following the analysis of its objects, structures and mechanisms, as well as its effects. We may take a specific case which has already been examined in the study. The ED presents many socio-economic problems and all architectural, urban and ecologic problems as *'environmental'.* Yet, as the notion of 'environment' is a vague generalization which defies definition and scientific specification, the problems that it supposedly defines are all reduced, purified, simplified and *displaced.* They are confined to a homogenous field where everything is classified according to a given pure principle, and where there is no contradiction (except perhaps between 'Man' and 'Environment'!). Once the stability of the field is presumed, different types of phenomena and relations are either dismissed, or labelled as pathological. This leads to a conservative ideology whereby that which exists is taken as the 'natural' and 'normal'. In this way 'stability', 'harmony' and 'normality' are assumed to be the *original state* of the M-E relationship that needs to be achieved. As to the ways in which this original state is proposed to be achieved different mechanisms are produced. Yet, all these mechanisms are based on the same (M-E or subject-object) problematic. The same problematic is present in the 'methodological' schemas of causality, correspondence and correlations as well as in reductions, shifts, confusions, analogies and anthropomorphisms.

On the basis of these central mechanisms, problems expressed in terms of a relationship between 'man' and 'environment' are treated as purely physical (hence, 'physicalism'), ecological (hence, 'ecologism'), technical (hence, 'technicism'), ethical (hence, 'moralism'), or psychological (hence, 'psychologism'). However, in all the reductions M-E schema is present as the universal, cosmological and ideal invariant.

As all these and other mechanisms are amply discussed in the text, there is no need to go further than these brief remarks. What we are really concerned with here in this *Conclusion* is that the study has *analysed* the ED in terms of these and other mechanisms as well as in terms of its objects, structures and relations. In doing these, it opened up the possibility of further and more specific studies on the *effects* of the discourse in different domains and practices.

Whilst some of the effects are implicit in the mechanisms concerned, some are not. For example, when architectural and urban problems are conceived of, and presented as purely physical and natural, the ideological effects of this mechanism penetrate certain domains far beyond the physical organization of objects and functions in particular settlements. It involves naturalization, hence, neutralization, of the fundamental social contradictions that lie behind or beneath the physical ones. The contradiction between labour and capital, between producers and consumers, between landlords and tenants are all transformed into those between 'Man' and 'Environment', planner and planned, designer and user . . . Not that some of the latter type of contradictions (if they are 'contradictions') are not in themselves worth looking at; but once the fundamental social relations of the first group are effectively obscured, distorted or ignored, the latter are not any longer conceived as the secondary or tertiary contradictions that they are. Thus, it is not only that such reductions produce many ideological and political effects, immediate technical solutions too may become distorted, ineffectual and inconsequential.

This produces several other effects. Many issues that would otherwise be identified are obscured or ignored. Misplaced solutions are transferred into utopian realms, mystic states of mind, global reorganizations, petty reforms, or individualistic and anarchistic interventions. One significant effect that has already been discussed in the text is the tendency to *blame* certain subjects as the 'sources' of problems. As with most of 'environmentalist' arguments, this one is quite consistent with the ideological arguments of the time. During the times of crises certain groups of people are blamed for the failures of a particular social system: it is the Jews, the blacks, the Arabs, the migrants workers or the squatters that are held responsible for all sorts of problems from unemployment to housing shortage. At a more specific level, all blame for the faults of urban and architectural products are put on the *apparent* decision-makers, namely architects and planners, or on the particular physical forms (such as tower blocks), or physical properties (such as high density). The significant point in this mechanism is that *it* is precisely the corresponding consequence of the technicist ideology that those technical professionals operate and argue within. Once socio-economic determinants are reduced to the technical domain, and once social structure is explained (!) by physical forms, there remains no reason why technical solutions, physical forms or their executioners should not be *seen* as the main sources of responsibility for the faults that are mostly the structural consequences of particular socio-political systems.

This is only one example for the effects of the ED in the conceptualization of problems. There are many cases where the individualist, relativist, subjectivist, hedonistic, consumerist, sentimental, elitist, and *basically a-theoretical*, arguments of the ED dominate architectural and planning practices as well as the mass-media. Yet, a concluding chapter is not the appropriate place to discuss more than one or two cases like those above. The main purpose of this discussion was to point out the incapacity (a) of the 'environmental' practices, and (b) of the ED, to understand the *non-technical* determinants of their technical involvements; and, as amply illustrated in the study, attempts to compensate this incapacity tends to fall into other types of reductions. For example, design activity is reduced to the cognitive processes that go on in the 'head' of the designer, or physical deterioration of cities and countryside are reduced to the "man's cruelty to his environment".

Surely, these rather brief and incomplete insertions into the *Conclusion* are not expected to give any new insight into the nature of the ED. What they lead to is a question which has already been posed earlier on: *"What did the present analysis do to this state of affairs, or, at least, what did it make possible?"*

First of all, by pointing out some problems that were (theoretically) non-existing it opened up the possibility of *questioning* certain obvious-looking positions, pre-defined issues, unquestioned assumptions, and closed arguments. This type of intervention is *even by itself* sufficiently suggestive of further efforts on the same lines. What is of primary importance in theoretical enterprises of this sort is the possibility of *opening up* the channels for new areas of inquiry, new modes of analysis, new terms and new problematics. *Criticizing* a whole discourse which is present in every conceivable field, *showing* its mystificatory effects, its relations to other ideologies and its a-theoretical structure, are the necessary, if not the sufficient, conditions of advances in understanding problems.

This 'opening up through a critique' could not be achieved without a whole set of other interventions that this study has attempted. First of all, the study has (hopefully) demonstrated that no problem is simple (both conceptually and practically), and that no problem can be explained in terms of simple, universal, schemas, single causes, or pure principles. For the same token, it was stressed that complex phenomena and objects, such as cities, buildings, regions and societies cannot be explained or described as obvious, empirical unities; and that their complexity cannot be analysed by reducing them to one or more of their aspects (e.g. spatial, functional, psychological, visual . . .). On the basis of this conception the study has analysed the *structure* of the ED in relation to the set of *mechanisms* on the one hand, and to its discursive and non-discursive *relations,* on the other. Unlike the environmentalist modes of treating the relations, this study saw them not in terms either of total autonomy or of total determinism, but as *the absolute condition of existence of the ED as a social practice.*

The internal complexity of a discourse is inevitably connected with many 'external' formations — whether discursive or non-discursive. Yet, preconditions of such an understanding were shown in the study to be
a) a shift from the abstract and schematic domain of M-E relationship,
b) abandonment of the terms and relations of the M-E problematic, and
c) making possible the analysis of specific problems without recourse to a-theoretical modes of explanation.
These preconditions involve a radical questioning not of particular definitions of 'Man' or 'Environment'; or, of suggested relations between them; but, of *whether there are such theoretical concepts, things or relations in the first place.* This, in fact, would lead to a deconstruction, and if necessary and possible, to a transformation, of the *problematic* itself.

Once such a radical strategy was initiated, the analysis could easily take up what is *absent* in the arguments of the discourse, as much as what is *present.* For, there are numerous cases where either certain questions were simply left out of the discourse; or, in what is *included,* certain problems, terms or frames of reference are *excluded.* The most common mechanism of this act of exclusion is, of course, the peculiar globality of the term 'environment'. While it leaves little outside its all-embracing generality, it is precisely that generality which excludes many fundamental objects and relations due to the inherent *lack of specificity* in its objects and relations. Demystification of this generality by deconstructing its unity was the most potential step in the analysis. For, once this generality and its supporting mechanisms were demystified, the whole concept of 'environment' can no longer be used without first 'bracketing', and then, scrutinizing, it. Disarticulating the environmental problematic leads to the disappearance from the field of inquiry many (pseudo-, or non-) problems. This deconstruction and disarticulation does not, as it may first be imagined, lead to a deprivation of the (already barren) field, but to the generation of new approaches. This rather paradoxical process (which might be conceptualized in the popular conception of 'dialectics') is inherent in the initial achievement of the study: *only by establishing the unity of the ED as a new object of study could it attempt to deconstruct it.* And, only by such a deconstruction could it suggest not a *void* to be filled, but a *clarity* to be exploited. After all, by dissolving the 'everythingness' of the term 'environment' those 'everything' that it refers to *do not all* disappear — though some may do so. Those objects or problems that disappear, however, are the ones which are the most 'environmental' of the field of 'environment'. Those whose definitions are dependent upon an undefinable and ubiquitous generality cannot be sustained once that generality is no longer the unquestioned term of reference. (This process is quite similar to the circular conceptualization of God that is sustainable only on the basis of a belief on its existence. Once the belief is shaken, the frame of reference can no longer provide its own proof.)

Now, as has already been remarked, despite the fact that the ED generates an immense amount of studies, statements and arguments, the latters' noticeable silence on the question of their own epistemological status, and on the theoretical viability of their terms and procedures is quite consistent with the specificity of the basis on which the whole discourse stands. It is to that basis that this study addresses itself.

In line with the initial decision of this *Conclusion* not to present a complete summary of the study, these fundamental points should be sufficient to indicate the nature of its intervention and intended contributions. Yet, in considering what the study has achieved, it is not only what it *did*, but also what it *did not do,* that deserves some attention.

Firstly, the study constituted a *new* object, i.e. the ED, though not to legitimize, but to deconstruct and to criticize it. By doing this, on the other hand, it had no intention of proposing an alternative discourse, or alternative definition of 'environment' or 'M-E relationship'. *Discourses are not simple objects that can be dismissed, ignored, created or proposed, by individual inquiries.* They are complex objects that have determinate places in social formations. They can, nevertheless, be used, defined, analysed, criticized and, if possible, transformed. Thus, as this study does not intend to propose an alternative discourse in place of the ED, nor can it be a substitute for the type of (mostly empirical) studies that the ED makes possible. Consequently, it has no intention of getting into a debate with endless positions on how 'M and E interact' by putting forward just *another* mode of interaction. As was repeatedly stressed in the study, *what is needed is a complete change of the terms and their relations* as they exist in the M-E problematic. In this way, the study does not prescribe an alternative way in which practicing designers and planners should (or should not) handle 'environment'. For, it is argued that contrary to the general conception in the ED, *what the designers design and the planners plan is not 'environment' but complex sets of objects and relations whose physical existence as well as theoretical conception are socially determined.*

The main reason for the particular level of analysis, its degree of generality and its conscious refusal to deal with the specific problems of the 'environment' have already been made clear. It must be said on this occasion that, this is in no way an escape from specific analyses. Due mainly to the theoretical conjuncture in which they were produced such specific studies *could not* be done — primarily for theoretical reasons. Nor could they be done in a way that would have satisfied the present author. Finally, the function of a discourse analysis is fundamentally different from that of some practical activities or empirical studies. The latter are to be considered in particular cautiousness so long as their theoretical status cannot be explicitly maintained.

The question of *what* this study did and did not do invokes that of *how* (as singled out at the beginning). Yet, as this question has already been examined in the *General Introduction*, we may only look at those issues that are directly relevant to an understanding of the intervention which is being described here.

As has already been remarked, this study was made possible by a radical shift of attention from *given answers* to *radical questions.* This was partly a reaction to the abundance of easy and specific, yet equally vague and undisputed, answers to unasked questions, or to questions which carried with them their own answers. (Any question which was asked in terms of M-E relationship had to be *governed* by the M-E problematic whereas this analysis questioned the validity of that very problematic.) Secondly, the study has attempted a shift of attention from entities and things to relations and discursive objects. This enabled the analysis to free itself from the limitations imposed by the preconceptions of things. But, this in no way impaired the development of a materialist analysis of the ED. On the contrary, only by refusing to recognize the cosmological conceptions of its objects could the ED be treated as a formation whose objects, structure, mechanisms and relations are its constitutive components. This approach implied the requirement that objects, phenomena and problems become objects of analysis only when they are theoretically identifiable unities. Prior to such an identification neither visually perceived objects, nor empirical individuals, nor their relations can be considered as *theoretical* objects. Ideal types, pure principles or ideological schemas preclude theoretical analysis, and precondition the objects to be studied.

Finally, there is the question of the *effects* that this critique might have on the ED itself. Having analysed the large variety of problems within the ED, it shouldn't be an excessive claim to suggest that *the very identification of these problems is likely to be the major effect of this analysis.*

As we have seen, the architectural and planning practices deal with many complex problems — technical, social, economic. Yet, they very seldom discuss their own fundamental problems — epistemological, discursive, ideological. The reasons for this inability or insularity have already been analysed in the study. It is on the basis of this observation that *showing* these practices and the ED their epistemological and discursive problems is expected to have some profound effects on them. If these practices are basically pragmatic, technicist, cosmological and substantially closed; a self-critical, theoretical and open-ended inquiry should be more than useful for the future of these practices. Similarly, once the closed arguments of the discourse are opened up, once their 'pure principles' and 'original unities' are deconstructed, disected and demystified, and finally, once the M-E problematic is shown to be the basis of majority of problems, it is expected that *the ED can no longer operate as if none of these has ever happened.* After all, this study assumed that even if the ED is vague, ideological, often confusing, and incapable of theoretical production, it is still justifiable to study it for reasons that are both internal and external to it. As to the *internal* reasons, this study and its extensions can perhaps evoke the need for self-criticism *within* the ED — since any field which does not, or cannot, question its own assumptions, its own problematic, its own modes of expression and its own con-

nections, is doomed either to unforgivable failures, or to eventual redundancy in the face of complex problems. It is on this background that this study believes to have prepared the ground for several potential lines of development:
— it opens up the possibility of *conducting* the activities of designing, planning, studying and describing without recourse to the questionable objects and mechanisms of the ED,
— it expects to *generate* further studies both on the discourse itself, and on some of the problems whose locations are indicated by the ED, (of course, after eliminating non-problems),
— in other words, it establishes some *starting points* for detailed (and if necessary empirical) studies,
— it suggests a possible *direction* that a critique or a discourse analysis can (or should) take,
— it suggests an *approach* to the understanding of the relationship between theoretical work and professional practices — which is totally different from the prevailing modes of isolationism and theoreticism, or pragmatism and anti-intellectualism,
— it puts forward the conception that while there is no 'Architecture' or 'Planning', there are *'architectural practice'* and *'planning practice'*. These practices are not, then, reducible either to their physical products or to their ideological self-images. Instead, they are complex social practices that are constituted by internal and external elements ranging from cultural and ideological to purely technical, from aesthetic to economic, from measurable to unmeasurable, and from spatial to conceptual, *instances* and *levels*,
— thus, it took as its object the *discourse* — i.e. the level at which the complex relationship between the above-mentioned instances and levels can be analysed, criticized and if possible, transformed. This approach was based on the principle that no problem, no object and no knowledge is possible without some *discursive* means to formulate them. In this sense, the present study presents not only the knowledge of a specific discourse, but also that of the complex whole of which that discourse is an element.

Finally, according to the *conjuncture* that was described in the *General Introduction* the present study was made possible by a striking abundance of theoretical problems, and an absence of theoretical tools and terms to deal with them. This, of course, was a *negative* condition for the study. The *positive* conditions of its existence, however, were described as the developments in the theoretical fields in social sciences and epistemology. It is in this sense that the study claims a place not only in the 'environmental' practices and their discourse(s), but also in the 'non-environmental' ones. While to the first area the study attempts to contribute a critical and theoretical mode of analysis, to the second, however, the message of the existence of a widespread ideology represented by the ED. Furthermore, in view of the fact that the *discourse analysis*, especially in the English-speaking world, is still an unknown mode of analysis, it is expected that this study will be an early example to this mode not only in the field of architecture and planning, but also in social sciences and art criticism.

These last points, however, need some explanation. As was stressed in the *General Introduction* as well as on several other occasions this study refuses to use or to propose a 'blue print' approach, and that it is against defining theoretical problems prior to their analyses. Similarly, it does not want to suggest specific areas where *its* mode of analysis can, or should, be used. First of all, the conditions of the ED *as well as* those of its analysis in this study may not be present in, or similar to, each and every domain; though, of course, different discourse analyses can be constituted for different problems or discursive formations with the present study as an *example* –and, *not* as a *model*. This suggestion should, however, be seen in terms of the specificity of the present

analysis. As it is a study at *discursive, epistemological* and *theoretical* level(s), its
'exemplary' function should primarily be at these levels whether in other analyses
of the ED, or in those of 'non-environmental' discursive formations.

Secondly, other studies may take the structure, arguments or criticisms provided
by this study as the bases or assumptions in their analyses in dealing with specific
theoretical problems of the ED. Many of these problems have already been defined
and analysed in the study, (e.g., the natures of architectural 'knowledge' and of
design and planning activities; the question of the relationship between social and
physical phenomena; the specific structures and effects of arguments on participation,
self-build, consumerism, vandalism, professionalism, . . .). These and some others
can (and should) be identified, formulated and analysed in greater detail, and, most
important of all, *in correct terms* in order not to reproduce the ideological structure
of the ED. As the present study has already cleared a theoretical terrain of some
of its obstacles and mystificatory structures, that terrain should now be open for
specific, precise, rigorous, and if necessary, empirical, studies on 'practical' problems
whose 'locations' are presently pointed out by the ED, and (supposedly) tackled
in 'environmental' practices in a rather narrow, reductionist, a-theoretical, and
often inconsequential, manner.

Finally, this study should enable several discourses and disciplines, (which are
not primarily concerned with so-called 'environment'), to identify the *effects*, in
them, of the ED. As was continuously stressed, the ED operates in many domains
where its epistemological structure and elements as well as its arguments (such as
those mentioned above) are *present* in a variety of ways. These domains (i.e., specific
disciplines or practices) take as given these elements, and the arguments based on
them, without questioning (a) the status of these elements in a (possible) discourse
on 'environment', and (b) their conditions of existence in the first place. This mode
of operation is indicative not only of their ignorance of the ED, but, most
significantly, of their own inabilities to specify and to criticize (a) their own
epistemological and discursive structures, and (b) their own conditions for borrowing
or sharing certain discursive elements. In other words, in whatever domain the
elements and the arguments of the ED, (as identified and criticized in this study),
are present, there is considerable reason to undertake studies of those domains
vis-a-vis the points just raised. It is to this process involving 'non-environmental'
domains that the present study expects to give an initial impetus. Furthermore,
it is in this sense that, whatever its starting point or initial focus of attention, by
its introduction of the discourse analysis this study addresses itself to the discursive
levels of many practices with or without *apparent* 'environmental' involvements.

In all these interventions the study should not, as has already been stressed, be
taken as a finished statement, a blueprint, or a model, but, as an *example*, an
attitude, and at best, as a *perspective.* The purpose of pointing this out again is not,
however, to emphasize any 'modesty' on the part of the author, but to assert one
of the fundamental requirements of theoretical work: Even a complex and rigorous
work as the present one cannot have the right to claim absolute validity or
applicability. But, *at the same time,* it has the right, on the basis of its own
experience and achievement, to assert that the attitude, the perspective or the
mode of analysis that it represents are indicative of *the way in which theoretical
work is, and should be, done.* Theoretical analysis *is* a complex and difficult process.
It involves (often painful and disappointing) efforts which cannot be expressed in,
or reduced to, the text(s) produced. It may produce more questions than answers,
more problems than solutions. But, in line with the expected interventions in

'environmental' and 'non-environmental' domains, it carries with it the implicit requirements of self-criticism and openness to development. Both the conscious denial *to itself* of establishing another orthodoxy or 'model', and the emphasis on self-criticism and openness are the prices to be paid for genuine theoretical achievements. The difficulties of such an approach is obvious. But, then, how else can the difficulties of the object of study be tackled if the *essential* difficulties of being open and self-critical are not accepted as part of the whole enterprise? After all, " can the river be crossed without getting wet?", or is it not the case that the easiest and the safest thing is *not* to tackle any problem at all?

These closing remarks are not meant to discourage others to undertake similar projects, but to warn them against the non-entities that easy approaches and given answers often lead to.

Finally, if this study carries the message that many explanations are themselves in need of explanations, and many answers themselves are in need of questions, it will also imply that not only the ('real') problems, but also their conceptions *can* be seen differently, and can be the objects of serious analyses.

What is most important, however, is to respond to the painstaking demonstration in this study that *epistemological and discourse analyses are not involved with just one more 'aspect' of problems, but with their very existence.* Consequently, *a critical awareness of what precisely it is that one is designing, planning, building, producing, studying, talking about or teaching;* and *an understanding of how the discursive level is responsible for most of the conceptions and misconceptions in all sorts of practices* is absolutely essential. It is primarily to the development of this awareness and understanding that the present study addresses itself.

Bibliography

ABBREVIATIONS USED: (Longer titles that are used frequently, and bibliographical abbreviations).

AAAG: Annals of the Association of American Geographers
AAQ: Architectural Association Quarterly
AD: Architectural Design
AJ: Architects' Journal
AIP J: American Institute of Planners'Journal
ART: Architectural Research and Teaching
B : Books
BD: Building Design
E & B: Environment and Behavior
Ed : Edition
(ed): Editor
(eds): Editors
et.al.: Others (authors)
E & S: Economy and Society
ES: Epistemologie Sociologiques
ISSJ: International Social Science Journal

J : Journal
JAR: Journal of Architectural Research
L'E G: L'Espace Géographique
L'H & S: L'Homme et la Société
M-E S: Man-Environment Systems
NLR: New Left Review
P : Publishers, Press
RIBA J: Royal Institute of British Architects' Journal
RP: Radical Philosophy
SSI: Social Science Information
TP: Theoretical Practice
Tr : Transactions of . . .
U : University
UP: University Press
US: Urban Studies

Abel, C. (1974) : 'The Learning of architectural concepts', (seminar paper), Portsmouth Polytechnic.
Adam, M.Y. (1973) : *A Theoretical Study of Industrial Housing Design Policies with regard to Potential Social Change in Turkey,* PhD Thesis, U. of Edinburgh.
Agron, G. (1974) : 'Behavior in institutional settings', in Moos , R.H. & Insel, P.M. (eds) (1974) : *Issues in Social Ecology,* P. Alto, National P.B. : 238–47.
Alberoni, F. (1972) : 'Technical progress and the dialectics of existence', *Human Context,* (4) 2: 285-305.
Alexander, C. (1966): 'A city is not a tree', *Design,* 206:46-55.
Althusser, L. (1969) : *For Marx,* London, Allen Lane.
Althusser, L., (1970) : Part I:' From Capital to Marx's Philosophy', 'Part II : The Object of Capital', in Althusser, L. & Balibar, E : *Reading Capital,* N. York, Pantheon.
Althusser, L. (1971) : *Lenin and Philosophy and Other Essays,* London, NLB.
Althusser, L. (1976) : *Essays in Self-criticism,* London, NLB.
Altman, I. (1973) : 'Some perspectives on the study of man-environment phenomena', in Preiser, W.F.E. (ed) (1973) vol II : 99–113.
Amir, S. (1972) : 'Highway location and public opposition', *E & B,* (4) 4 : 413–36.
Appleyard, D. (1976) : *Planning a Pluralist City : Conflicting Realities in Ciudad Guayana,* Mass, MIT.

Arendt, H. (1958) : *The Human Condition,* Chicago, U. of Chicago P.

Aubert, J. *et.al.* (1968) : 'L'architecture comme probleme theoretique', *L'Architecture D'Aujourd-hui,* 139 : 81–92 and CXXXVIII–CXXXIX.

Bachelard, G. (1948) : *Le Rationalisme Appliqué,* Paris, PUF.

Bachelard, G. (1975) : *Le Nouvel Esprit Scientifique,* Paris, PUF. (First ed. 1934).

Badiou, A. (1969) : *Le Concept de Modèle,* Paris, Maspero.

Baladier, C. (1976) : 'La carriere difficile d'un terme', *Architecture,* 397 : 42–3.

Bannister, D. & Fransella, F. (1971) : *Inquiring Man : The Theory of Personal Constructs,* Harmondsworth, Penguin.

Barbey, G. & Gelber, C. (eds) (1973) : *The Relationship Between the Built Environment and Human Behaviour,* Lausanne, IREC.

Barel, Y. (1972) : 'La reproduction sociale, itinéraire d'une recherche', *L'H & S,* 24–25 : 207–20.

Barthes, R. (1967) : *Elements of Semiology,* London, Cape.

Battisti, E. (1975) : *Architettura Ideologia e Scienza, Teoria e Practica nelle Discipline di Progetto,* Milan, Feltrinelli.

Bauer, E. (1971): 'Die Hilflosigkeit der Sociologie im Städtebau', in Korte, H. (ed) (1971): *Zur Politisierung der Stadtplanung,* Dusseldorf, Bertelsmann, U.V. 9–84.

Baum, A. *et.al.*(1974): 'Architectural variants of reaction to spatial invasion', *E & B,* (6) 1 : 91ff.

Bell, G. & Tyrwhitt, J, (eds) (1972) : *Human Identity in the Urban Environment,* Harmondsworth, Penguin.

Berdyaev, N. (1955) : *The Meaning of the Creative Act,* London, V. Gollancz.

Berndt, H. *et.al.* (1968) : *Architektur als Ideologie,* Frankfurt, Suhrkamp.

Bernstein, B. (1973) : *Class, Codes and Control,* London, Paladin.

Bhaskar, R. (1975) : 'Feyerabend and Bachelard : Two Philosophies of Science' *NLR,* 94 : 31–55.

Biolat, G. (1973) : *Marxisme et Environnement,* Paris, Ed. Sociales.

Blackburn, R. (ed) (1972) : *Ideology in Social Science,* London, Fontana.

Blackstone, W.T. (ed)(1975) : *Philosophy and Environmental Crisis,* Georgia, U. of Georgia P.

Blair, T.L. (1970) : 'Social Space', *Official Architecture & Planning,* Dec. : 1083–5.

Bonjour, G.P. – (1967) : *The Categories of Dialectical Materialism : Contemporary Soviet Ontology,* Dordrecht, D. Reidel.

Bonsiepe, G. (1975) : *Teoria e Practica del Disegno Industriale,* Milan, Feltrinelli.

Bose, A. (1975) : *Marxian and Post-Marxian Political Economy,* Harmondsworth, Penguin.

Boutourline, S. (1970) : 'The concept of environmental management', in Proshansky, H.M. *et.al* (eds) (1970) : 496–501, (repr. from *Dot Zero,* (4), 1967).

Brady, J.V. *et.al* (1974) : 'Design of a programmed environment for the experimental analysis of social behavior' , in Carson, D.H. (ed) (1974) : (7) : 187–208.

Brail, R.K. & Chapin, F.S. Jr. (1973) : 'Activity patterns of urban residents', *E & B.,* (5)2 : 163ff.

Bresson, F. *et.al.* (1974) : *De L'Espace Corporel à L'Espace Écologique,* Paris, PUF.

Brewster, B. (1971) : 'Althusser and Bachelard', *TP,* 3 + 4 : 25–37.

Broadbent, G. (1973) : *Design in Architecture,* London, J. Wiley.

Broadbent, G . (1975) : 'Bofill', *AD,* 7 : 402–17.

Broady, M. (1968) : *Planning for People,* London, Bedford Sq. P.

Broady, M. (1973) : 'Sociology in the education of architects', *AAQ,* (5)3 : 49–52.

Brown, H. (1973) : 'Man and his environment : a psychological introduction', in *The City as a Social System,* Bletchley, Open Univ. : 13–44.

Brown, N.O. (1966) : *Love's Body,* N. York, Vintage.

Bruvold, W.H. (1973): 'Belief and behavior as determinants of environmental attitude', *E & B,* (5)2 : 202ff.

Burch, W.R. Jr. *et.al.* (eds) (1972) : *Social Behavior, Natural Resources and the Environment,* N. York, Harper & Row.

Bycroft, P. (1973): *The Architect's Construct : 'Schools',* Brisbane, ERDG Pty. Ltd.

Campbell, R.D. & Roark, A.L. (1974) : 'Man-environment systems', *M-E S,* (4)2 : 89–99.

Candilis, G. (1968) : (no title), *Arkitektnytt,* 20 : 419–21.

Canter, D.V. (ed) (1970) : *Architectural Psychology,* London, RIBA.

Canter, DV. (1974): *Psychology for Architects,* London, Applied Science P.

Carey, G.V. (1971) : *Mind the Stop,* Harmondsworth, Penguin.

Carr, S. (1967) : 'The city of the mind', in Ewald, W.R. Jr. (ed) (1967) : 197–231.

Carson, D.H. (Gen.ed.) (1974) : *Edra 5,* Milwaukee, E.D.R.A. Inc.

Cassirer, E. (1955) : *The Philosophy of Symbolic Forms,* (Vol.I), New Haven, Yale U.P.

Castells, M. (1974) : 'Urban sociology and urban politics : from a critique to new trends of research', (paper given to ASA meeting, Montreal, mimeo).

Castells, M. (1975) : *La Question Urbain,* Paris, Maspero.

Castells, M. (1976) : 'Theoretical propositions for an experimental study of urban social move-ments', in Pickvance, C.G. (ed) (1976) : *Urban Sociology : Critical Essays,* London, Tavistock.

Castles, S. & Kosack, G. (1973) : *Immigrant Workers and Class Structure in W. Europe,* London, Oxford U.P.

Charter, S.P.R. (1972) : *Man on Earth,* N. York, Grove P.

Chisholm, M. (1970) : *Geography and Economics,* London, Bell.

Chizhov, N. & Lipets, Y. (1976) : 'Nature-society interaction modelling', *Soviet Geographical Studies,* 39 : 137–52.

Choay, F. (1973) ' 'Figures d'un discours meconnu', *Critique,* 311 : 293–317.

Choay, F. (1974) : 'Ghost Dance Exclusive', *Ghost Dance Times,* 7, (29 Nov) : 1.

Chombart de Lauwe, P.-H.(1974) : 'Eth(n)ologie de l'espace humain', in Bresson, F. *et.al.* (1974) : 233-41.

Chorley, R.J. & Haggett, P. (eds) (1967) : *Models in Geography,* London, Methuen.

Clark, W.A.V. & Cadwallader, M. (1972) : 'Locational stress and residential mobility', *E & B,* (4)4: 29–41.

Clarke, L. (1974) : 'Explorations into the nature of environmental codes', *JAR,* (3)1 : 34–8.

Cohen, J. (1970) : *Homo Psychologicus,* London, G. A. Unwin.

Colletti, L. (1974) : 'A political and philosophical interview', *NLR,* 86 : 3–28.

Colletti, L. (1975) : 'Marxism and the dialectic', *NLR,* 93 : 3–29.

Collings, P. (1965) : *Changing Ideals in Modern Architecture,* London, Faber & Faber.

Cooper, C. (1971) : *The House as Symbol of Self,* Berkeley, IURD.

Cooperman, D. (1974) : 'Density, design and social organisation', in Carson, D.H. (ed) (1974) : 87–100.

Cornforth, M. (1963) : *Dialectical Meterialism,* Vol. 3 : *Theory of Knowledge,* London, Lawrence & W.

Coulson, M.A. & Riddell, D.S. (1970) : *Approaching Sociology : A Critical Introduction,* London, RKP.

Craik, K.H. (1969) : 'Environmental psychology', in Craik, K.H., *et.al.* (eds)(1969) : *New Directions in Psychology : 4,* N. York, Holt, R. & W.

Critchlow, K. *et al.* (1973) : 'Chartres Maze : a model of the universe?' *AAQ,* (5)2 : 11–20.

Crosby, T. (ed) (1973) : *How to Play the Environment Game,* Harmondsworth, Penguin.

Cutler, A. & Gane, M. (1973) : 'Statement', *TP,* 7/8 : 37–50.

Daru, M. (1973) : 'Design and Linguistics', in *The Design Activity International Conference,* 1–13, London.

DeLong, A.J. (1973) : 'Aspectual and hierarchical characteristics of environmental codes', in Preiser, W.F.E. (ed) (1973); Vol I : 5–13.

Denike, K.G. & Parr, J.B. (1970) : 'Production in space, spatial competition, and restricted entry,' *J. of Regional Science,* (10) 1 : 49–63.

Derks, H. (1974) : 'Town-planning as ideology', *Newsletter,* 5 : 10–12, Rotterdam, Bouw-centrum.

Douglas, M. (1973) : *Natural Symbols,* Harmondsworth, Penguin.

Dubos, R.J. (1967) : 'Man adapting : his limitations and potentialities', in Ewald, W.R. (Jr.) (ed) (1967) : 11–25.

Durkheim, E. (1966) : *The Rules of Sociological Method,* New York, Free Press.

Eberhard, J.P. (1973) : 'Summary of EDRA 4', in Preiser, W.F.E. (ed) (1973) : v II : 514–19.

Eco. U. (1967) : 'Function and sign: semiotics of architecture', (Transl. manuscript of section C of *Appunti per una Semiologia delle Comunicazioni   Visive,* Milan, Bompiani, 1967, or of *La Struttura Assente : Introduzione alla Ricerca Semiologica,* Milan, Bompiani, 1968.).

Ecologist, The, (1972) : 'A Blueprint for Survival', *The Ecologist,* (2) 1.

Eisenschitz, A. (1973) : *Planning and Inequality,* London, AA Planning Dept. (mimeo).

Eliade, M. (1959) : *The Sacred and the Profane : The Nature of Religion,* N. York, Harcourt, B & W.

Engels, F. (1969) : *L. Feuerbach and the End of Classical German Philosophy,* in Feuer, L.S. (ed) (1969) : *Marx and Engels : Basic Writings on Politics and Philosophy,* London, Collins: 236–82.

English, P.W. & Mayfield, R.C. (ed) (1972) : *Man, Space, and Environment,* N. York, Oxford U.P.

Enzensberger, H.M. (1974) : 'A critique of political ecology', *NLR,* 94 : 3–31.

Esser, A.H. (ed) (1971) : *Behavior and Environment : The Use of Space by Animals and Man,* N. York, Plenum.

Esser, A.H. (1972) : 'Research in man-environment relations', *M-E S,* (2) 3 : 72–5.

Evans, G.W. (1973) : 'Personal space : research review and bibliography', *M-E S,* (3) 4 : 203–15.

Evans, R. (1971) : 'The rights of retreat and the rights of exclusion', *AD,* 6 : 335–9.

Ewald, W.R. (Jr.) (ed) (1967) : *Environment for Man : The Next Fifty Years,* Bloomington, Indiana U.P.

Faye, J.P. (1976) : 'The critique of language and its economy', *E & S,* (5) 1 : 52–73.

Fellman, G. & Brandt, B. (1970) : 'A neighbourhood a highway would destroy', *E & B,* (2) 3 : 281 ff.

Finnie, W.C. (1973) : 'Field experiments in litter control', *E & B,* (5) : 2 : 123–144.

Fischer, C.S. & Baldassare, M. & Ofshe, R.J. (1975) : 'Crowding studies and urban life : A critical review', *AIP J.,* November; 406–18.

Fitch, J.M. (1970) : 'Experiential basis for aesthetic decision', (reprinted) in Proshansky, H.M. *et al* (eds) (1970) : 76–84.

Foucault, M. (1965) : *Madness and Civilization,* New York, Random, Vintage.

Foucault, M. (1970) : *The Order of Things : An Archeology of the Human Sciences,* London, Tavistock.

Foucault, M. (1971) : 'Orders of discourse', *SSI,* (10) 2 : 7–30.

Foucault, M. (1972) : *The Archaeology of Knowledge,* London, Tavistock.

Foucault, M. (1973) : *Birth of the Clinic,* London, Tavistock.

Foucault, M. (1977a) : 'Prison talk : an interview with M. Foucault', *RP,* 16 : 10–15.

Foucault, M. (1977 b) : 'The political function of the intellectual', *RP,* 17 : 12–14.

Freedman, J.L. (1975) : *Crowding and Behavior,* N. York, W.H. Freeman.

Fried, M. & Gleicher, P. (1961) : 'Some sources of resident satisfaction in an urban slum', *AIP J,* (27) : 305–15.

Friedman, Y. (1975) : *Towards a Scientific Architecture,* Cambridge, MIT P.

Gabor, L. (1975) : 'Architecture, structure, manufacture', *Periodica Polytechnica Architecture,* (19) 1–2 : 3–13.

Galtung, J. (1973) : ' 'The Limits to Growth' and Class Politics', *J. of Peace Research,* 1–2 : 101–14.

George, P. (1973) : *L'Environnement,* Paris, PUF.

Gerard, R.W. (1942) : 'Higher levels of integration', *Biological Symposia,* (8) : 67–87.

Gied ion, S. (1960) : *Space, Time and Architecture,* Boston, Beacon.

Gied ion, S.(1969) : *Mechanization Takes Command,* N. York, W.W. Norton. (or.ed. 1948).

Glucksmann, A. (1972) : 'A ventriloquist structuralism', *NLR,* 72 : 68–92.

Glucksmann, M, (1974) : *Structuralist Analysis in Contemporary Social Thought,* London, RKP.

Goddard, D. (1972) : 'Anthropology : the limits of functionalism', in Blackburn, R. (ed) (1972) : 61–75.

Godelier, M. (1972) : *Rationality and Irrationality in Economics,* London, NLB.

Gokhman, V. (1976) : 'Theoretical Geography', *Social Sciences*, 2 : 66–79.

Goldmann, L.)1956) : *Le Dieu Cache*, Paris, Gallimard.

Goodchild, B. (1974) : 'Class differences in environmental perception : an exploratory study', *US*, (11) : 157–69.

Goodey, B.R. (1970) : 'Mapping "Utopia" ', *Geographical Review*, January, 15–30.

Goodey, B.R. (1974) : 'Exploring the environments of "Us" and "Them" ', in *Images of Place*, Birmingham C.U.R.S.

Gould, P.R. (1963) : 'Man against his environment : a game theoretic framework' *AAAG*, (53) ; 290–7.

Gray, J.A. (1966) : 'Attention, consciousness and voluntary control of behaviour in Soviet Psychology', in O'Connor N. (ed) (1966) : *Present-day Russian Psychology*, Oxford, Pergamon P.

Gurevich, A. (1977): 'Representations of property during the high Middle Ages', *E & S*, (6) 1 : 1–30.

Gutman, R. (1968) : 'What schools of architecture expect from sociology', *J. of Architectural Education*, March : 69–83.

Gutnov, A. *et.al.*(1975) : *The Ideal Communist City*, N. York, G. Braziller.

Güran, A. (1976) :'T.C. Ziraat Bankası Ankara Eğitim Sitesi ve Genel Tesisleri', *Mimarlık*, 1976/3 : 133–6.

Hamlyn, D.W. (1971) : *The Theory of Knowledge*, London, Macmillan.

Hampden–Turner,C. (1970): *Radical Man*, London, Duckworth.

Handler, A.B. (1970) : *Systems Approach to Architecture*, N. York, Elsevier.

Harris, N. (1974) : 'Urban England', *E & S*, (3) 3 : 346–54.

Hartnack, J. (1968) : *Kant's Theory of Knowledge*, London, Macmillan.

Harvey, D. (1969) : *Explanation in Geography*, London, Arnold.

Harvey, D. (1973) : *Social Justice and the City*, London, Arnold.

Harvey, M. (1972) : 'Sociological theory : The production of a bourgeois ideology', in Pateman , T. (ed) (1972) : *Counter Course*, Harmondsworth, Penguin : 82–111.

Hatje, G. (ed) (1963) : *Encyclopaedia of Modern Architecture*, London, Thames and Hudson.

Hawkes, D. (ed) (1975) : *Models and Systems in Architecture and Building*, Hornby, Contruction P.

Heilbroner, R. (1970) : *Between Capitalism and Socialism*, N. York, Random.

Hekstra, G.P. (1973) : 'Environmental education and public environmental awareness', *Planning and Development in the Netherlands*, (7) 2 : 140–8.

Hesselgren, S. (1971) : *Man's Perception of Man-made Environment*, Lund, Studentliteratur.

Heumann, B. (1973) : 'Kapitalist ülkelerde günümüzün şehircilik sorunları' , *Mimarlık*, 10 : 17–25.

Hill, D.A. (1964) : 'The process of landscape change : bicultural implications', in *The Changing Landscape of a Mexican Municipio*, U. of Chicago, R.P. : 91. (repr. in English, P.W. & Mayfield, R.C. (ed) (1972) : 42–55.

Hillier, B. (1970) : 'Psychology and the subject matter of architectural research', in Canter, D.V. (ed) (1970) : 25–9.

Hillier, B. (1973) : 'In defence of space', *RIBA J.*, Nov : 539–44.

Hillier, B. & Leaman, A. (1973) : 'The Man-Environment paradigm and its paradoxes' *AD*, (43) 8 : 507–11.

Hillier, B. & Leaman, A. (1974) : 'How is design possible?', *JAR*, (3) 1:4–11.

Hillier, B. & Leaman, A. (1976) : 'Architecture as a discipline', *JAR*, (5) 1:28–32.

Hindess, B. (1973a) : 'Models and masks : Empiricist conceptions of the conditions of scientific knowledge', *E & S*, (2) 2 : 233–54.

Hindess, B. (1973b) : 'Transcendentalism and history', *E & S*, (2) 3 : 309–42.

Hindess, B. (1975) : 'Extended review', *Sociological Review*, (23) 3 : 678–97.

Hirst, P.Q. (1975) : *Durkheim, Bernard and Epistemology*, London, RKP.

Hirst, P.Q. (1976) : 'Althusser and the theory of ideology', *E & S*, (5) 4 : 385–412.

Hollingshead, A.B. (1940) : 'Human ecology and human society', *Ecological Monographs*, (10).

Hollis, M. & Nell, E.J. (1975) : *Rational Economic Man*, London, Cambridge U.P.

Honikman, B.   (ed) (1971) : *Proc. of Architectural Psychology Conf. at Kingston Polytechnic,* London, Kingston Poly. & RIBA.

Horton, F. (1974) : Review of Broadbent, G. (1973) , *JAR,* (3) 2 : 55–6.

Hurley, J. (1972) : 'Towards a sociology of architecture', *ARse,* 5/6 : 21–4 .

Ittelson, W.H. (1973) : 'Environmental perception and contemporary perceptual theory', in Ittelson, W.H. (ed) (1973) : *Environment and Cognition,* N. York, Seminar P. : 1–19;

Ittelson, W.H. & Proshansky, H.M. & Rivlin, L.G. (1970) : 'Bedroom size and social interaction of the psychiatric ward', *E & B,* (2) 3 : 255 ff.

Jacobs, J. (1965) : *The Death and Life of Great American Cities,* Harmondsworth, Penguin.

Jaffe, A. (1968) : 'Symbolism in the visual arts', in Jung, C.G. (ed) (1968).

Jardine, B. (1971) : 'Me, Not Me', *AAQ,* (3) 2 : 38–40.

Jeffery, C.R. (1971) : *Crime Prevention Through Environmental Design,* California, Sage.

Jellico, G. & S. (1975) : *The Landscape of Man,* London, Thames and Hudson.

Jencks, C. (1974) : 'A semantic analysis of Stirling's Olivetti Centre wing', *AAQ,* (6) 2 : 13–15.

Jencks, C. & Baird, G. (eds) (1969) : *Meaning in Architecture,* London, Barrie & Jenkins.

Joedicke, J. (ed) (1968) : *Candilis, Josic, Woods,* Stuttgart, K. Kramer.

Johnson, H.G. (1973) : *Man and His Environment,* British–N. Amer. Comm.

Joiner, D. (1971) : 'Social ritual and architectural space', *ART,* (1) 3 : 11–22.

Jones, E. (ed) (1975) : *Readings in Social Geography,* London, Oxford U.P.

Juillard, E. (1962) : 'The region : an essay of definitions', *Annales de Geographie,* (71), (repr. in English, P.W. & Mayfield, R.C. (ed) (1972) : 429–41).

Jung, C.G. *et al* (eds) (1968) : *Man and his Symbols,* N. York, Dell.

Kade, G. (1970) : 'Introduction: the economics of pollution and the interdisciplinary approach to environmental planning', *ISSJ,* (22) 4 : 563–75.

Kaplan, R. (1973) : 'Some psychological benefits of gardening', *E & B,* (5) 2 : 145–62.

Kay, J.H. (1976) : 'Ada kicks up a fuss again', *BD,* 19.11.76 : 23.

Keller, S. (1966) : 'Social class in physical planning', *ISSJ,* (18) 4, 494–512.

Kelly, G.A. (1955) : *The Psychology of Personal Constructs,* N. York, W.W. Norton.

Klausner, S.Z. (1971) : *On Man in His Environment,* S. Francisco, J-Bass. (Reviewed by B.B. Greenbie, *M-E S,* (3) 3 : 177–81).

Klausner, S.Z. (1972) : 'Some problems in the logic of current man-environment studies', in Burch, W.R. (Jr.), *et al* (eds) (1972) : 334–63.

Knewstub, N. (1974) : 'The new Australians . . .', *The Guardian,* 5.8.1974.

Knight, S. (1972): 'Notes on the history of art and architecture', *ARse,* 5/6 : 33–6.

Knowles, E.S. (1972) : 'Boundaries around social space : Dyadic responses to an invader', *E & B,* (4) 4 : 437 ff.

Koseki, S. (1972) : 'Pour une sociologie critique de la quotidienneté', *L'H & S,* 23 : 51–68.

Krieger, M.H. (1970) : 'Six propositions on the poor and pollution', *Policy Sciences,* 1 : 311–24.

Kuhn, T.S. (1970) : *The Structure of Scientific Revolutions,* Chicago, U. of Chicago P.

Labour Party (1973) : *The Politics of Environment,* London, Labour Party.

Lacoste, Y. (1976) : *La Géographie, ça Sert, d'Abord, à Faire la Guerre,* Paris, Maspero.

Lakatos, I (1968) : 'Criticism and the methodology of scientific research programmes', *Proceedings of the Aristotelian Society,* 69 : 149–186.

Lakatos, I & Musgrave, A. (eds) (1970) : *Criticism and the Growth of Knowledge,* London, Cambridge U.P.

Latouche, S. (1970) : 'La crise de L'économie politique et ses effets épistémologiques', *L'H & S,* 18 : 215–40.

Leach, E. (1970) : *Levi-Strauss,* London, Fontana.

Le Corbusier (1954) : *The Modulor : A Harmonious Measure to the Human Scale, Universally Applicable to Architecture and Mechanics,* London, Faber.

Lecourt, D. (1973) : *Une Crise et Son Enjeu,* Paris, Maspero.

Lecourt, D. (1975) : *Marxism and Epistemology ,* London, NLB.

Lee, T.R. (1968) : 'Urban neighbourhood as a socio-spatial schema', *Human Relations,* (21) : 241–68.

Lee, T.R. (1970) : 'Do we need a theory?', in Canter, D.V. (ed) (1970) : 18–25.

Lee, T.R. (1971) : 'Psychology and architectural determinism', *AJ*, Pt. 1 : 4.8.1971 : 253–62; Pt. 2 : 1.9.1971 : 475–83; Pt. 3 : 22.9.1971 : 651–9.

Leech, G. (1974) : *Semantics*, Harmondsworth, Penguin.

Lefebvre, (1968) : *Dialectical Materialism*, London, Cape.

Lefebvre, H. (1970) : *La Révolution Urbaine*, Paris, Gallimard.

Lefebvre, H. (1971) : *Au-de la du Structuralisme*, Paris, Anthropos.

Lefebvre, H. (1974) : *La Production de L'Espace*, Paris, Anthropos.

Leiss, W. (1972) : *The Domination of Nature*, Boston, Beacon P.

Lenin, V.I. (1970a) : *What the "Friends of the People" are and How they Fight the Social-Democrats*, Moscow, Progress.

Lenin, V.I. (1970b) : *Materialism and Empirio-criticism*, Moscow, Progress.

Levi-Strauss, C. (1967) : *The Scope of Anthropology*, London, Cape.

Lévy-Bruhl, L. (1912) : *Les Fonctions Mentales dans les Sociétés Inférieures*, Paris.

Lewin, K. (1936) : *Principles of Topological and Vector Psychology*, N. York, McGraw-Hill.

Lewis, A. (1970) : 'The schock of delight', *Int. Herald Tribune*, 14–15.3.1970.

Ley, D. & Cybriwsky, R. (1974) , 'The spatial ecology of stripped cars', *E & B*, (6) 1 : 53 ff.

Lintoft, Y. (1970) : *Planlegging for Undertrykkelse*, Trondheim, NTH.

Lipman, A. (1969) : 'Architectural belief systems and social behaviour', *British J. of Sociology*, June, 1969: 190-204.

Lipman, A. (1971) : 'Ideology and professional commitment : The architectural notion of community' in B. Honikman (ed) (1971) : 72–78.

Locke, E.A. (1969) : 'What is job satisfaction', *Organizational Behavior in Human Performance*, (4) :309-36.

Lojkine, J. (1976) : 'Contribution to a Marxist theory of capitalist urbanization', in Pickvance, C.G. (ed) (1976): *Urban Sociology : Critical Essays*, London, Tavistock.

Lorenzer, A. (1968), 'Städtebau: Funktionalismus und Socialmontage? Zur Sozialpsychologischen Funktion der Architektur', in Berndt, H., *et.al.*(1968) : 51–104.

Lowenthal, D. (1975) : 'Geography, experience and imagination : towards a geographical epistemology', in Jones, E. (ed) (1975) : 104–27. (repr. from *AAAG*, (51) : 241–60.)

Lund, N–O (1970) : *Teoridannelser i Arkitekturen*, Copenhagen, Arkitektens Forlag .

Lynch, K. (1964) : *The Image of the City*, Cambridge, MIT P.

Mabogunje, A.L. (1970) : 'Systems approach to a theory of rural-urban migration', in English, P.W. & Mayfield, R.C. (ed) (1972).

Mandel, W.M. (1973) : 'The Soviet ecology movement', *Science and Society*, (36) : 385–416.

Marin, L. (1971) : 'Discours utopique et récit des origines', *Annales*, March-April.

Marinov, H. (1974) : 'Optimum spatial, resources et environnement', *L'E G*, 4 : 287–93.

Martin, L. (1958) : (Talk on) 'Conference on architectural education' *RIBA J.*, June.

Maruyama, M. (1973) : 'Principle of heterogenization and symbiotization : Implications for planning and environmental design', in Preiser, W.F.E. (ed) (1973) v.II : 18–34.

Marx, K. (1969) : *Theses on Feuerbach*, in Feuer, L.S. (ed) (1969) : *Marx and Engels, Basic Writings on Politics and Philosophy*, London, Collins, 283–6.

Marx, K. (1970) v. I, (1970) v. 2 : *Capital*, London, Lawrence & Wishart.

Marx, K. (1971) : *A Contribution to the Critique of Political Economy*, London, Lawrence & Wishart.

Marx, K. & Engels, F. (1970) : *The German Ideology*, (Part One), London, Lawrence & Wishart.

Mason, H.L & Langenheim, J.H. (1957) : 'Language analysis and the concept *Environment*', *Ecology*, (38) 2 : 325–40.

Massey, D. (1973) : 'Towards a critique of industrial location theory', *Antipode*, (5) 3 : 33–39.

Massey, D. (1974) : 'Social justice and the city : a review', *Environment and Planning–A*, (6) : 229–35.

Medawar, P.B. (1960) : *The Future of Man*, London, Methuen.

Medvedkov, Y. (1976) : 'Ecological problems highlighted by urban environment modelling', *Social Sciences*, 2 : 80–91.

Mepham, J. (1972): 'The theory of ideology in *Capital*', *RP*, 2:12-19.
Mepham, J. (1973):The structuralist sciences and philosophy,' in Robey,'D. (ed) (1973): *Structuralism: An Introduction*, London, Oxford U.P. :104-37.
Mercer, C. (1976) : 'Of rats and men', *New Society*, 8 Jan. 1976 : 64–5.
Michelson, W. (1970) : *Man and His Urban Environment*, Mass., Addison-Wesley.
Mills, C.W. (1970) : *The Sociological Imagination*, Harmondsworth, Penguin.
Moholy-Nagy, S. (1969) : *Matrix of Man : An Illustrated History of Urban Environment*, London, Pall Mall.
Moles, A. (1971) : 'La théorie des systèms fonctionnels comme cadre du design de l'environnement', *Environnement*, 1 : 29–35.
Montgomery, R. (1966) : 'Comment on fear and house-as-haven in the lower class', *AIP J*, (32) : 31–37.
Moore, G.T. (1973) : 'Developmental differences in environmental cognition', in Preiser, W.F.E. (ed) (1973) vII : 232–9.
Moore, G.T. (1974) : 'The development of environmental knowing : An overview of an interactional-constructivist theory and some data on within-individual development variations', (photocopied paper).
Moriarty, B.M. (1974) : 'Socio-economic status and residential locational choice', *E & B.*, (6) 4 : 448–69.
Morin, E. (1974) : 'La nature de la société', *Communications*, 22 : 3–32.
Morris, D. (1969) : *Human Zoo*, London Cape.
Morrison, B.M. (1974) : 'The importance of a balanced perspective : The environments of man', *M-E S*, (4) 3 171–8.
Mugnaioni, P. (1976) : *Towards a Theory of Planning Fetishism*, London, U.C.L. M.Sc. thesis, (unpublished).
Mulhern, F. (1974) : 'The Marxist aesthetics of Christopher Caudwell', *NLR*, 85 : 37–58.
Mumford, L. (1966) : *City in History*, Harmondsworth, Penguin.
McKencnie, G.E. (1973) 'The environmental response inventory', Berkeley, U.of California, Inst. of Personality Assessment.
McKinley, D. (1969) : 'The new mythology of "Man in Nature" ', in Shephard, P. & McKinley, D. (ed) (1969) : 351–62.
McLeish, H. (1976) : 'Politics and Planning : the radical perspective', *RTPI News*, Autumn : 77–9.
Nettler, G. (1970) : *Explanations*, N. York, McG. Hill.
Newman, O. (1973) : *Defensible Space : Crime Prevention Through Urban Design*, N. York, Collier.
NLR, (1972) : 'Introduction to Glucksmann' *NLR*, 72 : 61–67.
Norberg–Schulz, C. (1971) : *Existence, Space and Architecture*, London, Studio Vista.
Nutini, H.G. (1968) : 'On the concepts of epistemological order and coordinative definitions', *Bijdragen Tot de Taal-Land en Volkenkunde*, 124 : 1–21.
Oakley, D. (1970) : *The Phenomenon of Architecture in Cultures in Change*, Pergamon P. Oxford.
Odum, H.T. (1971) : *Environment, Power and Society*, N. York, Wiley.
Odum, H.T. & Peterson, L.L. (1972) : 'Relationship of energy and complexity in planning', *AD*, 10 : 624–29.
Oishi, I. (1970) : 'Some applications of economic theory to architectural theory', (abstracted in *DMG Newsletter*, March).
Olivegren, J. (1971) : 'A better sociopsychological climate in our housing estates', in Honikman, B. (ed) (1971) : 65–9.
Ollman, B. (1971) : *Alienation*, London, Cambridge U.P.
O'Malley, J.B. (1970) : *Lexicon*, Liverpool, unpublished.
O'Malley, J.B. (1971) : *A note on ontology, phenomenology, semiology*, Liverpool, unpublished.
O'Malley, J.B. (1972) : *Sociology of Meaning*, London, Human Context B.
O'Malley, J.B. (1974) : *Basic categories of being as the being of beings*, Liverpool, unpublished mimeo.
O'Neill, J. (ed) (1973) : *Modes of Individualism and Collectivism*, London, Heinemann.
Özkan, S. (1973) : 'Arkoloji-Profitopolis'/ iki sergi eleştirisi, *Mimarlık*, 9 : 29.
Paci, E. (1972) : *The Function of the Sciences and the Meaning of Man*, Evanston, Northwestern U.P.

Park , R.E. *et al* (1925) : *The City*, Chicago, U. of Chicago P.

Pastalan, L.A. & Carlson, D.H. (eds) (1970) : *Spatial Behavior of Older People*, Michigan, Ann Arbor.

Pawley, M. (1976) : 'Symbols of change', *BD*, 310, (6.8.1976) : 2.

Perin, C. (1970) : *With Man in Mind : An interdisciplinary prospectus for environmental design*, Cambridge, MIT Press.

Pevsner, N. (1964) : *An Outline of European Architecture*, Harmondsworth, Penguin.

Pevsner, N. (1976) : *A History of Building Types*, London, Thames & Hudson.

Piaget, J. (1971) : *Structuralism*, London, RKP.

Piaget, J. (1972) : *Psychology and Epistemology*, Harmondsworth, Penguin.

Piaget, J. (1973) : *Main Trends in Interdisciplinary Research*, London, G. Allen & Unwin.

Popper, K.R. (1963) : *Conjectures and Refutations*, London, RKP.

Popper, K.R. (1972) : *Objective Knowledge: An Evolutionary Approach*, London, Oxford U.P.

Porteus, J.D. (1977) : *Environment and Behavior : planning and everyday urban life*, Massac., Addison, Wesley.

Porter, P.W. (1965) : 'Environmental potentials and economic opportunities', *American Anthropologist*, (67) 2 : 409–20.

Poulantzas, N. (1972) : *'The problem of the capitalist state'*, in Blackburn,R. (ed) (1972) : 238–53.

Poulantzas, N. (1975) : *Classes in Contemporary Capitalism*, London, NLB.

Preiser, W.F.E. (ed) (1973) : *Environmental Design Research*, (EDRA 4), 2 vols, Stroudsburg, Dowden, H & R.

Price, C. (1966) : 'Life-conditioning', *AD*, Oct : 483.

Project Environment, (1975) : *Ethics and Environment*, London, Longman.

Proshansky, H.M. & Ittelson, W.H. & Rivlin, L.G. (eds) (1970) : *Environmental Psychology : Man and his physical setting*, New York, HRW.

Raffestin, C. (1976) : 'Peut-on parler de codes dans les sciences humaines et particulièrement en géographie?', *L'E G*, (5) 3 : 183–8.

Rainwater, L. (1966) : 'Fear and the house-as-haven in the lower class', *AIP J.*,(32) : 23 – 31.

Rambourg, C. (1973) : 'Un essai de formalisation dialectique', *ES*, 15–16 : 137–51.

Ranciere, J. (1973) : *Lire le Capital III*, Paris, Maspero.

Rapoport, A. (1969) : *House Form and Culture*, Englewood Cliffs, Prentice-Hall.

Rapoport, A. (1971) : 'Some observations regarding man-environment studies', *ART*, (2) 1 : 4–15.

Rapoport, A. (1973a) : 'Some perspectives on human use and organization of space', *AAQ*, (5) 3 : 27–37.

Ray, P. (1976) : 'Where the ecologists are going wrong', *BD*, 301, 4.6.1976.

Raymond, M-G (1968)·: 'Idéologies du logement et opposition ville-campagne', *R. Française de Sociologie*, (9), 191–210.

Reichardt, R. (1970) : 'Approaches to the measurement of environment', *ISSJ*, (22) 4 : 661–71.

Reichenbach, H. (1957) : *The Philosophy of Space & Time*, N. York, Dover.

Remøren, E. & T.I. (1975) : 'Marx and ecology', *Science Bulletin*, 8 : 5–9. (Abridged transl. of 'Marx und die Ökologie', *Kursbuch*, 33 : 175–187, 1973).

Rex, J. & Moore, R. (1967) : *Race, Community and Conflict*, London, Oxford U.P.

Richardson, H.W., *et al* (1974) : 'Determinants of urban housing prices', *US*, (11) 2 : 189–99.

Ritterbush, P.C. (1968) : 'Environmental and historical paradox', *General Systems*, (13) :107–14.

Rosenthal, M. & Yudin, P. (eds) (1967) : *A Dictionary of Philosophy*, Moscow, Progress.

Rowe, J.S. (1961) :'The levels-of-integration concept and ecology', *Ecology;* (42) 2 : 420–7.

Russell, B. (1973) : 'Barbarians in the living room or systems, patterns and design', *AD*, 12 : 792–5.

Rychlak, J.F. (1968) : *A Philosophy of Science for Personality Theory*, Boston, H. Mifflin.

Rykwert, J. (1973) : 'The lessons of the past', in Crosby, T. (ed) (1973) : 11–37.

Rykwert, J. (1976) : *The Idea of a Town*, London, Faber & Faber.

Sachs, I. (1972): 'Approaches to a political economy of environment', *SSI*, (5) 10 : 41–53.

Sandow, A. (1972) : 'Modern biology and dialectics', *Science and Society*, (36) : 463–69.

Santos, M. (1974) : 'Geography, Marxism, and underdevelopment', *Antipode*, (6) 3 : 1–9.

Schmidt, A. (1971) : *The Concept of Nature in Marx*, London, NLB.

Schumacher, E.F. (1968) ' 'Buddhist economics', *Resurgence*, (1) 11.

Seablom, S.H. (1970) : 'Udviklingen af en socio-kritisk institution', *Arkitekten*, 26 : 609–27.

Searles, H.F. (1960) : *The Non-human Environment in Normal Development and in Schizophrenia*, N. York, Int. Univ. P.

Seymour, J. (1974) : 'When good husbandry replaces the rape of mother earth', *Resurgence*, (5) 1 : 4–5.

Shepard, P. & McKinley, P. (eds) (1969) : *The Subversive Science, Essays Toward an Ecology of Man*, Boston, Houghton Mifflin.

Shils, E.A. & Finch, H.A. (1949) : *Max Weber on the Methodology of the Social Sciences*, Glencoe, Ill., Free P.

Simon, H.A. (1969) : *The Sciences of the Artificial*, Cambridge, MIT.

Smithson, A. (ed) (1968) : *Team-X Primer*, London, Studio Vista.

Soja, E.W. (1971) : *Political Organization of Space*, Washington, Assoc. of Amer. Geographers.

Soleri, P. (1969) : *Arcology : The City in the Image of Man*, Cambridge, MIT.

Soleri, P. (1973) : *The Bridge Between Matter and Spirit is Matter Becoming Spirit*, New York, Anchor.

Sommer, R. (1969) : *Personal Space*, N. Jersey, P-Hall.

Sommer, R. (1972) : *Design Awareness*, San Francisco, Rinehart P.

Sonnenfeld, J. (1969) : 'Personality and behavior in environment', *Proceedings of the Assoc. of Amer. Geographers*, (1) : 136–40.

Sonnenfeld, J. (1972a):'Geography, perception, and the behavioral environment', in English, P.W. & Mayfield, R.C. (eds) (1972) : 244–51.

Sonnenfeld, J. (1972 b) : 'Social interaction and environmental relationship', (4) 3 : 267 ff. *E & B;* (4) 3 : 267 ff.

Spizzichino, R. (1971) : 'Hypothèse pour une théorie de l'environnement', *Environnement*, 2 : 1–12.

Steward, J.H. (1955) : 'The concept and method of cultural ecology', in *Theory of Culture Change*, Urbana, Illinois U.P., (reprinted in English, P.W. & Mayfield, R.C. (ed) (1972) : 120–9.)

Stewart, T.C. (1970) : *The City as an Image of Man*, London, Latimer.

Stoddart, D.R. (1965) : 'Geography and the ecological approach', *Geography*, (50) : 242-51.

Stokols, D. *et al* (1973) : 'Physical, social and personal determinants of the perception of crowding', *E & B*, (5) 1 : 87–115.

Strum Group (1971) : *Utopia Foto-romanzo*, Milan, Ed. Casabella. (3 exhibition pamphlets).

Stringer, P., (1970) : 'The Architect is a Man', *AD*, August, 411-2.

Studer, R. (1969) : 'The dynamics of behaviour contingent physical systems', in Broadbent, G. & Ward, A. (ed) (1969) : *Design Methods in Architecture*, London, L. Humphries.

Swenarton, M. (1974) : A theory of artistic production, (paper presented to a conf. at RCA, London).

Tafuri, M. (1976) : *Architecture and Utopia : Design and Capitalist Development*, Cambridge, Mass., MIT.

Tekeli, İ. (1969) : *Sosyal Sistemler, Sosyal Değişme ve Yerleşme Yapısı*, Istanbul, İTÜ.

Tekeli, İ. (1972) : *Bölge Planlama Üzerine*, İstanbul, İTÜ.

Tekeli, İ. (1973) : 'Mekân organizasyonlarının incelenmesinde bilimsel stratejiler ve dil sorunu', *Mimarlık*, 9 : 5–12.

Teymur, N. (1973) : 'Architecture and/in/of apathy', *Assent*, 4.

Teymur, N. & E. (1973) : 'Demystification of techniques', in *Design Activity Conference*, London, DMG-DRS, (reprin. in *Mewspaper*, 11/1973) (abstract in *DMG–DRS Journal*, (7) 2 : 112).

Teymur, N. & E. (1974) : 'Understanding Society and Environment:– as a system?', London,· (seminar paper, UCL), (rev. version in *J. of the Faculty of Architecture*, 1980, (6) 1: 55-66.)

Teymur, N. & E. (1978): 'Mimarlıktaki tartışmaların statüsü üzerine', in Pultar, M. (ed): *Mimarlık Bilimi Kavram ve Sorunları*, Ankara, ÇMBD: 1-8.

Therborn, G. (1971) : 'Jurgen Habermas : A new eclecticism', *NLR*, 67 : 69—83.

Thiel, P. (1973) : 'On the discursive notation of human experience and the physical environment', in Preiser, W.F.E. (ed) (1973) v. 2 : 374—78.

Tibbetts, P. & Esser, A.H. (1973) : 'Transactional structures in man-environment relations', *M-E S,* (3) 6 : 441—68.

Tinker, J. (1975) : 'Stockholm,Nairobi, and then what?' *New Scientist* (66) 953 : 600—4.

Tognoli, J. (1973) : 'The effects of windowless rooms and unembellised surroundings on attitudes and retention', *E & B,* (5) 2 : 191 ff.

Tribe, K. (1973) : 'On the production and structuring of scientific knowledges', *E & S,* (2) 4 : 465—78.

Tschumi, B. (1975) : 'A chronicle of Space', in *Chronicle of Space,* London, Arch.Assoc.

Tuan, Y-F. (1968) : 'Discrepancies between environmental attitude and behaviour : examples from Europe and China', *Canadian Geographer,* (12) 3 : 176—91.

Tuan, Y-F (1970) : 'Our treatment of the environment in ideal and actuality', *American Scientist,* (58) : 244—9.

Tuan, Y-F. (1971) : *Man and Nature,* Washington, Assoc. of Amer. Geographers, R.P. 10.

Turan, M. (1973) : 'Environmental Stress and flexibility in the housing process' , in Preiser, W.F.E. (ed) (1973) : vol I,47—58.

Turan, M. (1974) : 'A concept of environmental flexibility : with special reference to squatter housing', in Carson, D.H. (ed) (1974) : 175—90.

Tyng, A.G. (1969) : 'Geometric extensions of consciousness', *Zodiac,* 19 : 130—162.

Ural, S. (1974) : 'Türkiye'nin sosyal ekonomisi ve mimarlık', *Mimarlık,* 1/2 : 5—53.

Vandenbroeck, A. (1972) : *Philosophical Geometry,* N. York, Sadhana P.

Victory Tract Club (1974) : *The Little Green Book,* S. Croydon.

Vidal de la Blanche, P. (1926) : *Principles of Human Geography,* (ed. by E. de Martonne), London, Constable.

Vilar, P. (1973) : 'Marxist history, a history in the making', *NLR,* 80 : 65—106.

Vipond, J. (1974) : 'City size and unemployment', *US,* (11) 1 : 41—48.

Wagner, P.L.)1972) : 'Cultural landscapes and regions : Aspects of communication', in English, P.W. & Mayfield, R.C. (eds) (1972) : 55—68.

Wagner, P.L. (1976) : 'Reflections on a Radical geography', *Antopode,* (8) 3 : 83—5.

Wall, G. (1973) : 'Public response to air pollution in S. Yorkshire, England', *E & B.* (5) 2 : 219—48.

Wa pner,S. *et.al.*(1973) : 'An organismic — developmental perspective for understanding transactions of men in environments', *E & B,* (4) 3:255—89.

Watkins, J.W.N. (1973) : 'Ideal types and historical explanation', in O'Neill, J. (ed) (1973) : 143—65.

Watts, A.W. (1969) : 'The individual as Man/World', in Shephard, P. & McKinley, D. (ed) (1969) : 139—148.

Watts, A.W. (1973) : *Nature, Man and Woman,* London, Wildwood House.

Watts, D.G. (1969) : *Environmental Education,* London, RKP.

Weisberg, B. (ed) (1970) : *Ecocide in Indochina : The Ecology of War,* S. Francisco, Canfield P.

Weiss, P.A. (1947) : *Nature and Man,* N. York, H. Holt.

Wells, B.W.P. (1965a):'The psycho-social influence of building environment', *Building Science,* (1) : 153—65.

Wells, B.W.P. (1965b) : 'Towards a definition of environmental studies', *AJ,* 22.9.1965 : 677—83.

White, L. Jr. (1969) : 'The historical roots of our ecologic crisis', in Shephard, P. & McKinley, D. (ed) (1969) : 341— 51.

Whitehead, A.N. (1955) : *Adventures of Ideas,* N. York, Mentor.

Whorf, B.L. (1963) : *Language, Thought, and Reality,* Cambridge, MIT Press.

Wilden, A. (1972) : *System and Structure,* London, Tavistock.

Willems, E.P. (1973) : 'Behavior— Environment systems : an ecological approach', *M-E S,* (3) 2 : 79—110.

Willer, D.E. (1967) : *Scientific Sociology,* Englewood Cliffs, Prentice-Hall.

Willer, D. & Willer, J. (1973) : *Systematic Empiricism : Critique of a Pseudoscience,* N. Jersey, Prentice-Hall.

Williams, K. (1972) : 'Problematic history', *E & S*, (1) 4 : 457–81.

Williams, K. (1974) : 'Unproblematic archaeology', *E & S*, (3) 1 : 41–68.

Wirth, L. (1968) : 'Urbanism as a way of life', *Amer. J. of Sociology*, (44) : 1–24.

Wohlwill, J.F. (1973) : 'The environment is not in the head!', in Preiser, W.F.E. (ed) (1973) v.II : 166–81.

Wolf, L. (1972) : *Idéologie et production : le Design*, Paris, Anthropos.

Wolman, B.B. (ed) (1965) : *Scientific Psychology*, N. York, Basic B.

Wolpert, J. (1965) : 'Behavio ral aspects of the decision to migrate', *Papers of the Regional Science Assoc.*, (15) : 159–69.

Workers and Peasants, (1972) : *Serving the People with Dialectics*, Peking, Foreign Languages P.

Worsley, P. (1973) : 'A sociological survey', *The Guardian*, 31.5.1973.

Wright, F.L. (1958) : *The Living City*, N. York, Horizon.

Wright, F.L. (1970) : *An Organic Architecture*, London, L. Humphries.

Yanker, G. (ed) (1972) : *Prop Art*, London, S. Vista.

Yavuz, F. (1975) : *Çevre Sorunları, Genellikle ve Ülkemiz Açısından*, Ankara, S.B.F.

Yeang, K. (1974) : 'Bionics : the use of biological analogies for design', *AAQ*, (6) 2 : 48–57.

Young, M. & Willmott, P. (1962) : *Family and Kinship in East London*, Harmondsworth, Penguin.

Zeisel, J. (1975) : *Sociology and Architectural Design*, N. York, R. Sage Found.

Zlutnick, S. & Altman, I. (1972) : 'Crowding and human behavior' , in Wohlwill, J.F. & Carson, D.H. (eds) (1972) : *Environment and the Social Sciences*, Washington, Amer. Psychological Assoc. : 44–58.

Bibliographical Addendum

Whilst the Bibliography *serves as the source of references for the text as published and it need not be updated in a first edition, the relevant and complementary studies by the author can probably be added here. I have done further research and writing over the past four years partly to develop the arguments and the approach of this book and partly to extend the scope of my own 'discursive' awareness. The following is therefore a list of texts which owe their existence to the present study and in which I thought the readers might be interested.*

1978a 'Questioning the Terms of our Discourse: "Architecture" and "Development",' (paper presented to the U.I.A. World Congress, Mexico).

1978b 'Knowledge of Knowledges', (Design Theory and Epistemology paper, London, P.S.B.).

1978c 'From ELMA to AD', (Design Theory and Epistemology paper, London, P.S.B.).

1978d 'Konut Sorununun Kavranması Sorunu', (= The Question of Housing Question), *Mimarlık*, (16)3: 19-22, (with E.Teymur).

1979a *Architectural Practice and its Education*, South Bank Architectural Papers, No.2, London.

1979b 'Mimarlık Dilinin "Mimarisi"' ', (= The 'Architecture' of Architectural Language), in Pultar, M. (ed): *Çevre, Yapı, Tasarım*, Ankara, Ç.M.B.D.: 7-25.

1980a 'Design Discourse: Doing vs. Saying – a dubious dichotomy', *9H*, 2: 47-49.

1980b 'Understanding Society and Environment:– as a "System"?', *M.E.T.U. J. of the Faculty of Architecture*, (6)1: 55-66, (with E.Teymur).

1981a 'Materiality of Design', *Block*, 5: 19-27, (shorter version in Jacques, R. & Powell, J.A. (eds): *Design: Science: Method*, Guildford, Westbury House: 111-116).

1981b *Problems in Professional Education*, South Bank Architectural Papers, No.7, London.

1981c   '"Aesthetics" of Aesthetics: Aesthetic question in architectural and urban discourses', *M.E.T.U. J. of the Faculty of Architecture*, (7)1.

1981d   'İlişkilerin İlişkileri Üzerine', (= On the Relations of Relations), *Mimarlık*, 19(7): 7-9.

1982a   ' "Vernacular" in the Classroom', (paper presented to the E.A.A.E./M.E.T.U. Workshop, Ankara), (with Y. Aysan).

1982b   'Design without Economics?', (paper presented to the Design Policy Conference, London, Royal College of Art).

1982c   'Economic Signification of Physical Surroundings', (paper presented to the I.A.P.S. Conference, Barcelona).

In preparation:

   Theory in Architectural Education, (results of a two-year study of UK Schools of Architecture sponsored by P.S.B. and R.I.B.A.).

   Architectural Discourse, (on design and architectural knowledge, language and theory).

Index

Name entries do not include all the names referred to, but those that are either central to the argument or are the authors of important quotations. References of particular importance, detail or length are in bold numerals.

A

absence/presence, 17, 20, 25, 190
action, 85
adaptation, 70
Africa, 122
Africans, 128n
alienation, 97-100, 138-9, 159
Althusser, L., XII, 10n, 16n, 18-21, 26, 50n, 60, 65n, **68-74**, 76, 78n, 95, 134n, 153, 176, *and passim*
amphibologies, 37, 38n, 116, **125**
analogies, **37**, 140, **141-4**, 164
   biological, 143n, 159
   circular, 143
   linguistic, 143
   natural, 143
analysis, 6, *and passim, see also*: discourse
   analysis
   mode of, **1-12**, 22-3, 52, 187ff
   objects of, 192
   scientific, 128
   theoretical, 12
animal-, 87
anthropocentrism, 138
anthropology, 56
anthropomorphism, 95, **140-1**
application, 7, 8, 170
a priori, 31
approach(es), 14
   choosing, 2, 5
   epistemological, 7
   interdisciplinary, 5
   traditional, 3
appropriation, 61, 139, 163, **166-7**
Aquinas, T., 97
Archigram, 106
architect, 42n, 128, 177, *and passim*
   as artist, 170
   as Man, 77n
   as intellectual, 178
   as intellectual artist, 126n
   blaming, 189

   self-image of, **170-2**, **170nf**
architecture, 132, 143, *and passim*
   and economics, 158n
   and social sciences, 157n
   and society, 3, 4, 98, 168ff
   as physical symbols, 121
   Architecture/building, 108, 182
   classification of, 142n
   conception of, 3, 31, 126
   definition of, 45
   field of, **13**
   material of, 42n
   materialist conception of, 4
architectural-
   criticism, 35, 37, 128
   design, *see*: design
   discipline, 142
   discourse, **14**, 165, *and passim, see also*:
     environmental discourse
   education, *see*: education
   form, 84
   ideology, 106, **170-2**
   language, 143, 177
   production, 157n
   profession, **170-2**
   reductionism, 124
   semiotics, 133, 158, 168
   theory, 125, *and passim*
   typology, 128
   utopias, 106
architectural practice(s), 3, 5, 127, 142, **170-2**,
     193, *and passim*
   and ED, 182
   epistemological problems of, 192
   knowledge of, 184
   techniques of, 185
Arcology, 36n, 106n, 142n
Arendt, H., 138n
art, 107, 159, 177
artist, 172n
ASMER, 67n
awareness, 29